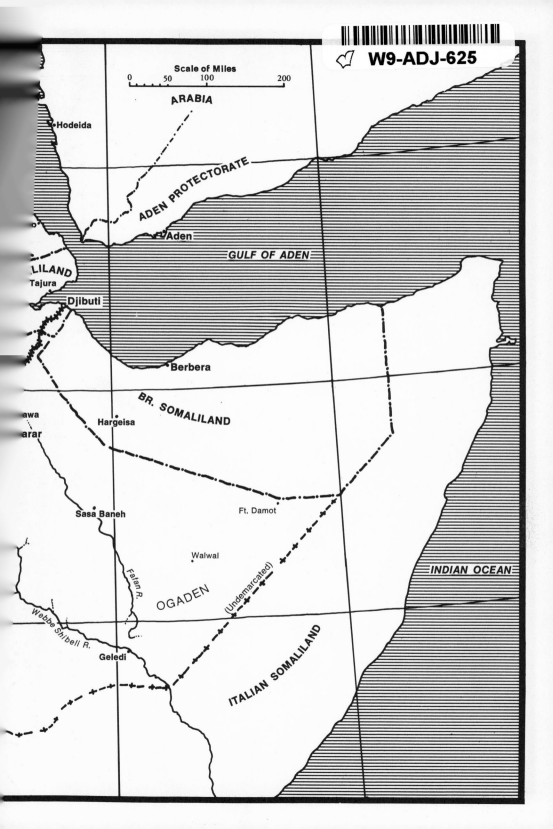

Scale of Miles

0   50   100   200

ARABIA

Hodeida

ADEN PROTECTORATE

Aden

GULF OF ADEN

LILAND

Tajura

Djibuti

Berbera

BR. SOMALILAND

awa

Hargeisa

arar

Sasa Baneh

Ft. Damot

Walwal

INDIAN OCEAN

Fafan R.

OGADEN

(Undemarcated)

Webbe Shibeli R.

Geledi

ITALIAN SOMALILAND

THE CIVILIZING MISSION

THE CIVILIZING MISSION

A History of
the Italo-Ethiopian War
of 1935-1936

A. J. BARKER

---

*There are those who have to be crushed with truth
before they can understand it.*

MUSSOLINI

THE DIAL PRESS, INC. NEW YORK 1968

Preface

In May 1936 a decree was issued in Rome placing the territories and peoples of Ethiopia under the sovereignty of King Victor Emmanuel. In seven months Italian troops had avenged a defeat which had rankled for forty years, and added Abyssinia's cool, green highlands to Italy's African empire. The barefoot army of His Imperial Highness, Haile Selassie I, had been routed, and the deposed Emperor had fled to Britain. The last African country free from European domination had been overrun; collective security—the accepted formula for world peace—had proved unworkable and the League of Nations had been discredited. Italy had been permitted to resolve her problems by force of arms and, in allowing her to do so, Britain and France had accelerated the decline of the concept of international law. A crucial corner in world history had been turned and Europe was fast heading toward the Second World War.

Because this episode was directly responsible for the breakdown of the League of Nations, the Italo-Ethiopian war is of high symbolic importance. Italy's aggression was the first test case of the League's ability to enforce the sanctity of peace which the democracies regarded as an article of faith. In failing to protect one of its fellow members, the League was discredited and doomed. Britain, as one of the dominating members, had been looked to for a lead by other lesser nations, and so Britain's share of responsibility in the League's failure was considerable. Furthermore Britain was also the holder of a great colonial empire, and it was understood that she had renounced her own imperialist ambitions and stood against those of others. Thus, the conquest of Ethiopia had a second significance in the eyes of politically conscious Africans and in countries such as the United States where there was a background of anti-imperialist tradition. In this respect, Britain could not be considered exonerated until Haile Selassie I was restored to his heritage and Ethiopian independence re-established.

At the time of the Italian invasion, opinion inside Britain was generally sympathetic toward Ethiopia. Indignation was tempered with a sense of responsibility arising from the widely held belief that sanctions were not applied with sufficient resolution, and that arms and other help had not been supplied to the victim of what was clearly an act of naked aggression. The reaction against the Hoare-Laval proposals testified to the character of British concern and, in its way, was typical of the nature of the British people and of the times. On the other hand, certain humanitarian organizations, such as the Anti-Slavery Society, showed mixed feelings. But on the whole, when British and Commonwealth troops swept the Italians out of East Africa five years later, there was a feeling that a wrong had been righted.

The purpose of this book is to tell the story of the Italo-Ethiopian war. Since the diplomatic battles were so important, as much of the account is set in Europe as on the battlefield of East Africa, and far more of its principals wear the plain clothes of civilians than the uniforms of the Italian or Ethiopian fighting services. Because it was an episode which occurred during my impressionable youth, and because of my personal involvement in the campaign to clear the Italians out of East Africa, the events have a special personal interest. But apart from my own concern I am convinced that it is a story which ought to be widely known. A knowledge of history—and more sadly still, an historic sense —is lacking in this computer age. So many people seem to believe that technocracy will solve all our problems. They cannot realize that the present has grown out of the past, that the future will grow out of the present, and that if one is to understand current affairs lack of historical knowledge is lack of understanding.

We are near enough to the 1930s for half the present population to have lived through the period of this episode, yet far enough away to begin to view it dispassionately. Looking back from the perspective of the Cold War, the problems then seem considerably less complex than those facing the world today; but they have shaped our present, so influencing our future. While no real comparison between the mid-sixties is possible, one lesson of this episode may still apply if we remember that right-sounding sentiment is no substitute for the will to translate words into deeds.

In compiling this account I have been encouraged and helped by many people. Those to whom I particularly wish to express thanks include Ato Admassu Badima, Signor Luigi Barzini, the Comte René de Chambrun, Colonel E. H. M. Clifford, Colonel A. Christmas, Mr. David Dilks, and Professor Renato Mori. For the valuable comments of the Earl of Lytton I am especially grateful.

Finally I must thank the following institutions, newspapers, authors or authors' heirs, publishers, and agents for permission to quote from works in their copyright:

The Royal Institute of International Affairs; *Il Giornale d'Italia; The Times* (London); *The New York Times*.

The Earl of Avon (*The Eden Memoirs: Facing the Dictators*), Cassell & Co.; General Pietro Badoglio (*The War in Abyssinia*), Arnaldo Mondadori Editore; Earl Baldwin of Bewdley (*My Father: The True Story*), Allen & Unwin, and Oxford University Press; Hubert Cole (*Laval*), Heinemann, and Putnam; Ian Colvin (*Vansittart in Office*), Gollancz; General Emilio de Bono (*Anno XIIII: The Conquest of an Empire*), Barrie Group of Publishers; Pierre Laval (*Unpublished Diary*), Charles Scribner's Sons; George Martelli (*Italy Against the World*), Chatto & Windus; Webb Miller (*I Found No Peace*), Gollancz; Leonard Mosley (*Haile Selassie: The Conquering Lion*), Weidenfeld & Nicolson, and Curtis Brown Ltd.; Kathleen Nelson and Alan Sullivan (*John Melly of Ethiopia*), Faber & Faber; Joachim von Ribbentrop (*Memoirs*), Weidenfeld & Nicolson; George Steer (*Caesar in Abyssinia*), Hodder & Stoughton, and Curtis Brown Ltd.; Sir Luke Teeling (*The Pope in Politics*), Peter Davies Ltd.; Lord Robert Vansittart (*The Mist Procession*), Hutchinson; Messrs. A. P. Watt & Son and Lady Vansittart.

A. J. B.

December 1967
London

Contents

Maps

THE TIMETABLE OF A WAR

Sequence of Events in "The Civilizing Mission"

in Europe	in East Africa
Secret contingency plans for military operations in Ethiopia are drawn up in Rome during the summer of 1933. In May 1934 Mussolini publicly declares that Italy has a "civilizing" duty in Africa.	

1934

November 23rd — The Anglo-Ethiopian Boundary Commission arrives at Walwal. Appreciating that trouble is brewing, the British contingent returns to Ado.

December 5th — Fighting breaks out between Italian and Ethiopian troops at Walwal. The Ethiopian force is routed; Mussolini demands an apology and compensation; Emperor Haile Selassie invokes the Italo-Ethiopian Treaty of Friendship.

1935

January 3rd — Laval, French Foreign Minister, travels to Rome.

	in Europe	*in East Africa*
January 7th	Announcement of a Franco-Italian Pact.	
January 11th	Haile Selassie appeals to the League of Nations over Walwal.	
January 29th	The Italian Ambassador in London asks for talks to discuss jointly British and Italian interests in Ethiopia.	
	During this month the G.O.C. Italian troops in Eritrea and the Italian Military Attaché in Addis Ababa are summoned to Rome to advise Mussolini on the plans for a campaign in East Africa. The provisional date for starting the campaign is fixed for October 1; General de Bono is appointed High Commissioner for Italian East Africa.	
February	The Maffey Commission is set up to study the effect of an Italian invasion on British interests in Ethiopia.	Under De Bono's direction, base preparations for large-scale operations start in earnest in Eritrea and Italian Somaliland.
April 11th	*The Stresa Conference.*	
	Two regular infantry divisions and four Blackshirt divisions are put on a war footing in Italy.	
May	The League of Nations Council decides that it will not interfere in the arbitration over Walwal, unless no settlement is forthcoming by August.	
June	Stanley Baldwin takes over as British Prime Minister, Samuel	

Hoare as Foreign Secretary, and Anthony Eden as Minister of League Affairs.

The Anglo-German Naval Pact is signed.

June 24th Eden submits to Mussolini's proposals for a settlement of Italian-Ethiopian differences, but they are rejected.

Results of the National Peace Ballot are announced.

The Maffey Commission reports that an Italian invasion of Ethiopia is not likely to affect British interests.

Deadlock in Italian-Ethiopian arbitration talks on Walwal.

August 17th An Anglo-French plan for settling Italy's claims on Ethiopia is rejected.

September 6th– 26th The League Council appoints a Committee of Five to find a peaceful solution to the Italian-Ethiopian dispute. Italy rejects the Committee's suggested solution.

September 11th Samuel Hoare addresses the League Assembly and declares that Britain will remain loyal to the League Covenant.

September 13th *The British Home Fleet sails for the Mediterranean.*

September 26th The League appoints a Committee of Thirteen to take over from the Committee of Five.

	in Europe	*in East Africa*
October 3rd	The Walwal dispute is settled.	*War.* Italian troops cross the Ethiopian-Eritrean border.
October 5th	Committee of Thirteen report to the League Council. Committee of Six is appointed.	Haile Selassie orders Ethiopia's mobilization.
October 6th		Adowa, Dolo, and Gerlogubi occupied.
October 7th	Committee of Six reports to the League Council that Italy has gone to war in disregard of the League Covenant.	The Italians capture Makale.
October 11th	Committee of Eighteen elected to decide what action should be taken to halt the war.	
October 17th		The main body of the Ethiopian Army under command of Ras Mulugeta starts to march north.
October 19th	*Sanctions recommended by the Committee of Eighteen are adopted.*	
November 7th		The Italians capture Makale.
November 14th	General Election in Britain.	
November 17th		De Bono is replaced by Marshal Badoglio and the war enters a new phase.
December 6th		Dessie bombed.
December 7th	Hoare meets Laval in Paris to discuss the proposals which are to become notorious as the "Hoare-Laval plan."	
December 10th	Baldwin officially denies prior knowledge of the Hoare-Laval plan but declares his "lips are sealed."	

	in Europe	*in East Africa*
December 12th	The League Council meets, considers the Hoare-Laval plan, and postpones indefinitely consideration of an oil embargo on Italy.	
December 15th		The Italians suffer a setback when Ras Imru attacks an Italian outpost. *Gas is used by the Italians for the first time.*
December 16th	Hoare returns to London.	
December 19th	Hoare resigns as British Foreign Secretary.	
December 30th		Red Cross units in Ethiopia bombed by Italian aircraft.
1936		
January 19th		Graziani defeats Ras Desta and occupies Neghelli.
January 21st–24th		The first battle of Tembien.
February 10th–17th		The Battle of Amba Aradam.
February 19th	Excerpts from the Maffey Report are published in the *Giornale D'Italia*.	
March		The battle of Shire sees the defeat of Ras Imru. Two more infantry divisions arrive in East Africa from Italy; Addis Abbi, Sardo, and other important centers are occupied during the course of the month.
April 1st		An Italian mechanized column captures the old Ethiopian capital of Gondar.

	in Europe	in East Africa
April 2nd		Following a last desperate attack by the main Ethiopian army under the Emperor's personal command, the Italians counterattack at Mai Ceu. Haile Selassie's warriors are routed and flee in disorder toward Dessie.
April 14th		The Battle of Ogaden opens.
April 16th		Dessie is occupied by the Italians.
April 17th–24th		A mechanized column assembles at Quoram for a final Italian sortie to capture Addis Ababa.
April 30th		Haile Selassie, tired and disillusioned, arrives back in Addis Ababa and vainly tries to rally his broken army.
May 2nd		Haile Selassie leaves Addis Ababa for Djibuti and exile.
May 5th		Badoglio unceremoniously enters Addis Ababa.
May 9th	*Mussolini announces that the War is over.* Badoglio is appointed the first Italian Viceroy to Ethiopia.	Diredawa captured, and the troops of Badoglio and Graziani link up.
June 3rd		Haile Selassie arrives in London.
June 30th	Haile Selassie addresses the League Assembly.	
July 15th	Sanctions against Italy are lifted.	
August		Badoglio is replaced as Viceroy by Graziani.

	in Europe	in East Africa
December		Italian mopping-up operations in the south and west.
1937		
February 19th		Attempted assassination of Graziani leads to savage Italian reprisals against the Ethiopian population of Addis Ababa.
1938		
November 3rd	Lord Halifax announces British recognition of the Italian regime in Ethiopia.	

CHAPTER I

Casus Belli

Our future lies to the east and south, in Asia and Africa.
MUSSOLINI

There are few areas in the world less attractive than the lands lapped by the Red Sea. Dominated by monsoons, the climate is hot and humid; thousands of square miles of the terrain are dull, featureless sandy tracts, where sources of drinking water are few and far between; and, as may be expected in such an unfriendly environment, the few people who live there are tough and virile. From Egypt in the north, along the coast of the Sudan, past Eritrea and French Somaliland, to the Republic of Somalia on the shores of the Indian Ocean, there is little to commend the coastal plain of the northeast corner of Africa. Economically, the region is practically worthless but because the Suez Canal provides a shortcut waterway linking the oil-rich Persian Gulf with Europe, it has considerable strategic importance.

As one travels inland, it is not until one reaches the eastern slopes of the Ethiopian plateau that the countryside—and with it the climate—starts to improve. This plateau, rising like a great island above the desolate sandy waste, covers 350,000 square miles of Africa, an area the size of France and Germany combined. At its northern extremity, where the Great Rift Valley nears the Red Sea, the desert plain narrows to a strip only a few score miles broad. But farther south, along the edge of the eastern escarpment, it widens out, and here lie the long scrub-covered plains, sloping slowly to the sea, which are known as the Ogaden. Although some of the region includes areas of agricultural promise, most of the Ogaden is a vast dry wilderness of thornbush and elephant grass. Over this arid waste Somali tribes, with their herds of camels, goats, sheep, and long-horned cattle, have wandered for centuries, ordering their movements in accordance with the distribution of pasture and water. The limits of their movement are set by the seasons and meticulously regulated by the tribes and clans whose pattern of life has been established and adjusted through the years. After the rains, when the grazing is fresh and green, the nomads and their livestock are widely deployed. But in the dry season they are compelled to concentrate near the water holes in the rough stony desert and make do with the nearby grazing.

The wells at Walwal are one such place and it was at this insalubrious spot on the map that the unhappy incident occurred which provided Italy with the pretext for an invasion of Ethiopia. Like so many of the other little places which have suddenly become famous by their association with international complications—Fashoda, Agadir, Sarajevo, and even Danzig—Walwal has sunk into obscurity. But in December 1934, the atmosphere of distrust existing between Ethiopia and Italy was such that the first shot fired at Walwal brought ephemeral fame to a place that few people could even find on the map.

The first news that something untoward had occurred in this area reached the outside world at a time when most people were thinking about Christmas. "Bloody incident in Abyssinia" declared one London newspaper poster; "135 killed" said another. The press reports were all fairly short and had originated in Rome; as yet correspondents in Addis Ababa, the capital of Ethiopia, knew nothing of the incident at Walwal. According to the Italians, a strong force of Ethiopians had attacked an Italian outpost on the Somaliland frontier and had been routed after a stiff fight. Since the affair was given little prominence, and few of those who read the newspapers had any idea of where Walwal was—and, more often than not, only a vague notion of the precise location of either Somaliland or Abyssinia—it excited little interest. Fighting was always going on somewhere; Africa was a long way from Europe and America, and there were other things to think about. The world was still suffering from the effects of an economic blizzard; in Britain alone, over two and a quarter million people were still out of work, and no one could be quite certain that the end of the crisis was yet in sight. The last thing that most people in Europe and the United States wanted was to have anything to do with another war. Most of their current troubles could be ascribed, directly or indirectly, to what was then so aptly described as the Great War, and they were not prepared to even consider the possibility of another. Consoling themselves with the thought that the journalists, in their constant search for sensationalism, were too ready to cry wolf, most of those who read the paragraphs about Walwal dismissed it as a storm in a teacup. Few people saw it as an evil omen.

With this sort of background, the incident at Walwal might have been expected to fade quietly out of the news. But the fact that Italian newspapers continued to give prominence to it gradually stimulated interest, and as more and more reports were received by the international press agencies it became clear that what had happened could not be so lightly dismissed. The dispute seemed to have arisen over the territorial rights to a water hole, and whether it was an Ethiopian or Italian colonial water hole depended on which side of the Ethiopian-Somaliland frontier Walwal was considered to lie. As this border had never been properly established the question was not so simple as it might have appeared at first sight. On the face of it, whether a few square miles of the disputed area was Ethiopian or Italian territory could hardly seem to matter very much, and only those who know the vital importance of water in a vast dust bowl almost devoid of this commodity could really appreciate what the wells at Walwal meant to the Somali nomads who used them. Except during the twenties, when the activities of a certain Sayyid Muhammad 'Abdille Hassan* forced them to divert their tra-

* A Somali patriot who held the British at bay for over twenty years and

ditional routes, these Somalis had wandered freely backward and
forward along the water line in the disputed region. It had been
the Italians who had introduced restrictions, and it had been
restless elements among the tribes in Italian Somaliland who had
opposed them.

Obsolescent rifles had been handed out, and a militia known as
"Banda" had been formed, ostensibly to deter Ethiopian raiding
parties. Sixty Somali "Dubats," as the men were called, commanded by an Italian officer, formed a single section of Banda.
Wearing a simple uniform comprising a turban, a white Somali
skirt, a colored sash, and a bandolier, the men of these quasi-
military units had been ordered to "dominate" the region between what was generally accepted as Ethiopia proper and Italian territory. Since the frontier had not been delineated and there
were no Ethiopian troops to oppose their activities, the risk of
frontier incidents was small. Officially, their task was to police
the frontier zone and deal with Ethiopian raiding parties whose
activities were common in this part of the world, and ignored—if
not encouraged—by the Ethiopian Government in Addis Ababa.
But the role of the Dubats went further than the normal func-
tions of a frontier police force; what they were expected to do
was to encroach into the wasteland, for by so doing the new
Caesar in Rome sought to emulate his forbears and create an empire in the desert wastes of Somalis.

Starting about 1930, the Dubats began to occupy the wells
across the Italian Somaliland border and systematically to extend
Italian-controlled territory. First, they would set up camp and
build their ball-like huts in the vicinity of the water holes; then
they would begin to lay down rules for use of the wells by the
tribes that frequented them. By the time an Italian officer arrived
to negotiate with the nomads, the Italian tentacles were well and
truly established. It was only when Emperor Haile Selassie, fresh
from his coronation, ordered the intruders to be driven from his
territory that the creeping invasion was halted and some of the

---

who was known by his detractors as "The Mad Mullah." An idealist, Muhammad 'Abdille Hassan believed that the Islamic faith of his people was threatened by Christian colonization.

disputed territory recovered. Two Ethiopian armies, totaling fifteen thousand men, marched south from Harar and Jijiga toward the frontier of Ogaden, and before them the Dubats melted away into the bush. But at Moustahil, where the Italians had built a fort, the Ethiopian armies came to a halt. The Italians were a few miles inside the line Haile Selassie assumed to be his frontier, but they were not prepared to move. As the encroachment was only marginal, Gabre Mariam, the Dejazmatch—or governor—of Harar, decided he had done all he had set out to do, and that the time was not propitious for a trial of strength. A small force was left to garrison the village of Tafere Katama near Moustahil, and the Ethiopians withdrew north along the shallow sandy gorge of the Fafan. Honor had been satisfied—for the time being anyway.

In effect, since the route taken by his army had bypassed the 20,000-square-mile triangular section of Ethiopian territory between the undemarcated borders of the British and Italian Somalilands, Gabre Mariam had failed to complete his mission. This triangle, containing the complex of wells which includes Walwal, remained under Italian control. Since communications in Ethiopia were rudimentary and Haile Selassie's administrative machine primitive and leisurely, news took weeks, if not months, to reach the capital from the outlying districts; months again before such news was assimilated and decisions taken, and even more months before the decisions were acted upon. But by 1934, when Haile Selassie was protesting about a buildup of Italian troops in Eritrea, he knew what was going on in the remote corner that Gabre Mariam had failed to flush. In August of that year the Italians had sent a white *commandatore* to Walwal to establish it as a proper frontier post and build a fort; the stage was set for the incident.

On November 23, a joint Anglo-Ethiopian Boundary Commission, investigating the question of common grazing grounds and endeavoring to map out the precise line of the Ethiopian–British Somaliland frontier, approached the oasis of Walwal. The party comprised two small British and Ethiopian technical contingents, escorted by what in retrospect may well seem to be an

unusually large force of about six hundred Ethiopian troops.
The British Commissioner, Lieutenant-Colonel E. H. M. Clifford,
was a large, good-natured, suave and tactful sapper who knew
the country well. According to his map Walwal was well
inside Ethiopian territory. Thus, it was obvious to him that
the green-white-red standard of Savoy fluttering over the water
hole was likely to invoke a delicate situation. That the Italians
should be there came as no surprise; the British Government
knew that a military outpost had been established at the wells,
and from what has been said already it may be taken that Haile
Selassie's Government also knew that the Italians had taken over
the wells. Nevertheless, Clifford was not expecting trouble; the
Ethiopian Government had informed Mussolini's Government in
Rome that the Commission would be operating in the Ogaden
area close to the border and had asked for it to be afforded every
reasonable facility. Possibly this was Haile Selassie's polite way
of suggesting that the Italians should withdraw, but if so, the
suggestion was ignored. Subsequently the Italians denied any
prior knowledge of the approach or intentions of the Commission.

Clifford's request for permission to camp near the water hole
met with a point-blank refusal, and by the tone and manner of
Captain Roberto Cimmaruta, the officer to whom it was addressed, it was crystal clear that the Italians were not prepared to
allow the Commission any facilities whatsoever. "I have had my
orders," the Italian said and when Clifford's attempts to humor
Cimmaruta proved to be abortive, there was nothing to be gained
by further argument. At this point, however, the issue was decided somewhat dramatically, by the officer commanding the
Ethiopian escort, Fitorari Shiferra, ordering his men to make
camp. Outnumbered four to one, the garrison of Italian native
troops looked on sullenly while the Ethiopians settled in. Meantime, foreseeing the possibility of an armed clash and being unwilling to become embroiled in any argument over Italian-
Ethiopian rights to Walwal, Clifford decided to withdraw the
British contingent. As his party retired to Ado, about twenty
miles northeast of where the trouble was brewing, Italian aircraft

made threatening passes over the Ethiopian camp. The Ethiopian Commission withdrew with Clifford, but the escort stayed and for the next ten days Ethiopian and Italian troops faced each other, "at a distance, which in places was not more than two metres; their loaded rifles in their hands, challenging, insulting and provoking each other." [1]

During the next few days both sides were reinforced, and under a scorching sun the situation grew steadily more tense, so that by the time the Ethiopians had collected a force of fifteen hundred and the Italians five hundred, it was quite certain that a clash was bound to eventuate unless one side or the other gave way and withdrew. The inevitable climax came during the afternoon of December 5. Who fired the first shot has never been established; each side said it was the other. One of the first casualties was the Ethiopian second-in-command, and Fitorari Shiferra—a mild man with no love of war—hurried off "to bury the dead in consecrated ground." Meanwhile his troops were left to carry on the fight under command of a resolute Muhammadan, Ali Nur. The issue could never really have been in doubt, for when the Italians brought up an armored car and called for air support, Ali Nur and his men were hopelessly outmatched. Since most of the bombs fell well outside the battle area, the reported bombing by the Italian aircraft appears to have had little effect on the Ethiopians. But the machine guns of the armored car were a different matter, and after more than one hundred Ethiopians had been killed, Ali Nur withdrew and the Italians were left in possession of the wells.

In the normal course of events an incident like this would quickly be forgotten; frontier clashes are common enough in remote regions, especially where frontiers are only vaguely defined. What happened at Walwal was no worse than dozens of other similar affairs that have occurred, and are occurring, on the borders of countries in Africa, Asia and the Middle East, and in ordinary circumstances the whole business could have been settled amicably.* Unfortunately circumstances were not normal;

* In the Northern Frontier District of Kenya a war against Somali secessionists has been raging since 1963, and in the Ogaden Ethiopian troops have

within hours there was a howl of indignation from Rome, and from then on events followed the precedents of other such affairs when one power is encroaching on a weaker or more backward state. Mussolini demanded an apology, a salute to the Italian flag, recognition of Italy's legitimate rights to Walwal, punishment of the offenders, and the equivalent of $100,000 compensation. To the Ethiopian Government such demands were wholly preposterous and Haile Selassie's reply was to "invoke the Treaty of Friendship, arbitration and conciliation" that had been drawn up and signed by the two countries six years before. Haile Selassie was well aware of the dangers inherent in the situation and he was less stubborn in his views than many of the people over whom he ruled. Indeed, the fact that he was prepared to make amends when the circumstances warranted an apology is evident from his willingness to do so in respect of an incident which had occurred only a few weeks earlier at Gondar in Northern Ethiopia when a group of Ethiopians had attacked the Italian Consulate. But with Walwal it was different. The Italians had set up a military post more than sixty miles inside Ethiopia and there was no cause for the aggressive attitude displayed toward the Boundary Commission. Nevertheless, though the legality of his case could not be disputed, he might still have been prepared to stomach another act of submission if he had really believed that it would have stemmed the tide. In his view it would not; the time had come to make a stand.

Yet, the Italian explanation of their grievances over Walwal was straightforward enough. Italian troops, Mussolini claimed, had been at Walwal for over five years without being disturbed, and this demonstrated quite clearly that the Ethiopian Government exercised no authority over the region. This fact of Ethiopian passive acquiescence to their presence alone was sufficient to justify the Italian outpost—even if it was accepted that there was any quibble about Italy's territorial entitlement to the region, which there was not. The Ethiopians replied that they had certainly never acquiesced, passively or otherwise, to the Italians be-

---

inflicted heavy casualties on other Somali nationalists. Yet reports of operations in these areas rarely reach the newspapers.

ing in the Ogaden, and were certainly not prepared to tolerate the illegal occupation of a single square yard of their country. The Italians had absolutely no right to be at Walwal; the frontier had been clearly defined in a treaty signed in 1906 and there could be no disputing that the place properly lay well inside Ethiopia.

The clause in the treaty to which the Ethiopian Government was referring read: "From the Webbe Shibeli, the frontier proceeds in a northeasterly direction, following the line accepted by the Italian Government in 1897; all the territory belonging to the tribes toward the seacoast should remain dependent on Italy; all the territory of the Ogaden and all that of the tribes toward Ogaden shall remain dependent on Abyssinia." The difficulty lay in the interpretation, and as the tribes concerned were nomadic, this method of defining the Ogaden frontier must be regarded as imprecise, to say the least. Undoubtedly what had been intended was the demarcation of the boundaries on the ground subsequent to the signing of the treaty, and in the argument which followed, the Italians claimed that they had pressed for this and in 1910 had actually sent a mission to the border for this very purpose; unfortunately, they said, its work had been hampered by the hostility of the Ethiopians. As a counter, the Ethiopians stated that they had never got around to the task. Oddly enough the suggestion that either side could set the limits of a frontier unilaterally excited little comment from the world outside. Perhaps this was because it could be argued that the line "accepted in 1897"—an arbitrary line running parallel to the Red Sea coast, which had no ethnic, racial, or tribal justification—was sufficient in itself. Yet if this were so, the Italians had no case, for the 1897 line put the boundary about 108 miles from the coast, and Walwal is 240 miles inland. There could be no arithmetical argument over 60 miles and, in fact, the most recent Italian maps then current showed the disputed area to be well inside Ethiopia. (It is relevant to add that these maps were quickly withdrawn, and new ones issued which put the border beyond Walwal.)

One Italian newspaper claimed that Walwal belonged to one of "the tribes towards the coast"—the Mijjartens, who live in the northern part of Somaliland—and that the Obbia region, put under Italian protection by a treaty of 1885, extended "twenty-five days' march inland." But little credence could be given to such reasoning, since none of the Italian maps showed the former Sultanate of Obbia or the territory of the Mijjartens to be within a hundred miles of Walwal. The Duce's Government made no attempt to enter into this argument or to try to refute it. What Mussolini did say was that Italy was fully prepared to agree to any properly constituted investigation of the Walwal incident, *but only in regard to the rights and wrongs of the fighting*; whether it took place inside or outside Ethiopia was not relevant. Clearly the sort of investigation he was looking for was analogous to an inquiry into the rights and wrongs of a fight developing when a burglar is caught in someone's house making off with the family jewels. The fact that the burglar had been caught red-handed was to be disregarded; the criminal would be the one judged to be the first to start the fight. Not unnaturally Ethiopia could not agree. To Haile Selassie a limited inquiry was as unacceptable as the wider considerations of the incident were to Mussolini; so, as Italian troops poured into the Eritrean port of Massawa, he invoked a new and little tried authority—the League of Nations—and Mussolini, not without a sense of humor perhaps, retaliated with his own appeal to the League for "redress in consideration of this outrage."

At this moment Haile Selassie knew exactly what to expect. Eight months previously, in May 1934, Mussolini had delivered a significant speech[2] to the second quinquennial assembly of Fascists in Rome. In his usual bombastic manner he had declared: *"There is no question of territorial conquest* [author's italics]— this must be understood by all both far and near—but of natural expansion which might lead to collaboration between Italy and Abyssinia," and he then went on to say that "Italy could above all *civilize* [author's italics] Africa, and her position in the Mediterranean gave her this right and imposed this duty on her. . . ." Italy demanded no privileges and monopolies, but she "did not want earlier arrivals to block her spiritual, political, and economic expansion." If the warning in the peroration of the speech was

lost on Britain and France—at whom it was clearly directed—
Haile Selassie had a shrewd idea of what portended and he was
not at all happy about Mussolini's plans for civilizing Ethiopia.
Imposing western culture on backward peoples has usually demanded more than a missionary crusade, and the Emperor found
it difficult to envisage the Italians moving into Ethiopia equipped
only with Bibles, bound copies of the dictator's speeches, and
samples of spaghetti and canned tomatoes. If and when they did
come, it would be more in keeping with Il Duce's style for them
to arrive wearing steel helmets and supported by tanks and aircraft.

That Italy was looking predatorily at Ethiopia there could be
no doubt. As early as October 1933 rumors of the award of a
cotton-growing concession in Ethiopia to a Japanese consortium
had triggered off a violent reaction in Italy, and when the engagement of a nephew of Haile Selassie to a Japanese princess
was announced a few months later, Italian diplomatic pressure
was brought to bear to get it canceled. Italy did not intend to
allow any other country to gain a foothold in a region to which
she considered a treaty signed twenty-six years previously had
given her exclusive rights. Two months after this Japanese affair
a military mission, headed by Marshal Badoglio, the chief of the
Italian General Staff, had visited Eritrea. Ostensibly its task had
been to inspect the colony's defenses, but rumors that its real
purpose was to assess the "requirements for a campaign in Ethiopia" were too strong to be ignored (and indeed in October they
had been partially substantiated by a newspaper report.*) According to one of its correspondents, the forthcoming campaign
would be directed by General Emilio De Bono, and the operations carried out largely by native troops supported by large
numbers of aircraft of the Regia Aeronautica. Finally, another
warning note had come by way of a speech to a gathering of
fifty thousand Blackshirts in Bologna. Farinacci, one of the more
virulent of the early Fascists and one of Mussolini's known
spokesmen, had told them, "Be always ready to march."

As the summer months passed the tension had grown, and

* The Italian émigré paper *Giustizia*.

Haile Selassie, thoroughly alarmed by the trend of events, had ordered his Ambassador in Rome to ask the Italian Government for a reaffirmation of the "friendship" that had been proclaimed by the Duce six years before. A somewhat shaky reassurance had come in the joint Italo-Ethiopian communiqué issued on September 28, 1934; "Italy," it read, "has no intention that is not friendly toward the Ethiopian Government." But as the Duce was vociferously declaring elsewhere that treaties were "not eternal" it was obvious that the joint communiqué had little real meaning, and all that it did was to lend color to rumor and give further ground for Ethiopian suspicion of Italian motives.

In circumstances like this it needed only a small spark to det-onate the powder keg, and the spark was supplied by Walwal. Undoubtedly Italy wanted an excuse, and there can be little doubt that there was an intention to stage an incident at some time or other. Whether the incident at Walwal occurred prematurely is a matter for conjecture. The arrival of the Anglo-Ethiopian Commission at Walwal may have been unforeseen and precipitated the event, but some trouble was inevitable if only because of the continual Italian incursions into the Ogaden. The possibility that Haile Selassie in December 1934 might have wished to force the Duce to reveal his hand is one which also cannot be completely disregarded. The Ethiopians knew that trouble was brewing, and the fact that the Boundary Commission's escort was of a strength which could cope with the Italian garrison at Walwal suggests that they felt that it was time that the whole business of Italy's intentions should be revealed to the world. If a colonial war was about to begin it would be well to establish who was the aggressor beforehand; by mobilizing world opinion it might even be possible to compel Mussolini to change his tune.

Yet, if this was the Ethiopian intention, things certainly did not work out that way. The probable outcome of the situation became increasingly clear as the months passed, although the curtain for the final act was not raised for nearly a year. From the day the first shot was fired at Walwal on December 5, 1934, until an Italian advance guard crossed the Ethiopian frontier on

October 3, 1935, no one could say for certain that Mussolini was not prepared to settle for something less than an armed invasion; everybody hoped that a face-saving solution could be found and a war averted.

Whether there could have been any other outcome to the Walwal affair is unlikely, for it must be stressed again that if the incident had not taken place there, then it would have happened somewhere else. Similarly, whether the course of history would have run differently if Haile Selassie had apologized, saluted the Italian flag, and punished Ali Nur (who, in fact, was promoted to 'Balambaras'—"captain of the hill fort") is also doubtful; Mussolini would still have found a pretext for invasion.* And the plain fact is that Haile Selassie felt that he could not in all honor comply with the Duce's preposterous demands. Walwal was Ethiopian territory, the Italians had no business being there, and whether or not an Ethiopian fired the first shot—a fact which has never been established—justice was still on the Ethiopian side. Furthermore, the feeling that the challenge which Italy had been sounding for many months would have to be answered sooner or later was also an important factor; better to resist before the incursions into Ethiopian territory became the accepted way of eroding the Ethiopian Empire; it might not yet be too late to arrange an amicable compromise.

That the Italian Government was in no mood to compromise was very quickly made clear in the Italian press. The Walwal incident occurred "in circumstances so definite and clear" that there could be "no doubt as to its nature," declared the *Giornale d'Italia* portentously. Italy, the report went on, did not see how there was room for arbitration on an incident of this nature, and it reiterated the demand for an apology and "proper" indemnity. The news of the incident might have passed almost unnoticed in the Western world when it broke on December 7, but before very many weeks had passed it was becoming increasingly clear —even to a disinterested public—that Italy meant business; Haile Selassie's Ethiopia was in danger.

* Coincidentally, Captain Cimmaruta, the Italian *commandatore*, was also promoted—to Major.

But it was not just the affair at Walwal, nor even the events of 1934 which have been recounted, that gave cause for anxiety. The causes and effects of the tension between Italy and Ethiopia had much deeper historical, emotional, and economic roots.

CHAPTER 2

The Argument from History

. . . history, which is, indeed, little more than the register of the crimes, follies, and misfortunes of mankind.

EDWARD GIBBON, *History of Decline and Fall of the Roman Empire*

Any idea that the rape of Ethiopia and the Italian dreams of a great new Roman Empire originated with Mussolini is utterly false. English newspapers of the thirties give the impression that Italian expansionist policy was devised and pursued by this single ambitious and self-centered Romagnol dictator, and suggest that totalitarian Fascist Italy had never had any imperalist designs until the Duce decided that certain areas of the world would be better off under Rome; that it was he who created the warlike spirit and the Italians themselves were wholly apathetic. Nothing could be farther from the truth, and to suggest that the Italian people were driven to fight a war they did not want, against a nation of whom they were scarcely aware until 1934, is refuted by the testimony of history. In seeking to carve out an overseas empire by force of arms in the twentieth century, the Italian warlord's legions were only aping what the British and French did in the eighteenth and nineteenth centuries, the Dutch and

Swedes in the seventeenth, and the Spaniards and Portuguese in the sixteenth.

History bears witness that when modern Italy first became a nation, a succession of patriotic Italians—politicians like Francesco Crispi, explorers like the Duke of Abruzzi—all harbored thoughts of recreating an empire governed by Rome. Yet by the end of the First World War Italy had not got very far with colonial expansion. Three great powers had already taken over the most desirable and potentially profitable regions in Africa and Asia, and all that was left were strips of desert. But the will was there, and when the time did come, the fact that she had been denied the opportunity to fulfill her imperialistic aspirations because others had got there first was exploited as justification for aggression. The curtain was raised at Walwal, but the sin which was committed in 1935 had its beginnings in 1857. In that year at least one Italian saw possibilities in Africa, and a certain Cristoforo Negri suggested the value of a commercial treaty with the most powerful of the several rulers of the divided Abyssinia, of which the two most important parts were Tigre in the north and Shoa in the south. Nothing came of the proposal. Nevertheless the idea took root and in 1869 Assab, a small port at the eastern extremity of the Red Sea, was purchased on behalf of the Florio-Rubattine trading company by a Lazarist missionary, Guiseppe Sapeto. Succeeding generations of Italians then gradually extended Italy's interests. A long five-mile-wide strip of the littoral around the port was purchased by the company in 1879, and six years later, following the massacre of some missionaries by local tribesmen, the Italian Government took over the company's African interests. Within a month Italian troops had occupied the port of Massawa at the direct invitation of Britain and in defiance of a treaty between Britain and Emperor John of Abyssinia concluded in the same year.* With the opening of the

---

* This treaty was a sequel to a punitive expedition against the Emperor Theodore, John's predecessor, by Sir Robert Napier in order to free British subjects held in captivity at Magdala. The assistance of Emperor John, ruler of Tigre, then Ras Kassa Merriccia, materially contributed to Napier's success, and in recognition of his help the British Government promised that Abyssinian traders should have free access to the Red Sea through Massawa.

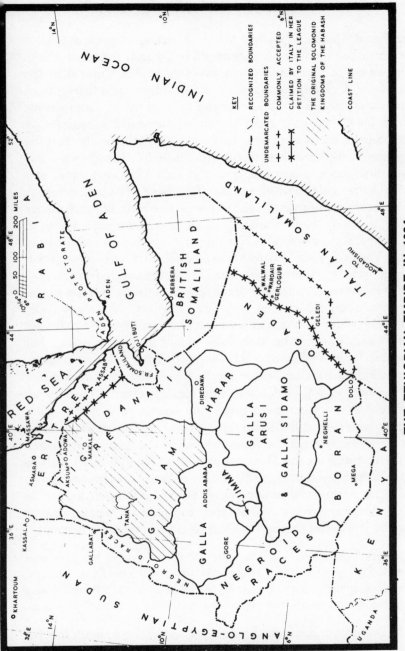

THE ETHIOPIAN EMPIRE IN 1934

(Showing development from the original Solomonid Kingdoms)

Suez Canal, the Red Sea had assumed a new strategical importance and Britain was concerned about French influence there.
Massawa is one of the hottest places on the Red Sea, and although
it had been decided that it was unsuited to become a British base,
Britain was anxious that it should not be used by any competitive
power. Faced with the rapid spread of the Mahdi's insurrection
in the Sudan, she was anxious that the vacuum created when the
Egyptians withdrew their troops should be filled, and in the circumstances lending encouragement to Italy's colonial aspirations
seemed to provide an ideal solution. Italy was a friendly country,
not powerful enough to be dangerous on her own, but sufficiently
strong to maintain the balance of power in Britain's favor. It
might well seem ironic that the country which first started Italy
on the road to Addis Ababa should be the first, fifty years later,
to oppose the inevitable outcome of her earlier machinations.

Invited and encouraged, Italy seized the opportunity to en-
large her foothold on the Red Sea littoral with alacrity. The
Gladstone Government had led her to believe that by combining
with Britain to fight the Mahdi she would be able to extend her
influence up the Nile, and Italian politicians began to refer to
Massawa, two thousand miles south of the Mediterranean coast,
as the "key" to Italy's destiny. The idea of reviving the Roman
Empire had now become a novel and attractive possibility and
for any who may still cherish the illusion that Italian imperialism
was born with Fascism, a consideration of the gusto with which
Italy embarked on the Massawa enterprise should be enough to
dispel it. On January 1, 1885, five weeks before Italian troops
landed in Africa, the newspaper *Il Diritto* published an article
which bears a curious resemblance to some of the statements
made by Mussolini during his years of posturing and strutting.

Italy must be ready. . . . The year 1885 will decide her fate as a
great power. It is necessary to feel the responsibility of the new era;
to become again strong men afraid of nothing, with the sacred love
of the fatherland, of all Italy, in our hearts. . . .

Italy was enthusiastic; France was concerned about the future; Russia flatly refused to recognize the propriety of the

move. And in Britain only one man spoke out against it. Yet he
was the man who had led the expedition against Theodore and
therefore probably the best authority in the country to speak.
His words were strangely prophetic. Britain had broken faith
with Abyssinia, said Napier in the House of Lords. "No good will
come of it."

Despite this enthusiastic start on their first colonial adventure, Italian hopes of reaching the Mediterranean via Massawa
were dashed when the death of Gordon led to the withdrawal of
all British troops from the Sudan. The Italians were disappointed. All that was left to them was a barren strip of territory
which was of little use to man or beast; only the hinterland
offered any prospect of riches, and apparently that was denied to
them. Whether the country had any natural wealth or not could
only be conjectured. Italian imperialists preferred generally to
take an optimistic view but nobody really knew the extent of
Abyssinia's natural resources. Two things were quite clear, however; settling Europeans there would prove costly, and the indig-
enous warrior tribes were unlikely to make a conquest of the
country easy.

But so far as Italy was concerned the main point was that
there was nowhere else; all the other colonial fruit had been
picked. If she was to expand anywhere it would have to be
Abyssinia. As she wanted to expand, it is not altogether surprising that the policy she pursued during this era bears a close resemblance to that followed in the decade preceding the Walwal
incident. From Massawa, an Italian tide oozed steadily outward,
encroaching further and further into Abyssinian territory. Protests made by Emperor John's chiefs met with no response and
matters finally came to a head when Ras Allula, the governor of
the province of Hamasen, next door to Massawa, attacked one of
the newly established Italian outposts. The attack was repulsed,
but the next day Ras Allula's men surprised, surrounded, and
massacred almost to a man a column of 650 Italians. Following
this the Italians withdrew their outposts and fell back on Massawa,
and it appeared that Ras Allula had at last stopped the erosion of
John's territories. In fact, the Italian Government had decided

that it had no intention of taking the defeat lying down. Italians were not going to be beaten by a lot of barbarians, and as it was considered that the column that had been ambushed had been overrun by sheer weight of numbers, the answer was simply more men and Maxim guns to correct the balance. The result was the dispatch of an expeditionary force of twenty thousand men.

Meantime the Ethiopian armies were also gathering strength, and by the time the Italian reinforcements reached Massawa toward the end of March 1888, Emperor John with one hundred thousand men was poised for an attack on the town. By one of those strange quirks of fate, however, he was suddenly compelled to halt, turn about, and tackle a different enemy—Sudanese dervishes who had penetrated to Gondar and burned his capital. Since John no longer represented a threat to Italian activities the projected campaign was called off, and twelve thousand of the expeditionary force were re-embarked and shipped off back to Italy. At the same time, the encroaching tactics were resumed. But this time there was one big difference. By now the benefits of an alliance with Emperor John's potential rival, Menelek, had become apparent; by cultivating his friendship it was clear that there were opportunities for pursuing a policy of divide and rule. So it was to prove. When Emperor John died at the hands of the dervishes in the following year, Menelek of Shoa automatically became the strongest claimant to the throne of Tigre, and in his own interests he was more than ready to open the road to his newfound friends. At his instigation, the Italians occupied Asmara in order to block supplies of arms reaching his rivals, with the result that the Italian colony of Eritrea came into being six months later and Menelek was able to proclaim himself Emperor of Ethiopia.

It appeared that Menelek was not ungrateful for the help he had received, for on May 2, 1889, on his way to Gondar to be crowned Negusa Nagast—King of Kings—he stopped at Uccialli to sign a treaty of alliance which, because of the subsequent controversy it aroused, made famous the name of an insignificant little town. To the Italians, this particular treaty represented a most outstanding advance in their empire-building program—

not only then, but later. Drafted by Count Antonelli, the Italian minister at Menelek's court, its terms were heavily weighted in favor of Italy. In return for a supply of arms and financial backing, there was to be "peace and friendship" between the two countries; mutual diplomatic representation; the establishment of a frontier commission to demarcate a border between Ethiopia and the newly expanded Italian protectorate; suppression of the slave trade; and most important of all, according to the Italian version, one of the articles—number XVII—laid down that "the Emperor consents to make use of the Italian Government in dealing with other powers."

Thus, in return for recognizing Menelek as Emperor and for the help they were giving him to establish his right to the throne, the Italians had promise of great reward; privately, Rome was now convinced that Ethiopia was well on the way to becoming an Italian protectorate. It was a case of prematurely counting their chickens, for what the Italians had not reckoned on was the astuteness of the man with whom they had signed the treaty. Menelek was fully prepared to accept the benefits it brought him —but only so long as the treaty furthered his interests. When it suited him he was quite prepared to denounce it and use Italian rifles against their donors. Nevertheless, for a time matters went rather as the Italians had hoped. The business of consolidating their power in the new colony of Eritrea went steadily ahead and by the end of the year the territory that had been taken over was well outside the limits laid down in the treaty. At this point Menelek voiced his objections and the result was the negotiation of a supplementary convention to the treaty to take care of the trespasses. The negotiations were conducted in Rome by Menelek's cousin, Ras Makonnen,* who—among other things— agreed that Menelek would accept the new frontiers of Eritrea in return for an Italian loan of 600,000 lire with which to buy ammunition. Everything seemed to be going swimmingly; for the equivalent of $60,000 the Italians had bought a very sizable piece of territory and they were well satisfied.

* Governor of Harar, and father of Lij Tafari, who is better known now as Haile Selassie I.

But Menelek, it seemed, was not going to sell his kingdom off quite so readily as Ras Makonnen may have suggested, and the first breach in the Italo-Ethiopian relationship came when Menelek refused to ratify the convention. From then on difficulty succeeded difficulty, and in September 1890 matters came to a head when Menelek, addressing himself to King Humbert, wrote to say it had "come to his notice" that the Italian interpretation of Article XVII was incorrect: that what the Italians had translated as "*consents* to make use of the Italian Government in dealing with other powers" read in the Amharic text "*may* make use of . . ." In order to avoid any misunderstanding in the future, Menelek continued, he wanted to establish that he had agreed that he *might* use Italy to negotiate with other European powers —nothing more; certainly he was under no compulsion to do so.

A slap in the face like this could hardly be ignored. It had become increasingly apparent to the Italians that Menelek had outlived his usefulness, and General Baldissera, the dynamic and eminently capable governor of Eritrea, promptly recommended that support should be switched to the man who had succeeded King John as the ruler of Tigre, Ras Mangascia. Baldissera was a strong believer in the divide-and-rule principle, but as his views were opposed to the policy of Count Antonelli, who still favored Menelek, he was recalled—ostensibly because he was suffering from ophthalmia, although Roman wags were openly referring to it as "Ophthalmia Antonelliana." After this the situation in Eritrea was so badly mismanaged as to set back Italy's expansionism for a whole generation. Baldissera was succeeded by General Ororo, and as soon as he also concluded that Ras Mangascia was the man to be cultivated, he too followed his predecessor back to Rome and retirement. Not until Menelek had actually repudiated the Treaty of Uccialli did Italian policy undergo a change, and by then it was too late. Menelek was firmly seated on his throne and Ras Mangascia had come to terms and accepted his suzerainty.

Yet, despite the signs of increasing truculence which went on during this period of Menelek's growing power, the Italians remained supinely confident of their ability to cope with any situation which might arise in Eritrea. General Baratieri was appointed governor in 1892, and in the next two years several successful actions against numerically superior forces led them to believe that disciplined troops equipped with modern weapons would always defeat primitive warriors. Indeed, Baratieri's early victories over the dervishes probably bred the overconfidence which eventually led to a reduction in the size of the garrison in Eritrea. But then Ras Mangascia decided to demonstrate his new-found loyalty to Menelek by assaulting the Italians. Crossing into Italian territory from Tigre in 1895 with an army of ten thousand men, Ras Mangascia was met by Baratieri and the offensive was promptly and skillfully crushed. Encouraged by this success, an Italian force of about nine thousand men then started to advance into Tigre and push rapidly up the road followed by Napier on his expedition to Magdala twenty-seven years before. In six weeks Baratieri's vanguard was 150 miles into Ethiopia, and when the Italians eventually clashed with the army which Menelek had collected and rushed up from the south, they had occupied the important towns of Adigrat, Makale, and Amba Alagi in northern Ethiopia. The Italians had in fact outrun their resources and the outcome of the short campaign was never in doubt. By sheer weight of numbers Baratieri's men were forced into the fortress of Magdala, where they were besieged and harried for two months. Finally, with no food and precious little ammunition, they hoisted a white flag and were permitted to march out of Magdala with the so-called honors of war—the white troops being marched south into captivity, while the native mercenaries were branded on the arm, warned never to fight against the Emperor again, and then released.

Although the campaign had lasted only a few short weeks, the Italians had suffered disaster after disaster. Not only had they lost everything they had gained in Tigre, but Eritrea was now threatened with invasion. In an action at Amba Alagi comparable to Custer's last stand, almost the entire Italian garrison of two thousand—including its commander, Major Toselli—was slaughtered. But in this and the other defeats it was the loss of prestige rather than the loss of life that rankled most, and Rome, seeking

a scapegoat, ordered the recall of the man in charge, who but a
few months before had been compared with Garibaldi. And it
was at this point that the worst disaster of all occurred—a disaster which excites uneasy memories even to this day. Goaded by
his official disgrace, and convinced that the well-armed, well-
trained reinforcements now pouring into Massawa from Italy
would overwhelm the savage hordes confronting him, Baratieri
decided on an advance into Tigre. The clash came at Adowa,
where Menelek was waiting for him, and the result was an ignominious and resounding defeat for the Italians. In a vicious and
eerie lunar landscape of black volcanic rocks, a force of twenty
thousand Italians, whose bravery is not in question, was broken
by an army of ninety thousand equally brave and hot-headed
Ethiopians. By the time the Italians were able to start to retreat,
six thousand of the original force lay dead on the battlefield, and
another four thousand had been taken prisoner. Baratieri's force
had ceased to exist as an army; what remained was little more
than a rabble. Fortunately for the wretched survivors, no serious
pursuit was attempted, and half of them were able to stumble
back to safety; fortunately also for Italy, Menelek made no attempt to invade Eritrea. The victory which had consolidated his
position as Emperor over a united Ethiopia was sufficient; he had
had enough of slaughter, he said. The dead were left to rot on
the battlefield, the wounded to die; the prisoners were rounded
up. Many of the latter were emasculated, and by order of Menelek, the native askaris who were found to have been branded
after Magdala had their right hands and left feet amputated.

When news of the defeat filtered back to Rome, the Italians
were dumbfounded. That their troops, well armed and well
equipped, should be defeated by what most people in Europe
regarded as a horde of primitive savages seemed unbelievable;
there could be no excuse. Adowa was regarded as a national disgrace, and racial pride produced a typical Latin reaction. A wave
of defeatism swept over the country; thoughts of imperial aspirations were put aside and all the high hopes of becoming a colonial
power were forgotten in a crisis of shame. Premier Crispi's Gov-

ernment was compelled to resign; the newspapers clamored for an end to what was now termed a "sinister African adventure," and Baratieri's returning warriors were booed and hissed when they disembarked at Naples. Italian imperialism had received a setback. Nevertheless it was not dead, only dormant; Italy still wanted an empire, with living space to develop her cultural and economic capabilities. It was just that in 1896, it seemed as if the time was not propitious. Adowa was the end of a phase, but it was written on Italian hearts.

Judged in the perspective of time, Italy was very lucky to be able to retain Eritrea in view of what had happened on the battlefield. Because the Government which replaced that of Crispi put country before politics and poured money into Africa, some of the luck was probably well deserved. And in the field the military operations were helped by Menelek's unaccountable conclusion that he was sick of war.* Consequently Kassala on the Sudanese frontier, which had been under siege, was relieved without much difficulty, and it was then handed over to Britain in order to reduce Italian military commitments. Peace was declared between Italy and Abyssinia in October 1896, and as the conditions of the Convention which concluded this first Italian colonial essay allowed the restoration of the original Italian boundaries of Eritrea, Menelek may be said to have shown considerable restraint. The Uccialli Treaty was repudiated, however, and with its abolition went any claim to prescriptive rights or special privileges in Ethiopia that Italy might have had. Nevertheless the fact that there had once been such a treaty was to be remembered in the years to come.

There was one important agreement which must be mentioned now, since its existence may be compared with a time bomb ticking away in a cupboard. By the Anglo-Italian Protocols of 1891 and 1894, Britain accepted that most of Ethiopia was an Italian sphere of influence, in return for which Italy agreed to recognize British interests in the Nile basin—interests

---

* Later, in 1899, he appears to have got over his aversion to bloodshed, since his troops shot down, like rabbits, luckless members of the Boran tribe—one of his "subject" races.

which included Lake Tana, near the source of the Blue Nile. The nineties were a period of intense rivalry in Africa between Britain and France, and the Protocols were a direct result of Britain trying to boost Italy as a junior partner in her own efforts to counteract French influence on Menelek. But Adowa appeared to make the value of Italy's contribution to the partnership questionable at a time when the international scene was starting to change. Discordant Anglo-French feelings reached their climax at the time of the Fashoda incident,* and the increasing activities of Germany then gradually drew the two countries together. For some years after Adowa, both cast hungry glances at Ethiopia, but so long as Italy remained in Eritrea she still held the balance of power in Africa, and neither Britain nor France felt strong enough to move into Ethiopia by themselves. Both sent missions to Menelek's court—as indeed did the Russians, Turks, Italians, and Sudanese dervishes—in endeavors to develop their individual interest. Very little came of the efforts of these missions and it is true to say that if anyone benefited at all, it was Menelek; by his success at Adowa he had consolidated his position in a way which he probably never fully appreciated at the time. He was concerned with bringing his country forward, and as the outside world recognized that he was clearly the man who spoke for the whole of Ethiopia—the one with whom to negotiate—Menelek basked in the attentions of the official missions and swarms of adventurers who descended on his capital.

In May 1897, a Treaty of Friendship between Ethiopia and Britain was signed in Addis Ababa, and nothing untoward occurred until rumors of Menelek's failing health disturbed the status quo. When it became clear that Queen Taitu, Menelek's consort, was pro-German and that a German influence at the court of Addis Ababa was increasing, all three colonial powers whose territories bounded the landlocked country decided that

---

* Kitchener, after his victory at Omdurman in 1898, found a certain French Captain Marchand installed at Fashoda. Marchand, who had left the French Congo two years before, had been ordered to forestall the British in the Upper Nile. Kitchener protested the presence of the French flag on territory belonging to the Khedive; a British ultimatum was issued and eventually Marchand received orders from Paris to evacuate Fashoda.

something would have to be done to counter it. A series of secret meetings followed, and the upshot was that a Tripartite Treaty was concluded in 1906 without any reference to Menelek. It was agreed that none of the three signatories would "infringe in any way the sovereign rights" of the Emperor of Ethiopia, but asserted their right "in the event of rivalries or internal changes in Ethiopia, to intervene to protect their nationals and to act always in concert to safeguard their *respective interests* [author's italics]." This meant that the country had been arbitrarily divided into three spheres of influence. To Britain would go the Nile basin; to France the railway linking their port of Djibuti in French Somaliland with Diredawa—and, it was hoped, eventually with Addis Ababa; to Italy was allotted a *territorial connection between Eritrea and Italian Somaliland to the west of Addis Ababa*. In addition, all three pledged not to undertake the building of any railway or initiate any other form of economic penetration without previously coming to a three-way agreement.

The whole treaty was in fact an arrogant example of pre-1914 imperialistic diplomacy, and when the news of its existence eventually reached the ears of Menelek he was furious. Angrily he demanded details from the British, Italian, and French ministers in Addis Ababa, and no doubt if he had not been a sick man he would have instituted some form of reprisals against all three countries. But Menelek in 1906 was not the Menelek of Adowa, and once he had been assured that the Treaty dealt with purely hypothetical contingencies his reaction was surprisingly mild:

We have received the arrangement made by the Three Powers. We thank them for . . . their desire to keep and maintain the independence of our Government. But let it be understood that this arrangement in no way limits the Sovereignty of Ethiopia or affects her territorial integrity or political independence.

The Emperor's time was fast running out, and after a stroke in the following year, he delegated his responsibilities to a Council of Ministers; 1907 was the end of Menelek's autocracy and the end of a long period of anything approaching authoritative rule in Ethiopia.

For the next two decades after this, Ethiopia was rent by domestic struggles. In the ambiguity and loose wording of the dis-
ingenuous Treaty of 1906 Italy was promised the lion's share of
Ethiopia. The clause concerning the "connection" between Eritrea and Italian Somaliland was the one which had the greatest
significance, for such a link could be interpreted as assigning to
Italy virtually the whole of Western Ethiopia. The only problem was how she was actually going to claim the concession;
when the treaty was signed she had little hope of doing so and
her opportunity really depended on a change in the *status quo*—
on rivalries or internal changes. If one were to be charitable, it
might be assumed that Italy wanted nothing more than to abide
by the treaty—that she had no intention of asserting her rights
unless the situation in Ethiopia did deteriorate. Such a theory
seems improbable and no doubt she muffed her chance because
she did not know how to propagate circumstances which would
enable her to turn the situation to her advantage. Unlike her
more powerful cosignatories, Italy did not have sufficient experience of empire-building to appreciate the tricks of the trade
which brought about disturbances leading to the sort of internal
changes to which the treaty referred. In matters of "frontier incidents," exploitations by "financial advisers," military and religious missions, "concessions," and ambiguous treaties, Italy was
extremely naïve. A catastrophic war was to rock the world before she had absorbed the technique, and by that time Britain and
France, no longer concerned with empire-building themselves
and paying lip service to the ideal of "making the world safe for
Democracy," looked with disfavor on the Duce's heavy-handed
attempts to emulate their earlier imperialism.

It was nine years before Italy again had an opportunity to
pursue her colonial ambitions. As a condition for entering the
war against Germany on the side of the Allies, she was promised
"equitable" compensation if Britain and France obtained any territorial benefit at Germany's expense, and it was understood that
such compensation would include a settlement of "questions
concerning the frontiers of Eritrea and Italian Somaliland." [1]
Fortunately for Ethiopia, which had dissolved into chaos after
Menelek's death, there the matter rested until after the war. Had

Italy, Britain, France—or Germany, for that matter—had time or troops to spare, probably the country would have been occupied and split up between the colonial powers during the war years. But all were too embroiled in Europe.

A reckoning had to come eventually, however, and in 1919 Italy drew attention to the wartime agreement for the "equitable compensation" to which she then felt her contribution to the war had entitled her. What she asked for now was a logical extension of the 1906 Tripartite Agreement. Britain was asked to support her claim to build a railway between Eritrea and Somaliland; in return, Italy would press Britain's claim for the right to build a dam on Lake Tana. Britain, for whom such a dam was not a particularly live question and who was not anxious to extend Italian influence in Africa if she could avoid it, jibbed and procrastinated. The result was that Italy got no compensation either in Ethiopia or anywhere else that mattered. In the Treaty of Versailles Germany renounced "all her rights and titles over her overseas possessions" and surrendered Tanganyika, South-West Africa, Togoland, and the Cameroons. South-West Africa went to South Africa as a mandate; Tanganyika, parts of Togoland, and the Cameroons to Britain; the rest to France.[2] There was nothing for Italy, and as it took five years of patient negotiation before she even managed to get a worthless strip of desert known as Jubaland on the northern borders of Kenya, and a further fifteen years of less patient discussion before France would even agree to make any concessions to her wartime partner, Italy came to feel that she had been badly served.

Frustrated and discouraged, Italy did not need a Mussolini to give vent to her feelings of discontent, and even before the Duce had mounted the stage, Italian politicians were voicing their opinions about Italy's "rights" in Africa. On November 10, 1920, Signor Tittoni ventured to put his country's case to the assembly of the newly formed League of Nations in restrained and mild terms:

To those privileged states which enjoy a monopoly with regard to raw materials and to those whose wealth has permitted them to acquire a monopoly of those materials outside their territories, I say:

Do not wait to be appealed to by the poorer states which are at the mercy of your economic policy, but come forward spontaneously and declare to this Assembly that you renounce all selfish aims, and before the bar of the League of Nations declare yourselves ready to support the cause of international solidarity.

Needless to say, although a number of delegates declared earnestly that their countries had "renounced all selfish aims," nobody came forward with any concrete suggestions for helping Italy.

Nevertheless, as time passed, the tide of the rapidly changing international situation seemed to be flowing in her favor. In 1923, Ras Tafari, the heir apparent to the throne of Ethiopia, having restored a minor degree of order in his country, applied for Ethiopia's admission to membership of the League of Nations. France was at loggerheads with Britain at this time over what the latter considered to be an unreasonable attempt to sabotage German recovery by sending troops into the Ruhr. Similarly, because of the recent Corfu incident,* relations between Italy and Britain were strained and Paris and Rome were on cordial terms. Consequently when Ethiopia's application was opposed by Britain and a number of other countries who sided with her—Australia, Norway, and Switzerland among them—on the grounds that the Government in Addis Ababa appeared to exercise only a precarious control over large areas of the country and had made little effort to stamp out slavery or control the widespread arms traffic that existed there, it is not altogether surprising that Italy and France should undertake to sponsor the application. Owing almost entirely to the energetic lobbying of other delegations by the representatives of these two countries, Ethiopia eventually secured a unanimous election and so, thanks to Italy and France, Ras Tafari was allowed to affix his signature to the

---

* The assassination in 1923 of an Italian general on a boundary commission in Greece resulted in Italian warships shelling Corfu. A large number of refugees from Asia Minor were killed in the bombardment and as Greece had to pay a fine of $2,500,000 to secure Italy's withdrawal, the incident could be regarded as a triumph for the aftermath of the Italian *Risorgimento* and newfound "sacro egoismo."

Covenant which pledged that all signatories should guarantee the full independence and territorial integrity of each other. It turned out to be the most shrewd move that Ras Tafari could have made, for no doubt what happened in 1935 would have been little more than a passing squall on the political scene if it had not been for the fact that Ethiopia was a member of the League. British and French statesmen, reflecting on their own colonial history, would hardly have been likely to go beyond limited comment on a situation which could have been represented as a virtue rather than a case of naked Italian aggression.

In 1924, Ras Tafari visited Europe in order to establish a regular relationship with the countries of "superior civilization," and Mussolini, looking for favors in return for his role of godparent, prepared a cordial welcome. Unfortunately Ras Tafari arrived at a time when the Fascist regime was rocked by the Matteotti scandal and the body of the murdered man was being sought without success.* In deplorable and unusual taste, a cartoon appeared in Rome depicting the scion of King Solomon and the Queen of Sheba as a black cannibal, whispering in the ear of the Italian Chief of Police: "You can tell me in all confidence, did you eat him?" If the future Emperor saw it, the picture can hardly have endeared him to the "superior civilization" of his Latin hosts. Ras Tafari was no fool, and whether or not he was disillusioned, there were no return favors or concessions forthcoming for Italy, or for anyone else for that matter. Having appreciated that he was making no headway, the disappointed Duce turned back to his earlier negotiations with Britain. The relationship be-

---

* Matteotti was a Socialist deputy who had been particularly outspoken in his criticism of Mussolini and Fascism. On June 10, 1924, a number of men were seen to bundle him, struggling, into a car which had been waiting outside his house. A bystander took the registration number of the car and reported the incident to the police. The car and the owner were traced but there was no sign of Matteotti. He had been stabbed to death and it was two months before his body was found in a shallow grave about twelve miles from Rome. Matteotti's disappearance caused an outcry in Italy, and Mussolini and the Fascist Party were accused of his abduction and death. Like Henry II of England, who benefited by the murder of Archbishop Becket in 1170, Mussolini was able to say that he was not directly involved. In 1947 it was established that Fascists, who were hoping to intimidate the Socialist opposition, were responsible for Matteotti's murder.

tween the two countries had improved since the settlement of
the Corfu affair, and as Britain had also decided that she was
making no headway with Ethiopia over the question of the Tana
dam, it was a propitious moment for a renewal of Anglo-Italian
cooperation.

In November 1925, while cruising in the Mediterranean, Sir
Austen Chamberlain, the British Foreign Secretary, combined
holiday and statesmanship, and invited Mussolini to lunch. The
Tories liked Fascism in those days; it had stamped out Bolshevism in Italy, they said, and Chamberlain was as anxious to extend the hand of friendship to the Duce as the latter was to accept it. Mussolini admired the British Empire; something similar
was what he hoped Italy would have some day. The meeting
appears to have been an unqualified success. An official communiqué announced that Chamberlain and Mussolini "found themselves in perfect agreement on the policy to be pursued to assure
the continued good relations between Italy and Great Britain,"
and Chamberlain wrote that his host was "the simplest and sin-
cerest of men when he was not posing as the dictator."

It is no part of my business as Foreign Secretary to appreciate his
action in the domestic policies of Italy, but if ever I had to choose
in my own country between anarchy and dictatorship I expect I
should be on the side of the dictator. . . . I believe him to be accused
of crimes in which he had no share, and I suspect him to have con-
nived unwillingly at other outrages. *But I am confident that he is a
patient and a sincere man; I trust his word when given* [author's
italics], and I think we might easily go far before finding an Italian with whom it would be easy for the British Government to
work. . . .

No doubt it was in this frame of mind that Chamberlain
agreed to reopen the negotiations on Ethiopia, and the exchange
of "notes" between the British Ambassador to Rome, Sir Ronald
Graham, and Mussolini which followed is again characteristic of
the attitude of mind in those days of imperialistic arrogance. The
outcome of these notes was a bilateral agreement to approach the
Ethiopian Government with certain demands, and these can best
be summed up by quoting an extract from Mussolini's letter to
Graham dated December 20, 1925:

. . . I have, therefore, the honour to state to your Excellency that the [Italian] Royal Government will support the British Government with the Ethiopian Government, in order to obtain from the latter the concession to construct a barrage at Lake Tana, together with the right to construct and maintain a motor road for the passage of stores, personnel etc. from the frontier of the Sudan to the barrage. The Royal Government take note, on the other hand, that the British Government will, in return, support Italy in obtaining from Ethiopia the concession to construct and operate a railway from the frontier of Eritrea to the frontier of Italian Somaliland, it remaining understood that this railway, together with all the necessary works for its construction and operation, shall have free transit across the motor road mentioned above. . . .*

Ostensibly the agreement had the appearance of an economic arrangement and concluded with the pious determination that if only one of the two signatories should be granted concessions, the successful one would not "relax his wholehearted efforts to secure a corresponding satisfaction for the other Government concerned." In exchange for an assurance that Italy would not challenge Britain's "special interests" in the Lake Tana region, Mussolini had got a pledge that Britain would uphold Italy's rights to build a railway right across Ethiopia. How Mussolini would have done this without an entitlement to military action if Ethiopia said No is difficult to understand, so that one is left with the conclusion that Britain pledged herself not to interfere even if the Italians became involved in a war with Ethiopia.

As neither the British nor the Italians had consulted the Ethiopians, it was only to be expected that Ras Tafari would boil with indignation when he learned of the agreement. But once again he was to show that diplomatic skill which was to characterize his every move, and what he appreciated could be a very delicate situation was handled extremely adroitly. To Britain he wrote in terms of pained reproof: "We should never have suspected that the *British* Government would come to an agreement with another Government regarding *our* Lake [author's italics]." To Italy he was frostily curt; and it was to the greater audience

---

* Although in September 1935, referring to the document, Mussolini declared angrily that "it divided—you understand me—virtually cut up Abyssinia."

provided by the League of Nations that he addressed himself at length.

Our Government has recently received from the British and Italian Governments identical notes informing us that these Governments have arrived at an agreement to support each other with a view to obtaining [the concessions mentioned above]. We have been profoundly moved by the conclusion of this agreement arrived at without our being consulted or informed, and by the action of the two Governments in sending us a joint notification. In the first place, on our admission to the League of Nations we were told that all nations were to be on a footing of equality within the League, and that their independence was to be universally respected, since the purpose of the League is to establish and maintain peace among men in accordance with the will of God.

We were not told that certain members of the League might make a separate agreement to impose their views on another member even if the latter considered these views incompatible with its national interests. . . .

We cannot help thinking, therefore, that in agreeing to support each other in these matters, and in giving us a joint notification of that agreement, the two Governments are endeavouring to exert pressure on us in order to induce us to comply with their demands prematurely, without leaving any time for reflection or consideration of our people's needs. . . . Throughout their history, they have seldom met with foreigners who did not desire to possess themselves of Abyssinian territory and to destroy their independence. . . .

Nor must it be forgotten that we have only recently been introduced to modern civilisation and that our history, glorious though it may be, has not prepared us for ready adjustment to conditions which are quite often beyond the range of our experience. Nature herself has never gone forward by sudden bounds, and no country has been metamorphosed in a night. With our well known eagerness for progress—given time and the friendly advice of countries whose geographical position has enabled them to outdistance us in the race— we shall be able to secure gradual but continued improvements which will make Abyssinia great in the future as she has been throughout the past. But if we try to go too fast accidents may happen. . . .

The appeal concluded with the words:

We should like to hear from members of the League whether they think it right that means of pressure should be exerted upon us which they themselves would doubtless never accept. We have the honour to bring to the notice of all States Members of the League of Nations the correspondence we have received, in order that they may decide whether that correspondence is compatible with the independence of our country, inasmuch as it includes the stipulation that part of our Empire is to be allotted to the economic influence of a given Power. We cannot but realise that economic influence and political influence are very closely bound together; and it is our duty to protest most strongly against an agreement which, in our view, conflicts with the essential principles of the League of Nations.

> Addis Ababa, this 12th day of Senie in the year of grace 1918 [12 June 1926]
> TAFARI MAKONNEN. HEIR TO THE THRONE OF ABYSSINIA.

The publicity given to the Ethiopian appeal had an immediate and shattering effect, and both Chamberlain and Mussolini had little option but to climb down and issue public assurances to the effect that neither Britain nor Italy had ever had the slightest intention of suggesting that Ethiopia was being allotted to Italian economic influence. Ras Tafari had gained a respite and was hoping that time would be on his side, that he would be able to bring Ethiopia into the twentieth century before there was any physical infringement of Ethiopian sovereignty.

Faced with such evidence of the League's protective capabilities, it is not surprising that Italy should begin to regret that she had ever sponsored Ethiopian membership. By 1925 it was already becoming apparent that imperialist diplomatic methods were outmoded. Mussolini swallowed the snub administered by Ras Tafari through the League, and attempted a new approach. An elegant emissary, the silver-tongued Duke of Abruzzi, was sent to placate Ras Tafari, and in August 1928 a treaty of friendship, arbitration, and sincerity was signed as a result of this individual's persuasive charm.

The new treaty was to run twenty years, and it pledged that neither Government would *"under any pretext whatsoever* [author's italics] take any action that may prejudice or damage the independence of the other" and that both countries would submit all disputes which could not be solved through normal diplomatic channels to "processes of conciliation or arbitration." As a concomitant, there was also an agreement by which Ethiopia would be allowed free port facilities at Assab, and in return the Italians were to enjoy a number of economic trading benefits. At long last it appeared that the two countries had reached a working arrangement from which both could expect mutual profit in the years ahead; everything, in fact, seemed to augur well for the future. Italy especially appeared to be doing her utmost to be friendly, and for his coronation in November 1930 Ras Tafari was presented by Mussolini with a brand-new modern tank as a token of the latter's sincerity. At the same time by conferrance of the highest decoration within the prerogative of the Italian Crown—the Collar of the Most Holy Annunciation—the new Emperor was raised to the rank of cousin to Victor Emmanuel. Everything, it seemed, was sweetness and light.

The newfound friendship could not last. The latest treaty was but a camouflage for the old white imperialism which Mussolini was now describing as Fascist "destiny," and the heavy-handed encroachment tactics on the Italian Somaliland borders which now got under way were hardly calculated to encourage the new Emperor, surrounded as he was by xenophobic, reactionary chiefs imbued with the consummate conceit which Menelek's victory had bred in them. Assab was scarcely used, no economic benefits accrued to Italy in return, and when the guns spoke at Walwal in December 1934, Mussolini was not prepared for any serious attempt to settle the dispute by any of the processes of conciliation or arbitration to which he had solemnly agreed in 1928. Walwal, it is clear, was the spark to ignite a fire for which the fuel had long been stored.

CHAPTER 3

The Quarry

Oh Ethiopia, be happy,
By God's power and your Emperor. . . .
            The first words of the National Anthem of Ethiopia

To understand the events which followed on the heels of the
Walwal incident it is necessary to take a brief glance at the internal affairs of Italy's projected victim. Inevitably this scrutiny
must center around the one man who has controlled them for so
long, Haile Selassie I, Elect of God, King of the Kings of Ethiopia, Lion of the Tribe of Judah—the benevolent despot who
may be praised or blamed for everything that has happened in his
country during the last fifty years.* Born Lij Tafari Makonnen
on July 23, 1892, Haile Selassie had spent nearly twenty years
trying to drag his country out of a medieval slough when events
overtook him and showed that he had not been able to move fast

---

* Although only 5′2″ tall, His Imperial Highness is a man of great dignity,
soft spoken, polite, and approachable. But at times this rather stiff and formal
Emperor can strike terror into his Ministers. He has been in power for almost
fifty years and consequently has come to be regarded as the one permanent element among the vast changes which have taken place in the half century of his
rule—the father figure of Ethiopia. To many, Ethiopia is inconceivable without him; to a few young intellectuals he is now sometimes seen as a barrier to
progress.

enough to cope with a predatory nation equipped with the advantages of modern industrialism and obsessed with imperialist ambitions. His race against time failed because the odds against him were too high.

In the thirties, as now, the ruling caste of Haile Selassie's subjects preferred to be called Ethiopians rather than Abyssinians. *Abyssinia* has an Arabic derivation—*habesci*—which signifies a number of races. *Ethiopia* has no ethnic significance; according to legend ic is the name of an empire which was founded as a result of the union of King Solomon and the Queen of Sheba. Because of its proud associations with the distant past the name was adopted by Haile Selassie's illustrious forbear, Menelek, and given to the heterogeneous collection of tribes of different religions, customs, and outlooks that make up the political state known by that name. The most important race of Ethiopia, the Amhara, who inhabit the central Ethiopian highlands, are a virile people of mixed Hamitic and Semitic origin. Their history is one of sporadic expansion southwards and eastwards, and up to 1935 they were inclined to boast of their ability to withstand invasion for many years after the rest of Africa had yielded up its secrets to the white man—a fact largely attributable to geography. Almost the size of France and Germany combined, much of the country is low-lying rocky desert, difficult and dangerous to travel. But beyond the deserts lies the fertile plateau constituting the greater part of the inhabited region and here, at a height of over 6,000 feet, the climate is cool and salubrious—ideal, in fact, for Europeans. Since the plateau is out of reach of the tsetse fly, it is also ideal for cattle, and could one day become the Argentine of Africa. Through the centuries, incursions by Arab and Sudanese invaders who succeeded in penetrating beyond the low-lying regions—and to do so meant traveling over the scorching sands of the eastern desert or up the sweltering tributaries of the Nile—invariably came to a halt when they reached the craggy ranges that form the foothills of the plateau. With their camels dead, they soon lost heart in the rarefied rainy atmosphere, and there also the savage, barefoot Abyssinians were usually waiting to smash, slaughter, and mutilate.

Physically, the dominant Amharas closely resemble the Yemenis, and like them they are a fighting people. Their customs—such as that which permits a man who has killed a lion the right to wear its mane on ceremonial occasions—denote their pride in courage and the heritage of their independence. To the north of the Amharas are the Tigreans, akin to the Amhara and belonging to the same Christian church, but speaking a different language. Both are of mixed Hamitic and Semitic stock, mixed by intermarriage with some of the other races. The majority of the other races, including the nomad Somalis, are Moslems, who in the past have resisted Christian rule from the plateau. In the west, a large area south of the Blue Nile is occupied by Gallas who, until recent years, were mostly pagans, and farther south there are large numbers of Negroes—Shankallas. To this day, despite the present Ethiopian Government's identification with Pan-Africanism, these Negroes are looked down upon by the Amharas. In the northeast there is also a group of Jews, called Fallashas, whose origin is said to go back to the time when Solomon's son by the Queen of Sheba, having been rejected by the Israelites as his father's successor, was sent back to Ethiopia under a Jewish escort. Subsequently the escort remained in Ethiopia, preserving their race and religion in pristine purity, and through the ages these "Black Jews" became the blacksmiths of the country. As such they were feared and detested by the superstitious Amharas, many of whom in the outlying districts still believe anyone who works in iron is liable to become a hyena at night and eat the bodies of the dead. To a people who harbor superstitions like this, progress in the modern sense is a tedious business.

Agriculture has always been the main preoccupation, and the deep, rich red earth of the uplands with its rivers and its rains can support almost every known crop. For centuries this same land could supply little beyond the modest requirements of the population, and before the Italians came along most of the tips of the primitive wooden instruments used for cultivation were not shod with iron, and the plows were merely crooked sticks. (More than thirty years after the start of the Italian adventure, both landlords and peasants tend to be very conservative about mod-

ern farming methods, preferring to stick to the ox plow and hand
hoe rather than work with machines.)

In 1916, when Ras Tafari Makonnen entered the lists for
power in what was loosely described as the Ethiopian Empire,
Abyssinia was probably one of the most savage, uncivilized, and
unknown areas in the world. Over seventy different languages
and two hundred dialects were spoken, and only a mere handful
of people were capable of reading or writing in any of them. The
majority of the population lived in comparative poverty and
wretchedness; the social fabric of the ruling Amharas rested on
slavery; fighting was the national pastime and men were honored
according to the number of people they had slaughtered. Criminal punishments generally were barbarous in the extreme—a
hand or foot being struck off for the most venial offenses; tuber-
culosis, syphilis, malaria, and leprosy were rife. The Ethiopians
were, in fact, at about the same stage of culture as the American
Indians had reached fifty years after the arrival of the white man.
They had adopted the rifle in place of the steel-tipped spear; su-
perstition, it seemed, did not extend to the use of iron instruments manufactured abroad, and the rifle became a symbol of
manhood and status. Yet the wheel, one of the earlier blessings
and indications of civilized society, was rarely used and roads
suited to wheeled transport were in consequence few and far between. Communication within the country was mostly by pack
transport over rocky trails that the feet of horses, mules, donkeys, and camels had worn through the centuries. In spite of this,
the few wealthy Abyssinians who visited Europe at this time
often became obsessed with a desire to own an automobile.

Ethiopia's Government was based on a feudal system, as it
still is. Provinces were ruled by princes, Rases, and Dejazmatches,
who levied their own taxes, maintained their own troops, made
their own laws; and, as each of these barons was responsible only
to the chief next above him, fealty to the Emperor meant little.
They received no salaries and lived on what they could extract
from their wretched subjects, who had to pay taxes in kind
amounting to a tenth of a man's food and animals, and work for
one day in four in the service of his master. Supplies of food for

the baron's troops or guests were levied additionally, as were the taxes aid to the Emperor and the central authority. As might be expected, the result of all these extractions left the mass of the population at a bare level of subsistence and the main preoccupation of the peasants was how to get enough food to live on.

Of all the landlords, it was the monophysitic Ethiopian Orthodox Church, owning a third of the country outright, which can be said to have had the most obnoxious and repressive influence. As a branch of the Coptic Sect, its doctrine is basically Christian, although the pagan ritual and superstitious practice with which it is overlaid sometimes makes it difficult to appreciate this fact. Within Abyssinia proper, the Church had exerted a unifying influence for more than two thousand years, but once its missionary activities ceased during the sixteenth century, it adopted an introspective and regressive role. What made it so obnoxious was not the ignorance of the priests, but the fact that it was so bitterly opposed to any kind of progress which threatened its authority. The power it wielded with the feudal barons gave added strength to this resistance; all the worldly and spiritual advantages that accrued to the priests were stubbornly guarded, and any policy which had the aim of unification of the Ethiopian Empire or the breaking down of Ethiopia's isolation from the world was loudly decried. On the other hand the priests made little or no effort to influence the morals of the people. The usual way to contract a marriage was for a man and woman simply to live together until one or the other decided to conclude the arrangement. (For a formal marriage they went before the local magistrate and entered into an agreement to share their property if they should divorce—a process accomplished rather like the Moslems by simply stating that the marriage had ended.) For men who sought an outlet outside marriage there were plenty of *tej* houses—little shacks where prostitutes outnumbered the customers—where sex and *tej*, the national alcoholic drink made from wild honey, were provided cheaply. As might be expected in the circumstances, most of the population was drawn to gross superstitious practices; the power of the "evil eye" was respected, witch doctors or priests treated diseases simply by writing down the name of the sick person or cutting it on a tree, criminals were "smelled out" by small boys who had been drugged. Administration of criminal justice was based on the ancient Mosaic law of "an eye for an eye, a tooth for a tooth" and in the case of murder or manslaughter, the relatives of the dead man had the right to demand that the criminal should be killed by the same means; a thief had his arm or leg cut off in public; debtors were chained to their creditors until their debts were paid off. All this may sound bad enough. But to the outside world the real black spot in Ethiopia was not religious obscurantism or a feudal system; it was something that was associated with both: slavery.

When slave trading fell from its high estate with the disappearance of the forced labor markets in America and the West Indies, the obnoxious practice lingered on in North Africa because of the continued existence of markets in the Middle East. Many of the slavers operated from Northern Ethiopia and the Danakil country, and as the slavers' sources of supply lay in the territories of Ethiopia's immediate neighbors—British, French, and Italian colonies—it is hardly surprising that their raids embittered these neighbors and led to pressure being applied on the Ethiopian Government in Addis Ababa. But for the Ethiopian Government to agree to stamp out the slavers' activities was one thing; to do so was quite another matter. Without a frontier police or any other means of bringing the raiders to book, it had little control of Ethiopia's frontiers or indeed of her outlying regions. Only tenuous communications existed between the capital and the provinces, and apart from the fact that the local barons tended to ignore orders coming from Addis Ababa, there were some places where people believed that Menelek was still alive. Not that all the blame could be laid on Ethiopia. To ship their human cargoes across the Red Sea, the slavers had to get them to the coast, and to do this meant further incursions into British or Italian territory since Djibuti was too small to provide suitable embarkation points. Probably a good deal of the traffic which was not absorbed in Ethiopia went from Southern Ethiopia to a point on the coast in Italian Somaliland. The Italians must have known this, but apparently there were officials who were prepared to wink at what was going on. Nevertheless, the fact that Ethiopia had not succeeded in stamping out the trading within her own borders was taken as proof that the Central Government exercised little control over the outlying regions. This, of course, was true.

Nobody understood the inherent weaknesses of this country, its problems, and its people, better than Ras Tafari. It was only too clear to him that the Coptic Church and the feudal system were serious obstacles to change, and that he would constantly be faced with the danger of some disgruntled Ras overthrowing the Government, destroying him and everything he was working for. There was, after all, the lesson of Afghanistan—a country situated similarly to Ethiopia and facing similar problems. Trying to force the pace there had cost Amanullah his throne and Ras Tafari had no wish to make the same mistake. There is a Swahili proverb, *Haraka, haraka, haina baraka*—"Hurry, hurry hath no blessing"—which seemed particularly appropriate. In the light of after events the Emperor (as he was to become) has been criticized for being overcautious but the point must be stressed that any reform he ever undertook, any measure he ever introduced, had to be forced through in the teeth of a powerful xenophobic ruling class and the recalcitrant clergy. Not without some justification, most of the elder Rases distrusted all foreigners and all alien influence intensely. To a certain extent this feeling was shared by Ras Tafari, who once wryly commented that Ethiopia's contact with foreigners had been limited to those who wanted bits of her territory. Yet he knew that he would have to employ foreign advisers and technicians, for Ethiopia had few people trained for the task of reorganization. As the powers on his borders could all be said to have a vested interest in Ethiopia, he deemed it wise to recruit most of them from countries other than Britain, France, and, least of all, Italy. This explains why, when the crisis came, his financial adviser was an American, his expert on foreign affairs a Swiss, his military experts a Swede, a White Russian, and a Turk.

The process of reform had been started by Menelek after

Adowa. However, as soon as his hand was removed from the tiller, the Ethiopian ship of state started to flounder, and by 1913, when Menelek died, the country had fallen into a state of near anarchy. Menelek's immediate successor, his seventeen-year-old grandson Lij Yasu, was a wild, incompetent, and irresponsible youth and a Moslem convert who shortly after assuming the throne declared Ethiopia to be in religious dependence on Turkey. Even before this the Rases had reasserted much of the authority they had surrendered to Menelek, and faced with the threat of Islam, the Coptic Church was not slow to support moves to depose Lij Yasu. Nor were Britain, France, and Italy, who had all been watching his flirtations with Turkey with considerable misgivings, and the revolt which brought the end of this regressive phase in Ethiopia's history was in fact prompted by an ultimatum issued by the three Western powers' representatives in Addis Ababa.* For the next phase Princess Zauditu, a daughter of Menelek and a great admirer of Queen Victoria, was installed on the throne; and the young Ras Tafari was appointed Regent and heir. Since this was the first step toward becoming Emperor, Ras Tafari might seem to have just cause to be grateful for the tri-power ultimatum, but as it was the same three countries which were eventually responsible for toppling him—albeit temporarily—in the perspective of time the situation has a certain irony.

For the next fifteen years, from his election as Regent until his coronation as Emperor Haile Selassie, much of Ras Tafari's time and energy was spent establishing his authority. These were years of constant struggle for power, and there is little doubt

---

* Lij Yasu did not completely disappear from the scene. Having been excommunicated by the Abuna, the Ethiopian Pope appointed by the Coptic Patriarch who had previously released the Rases from their oath of allegiance to him, the deposed monarch fled to shelter among the Danakils. He was captured in 1921 when they tired of him, bound in the gold chains to which his rank entitled him, and handed over for safekeeping to Ras Kassa, a relative of the future emperor. Kassa, the powerful governor of Gondar, was Ethiopia's elder statesman and a man with more royal blood in his veins than the man who had been nominated as heir to the throne. He had been a claimant to the throne himself, but once he had declared his fealty to the man who had superseded him, he proved to be one of Ras Tafari's most reliable henchmen, serving him as prince and emperor with almost fanatical loyalty.

that they sharpened his wits and developed the skill for political maneuver that he was to show later. On the whole he tended not to interfere with the old established governors unless they compelled him to do so by resistance to the changes he considered necessary. They were too entrenched and too powerful to be overthrown; it was useless to alienate them, and in time he hoped they might be induced to accept his methods. Nevertheless, at one time or another in his efforts to reform the constitution he clashed with most of the feudal Rases, the Empress herself, and the aged War Minister, Hapta Giorgis, who supported the idea of a traditional regime. The climb to power was especially difficult because Ras Tafari was not a warrior like Menelek, and for him to retain loyalty of a people who respected physical force above all else demanded prudence. But Ras Tafari was an intelligent and astute individual. From his father he had inherited Amharic traits of ruthlessness, arrogance, and keen intelligence; from his schooldays at the French Catholic Mission in Harar he had got a taste for Western culture; and by nature he was extremely ambitious. It was this combination of qualities which enabled him to see what had to be done for Ethiopia and to work to that end. Of necessity, in a country which could not be ruled without cruelty, his reputed distaste of violence and bloodshed had to be concealed—although to what extent this loathing was superficial is difficult to assess. With Europeans—including Italian prisoners of war—he came to be known as a kind and gentle man.

The problem confronting Ras Tafari was the same as that which Menelek had tried to resolve. To give Ethiopia internal stability and make her powerful enough to withstand external pressures, the provinces had to be welded into a single homogeneous state. Against the background that has been so briefly described it should now be apparent that progress toward this end was bound to be very slow. But progress was made. In 1923 Queen Zauditu was persuaded to allow the application for Ethiopia's admission to the League of Nations to go forward to Geneva. When Hapta Giorgis heard that it had been approved, his reaction was a comment to the effect that "we are now under the evil eye of the foreigner." He died in 1926, before the dividends of the move which he had condemned were apparent, and the Empress was left to fight alone a rearguard action against Ras Tafari's reforms. No match for the Regent, by 1928 she was virtually out of the battle—a tired, sad, acquiescent, and impotent old lady confined to the palace.

Even prior to Ethiopia's admission to the League, Ras Tafari had reaffirmed an edict published by Menelek against the slave trade: "Any person is liable to the death penalty who, without the King's authorization and except in case of war, seizes any person by violence with the object of enslaving him." This was followed by the public execution of several dealers caught red-handed contravening the slave laws and their bodies were hung at the gateways of their native towns to serve as a grim warning of the dangers of defying the Government. But this was not enough for the outside world, and following mutterings at Geneva in 1924, a further step was taken. Another edict, issued by the Empress but prompted by Ras Tafari, provided for the liberation of any slave who could "prove cruelty or underfeeding against his master; of all those slaves who had been sponsored by their owner at their baptism; of all those who with their owner's permission had entered the Army or Church; of any slave whose master had not claimed him within a week of his arrest." Further clauses in the same decree provided that slaves who were not freed on the death of their master—as frequently happened—should serve for seven years only in the heir's household, after which they should be considered free. These were modest reforms; Ras Tafari had decided that nothing spectacular was physically possible and that if he was to avoid his own downfall, the best that could be hoped for was to effect a change of heart toward slavery as an institution in Ethiopia.

Yet even such comparatively mild measures showed that the drastic reforms which some members of the League were advocating could produce economic chaos in Ethiopia. The immediate effect of the second edict was to release thousands of men from unpaid domestic service, and on the face of it this might well seem to be a humane and progressive step in the right direction. Unfortunately there was practically no alternative employment into which the former slaves could be absorbed; they were jobless in an area where the cash incentive did not exist. Most came to some sort of terms with their old masters, many of whom were only too glad to be free of the traditional social responsibility to which slave retainers were entitled. But the rest, destitute of support, drifted into the towns to swell the unemployed, and Ethiopia suddenly became aware of the fact that progress brought a whole new set of problems.

At a time when many of the powerful barons were merely awaiting a suitable opportunity to unseat him, Ras Tafari next decided to make a tour of the Near East and Europe, and the problem of his authority being undermined in his absence was met by the expedient of splitting his rivals and taking the most dangerous of them to Europe with him. Thus, when the Regent sailed from Djibuti in April 1924, his entourage included Ras Hailu and Ras Seyoum Mangascia; there were also thirty servants, six lions and four zebras.* Ras Hailu, a shrewd and wealthy man of commerce immensely powerful in his own territory, was known to be obsessed with the idea of becoming King of Gojjam, as a step toward becoming Emperor; Ras Seyoum, a grandson of Emperor John, was also suspected of having ambitions toward the occupation of Ras Tafari's seat. In Ethiopia the task of keeping an eye on Hapta Giorgis and the Empress was given to the faithful Ras Kassa. The tour took in Jerusalem, Cairo, Marseilles, Rome, Paris, and London; and it did not produce any diplomatic triumphs. In Rome Mussolini made a vague promise of financial aid; in Paris the French talked about free port facilities at Djibuti, and in London, while Britain made no promises for the future, the crown of Theodore which Napier had confiscated after Magdala was ceremoniously handed back to the future Emperor. Each country proffered the customary official courtesy afforded to a foreign potentate, but there was little more, and the tendency of the man in the street in Rome, Paris, and London, was to look on the Prince Regent as something of a curiosity. "We

* The lions were for King George V, President Millerand (who also got the zebras), and the Paris zoo.

Londoners" pontificated the London *Evening News* in its edi-
torial of July 7, 1924, "dearly love a foreign ruler . . . Londoners like people who are 'different'. 'There are seven million white
faces here' they say in effect, 'and white faces become monotonous—so that to see a dark one now and again cheers you up.' "
Most of the Press comments were concerned with the elaborate
dress of the visitors, however, and as London was experiencing
one of its rare heat waves that summer, the fact that the Ethiopians in their thick garments managed to look cool was the main
interest.

To see conditions and inspect modern inventions in the so-
called enlightened countries, Ras Tafari had spent a lot of
money, and on his return to Ethiopia the only tangible evidence
of success among the foreigners was Theodore's crown. Fortunately it was something which appealed to the populace and was
sufficient to ensure an enthusiastic reception when he stepped off
the train at Addis Ababa. In effect, what Ras Tafari had seen in
Europe was of far greater value than Theodore's jewels. Europe
had been an educational revelation to him and if the enthusiastic
and ignorant crowds in his capital had realized that his fertile
brain was already planning further reforms, they might not have
cheered quite so heartily. The Regent had seen something of the
industrial capacity which bred military might; he had also heard
influential individuals in Europe talking scathingly about the
backwardness of Ethiopia and enviously of its open spaces and
potential as a new Eldorado. To him it was apparent that reveille
could not long be deferred. So long as Ethiopia lacked unity and
the wherewithal to defend herself against an all-out attack by an
aggressor equipped with modern weapons of war, there was always the risk of foreign intervention. His problem was that the
existence of such a threat meant that money which might be
spent on schools or hospitals would have to be spent on armaments. And, because it was spent on armaments and not on social
development, the process of stabilizing the internal situation
would be slowed; in turn this meant that the army created to
meet the menace from outside would have to be used to suppress
internal revolts financed by foreign gold.

In a vicious circle of this nature the problem is how to secure a breathing space in order to decide which causative factor should be tackled first. With money the solution would have been relatively simple. Arms could have been bought, foreign technicians hired, and the only problem then would have been in overcoming his people's natural suspicion of foreigners. But there was very little money in the exchequer; the Ethiopian budget was in a perilous state and only the supposition that there were great untapped mineral resources in Ethiopia—including deposits of the precious metals—offered any immediate hope of further revenue. Despite the fact that much of the country had been prospected without any very definite results, rumors that the mountains were full of minerals persisted. The existence of any economically worth working has since been disproved, but in the twenties the fact that they were believed to be there was a situation capable of exploitation. By permitting concessions to foreigners the Regent was in a position to raise capital and cultivate powerful friends. On the other hand, in doing so he was bound to open the way to political exploitation by the foreigners concerned, and at the same time he would incur the risk of alienating the suspicious Rases. The alternative was to accept the implications of a smaller budget and seek the support of the Rases by deferring reforms and excluding the foreigners; such a policy might be more acceptable internally but it would increase the likelihood of foreign aggression and the country would be more vulnerable. The answer could only be a compromise of these alternatives, and it is doubtful whether any policy different from the one which Ras Tafari decided to follow would have stood a better chance of success.

Ras Tafari's own appreciation that the history of Afghanistan had lessons for Ethiopia has been mentioned already. By concentrating on a domestic policy with only three major objectives, he hoped to avoid the Afghan king's unhappy fate and make his own plan work. Simultaneously he planned to build an efficient civil administration linked to the world outside Ethiopia, and to create a standing army equipped, organized, and trained for modern warfare, while encouraging the gradual spread of general education. As the program developed he hoped that solutions to other problems would tumble out as dividends. These were clear, simple, and reasonable aims. But they represented a Herculean task, and because he had to tackle them almost single-handed Ras Tafari was unable to give the objective attention needed in the field of foreign affairs.

The twenty-year "Treaty of Friendship" with Italy was signed in 1928; in the same year the Regent was crowned Negus Tafari Makonnen—"King" Tafari—and the modernization program appeared to be making modest progress. In 1929 a Belgian military mission was engaged to train the Imperial Guard from which the nucleus of a new regular army would be formed. No national army in the accepted sense then existed. As has been noted, under the existing system the feudal Rases maintained their own small private armies; lesser chiefs raised and equipped levies who formed a sort of militia. As the levies were allotted land to farm in exchange for military service when required, their allegiance was wholly to the particular chief who engaged them. To quell a revolt or for a national emergency, the Emperor had to depend initially on his own Imperial Guard and the private armies of the provincial Rases; later, when they were mobilized, he might expect help from the independent levies. However, it is obvious that in any revolt he was bound to find at least some of them, and probably one or more of the private armies, arrayed against him. Thus the need for a regular army, whose existence would eliminate the need for calling up the levies except in dire emergency for an external war, is equally obvious. What Ras Tafari projected was a standing army of about forty thousand men, trained on European lines (under the direction of the Belgian military mission) by officers imported from Europe. The first step was a revitalized and reconstituted five-thousand-strong Imperial Guard. When it came into being it would be an elite corps, drilled, disciplined, uniformed, and equipped with the very latest rifles, considerably more powerful than any of the forces of the most important of the Rases. Furthermore, since its officers' ranks would provide a suitable calling for the more enterprising of the Rases' sons, it was hoped that Ethiopia's upper class would inculcate an *esprit de corps* that would bind them more closely to the throne. Unfortunately the whole program was limited by financial considerations and when the storm broke in 1935, the regular army had not reached the halfway mark toward its target figure and what there was of it was sadly deficient of arms and ammunition.

If the creation of a standing army was difficult, progress toward Ras Tafari's other two objectives was even more so. Underlying any development program was the same basic handicap as that which faced the defense planners—insufficient means in terms of money and men of the right caliber. An efficient administrative machine demanded educated men; Ethiopia had very few, and the extent to which foreigners could be used virtually restricted them to an advisory role. The fundamental problem was thus one of education, and it was clear that Ethiopia's future as an up-to-date nation would have to depend on the progressives of a new generation. With little to hope for from the old diehards, it was to the younger Ethiopians that Ras Tafari was compelled to turn his attention. Raising standards of education, even in countries where organized educational services already exist, takes time, and in Ethiopia there was no structure of state schools, colleges, and institutions which the Western world takes so much for granted. As in so many backward countries, the Church had a virtual monopoly of education. It tended to encourage the best pupils to enter the priesthood, and because it considered that universal education would undermine its authority, its clergy were resolutely opposed to the spread of knowledge. A few new schools were opened, but the number was limited by the lack of teachers; some young men showing special talent were sent abroad to study at the Regent's own expense, but there were not enough of them. The result was that the overall effort proved woefully inadequate; before the first fruits of Ras Tafari's educational enterprise were visible, a foreign invasion completely upset his program.

Meanwhile internal security problems continued to absorb much of Ras Tafari's energies. Toward the end of January 1930, rumors of an impending revolt against Negus Tafari were circulating in Addis Ababa. Ras Gugsa, Queen Zauditu's former husband, had collected an army and was preparing to march on the

capital in a bid for the throne; the forces of Ras Hailu and Ras
Seyoum—the two governors of doubtful loyalty who had accompanied the Negus on his European tour—were standing by
ready to lend their weight to the revolt. Ultimately, both were
bought off before the insurrection even got under way, and Ras
Gugsa himself was killed after his troops had been dispersed by
the bombs and machine guns of four French biplanes which the
Regent had bought only a few months before as the nucleus of
an Ethiopian Air Force. The news of Ras Gugsa's death precipitated Queen Zauditu's own demise, and on April 3, 1930, by
royal proclamation, His Imperial Majesty Negus Tafari Makonnen ascended the Imperial Throne as King of Kings.

Forty days of formal mourning for the old Queen, followed
by the rainy season which turned roads and tracks into quag-
mires and precluded the chiefs of outlying districts traveling to
the capital, were among the reasons for seven months' interval
between his succession and coronation on November 2. But the
main reason for the delay was Haile Selassie's own desire to make
the coronation a show that would persuade the European powers
that his accession was considerably more important than the
mere elevation of a king of an "African shambles." In this he was
extraordinarily successful, and undoubtedly the coronation—
even more than her admission to the League of Nations seven
years earlier—put Ethiopia on the map.

Addis Ababa in 1930 was little more than a shantytown of
mud huts with corrugated iron roofs; few buildings had more
than one story, the only ornate edifices were of religious origin,
and the name of the solitary hotel, the Imperial, gave promise of
far more than its facilities offered. For the coronation, however,
the whole capital was refurbished; the police were given new
uniforms; the town's twenty thousand prostitutes and *tej*-house
girls prepared for a big influx of foreign customers, and the main
road up to the palace was resurfaced. Arrangements were made
for distinguished guests to be brought by special train from
Djibuti, and, as expected, the host of journalists flocking in to
report the celebrations proved to be a guarantee of world publicity. Sufficient to say that in ten days of feasting and dancing, the
new Emperor accomplished what he had been hoping for during

a lifetime—Europe and America became conscious of Ethiopia's existence as an independent kingdom.

After the coronation the tempo of modernization was speeded up. Negotiations with the National Bank of Egypt for the purchase of its subsidiary, the Bank of Abyssinia, had already been concluded during that year; a Sudanese-sponsored American engineering survey of Lake Tana had been agreed on; and an arms traffic act with Britain, France, and Italy, regularizing the import of arms and ammunition for the new army, had also been signed. Then, in 1931, after the first constitution in the history of the country had been promulgated, a rudimentary parliament, which, in theory, set a limit to the Emperor's hitherto absolute power, came into being. Ostensibly, the new parliament represented a form of constitutional government, but as its members had to be approved by the Emperor and its ministers took their orders from him, it was hardly any more democratic than the Government of Fascist Italy or Nazi Germany. With the judiciary it was the same. During his Regency, the Emperor had introduced a number of codified laws covering such subjects as loans, bankruptcy, partnership, and limited-liability companies, but outside these limited zones, criminal justice was still administered according to the customs and habits of local committees, just as it had always been.

When the Walwal incident exploded into war, Ethiopia was still struggling toward what nowadays is popularly and frequently termed "emergence." Under Haile Selassie's direction no doubt she would have emerged as an up-to-date nation in a more tranquil fashion than has been her lot. Whether the six years under Italian occupation slowed or accelerated the process of advance is arguable; the fact is that in 1934 Ethiopia was at the end of a phase of her development. The mutual jealousies of her powerful and predatory neighbors had allowed her to continue an independent existence for a long time. But when one of them, with the connivance of the others, decided that her fruit was ripe for plucking, only military and economic strength could have saved her. As she had neither, her days of independence were numbered.

CHAPTER 4

Incentives and Excuses

Italy is a nation on the march. . . .

MUSSOLINI

Until the autumn of 1934 a casual observer of the international
scene had little reason to suspect the existence of any rift in the
relations of Italy with Ethiopia. Indeed, from a distance the
treaty signed in the year of Haile Selassie's first coronation appeared as a clear indication that both countries had buried the
hatchet and entered into a bright new phase of understanding.
Consequently it is not altogether surprising that the bellicose sentiments expressed by Mussolini in a speech at the conclusion of
the Italian army's maneuvers during August 1934 were not related to Africa by the foreign press. "It is necessary to prepare
for war," the Duce declared in his customary bombastic manner:
"Not tomorrow, but today. We are becoming, and shall become
increasingly—because this is our desire—a military nation. A mil-
itaristic nation, I will add, since I am not afraid of words. . . ."
The significance of this pregnant passage was lost on people outside Italy for a variety of reasons. First, there was Mussolini's
own reputation to consider. In 1934 the Italian dictator had
many admirers in Europe. To them his unsurpassed capacity to

dominate a mob of Latins with stark, monumental, masculine vulgarity while directing Italy's policy with cunning statesmanship was little short of miraculous. Secondly, the Duce was known to be a man capable of sudden change; there were few political opinions which he had not held at one time or another. Admittedly, his preference had always been for the violent and extreme, but experience had shown that his public utterances were not necessarily an index to his future actions. Thirdly, what he had said on this occasion had been addressed to a military audience, and the morale of the Italian army probably needed a boost anyway. Finally, what was probably the best reason of all for ignoring sinister forebodings was the fact that every one of the major powers was too engrossed with its own internal problems to be moved by Mussolini's words.*

In the thirties Britain and France were still the hub of the Western world, so it was their reactions to what went on in the West which usually counted. Neither of them saw Italy as a potential threat to peace; what is more, neither of them wished to see a problem. Apart from those who actively sympathized with the Duce—and in both countries these constituted powerful and vociferous factions—memories of the cost in lives and treasure of the war that was to end all wars had produced an almost hysterical dread of another.

From an orator as flamboyant and verbose as Mussolini, it is relatively easy in retrospect to select statements which show that his imperial ambitions had developed long before 1930, and that contrary to popular belief he always did give ample public notice of his intentions. On January 1, 1919—three years before he was invited to form a government—he wrote in *Il Popolo d'Italia*: "Imperialism is the law of life, eternal and unchanging. At bottom it is nothing but the need, the desire, the will to expand felt

---

* Benito Mussolini ruled Italy for twenty-three years. The ambitious son of a blacksmith, he was in turn a Socialist agitator, a journalist, and, during the First World War, an enthusiastic soldier in the Bersaglieri. His life was full of stormy incidents and he aroused feelings of hatred and of love, of contempt and of admiration. Called everything from a rabbit to a lion during his lifetime, his character remains a fascinating enigma. Grandi summed it up in two words: "Poor Mussolini." Since his demise, Italians have proved that great things can be achieved without a dictator, but they cannot forget Mussolini or Fascism.

by every individual and by every nation with *vitality.*" *Vitality,* *vigor,* and *virility* were words which meant a great deal to Mussolini, for it was these qualities, which he admired in the British, that he was trying to inculcate in the Italian people. As a young man in exile in Lausanne he had been impressed by Professor Vilfredo Pareto's exposition of the so-called imperial-cycles theory, which postulates that countries remain powerful only so long as their rulers retain the will to command.* As he saw it, the world of the thirties stood on the threshold of a new imperial cycle which could be Italy's opportunity. To his titian-haired mistress Margherita Sarfatti† he confided that he was determined ". . . to get this people into some kind of order. Then I shall have fulfilled my task. I shall feel that I am *someone* . . . I am obsessed by this wild desire which consumes my whole being. I want to make a mark on my era with my will—like a lion with its claw."

The history of the growth of Fascism is too well known to warrant anything more than a cursory glance. But, as with Ethiopia, it is impossible to understand the fateful march of events without considering both the development of the Fascist totalitarian regime in Italy and the personality of the man who directed it.‡ "I have always held that having broken the pride of Bolshevism," Mussolini declared before the March on Rome, "Fascism should become the watchful guardian of our foreign policy." Probably the Red bogey brought Fascism its greatest stimulus, since the big Italian industrialists, disgruntled with the incompetence of the Socialists then in power and fearing that

---

* An imperial cycle starts with the creation of an empire by a virile race seeking outlets for their vitality. After a period of rule, however, the virility of the master race degenerates in the affluence brought by possession of the empire. At the same time the virility of the colonial subjects increases until eventually the existing order is toppled and a new cycle starts.

† Signora Sarfatti was an intellectual Jewess, the widow of a distinguished Milanese lawyer. She was expelled from Italy when anti-racial laws were enacted at Nazi instigation and fled first to France and later to South America.

‡ The existence of the Roman Catholic Church made Italian Fascism imperfectly totalitarian—as distinct from the German version, National Socialism, which Hitler attempted to impose as a form of national religion. Mussolini himself was not a religious man but he was realistic enough to see in religion a formidable and possibly useful power.

Italy was heading straight toward communism, decided to back the new movement. Later many of them were to rue the day they had ever seen a black shirt; nevertheless, largely as a result of their financial backing, Fascism grew, and to avoid a civil war in 1922, King Victor Emmanuel invited Mussolini to form a new government.

That Fascism would oversee Italy's foreign policy was but a half-promise: Mussolini intended to lead Italy to a more respected position in Europe. The Duce's first task was to consolidate his position, but his first speech in the Chamber was clearly intended for an international audience and designed to allay any foreign concern about Italian intentions. "We wish," he said, "to pursue a policy of peace, but not of suicide." A few days later he returned to this theme in the Senate. "Above all," he announced, "I intend to pursue a foreign policy that will not be adventurous, but will be in no way renunciatory." And again: "Our policy will not be one of Imperialism which seeks the impossible." As in the case of so many political speeches, one could read almost anything into these phrases, but on the face of it Mussolini's attitude toward Italy's foreign policy seemed to be one of sweet reasonableness, and his political adherents were quick to point out that what he had said from a position of power was no different from what he had said before he was called to office. The Duce had always taken a "realistic" attitude, especially in foreign affairs. Mere territorial gain had never appealed to him and he was still the same man who had said he would rather be a citizen of Denmark than a subject of the Chinese Empire—honest, straightforward, pragmatic.

There was just one sentence in that first speech to the Chamber which ought to have given rise to comment, however. Like so much of what Mussolini said, it passed unnoticed at the time, but in the light of subsequent events the words "Treaties are not eternal, and they are not unalterable; they are the chapters of history, not its epilogue" were significantly loaded. Although it would be farfetched to suppose that Mussolini was already plotting his Ethiopian adventure, his utterance on treaties may be deemed to have prophetic importance. Why nobody bothered to question Mussolini's motives seems strange in an age of constant suspicion. In the twenties and early thirties, a pact was a pact, and once a treaty was signed and sealed, although it might have to be amended, it was a matter of national honor to see that its terms were kept; certainly they were not meant to be abrogated without very good cause. Such behavior was unthinkable to people outside Italy; what Mussolini had said probably meant something quite different; besides, there were few treaties with Italy that were worth mentioning.

Inside Italy, people were scarcely in a position to criticize. Apart from a controlled press and the threat of castor oil and clubs, the fact is that the Duce's passionate physical magnetism drew the majority of Italians to him. Few will concede it nowadays, but at that time they enjoyed his histrionics, cherished his holy egoism, and rejoiced in the fact that they had found a man of action to lead them to a better life. In stature Mussolini was a much smaller man than photographers usually made him appear.* But when he spoke, his words had a hypnotic effect. This effect was not confined to Latin audiences; many foreign correspondents and diplomats spoke of the aura of impressive sincerity and impregnable rectitude that attended their discussions with him.

Whether or not the Italian dictator had already decided on a policy of colonial aggrandizement when he came to power, Italy's economic situation necessarily delayed its implementation. On the narrow Italian peninsula 45 million people were living a hand-to-mouth existence, and in the south especially many of them existed in conditions of grinding poverty. The bulk of the population, most of whom were illiterate, worked on the land, and no matter how the peasants toiled it was impossible to get by without large imports of food. Nor was the industrial picture much better. Lacking so many essential raw materials, Italy, like Britain, had to rely on imports in order to maintain her industries and her standard of living. The statistics have not changed

---

* Nor was his jutting lower jaw as monumental as it usually appears in photographs. To make it look impressive photographs were taken with the camera placed near and slightly below the Duce's jaw.

greatly since 1930, and Italy still has to import nearly all the oil, cotton, and wool, most of the coal, and over 80 percent of the iron and steel she needs. Thus, to make up the difference between food consumption and production, and to buy raw materials for the manufacturing industries, Italy relied on exporting vegetables, fruit, cheese, textiles, silk, hemp, wire, marble, cars, and machinery. But even this was not enough. Then, as now, tourists had to be lured to Italy's resorts and ruins; other countries encouraged to send freight in Italian ships; and Italians living abroad urged to send money home. Only by doing all these things successfully could Italy hope to make ends meet. Even then, she still had a major unemployment problem, and when a job fell vacant in Italy there were scores to fill it. In simple terms Italy was overcrowded, and with the Roman Catholic church doctrine ruling that "unnatural" methods of birth control were heresy, the situation was steadily deteriorating. When Mussolini said, "We are hungry for land; we are hungry because we are prolific," he expressed the economic problem clearly and concisely. When he added, "We intend to remain prolific," he was announcing his inability to come to grips with the crux of a matter which the Roman Catholic Church regarded as its prerogative.

For decades, large-scale emigration to the United States had alleviated the deleterious effects of Italy's expanding population, providing Italy with a source of income as well as reducing the unemployment problem, since the Italians who made good in America invariably sent remittances home. In 1921, however, the U.S. immigration laws were drastically amended. During the controversies about America's attitude toward the war between 1914 and 1917 it had become apparent that the merits of an open-door policy to what previously had been regarded as an empty continent had lost their validity. Demobilization had created unemployment, and to prevent a further influx it was decided to control immigration. Quotas were established on a nationality basis and the effect was to reduce Italian immigration to a trickle. In 1914, over a quarter of a million Italians had taken out American nationality, but ten years later the quota for Italy was less

.than four thousand. Measures like this were bound to create resentment, and as the new U.S. immigration laws appeared to put
them in the same category as Asiatics, the Italians were nettled
for psychological as well as economic reasons. It was a bitter
blow for the new Fascist state.

It is popularly supposed that economic reasons are the underlying cause of any war, and many writers have seen the key to
the Italo-Ethiopian tragedy in Italy's economic difficulties; and
the economic crisis which developed as a result of the world depression probably was a major factor in Mussolini's decision to
launch the colonial enterprise when he did. Within a year of taking office, he had built up the Fascist party into a nationwide and
all-purposeful organization and had restored order in the country. By 1925, Italy's finances were improving and despite many
of the unpleasant facets of the regime—press censorship, the suppression and murder of political opponents, and the philosophy
of the corporate state, whereby private property and private
profits were preserved but under state control—the Fascist state
was in a much better shape economically than it had been for
very many years. "Discipline, work, and order" was the cry, and
Italy's economy was regulated according to Mussolini's ideas of
what was best. In 1926, in order to create confidence in the currency, he took a solemn vow to maintain the value of the Italian
lira at a fixed level based on gold, and for prestige rather than for
economic reasons, the lira was stabilized at nineteen to the dollar.
This rate, which was far too high, was chosen in order to better
the French figure, because Mussolini was unwilling for a franc to
rate higher than a lira. Consequently, when every nation tried to
hedge the effects of the international slump which suddenly descended on the world by raising tariffs and restoring trade,
Italy's difficulties were disproportionately worse than those of
her neighbors. As a result, the numbers of her unemployed shot
up in 1930 at a staggering rate. Rather than let these unemployed
rot in isolation (as happened with four million men in Britain),
attempts were made to cushion the crisis with grandiose and
costly public ventures. But these rapidly absorbed much of the
meager reserves of the Italian treasury, and restrictions on the

use of Italian currency abroad were introduced. Finally, when the United States devalued the dollar in 1934, Mussolini followed suit and devalued the lira by 40 percent. Financial juggling accomplished a good deal, as exemplified by the fact that Mussolini was able to raise four billion lire's worth of gold with which to wage war the following year.

No Italian surveying the monuments of antiquity with which his country is so liberally strewn can doubt that he is heir to a great tradition, and Fascism's response undoubtedly had considerable appeal—particularly amongst the younger generation. Historically it could be said that if one were to take five of the greatest men in any branch of human activity, two of them would be Italians. Of the poets, philosophers, scientists, inventors, and artists whose names are remembered, many bear illustrious Italian names, although it is not since the days of Caesar that Italy's soldiers have done anything by which they are remembered. But the Roman legend dies hard and the Italian of the thirties had an innate desire for his country to attain glory on the field of battle. Possibly this was why Mussolini's promises that if Italians followed him some day they would rule the world had such an appeal, and why the Duce exploited the symbols of the Roman age. The *fasces* symbol, the Fascist organization modelled on Roman military formations, the revival of old Roman names, and the emblems adopted by the Fascist legionaries were all designed to focus public attention on the achievements of the Caesars—to recall centuries of triumphs, of Roman holidays and Roman dominion; even the outstretched-arm salute of the Blackshirts had this purpose. Not that all the Fascist trappings were based on Roman traditions; but in the maturity of the movement emblems and tokens selected on practical grounds or hastily improvised were raised to tradition status. The opaque and unceremonial black shirt, for instance—originally chosen because it was cheap and seldom needed to be changed—became shiny, ceremonial full dress, while the Fascist march '*Giovinezza*' (Youth)—derived from an old Swiss melody—by law became a national anthem and when it was played the audience was expected to stand with bared head. The theme was patriotism, *esprit de corps,* and the spirit of ancient Rome. To an Englishman or Frenchman, for whom the period of national greatness is in the more recent past, a 2,000-year-old nostalgia may seem very far-fetched. But it must be remembered that with the exceptions of the Renaissance and the *Risorgimento* there had been little in the history of the Italian peninsula since the era of the Caesars that was particularly glorious. Thus, in appealing to Italian patriotism, Mussolini struck exactly the right note at exactly the right time.

As for the Duce himself: according to his own testimony it was war that had converted him from Socialist to Fascist, from pacifism to patriotism, and to the idea of Italy's imperial role. Political opportunism and personal ambition rather than some traumatic experience in the heat of battle is more likely to be nearer the truth. Posturing and flamboyant gesticulation is merely an adjunct to expression for the Latins, and while his orations might seem ridiculous to an Anglo-Saxon, their appeal to the Italians should not be underrated. Here was a man with spine and starch. Passionate ovations, full of patriotic platitudes and dramatic rhetoric about virility, racial pride, and national prestige, diverted thought from troubles at home and gave the Italians visions of riches and greatness. Furthermore, few could fail to be convinced by arguments that Italy had had a raw deal. She had lost nearly three-quarters of a million men in World War I and when it came to dividing the lion's pelt, Italy's share had been pathetically small. Britain and her Dominions had taken most of Germany's old empire; France had got Alsace-Lorraine and some other concessions. A portion of Anatolia had been allotted to Italy under the abortive Treaty of Sèvres with Turkey in 1920, but even that had been restored to Turkey under the Lausanne Treaty of 1923. So Italy was left with her old sterile colonies, a bit of the Austrian Tyrol, a patch of territory around Trieste, and the promise of the "rectification" of some of the borders to their uninhabited wastes—nothing of any value. In an era when the status symbols of a nation were colonies, Italy's prestige was bound to suffer, and for any of the "have" nations to repudiate the plaintive demands of Italy—one of the "have-nots" —seemed unjust. One of Mussolini's own arguments later was that the nineteen-twenties coincided with the end of Britain's colonial expansion and ambition: "As soon as the British have sated themselves with colonial conquests, they impudently draw an arbitrary line across the middle of the page in the Recording Angel's book and then proclaim: 'What was right for us till yesterday is wrong for you today.' " [1]

Indignation over the injustice meted out to Italy at Versailles and the whole question of colonial development provided the dominating background which lent itself to propaganda that could be used to divert attention away from Italy's internal difficulties. The result was that Italian newspapers published articles on the value of colonies as outlets for surplus population. Most of these were dissertations of muddled thinking, although there were some rather more germane appreciations of Italy's needs in terms of raw materials. As time passed and the complaints about Italy's pressing need for colonies grew louder, the old arguments were embroidered with versions of the Duce's imperial-cycle theory. Gradually a new theme developed. Law and order existed in Italian colonies, officially inspired articles stated, while Britain and France—who had so much land between them— were unable to keep their territories in order. And judged by what was happening in India, it was true that Cyrenaica was quiet. But nothing was said about it having taken three years to bring peace to the Libyan desert. Between 1914 and 1918 Italy had virtually lost complete control of her African colonies across the Mediterranean, and in 1916 Eritrea had been threatened by an Ethiopian invasion, principally because the garrisons of these places had been reduced when the troops were needed in Europe. In Eritrea the threat subsided, but in Libya and Cyrenaica, the tribal chiefs had defied the Italian authorities and asserted their own authority. And by 1918 Italy was holding only a strip of land along the Libyan coast and the interior was under the domination of these chiefs. Having decided to subdue the insurgents, Mussolini appointed a certain Rodolfo Graziani as "pacifier," and the savage way in which his task was accomplished has few parallels in contemporary colonial history.* Only when the

* Graziani came to be regarded as one of Mussolini's best soldiers. He was also one of the most ruthless, and known by the Arabs as "The Butcher."

population had been reduced to absolute docility were any concessions made, and the policy of conciliation which followed was
designed to promote the Duce as the "Protector of Islam." The
fact remains that by 1927 Italy felt that she had demonstrated
her ability to share the white man's burden, and that she was
ready to take on extra colonial commitments.

Enough has been said already to suggest that there were ample
reasons why Ethiopia should be selected for the first stage of
Mussolini's empire-building program. First, there was the old desire to avenge Adowa. This had been revived by Mussolini's
fighting talk and the Italians' wish to prove themselves as soldiers, stimulated not only by Adowa but by memories of a
different setting and a different enemy at Caporetto.* Possibly
Graziani's successes in Libya also contributed; Arab resistance
had been fierce, but it was no match for modern armament. If
Adowa were fought again with modern weapons, the Italians felt
certain that the result would be very different. Secondly, there
was Ethiopia's own attitude toward Italy. Despite the various
treaties, she had persistently adopted a disdainful attitude toward
Italy's rights to preferential treatment in the matter of concessions, and by 1930 it was obvious that she had not the slightest
intention of implementing the economic agreements of the 1928
Pact of Friendship. Thirdly, there was also a case on purely mili-

---

Trained as a lawyer, he never practiced. At twenty-one he joined the army and
as a junior officer spent the first nine years of his service in Eritrea and Somalia.
When the war started in 1914 he was a captain and by 1918, after three and a
half years of active service and being wounded twice, he had risen to the rank
of Colonel. After the war he was demobilized but returned to the army when
Mussolini came to power. His desert campaign in Libya consisted mainly of
raids into Arab-held territory but it is worth recording that he once fought a
joint punitive action at Kufra with General (later Field Marshal Lord) Wavell,
who, as Commander-in-Chief of British troops in the Western Desert, was his
adversary in the Second World War.

* At Caporetto, about forty miles north of Trieste, the Italian Army suffered
a crushing defeat. German divisions which had been sent to bolster the Austrian
Army attacked in October 1917 and in one battle Italy lost 305,000 soldiers, of
whom 275,000 surrendered. The rest of the defenders dissolved into a rabble
and fell back a hundred miles behind the Piave river. British and French divisions had to be rushed to Italy to keep her in the war, the Italian Commander-
in-Chief was sacked, and General Pietro Badoglio became the new commander's
Chief of Staff.

tary grounds. Once during the Italo-Turkish war in Tripoli and again in 1916, Eritrea had been threatened with an Ethiopian invasion. By 1934, Mussolini was postulating that with an army organized and trained by Belgians and Swedes, Ethiopia might well choose to stab Italy in the back if circumstances ever arose whereby she was unable to defend Eritrea—if, for example, Italy were to become embroiled in another war in Europe. Security, said the Duce, was important to Italy, and she "required such control over civil and military administration as to ensure that the removal of the menace that has hung over Italian East Africa ever since the Treaty of Uccialli was torn up and the Italian protectorate repudiated."

These three reasons each had some factual basis for complaint. But even when compounded together they were hardly enough to motivate a war of aggression. Fifty years had elapsed since Adowa; the commercial benefits to be derived under the 1928 treaty were of doubtful value; and, if security in East Africa worried Italy to the extent that Mussolini said it did, then it seemed strange that he had not been concerned about it when he had sponsored Ethiopia's admission to the League of Nations, or five years later when the Friendship Treaty was signed. It is true to say that security, which is a comprehensive term, has furnished the excuse for very many wars. But it is usually merely a contributory cause to the *casus belli* and not the prime factor—as indeed is a burning desire for revenge. Commercial benefits are another matter, particularly if a country's economic situation is as desperate as was Italy's in the twenties and early thirties. "Trade follows the flag" is an apposite cliché; Italy was seeking trade and Ethiopia was the only promising territory left by the other imperialist powers. Whether the Duce himself actually believed in the fabled riches of Haile Selassie's empire will never be known. If he trusted the reports of the numerous Italian consuls scattered over Ethiopia and the political officers at the frontiers, then he had reason to conclude that there was everything from pineapples to platinum there. But it is more likely that he hoped Ethiopia would allow some of the southern Italians, who live at a standard below that of most other Europeans, to settle there, and that there would be some oil and a few precious metals. One thing he could be sure of was that Ethiopia had infinitely greater possibilities than any of his existing African colonies.

The climate of world opinion is rarely suited to declarations of war based on the relief of one country's economic situation at the expense of another, and to state publicly that this is what lies behind an intent to aggress would probably be regarded as flippant. The brutal truth has to be camouflaged, and in the past there have been conventions amounting almost to a drill. In March 1934 Mussolini was talking about "the natural expansion which ought to lead to a collaboration between Italy and the peoples of Abyssinia." "There is no question," he declared, "of territorial conquest—this must be understood by all both far and near." [2] Three months later he was telling Fascists that it was Italy's mission to *civilize* Africa and that her position in the Mediterranean "gave her the right and imposed this duty upon her." For the benefit of Britain and France he added that he "did not want earlier arrivals to block her spiritual, political and economic expansion." In another six months, after he had reached an understanding with Laval, there was a sudden rise in the bellicosity of his pronouncements and he was demanding "a radical, unequivocal and definite solution" to what he was now pleased to call Italy's Ethiopian problem. Thus it may be seen that from the beginning of 1934, when he first started talking in earnest about Italy's colonial destiny, until October 1935, when Italian troops started to advance into Ethiopia, Mussolini's speeches followed a definite trend. And what was most interesting was the introduction of Italy's duty to *civilize* Africa when he defined the order of Italy's aspirations as: "spiritual, political, economic."

At the height of the trouble with the League that followed the invasion of Ethiopia, Mussolini lost the open support of the Vatican. But while he was making these earlier speeches and his agents were busy handing out bribes to the Ethiopian Rases, he was carrying the Pope along with him, and Italian missionaries were busy establishing the mission, known as Ethiopian College, in Addis Ababa. Few men in modern times have attacked the Roman Church with more acrid vehemence, and got away with it, than Mussolini, and in the early days of the regime he faced stern opposition from the powerful Catholic Party. Fortunately, he found in the septuagenarian Pius XI a man who was prepared to tolerate if not actually encourage Fascism. By upbringing a loyal Italian, by his experiences in Poland an ardent anti-Communist, the Pope was biased toward Fascism even before his accession, and when a policy of appeasement toward the Vatican initiated by Mussolini culminated in the Lateran Treaty in 1929, he found much to admire in the Fascist state. Under the treaty, the fifty-year-old quarrel between Italy and the Holy See was ended by the settlement of long-standing and dubious debts with the payment of a thousand million lire in Government bonds and about seven hundred million lire in cash by the Italian Government to the Vatican.* With a decline in contributions from other countries the papal income was beginning to fall off and so the settlement was doubly welcome; for it brought financial independence for the Roman Catholic Church as well as an end to a long-standing dispute. Both Pius XI and Mussolini had good reason to be satisfied with their bargain. With peace between Church and State secure, the Pope would cease to be the prisoner of the Vatican that he had been since 1870; both Italy and the Catholic Church would benefit from the other's support abroad, and that not least in Africa.

To Mussolini the problem was purely a political one. If Paris had been worth a Mass to Henri IV, then a settlement with the Vatican was worth the recognition of Catholicism as the State religion to the Italian dictator. Any question of conscience did not arise; Mussolini was anticlerical before he signed the Lateran Treaty and he did not change afterward. Like Napoleon he was bent on stabilizing the effects of a revolution, and in the Church he recognized one of the most stable factors in the community. Because the settlement was largely a paper transaction, and one which effectively bound the financial security of the Vatican to the continuance of the Fascist state, Mussolini had bought the support of the Church comparatively cheaply. During and after

---

* Details of the Lateran Treaty are reproduced in the *Survey of International Affairs 1929*, p. 466. One thousand million lire was then equivalent to about $50,000,000.

the Ethiopian war, the attitude of the Vatican vacillated, but the majority of the Italian clergy were to stand firmly and uncritically behind their Duce. Furthermore, with papal support he was assured of the help of Roman Catholic communities abroad in expressing and promoting the Fascist cause.

From what has been said so far, it may be reasoned that al- though he was laying the foundations, Mussolini was too preoccupied with Italy's domestic situation to be able to do anything about the colonial question until he was firmly in the saddle and the international situation was right for it. In fact, it was 1930 before he could properly devote his energies to it, and even in that year the world situation did not favor belligerent moves by Italy. Britain, with whom the stern factors of commerce, finance, and defense imposed a continuance of the traditional friendship, was on good terms with Italy but was playing down her imperialist role; in Germany the Nazis had not yet risen to rule; France was not disposed to be friendly. The United States remained aloof, and while she was out of the picture, Europe looked to the League of Nations as a means of establishing international law and as a solution to the imperial rivalries that had menaced the world for nearly fifty years. Two years later, the picture seemed rather different. An economic storm had swept across the Atlantic and in 1933, when Hitler came to power, the Duce saw his chance. As one country after another abandoned the gold standard and built tariff walls to safeguard their economies, the prospects of increased international trade—and with them the chances of better international cooperation—gradually diminished. With Britain uneasy, France frankly apprehensive, and the United States seemingly disinterested about developments in Germany, Mussolini quickly appreciated that the ingredients of a real devil's broth were all to hand. While others argued over the brew there should be opportunities for Italy to better her place at the international table.

From Marshal Emilio de Bono's candid and dispassionate disclosures,* it appears that plans for the annexation of Ethiopia

* All the quoted material that follows in this chapter is excerpted from De Bono, *Anno XIIII: The Conquest of an Empire* (see Bibliography).

were being formulated early in 1932. In the spring of that year, the sixty-six-year-old Marshal was sent by the Duce on a confidential mission to Eritrea. "Nothing definite," he wrote later, in 1936, "had as yet been settled as regards the character and method of a possible campaign against a probable enemy, nor in respect of the force which might have to be employed." The victim had been chosen but "nothing definite" had been settled because it was possible that without any actual fighting political manipulation could bring Italy the prestige for which Mussolini was striving. A little war was desirable; after all Adowa had to be avenged and national "honor" redeemed. But if Haile Selassie eventually agreed to come to terms and be content with a puppet role, the main object could be achieved peacefully.

On his return De Bono reported to Mussolini. ". . . I gave the Duce a succinct account of the state of affairs; an unvarnished account, but optimistic in spirit." What it amounted to was that there would have to be considerable preparations in Eritrea and Italian Somaliland before any military venture guaranteeing success could be launched in Ethiopia. Neither colony had any natural resources to speak of and both had been neglected since Adowa, and existing facilities—ports and communications—were totally inadequate for any large-scale operation. New roads, better ports, and bigger garrisons were needed first, and during 1932 Mussolini sanctioned a development program. De Bono, as Minister of Colonies, was given the task of seeing it through, and his memoirs explain that the preparations "were considered in the light of warlike eventualities, which it behooved one to regard as increasingly probable." In September, King Victor Emmanuel visited the two colonies, accompanied by De Bono, and this, he said, "gave me an opportunity of revising, on the spot, by knowledge of certain matters which would help me to shape the detail of the decisions which would have to be taken." Furthermore, from De Bono's account, it appears that the king must have had at least an inkling of which way the wind was blowing: "His Majesty is a keen and profound observer; nothing escaped him, and his judgements on what he saw were conspicuous for their practical good sense. The lack of roads and the insufficiency of the railway attracted his attention, and he discussed these matters with the Duce."

By the summer of 1933 the plans for a military operation had been drawn up. However, with the situation in Europe unsettled, Mussolini had not yet made any irrevocable decision. The Italian rearmament program was not yet complete and despite De Bono's urgings he was unwilling to undertake any campaign until he was convinced that it would be successful. De Bono himself was consoled by the promise that he would be given command of the operations when they did eventuate:

. . . one day I said to the Duce: "Listen, if there is war down there— and if you think me worthy of it—you ought to grant me the honour of conducting the campaign." The Duce looked at me hard, and at once he replied: "Surely." "You don't think me too old?" I added. "No," he replied, "because we mustn't lose time." *From this moment the Duce was definitely of the opinion that the matter would have to be settled not later than 1936* [author's italics], and he told me as much. . . . It was the autumn of 1933. The Duce had spoken to no one of the forthcoming operations in East Africa; *only he and I* [author's italics] knew what was going to happen, and no indiscretion occurred by which the news could reach the public.

De Bono's memoirs go on to say that he put the following considerations to Mussolini:

The political conditions in Abyssinia are deplorable; it should not be a very difficult task to effect the disintegration of the Empire if we work at it well on political lines, and it could be regarded as certain after a military victory on our part. The unruliness of the Rases, some of whom are open malcontents, may lead to a movement which will induce one or another of the stronger of them—even without the Emperor's wish—to rebel against the Emperor, and give us an opportunity to intervene. But, on the other hand, the possibility must not be excluded that those chieftains who are situated on our frontier may attempt to attack us, counting on our present weakness. This being so, it is incumbent on us to prepare ourselves, so that we could withstand the shock of the whole Abyssinian force in our present positions, and then pass to the counterattack, and go right in with the intention of making a complete job of it, once and for all. The Duce thought as I did, and ordered me to go full speed ahead. I must be ready as soon as possible. "Money will be needed, Chief; lots of money." "There will be no lack of money."

At the beginning of 1934, the general officer commanding the Italian troops in Eritrea and the Italian military attaché at Addis Ababa were summoned to Rome to advise Mussolini on what De Bono was calling his "defensive-counteroffensive" plan. Both apparently agreed with the method that was advocated, and it was decided to let those who were to be concerned with implementing the plan into the secret. Officially this was the first time that the "Minister for War, the Chief of the General Staff and the Staff Corps" had heard about it, and Marshal Badoglio, the Chief of Staff, was not happy to accept the plan at its face value. According to De Bono, "The Chief of the General Staff wished to send his Adjutant-General to Eritrea in order that he might report on the actual state of affairs. His report, though very able, was by no means optimistic, and the preliminary work that was necessary was so extensive that no hope was left of completing it within the time-limit which we had fixed as desirable." In fact, Badoglio, according to his own memoirs, did not consider that any operations could start in Ethiopia before the autumn of 1936—exactly a year later than the date fixed by Mussolini. De Bono "was not impressed" with Badoglio's arguments and "went ahead in accordance with my fixed idea, which I knew was consonant with the Duce's wishes."

Mussolini had in fact fixed the time for the start of the campaign as October 1, 1935, and when de Bono was appointed High Commissioner and Commander of Troops in East Africa in January 1935, he had just under ten months to complete arrangements for which Badoglio had said he would need two years. "Not many thought it possible to accomplish such a gigantic work of preparation in ten months," Mussolini wrote in his introduction to De Bono's memoirs. "There were moments when the inextricable difficulties of the task took possession of men's minds: but De Bono's determination, his fifty years of experience, his sang-froid, his vigorous, youthful optimism, were elements that made for success." With the General Staff in mind the Duce continued, "The obstacles—even those that seemed insurmountable in the eyes of the timid and sceptical—were overcome, and overcome within the time-limit, which Emilio de Bono expected as though it had been divinely ordained."

Meanwhile, events outside the military sphere had been moving in Mussolini's favor. In September 1931 a storm had burst over the Far East: Japan marched into Manchuria and the League of Nations showed that it was completely ineffectual in dealing with the situation. Not only did the whole idea of collective security suffer a shock from which it was never to recover, but Mussolini was quick to appreciate the likely significance so far as his own adventure was concerned. France's interests in Indo-China had prompted her to remain on good terms with Japan; Britain had hastily made it clear that she was not interested in anything but safeguarding her own trading rights in the East, and when it appeared that Japan had guaranteed to do this, Britain's attitude was that she was prepared to let matters in Manchuria take their course. In the United States public opinion was apathetic and no support for any action was forthcoming from Congress; America was in fact slumping farther back into isolation.

Since it was now clear that the countries most likely to interfere with his plans were prepared to condone an aggressive war so long as their commercial interests were not affected, Mussolini must have rubbed his hands in glee. Despite its high-flown ideals the League of Nations appeared to offer no protection to its members if their territory lay outside Europe and unless they were of the right color physically or politically.

CHAPTER 5

The Deepening Shadows

War has a beauty of its own because it serves towards the aggrandisement of the great Fascist Italy.

F. T. MARINETTI, from a manifesto
"War has a beauty of its own" [1]

Whether or not it fell strictly within the timetable Mussolini's planning staff had sketched out, the Walwal affair was to become the main pretext for war. Not that this was apparent for some time. On December 10, 1934, according to the Rome correspondent of the *Daily Mail*, "Official circles in Rome were continuing to display optimism concerning the outcome of the Abyssinian frontier incident—when 1,000 Abyssinian troops attacked an Italian frontier post at Walwal." Three weeks later, even the *New Statesman* was airily predicting that Britain would be "surprised" if Italy and Abyssinia came to blows over the business.

At this point whether or not what happened at Walwal was deliberately provoked by the Italians is worthy of some further consideration. If it was, then—judging by the subsequent evidence of De Bono, Badoglio, and Mussolini himself—those re-

sponsible for the state management of the *casus belli* seem to have
had a poor sense of timing. Mussolini had no intention of coming
to blows until he was assured of absolute success. He was not
going to risk another Adowa under any circumstances, and as
the military wanted another year to complete their preparations,
there was much to be gained from a policy which exuded sweet
reasonableness to everybody except Ethiopia. Having got a pretext, the obvious course was to keep the situation simmering.
The more noise and stir created, and the longer a settlement was
held off, the more likely it would be that the clang of the Italian
war anvil would go unnoticed. As it turned out, the Duce's tactics
achieved a remarkable degree of success. By resorting to dilatory
tactics and provoking every manner of objection, Italy managed
to string out the arbitration negotiations and so provide the
Council of the League of Nations with an excuse for not dealing
with Haile Selassie's appeal under Article 15 of the Covenant.
For seven months, while Italian troops and war matériel poured
into Italian East Africa, the Council dealt with nothing but the
trumpery of Walwal.

That trouble was bound to arise eventually was quite certain;
there was too much Italian activity both inside and outside Ethiopia to allow for anything else. Apart from the Banda, Italian
consuls and agents within the country and Italian political officers at the frontiers were all working to create internal dissen-
sion, and from the moment that the decision in principle to invade Ethiopia had been taken in Rome their activities grew in
intensity. As a result, part of the complaint against Italy which
Haile Selassie ultimately tabled at Geneva was concerned solely
with those activities:

. . . At places where there is not a single Italian national, a consul
establishes himself in an area known as consular territory with a guard
of about ninety men, for whom he claims jurisdictional immunity.
This is an obvious abuse of consular privileges.

The abuse is all the greater that the consul's duties, apart from the
supplying of information of a military character, take the form of
assembling stocks of arms, which constitute a threat to the peace of
the country, whether from the internal or the international point of
view.[2]

Under the cloak of diplomatic immunity the consuls were in fact engaged in far more sinister activities—activities at which Haile Selassie could only guess. Under the direction of Signor Gasparini, the Governor of Eritrea, their main task was to foster dissent and cultivate the dissident elements among those of the Ethiopian chiefs who were dissatisfied with their lot under the Emperor. From the way in which the chiefs acted later it would appear that the consular reports to Rome on their progress in this field were overoptimistic. Nevertheless they did have some success. One important chief won over very early was Ras Gugsa, one of the two governors in Tigre and a son-in-law of the Emperor. Although he died in 1933, his two sons joined the Italians as soon as hostilities broke out. But this was an exceptional case, and although in the final stages of the war there was considerable demoralization among Haile Selassie's personal staff, this was probably due to the long series of defeats and strain rather than the consuls' early intrigues. Since many of the Rases continued the struggle long after the Emperor had fled the country, the blatant corruptive effects of Italian gold were undoubtedly much less than what had been hoped for by Signor Gasparini.

What is more important than the actual result of the consuls' activities is the belief in their estimated effect during the preparation period. De Bono shared the optimism of the consuls, and the opinion he passed to the Duce was:

The political conditions in Abyssinia are deplorable; it should not be a difficult task to effect the disintegration of the Empire if we work it well on political lines, and it could be regarded as certain after a military victory on our part.[3]

From this, Mussolini's deduction could only be that if and when it came to a question of force, little real fighting would be necessary. Nevertheless, at the beginning of 1935, Mussolini would probably have preferred to have attained his ends without resorting to force. As he saw it there was always the possibility that Haile Selassie might accede to his demands over Walwal. Had this happened it would have been clear that the Emperor had come to realize that resistance would be futile, and then with further bullying, more bribes, and deeper political infiltration,

Italy's grip on Ethiopia could have been extended until she had everything she wanted without the need for any military action. In January 1935 the position had not yet been reached where the Duce wanted glory quite as much as Ethiopian territory; the warlike preparations had not gone so far that they might not be halted without loss of face, and at the cost of becoming a puppet, Haile Selassie might have been able to retain his throne and a large part of his empire in apparent independence. The victory would have been less spectacular for Mussolini and would have meant a *volte-face*, but this was not something to which he was unaccustomed, and the fact that the Duce might have settled for the lesser triumph is borne out by his parting instructions to De Bono in January 1935:

You will go out with the olive branch in your cap. We shall see how the Walwal affair is settled. If it suits us to accept the conditions offered in consequence of the award you will announce your appointment to the Emperor telling him that you have been sent to remove misunderstandings and to collaborate as good neighbours in the moral and material interests of the two states. In the meantime, continue to make active preparations, such as you would make in view of the more difficult and adverse outcome of the affair. If no solution of the incident is offered or if it is not such as to satisfy us, we shall follow subsequent events exclusively in accordance with our own standpoint.[4]

Within but a few days of this briefing, Mussolini's attitude had started to harden; from Pierre Laval he had been given the tip that France would be prepared to look the other way while Mussolini "arranged" matters with Ethiopia.

It was on the evening of January 3, 1935—by strange coincidence the same day as that on which Ethiopia had referred the Walwal affair to the League—that the French Foreign Minister left Paris to make his first trip to Rome. It was also his first major effort in the cause of France, and his aim had nothing whatsoever to do with Ethiopia. Laval's prime concern was with Europe; what went on in Africa was of little importance when compared with the growing menace of a resurgent Germany, and if he had any thoughts about Ethiopia at all as the train carried him through to Rome, they would have been concerned only with its value as a bargaining counter. Thrifty, shrewd, and cautious, the "Nigger of the Auvergne" was a realist with the philosophy of one who believes that nothing can be obtained in this world without payment in one form or another. A lawyer of peasant stock, he possessed all the qualities that might be expected of such a combination in a Frenchman—especially one hailing from the deep vastness in south-central France which is Auvergne. The Auvergnese are the grimmest of all French peasants; hard-working, crafty, suspicious, close to the soil, they used to be the coal and wood dealers all over France, and Laval himself was often called "Le Bougnat"—slang Auvergnese figuratively describing "a coal and wood man." Many of the Auvergnese have a strong negroid cast of countenance, and with his stocky build, thick lips, and heavy black oiled hair, together with his black suit and perpetual white tie, Laval undoubtedly presented an unusual appearance for a French diplomat. Because Laval's particular form of patriotism carried him to an ignominious end, the tendency has been to relegate him to the role of villain and to extrapolate opinions formed on his behavior between 1940 and 1945 back into the preceding decade. This is unfortunate because his conduct throughout the whole Ethiopian crisis was crude in its frankness and, in contrast to that of some of his British colleagues, he left no doubt as to his intentions.

All his life Laval had been a passionate pacifist—and when he started his political career it took courage to be a pacifist. Twice within living memory France had been racked by war with Germany, and if it came within his power, Laval intended to see that the volcano did not explode a third time. In 1919, with Germany beaten to her knees, Russia relapsing into barbarism, the Austro-Hungarian Empire no more, and the chaos of postwar Italy giving no indication of the renascence shortly to take place, it had seemed as if France was about to enter an era recalling that of the great days of Louis XIV or Napoleon. But France's power had declined since then, and that of her rivals had grown. The army of France was no longer the most powerful in Europe and the morale of French conscripts was said to be poor. Cynics were

saying that France was prepared for war—perfectly prepared, in
1935, for the war of 1914, in the same way as she had been prepared for the war of 1854 in 1870. The basic trouble was deep-
seated. Corruption among French politicians, doubts about the
impartiality of the courts of justice, and suspicions of the police,
had all brought the country's administration into disrepute.*
Consequently, when the Stavisky scandal broke in January 1934,
public opinion attached little importance to the financier's alleged suicide, assuming that Stavisky had been done away with in
case he incriminated those in high places.† The disgust generated
by the scandal came to a climax the following month, when the
people of Paris rose against the Government. On the night of
February 6, thirty thousand demonstrators who had assembled in
the Place de la Concorde were fired on by the Garde Mobile,
with the result that seventeen people died, several thousand were
injured, and Laval became Premier.

When Hitler came to power Laval had quickly decided that
the potential danger to France came from Berlin. Consequently,
as Foreign Minister, he saw that his prime task was to contain
Germany. Yet it was obvious to him that if he was to be remembered for his contribution to French security and peace, there
was a good deal of difficult negotiation ahead. Much of this has
since been unfairly labeled double-dealing and appeasement, although Laval—too astute himself to trust anyone fully—would
have been the first to suspect others of underlying motives. The
Saar plebiscite, which lay in the background of his visit to Rome,
is one example serving to illustrate his approach to international
bargaining, which in later perspective could not truly be classed
as appeasement but which at the time was not fairly judged.

* During Clemenceau's term of office, one minister was imprisoned and
another exiled; several other prominent citizens were shot on charges of in-
triguing with the enemy. In January 1923, the acquittal of Germaine Berton,
the murderess of a Royalist, Marius Plateau, raised grave doubts as to the impartiality of the courts. In November the same year, when Philippe Daudet,
the son of a Royalist leader, was found dead in highly suspicious circumstances,
most Frenchmen believed he had been murdered by the police.

† Serge Alexandre Stavisky was a petty crook with influential friends, who
killed himself—or was murdered—when his fraudulent empire, worth forty million francs, collapsed. The case rocked France, and the implications reached to
the very heart of French political life.

Realizing that the plebiscite was not likely to go in favor of France, Laval decided that a gesture of generosity was called for. Since the Saarlanders would opt for Germany, his view was sensible; generosity on this occasion would cost nothing, and to question the decision would almost certainly bring trouble.

Having concluded that Nazi Germany was the growing menace, Laval decided that the best hope for France lay in lining up the rest of Europe against Hitler. Winning over Italy was the first move, and in December 1934, the situation seemed more suited to a *rapprochement* between the two countries than it had been for very many years. To Mussolini, it was as clear as it was to Laval that the potential threat to Europe was from Berlin. And if France might need Italy to help defend the Rhine, Italy might equally well require French assistance to stem German expansion into Austria. Indeed, in February 1934 the Duce had declared that it was essential that Austria should remain independent; France and Britain had both associated themselves with the declaration. A month later, he had emphasized Italy's determination to prevent German expansion across her northern and eastern borders by signing protocols with Austria and Hungary which provided for mutual consultation in the event of a threat to any one of the three countries. Then, when the two dictators had met briefly in June, their first meeting had been far from cordial. Mussolini, expecting to impress the man he regarded as his junior partner in Fascism, had found Hitler arrogant; Hitler, who arrived for the meeting in Venice in a raincoat, had been irritated to find that Mussolini and his staff were all in uniform. The confrontation had got off to a bad start and nothing of any importance had come of the meeting. Both had agreed that they disliked Russia on ideological grounds and France on practical ones, but Austria—the country which Hitler was committed to bring into the German Reich, and which Mussolini was resolved should remain an independent buffer on Italy's northern frontier —remained a bone of contention. Hitler had left Venice without reaching any agreement on this thorny problem, and the following month when the Nazis overplayed their hand and attempted a *coup d'état* by murdering the Austrian Chancellor Engelbert

Dollfuss while his family were guests of Mussolini in Italy, the Duce's reaction had been prompt and forceful. Three divisions of Italian troops were sent to the Brenner Pass to back a promise to the acting Chancellor, Prince Starhemberg, that Italy would not stand idly by while Germany swallowed up Austria. Hitler, realizing that his supporters had overstepped the mark, had been compelled to sit back while one of Mussolini's protégés, Kurt von Schuschnigg, Dollfuss's successor, put down the coup.

Meanwhile Mussolini had made no attempt to disguise his contempt for the man he had referred to after their meeting in Venice as a "mad little clown" or for the Germans themselves who were "still the barbarians of Tacitus and the Reformation in eternal conflict with Rome," and in a speech at Bari during September he had declared: "Thirty centuries of history allow the Italians to regard with supreme indifference certain doctrines taught beyond the Alps by the descendants of people who were wholly illiterate in the days when Caesar, Virgil, and Augustus flourished in Rome." By October, the month in which the Duce said, "An understanding between Italy and France would be useful and fruitful," it was evident that the chances of France reaching an agreement with Italy were better than they had ever been. Laval was delighted; if Mussolini was so eager for an understanding, the chances of striking a bargain seemed very good indeed.

Laval, accompanied by his daughter Josée, arrived in Rome on January 4, 1935, where he was received in style. A meeting with the Pope had been arranged and this occasion gave rise to a flood of anecdotes: Laval's imaginary protest, "They're saying I addressed the Pope as Your Reverence—everybody knows he's called the Holy See," or his supposed comment when being rehearsed for the audience, and told that he must make three genuflections: "Three what?" were all illustrative of the popular image of an uncouth self-seeking tough. The talks with the Italian dictator offered little scope for snide comment, however. The two men were closeted together in the Palazzo Venezia under strict security precautions, and it was not until the conclusion of the talks that the agreement which they had reached was revealed to the eager, waiting reporters. What was released made no mention of Ethiopia; there was only a brief hint that the subject might have been discussed.

On January 7, the newspaper headlines in London read: "Midnight Italian Pact," "Dramatic Palace Scenes," "Mussolini's Toast in Champagne." But the reports which followed made drab reading, and so far as one could see, the Laval-Mussolini understanding hardly seemed to justify champagne. According to the *Daily Mail*, four documents had been initialed before the conference broke up:

1. A statement recording the identity of views of France and Italy on the principal problems of general policy.

2. A joint recommendation to the neighbouring and successive states of the old Austro-Hungarian monarchy to conclude a convention with respect to frontiers and non-intervention.

3. A consultative pact in which France and Italy undertook to consult together should events threaten the independence of Austria. (Germany, Hungary, Czechoslovakia, Jugoslavia, Poland, Rumania are to be invited to join in this pact.)

4. A convention regulating colonial problems in Northern Africa.

Because of Germany's attitude, the first three documents scarcely seemed worth the paper they were written on, and ten years were to elapse before it was known that secret teeth had been put into these apparently innocuous statements. France and Italy had entered into a military alliance under which France would send troops to support Italy if Hitler moved into Austria, and conversely Italy would provide the French Army with air support if Hitler tried to occupy the Rhineland. It was the last document, so briefly described, that held the real meat of the bargaining for the other three ostensibly meager and nebulous agreements.

In the negotiations Laval's chief bargaining counters had been some of Italy's long-standing grudges. First was the question of Italy's existing colonies. The few square miles France had conceded on the Libyan-French border fell far short of what Italy considered was due to her under the terms of the London Agreement of 1915, and she wanted an extension. She also

wanted a strip of land across French North Africa to link Libya
with Lake Chad; lastly there were some old grievances concerning the position of Italian settlers in Tunis which had never been
settled. It was these that provided the most emotive issue, since
Italy claimed that Tunisia to Italians meant what Alsace-
Lorraine means to the French. Never having forgiven France for
appropriating the colony, she had kept the discontent alive by
insisting that children born of Italian parents retain Italian nationality and use their own language in Italian schools and institutions, and by clinging to a number of other outmoded privileges
—all of which hampered the French administration.

Three protocols to the pact which were published later pur-
ported to disclose the nature of the settlements in Africa. In return for recognizing France's rights in Tunisia, renouncing the
special treatment accorded to Italians there, and agreeing that
they should surrender their nationality, Italy had been given a
strip of desert on the southern border of Libya, 800 square kilometers of French Somaliland, and the right to buy 20 percent of
the shares in the Djibuti–Addis Ababa railway. To all intents and
purposes France had got the better part of the deal. So far as one
could see, Mussolini had traded Italian friendship and a principle
in Tunisia which successive Italian Governments had upheld for
over forty years for a few square miles of desert and some shares
in what was widely recognized as an uneconomic enterprise. That
Mussolini should have come to terms on Tunis so easily surprised
most Italians and even Laval recorded that:

When the extent of Mussolini's concessions became known at the
Palais Farnese [the French Embassy in Rome] I was surprised to hear
important officials state their dissatisfaction, and add "If we had a
Parliament, Mussolini would be overthrown." I remember that at
the time M. Payrouton, our Governor in Tunisia, reported that in
the Italian schools the teachers had removed from the walls the pic-
tures of Mussolini and thrown them on the ground, and that children
spat upon them. . . .[5]

Not unnaturally the current explanation was that the Duce had
been taken in by Laval in regard to the value of the ceded territory, and the story went around that when Mussolini com-

plained he was getting nothing but desert Laval smiled and replied, "Oh, there's bound to be a few villages there somewhere—though they won't be Rome or Aubervilliers of course." *

In point of fact, what the public had been permitted to see was only an insignificant part of the agreements, the tip of the iceberg; nothing was disclosed of the real bargain which had been struck at a private dinner party in the French Embassy on January 6. No record was kept of what was said either at the dinner table or afterward but, before leaving Rome, Laval is reputed to have told some of the reporters waiting to see him off that he had given Mussolini "A desert—I have given him Abyssinia." Subsequently, however, Laval strenuously denied that he ever traded Abyssinia for Italian support in Europe, and in the testimony published as his *Diary* he recorded: "With reference to Ethiopia. I urged Mussolini not to resort to force. My last words to him were: 'Follow the example of Marshal Lyautey.' †
He committed the blunder of going to war. He started war against my will and despite my solemn protest." This is sufficient evidence to prove that Ethiopia had come up for discussion in Rome, and Laval's own admission that he argued against the use of force makes it patently clear that the likelihood of military operations was raised during the talks. It is unlikely that the Duce disclosed his grand design—there was no reason why he should be particularly explicit anyway. Laval knew that he was not a collector of deserts, and the Frenchman was not so naïve as to expect Mussolini to trade Italian friendship and abandon Italy's claims in Tunis merely for a few square miles of barren waste and some railway shares of doubtful value. There was no need to spell it out; what Mussolini wanted was an assurance that France would be looking the other way when Italy was ready to deal with Ethiopia. And undoubtedly this is what he got.

This is not to say that Laval was not hoping that Italy would

* Mussolini said afterwards that in the whole area transferred there were only sixty-nine inhabitants.
† As High Commissioner for Morocco before the First World War, Marshall Lyautey earned a reputation for judicious methods of colonial government; as a soldier he was equally successful with his internal security arrangements. Quite how Mussolini was expected to follow in Lyautey's footsteps is difficult to understand; in 1912 Morocco was French territory, in 1934 Ethiopia was not an Italian colony.

get her own way without war—probably he was. But to him Hitler's growing truculence was of far greater importance than Mussolini's aspirations in an area outside Europe where France no longer had any ambitions, and even if he knew that De Bono was on board ship bound for Massawa at the time of the meeting, it is doubtful if Laval's attitude would have been any different. Like Winston Churchill when Russia was attacked by Germany, he was prepared to make a pact with the devil if he thought it would help to resolve the problem of Germany. Italy's political system might not be to everyone's liking but that was a matter for the Italians, and he had no time for those of his fellow Frenchmen who felt disinclined to prejudice their country's interests because of their allegiance to abstract international theories. "Those damned *ideologues*," he said of them. "The Rights of Man? Certainly. But the rights of Frenchmen first!" For the security of France Laval would bargain with any country that could help—and to hell with its political implications.

Both Mussolini and Laval were well satisfied with their contract when the latter left Rome. The French Foreign Minister could concentrate on other measures to contain Germany, and the Duce knew that he could rely on France for tacit, if not active, support for his venture. Britain still had to be "squared" but the Italian dictator had great hopes of Laval's influence in this direction. And even more important at that moment was French backing at Geneva, where he was anxious to keep the Ethiopian dispute simmering until he was ready to act.

Within days the newfound friendship was put to the test, and the result was much as Mussolini had hoped. From Rome, Laval went straight to Geneva, arriving on January 11, in time to take part in the discussion on the Ethiopian appeal under Article 15 of the Covenant, which dealt with the threat of war. Immediately, he threw all his influence into preventing the appeal coming before the League Council. In fact, the appeal had already been put on the Council's agenda, but largely as a result of pressure on Italy by Laval and Mr. Eden (now Lord Avon)—who as Lord Privy Seal was representing Britain on the Council—it was taken off. On January 16 Eden proposed that, in view of Italy's attitude, matters should be allowed to take their course at Geneva. This induced the Italian delegate, Count Aloisi, to adopt a conciliatory line with his Ethiopian opposite number, Mr. Tecle Harawiate, resulting in the League Council receiving written assurances from both countries saying that each would pursue a settlement in conformity with their own Treaty of Friendship. In Italy's letter there was an additional assurance that her negotiations would be in accordance with the spirit of the Covenant. Italy was stalling for time, delaying actions until her standing with Britain and France was clarified, and using the delay to complete her military operations.

Once Mussolini was confident that France was not going to stand in the way of Italy's empire-building, his next objective was to try to persuade Britain to stand aside. His first move in this direction came toward the end of January when the Italian chargé d'affaires in London called at the Foreign Office to inform the British Government officially of the agreements concluded by Laval and the Duce. Then, on January 29, the Italian Ambassador, Signor Grandi, followed up with an invitation to the British Government for talks "to consider pacific agreements for the harmonious development of Italian and British interests in Abyssinia." This was a tactfully worded proposal implying that Italy was ready to safeguard British interests in Ethiopia if Britain was prepared to allow Italy a free hand there, and no one was better qualified to put Italy's case than her ambassador in London. A man of great personal charm, the big, bluff, bearded Dino Grandi had been the Fascist Chief of Staff during the March on Rome, and in 1929, at thirty-four, Italy's youngest-ever Minister of Foreign Affairs. With his perfect command of both English and French, his work as a diplomatic negotiator in Rome had been brilliant, and he had in fact trained himself to be a perfect foreign minister—learning the languages, keeping himself slim on an ascetic's diet, and ordering his clothes from the only English tailor in Rome. When he fell from favor, as so many of the Duce's collaborators were apt to do, he was posted to England as Ambassador to the Court of St. James's, supposedly as a punishment for not doing his job properly and allowing France and

Britain to compose an agreement at the Lausanne Reparations Conference which excluded Italy. In Britain the Duce presumed that Grandi would learn better the ways of the subtle English. As it turned out, it was there that the former *squadristi* leader reached the peak of his career, for before long he was the most popular as well as the most fashionable diplomat in London. As an Ambassador his success came from his genuine understanding of and liking for the British, while his ability to weather the caprices of Fascist foreign policy dictated by Rome was something which says a great deal for his mental agility.

When Signor Grandi made his first overtures to the British Foreign Office, the man with whom he had to contend was Sir John Simon. A lawyer by profession—some said the greatest lawyer of the day—the not-so-simple Simon was an exceptionally shy and lonely man, desperately anxious to be liked. Unfortunately, popularity was the one thing which consistently evaded him, and by the time he was replaced by Sir Samuel Hoare on June 7, 1935, he had managed to make himself the most unpopular Foreign Secretary in modern times.* Trying to steer a middle course in order to avoid offending people inevitably led to nobody being pleased, and as the crisis over Ethiopia deepened he was reviled by both the friends and enemies of Italy. There can be little doubt that as Foreign Secretary to the MacDonald-Baldwin National Government then in power, he had an extremely difficult task—not made easier by the fact that he endeavored to interpret its policy, or lack of it, with legal exactitude. While the Government, with its wait-and-see-and-hope-for-the-best attitude, deliberated about Ethiopia, Simon was not prepared to commit himself on Signor Grandi's proposals until a

---

* The British working classes remembered him for an historic speech declaring the General Strike of 1926 illegal, and loathed him; over the all-important question of disarmament he had suceeded in antagonizing both France and Germany; and during the Manchurian crisis he offended the United States and weakened the League with his virtual advocacy of the Japanese case. Later, as Home Secretary, Sir John was responsible for civil defense and published the first handbooks on antigas precautions, which were sufficient in themselves to guarantee universal unpopularity in Britain. Despite their forebodings, most people preferred not to think about war. Instructions about gas masks and decontamination drills were unwelcome reminders of the harsh reality of what the unthinkable could bring in its wake.

definite policy emerged from the Cabinet Room. At the same time he had no wish to reject the offer of negotiations out of hand. All he felt able to do was to burke the issue by promising to look into the matter and let Signor Grandi know in due course. And to help the Cabinet to make up its mind, a departmental committee under the chairmanship of the Permanent Under-Secretary of State for the Colonies, Sir John Maffey, was set up to study the extent of Britain's material interests in Ethiopia and the likely effect on them of an Italian invasion.

Meanwhile, it may be presumed that Mussolini had taken Sir John Simon's evasive answer to mean that the British Government would hesitate to do anything to upset his agreement with Laval and was unlikely to raise any serious objections if he took some positive action against Ethiopia. If so, it was not an unreasonable assumption. Britain could hardly claim to be ignorant of the way things were shaping—there was so much evidence that Whitehall could not fail to know that something was brewing in Italian East Africa. By January a constant and growing stream of Italian ships carrying troops and easily recognizable war matériel was passing through the Suez Canal. Moreover, Italian political officers operating on the Sudanese border had been talking openly to their British colleagues for months about plans for provoking unrest in Ethiopia, and since September Sir Sidney Barton, the British Minister in Addis Ababa, had been sending a succession of warning signals and notes back to London. The British Foreign Office might prefer to keep quiet but it certainly knew what was going on.

When Haile Selassie first announced his intention of referring the Walwal dispute to Geneva, the Foreign Office told Barton that ". . . while Simon agreed to the Emperor doing all he could to reach agreement by direct negotiation, it seemed probable that the cooperation of the League would be needed in the end. We would do anything we could to help." [6] The suggestion meant less than might be inferred from such words. Britain's help was intended to be limited solely to mediation at Geneva, and Barton tried to explain to the Ethiopian Government that Britain did not wish to get involved in the dispute. "When the Counsel-

lor at the Italian Embassy in London, Signor Vitetti, called at the
Foreign Office on December 3, he was told that our interest in
Walwal and Wardair related to the ancient grazing and watering
rights enjoyed by the nomadic tribes of British Somaliland. While
we could not in any circumstances disregard these rights, the matter was certainly not one which should be allowed to do any
harm to Anglo-Italian relations." [7] The last thing that Whitehall
wanted was to be mixed up in a dispute between an upstart African kingdom and a European power whose cooperation in restraining Germany Britain was hoping to gain. Indeed, Sir Robert Vansittart, the Permanent Under-Secretary of State at the
Foreign Office, would have stopped at little to keep Italy sweet,
pro-British, and anti-Hitler. "International politics of this time
would not be intelligible without some reference to the part
played by Sir Robert Vansittart," Lord Avon wrote, looking
back on the period. "Vansittart held decided views on international affairs and his instinct was usually right, but his sense of
the political methods that could be used was sometimes at fault."
But seeing the menace of Nazi Germany, "he was determined to
keep the rest of Europe in line against Germany and would pay
almost any price to do so. He did not discern that to appease
Mussolini beyond a certain point in Abyssinia must break up the
alignment that Italy was intended to strengthen." In Vansittart
he had "never known one [head of the department] to compare
with Sir Robert as a relentless, not to say ruthless, worker for the
views he held strongly himself. The truth is that Vansittart was
seldom an official giving cool and disinterested advice based on
study and experience. He was himself a sincere, almost fanatical,
crusader, and much more a Secretary of State in mentality than
a permanent official." [8] Vansittart himself confessed that he
". . . laboured under a dualism which might look like duplicity.
. . . My real trouble was that we should all have to choose between Austria and Abyssinia. . . ." [9] This attitude was to lead to
differences between the Permanent Under-Secretary and the
young man who was to be Minister for League Affairs during the
real crisis—differences which were "amicable but defined."

The Maffey Commission reported to Whitehall in June 1935,
and excerpts from the report were published in the *Giornale*

d'Italia while it was still on the confidential list. The precise details of how the editor, the diminutive Signor Virginio Gayda, got possession of this highly controversial document still remain a mystery, but certainly it was not the journalistic scoop that was imagined at the time. Five years before the Second World War, it was learned later, official secrets—the quantity and importance of which were far more serious than the more publicized wartime exploits of Cicero in Ankara—leaked out of the British Embassy in Rome to find their way into the hands of Mussolini and Hitler. To some extent this explains the Duce's amazing self-assurance throughout the crisis which was to come; diplomacy is made easier if it is possible to read the opponents' appreciations and plans while you are dealing with them. Vansittart himself, reflecting on the leakages, said sadly that "such knowledge was fatal to compromise." * But there was no suspicion of a leakage when the report was received in Whitehall, and when the *Giornale d'Italia*'s disclosures were published the Foreign Office allowed a rumor to circulate to the effect that it was not displeased because the report gave the lie to inferences that Britain also had designs on Ethiopia. The suggestion was that this was one of those deliberate leaks which are the tricks of the skilled diplomat.

In retrospect the one thing that the Maffey Report accomplishes is to dispel once and for all any illusions about Whitehall not being aware of Italy's aims, since it proves that both the Foreign and Colonial Offices not only knew what Mussolini intended but also that, in their estimate, the operation he was about to embark on would likely be wholly successful. The gist of the report is contained in the Commission's second and third conclusions:

2) There are no vital British interests in Abyssinia or adjoining countries such as to necessitate British resistance to an Italian conquest of Abyssinia. Italian control of Abyssinia would on some

* When Vansittart got wind of the leakage in 1935 he thought at first that it had occurred at the Foreign Office, and the security there was tightened up. He was on the wrong scent. According to the Ciano diaries it appears that the Austrian Foreign Minister, Guido Schmidt, warned the Foreign Office that information was leaking out of the British Embassy in Rome. It was some time before an investigation there confirmed his information. The Italian staff, down to the boilerman, all appear to have been implicated.

grounds be advantageous, on others disadvantageous. In general, as far as local British interests are concerned it would be a matter of indifference whether Abyssinia remained independent or was absorbed by Italy.

3) From a standpoint of Imperial defence, an independent Abyssinia would be preferable to an Italian Abyssinia, *but the threat to British interests appears distant and would depend only on a war against Italy, which for the moment appears improbable* [author's italics].

In less than three years the situation depicted in this last paragraph would look very, very different. Yet if one disregards the events of 1938 and 1939 and tries to consider the report as might a contemporary judge, the last sentence is of special interest. What it suggests is that it had not occurred to the Permanent Under-Secretary of State for the Colonies, or to any of the other experts in his committee, that an Italian invasion of Ethiopia would entail breaches of treaties which might lead to a much bigger war. The point is that the British Government of 1935 appears to have looked on Ethiopia as a second-class member of the League, of secondary importance in regard to treaties made with her, and did not expect any serious international complications if Italy decided to march into her territory. Only the issue of a curious Order in Council toward the end of 1934 suggests there may have been some slight fear of what individual Englishmen might do in support of the Ethiopian cause, and this order, giving the Government power to control all activities of their nationals with regard to Ethiopia, appeared so unobtrusively that it went unnoticed in Parliament and the press. Under the Foreign Enlistment Act it was possible for an individual to volunteer to serve in the Ethiopian Army, but the effect of the new order was to make this illegal once fighting began.

Meantime, during the period between Signor Grandi's approach to the Foreign Office and the issue of the Maffey Report, the flow of events had quickened. In February 1935 Laval, accompanied by the French Premier, M. Flandin, arrived in London to discuss how the rearmament of Germany could be limited. What Laval proposed was that Britain and France should join with Italy in a new system of guarantees of European security. Simon did not have very much enthusiasm for the suggestion. He was not keen on a system of regional pacts. Nor did he consider there was any need of Italy as a bulwark against Germany at that moment; what was needed was to keep Italy in her place. Eden made proposals which were presented to Germany at the end of February in an Anglo-French Memorandum which contemplated an ambitious plan of regional pacts. The *status quo* in Central and Eastern Europe would be guaranteed by Germany concluding a treaty of mutual assistance with Russia and Poland, while another pact between the "Locarno Powers"—France, Britain, Germany, Belgium—would promise mutual support with each others' air forces if any one of them was attacked by another. Since Italy was not included in the proposals it was not considered necessary to consult her.

From Berlin came a request that a British Minister should visit Germany immediately, to discuss the Memorandum with the German Führer, and Simon decided to go on March 6. On March 4, however, the annual British Defense White Paper was presented to Parliament, and the resultant furore led to his visit being postponed.* Disarmament had failed, the White Paper announced, and it was Britain's intention to rearm. From the Labour benches came a motion of censure on the Government, and Major Clement Attlee (later to be Prime Minister of the post-1945 Labour Government) said that his party believed "that the policy as outlined here is disastrous, and it is rattling back to war." But it was Germany's reaction that was startling. Hitler, whose prestige had been given a distinct boost when the expected result of the Saar plebiscite became known, countered forcefully. It was a few days before the bomb burst, however, and on March 5, when the British Government was informed that the German leader had a severe cold which made it necessary to put off Simon's visit, Whitehall assumed that his affliction

---

* The White Paper was prepared during the latter half of 1934 and it had been sanctioned by MacDonald and Baldwin. The urgent need for a reassessment of British defense policy should have been underlined not so much by the clash at Walwal as Japan's notice to end in 1936 the Washington Naval Treaty by which Britain, America, and Japan agreed to preserve a capital ship ratio of 5:5:3 respectively.

was caused by the White Paper revelation that Britain was aware of Germany's growing military strength. It was in fact nothing of the sort. The Führer was totally unconcerned about what Britain thought about Germany's rearmament plans at this stage, and he had made up his mind to abrogate the Versailles Treaty. On March 10 the world was told that Germany had begun to rearm, and six days later a decree was issued in Berlin reintroducing compulsory military service with a view to raising the strength of the German Army to something over half a million men. Next day, Sunday, March 17, Germany's ambitions, which until this moment had been furtive and concealed, now appeared in the full light of day, as the whole country celebrated the official rebirth of militarism.

France, who had been given prior warning that German conscription was on the way, anticipated Hitler's decree by a few hours with a statement extending her own military service from one to two years. Remembering the sufferings and severity of the war of less than two decades before, the French also appealed to the League. Britain, aghast, frantically looked around for some sort of compromise, and Simon set off for Berlin in order to try to find some way out of a situation which had already deteriorated to a point where no solution short of war seemed possible. Both Laval and Mussolini tried to dissuade him from going on the grounds than an official visit by Britain's Foreign Secretary might be taken as British approval of German rearmament. But he went. Nothing came of the visit other than his returning to London with the glum but inaccurate information that Germany had reached air parity with Britain. Hitler—aware that his star was in the ascendent, knowing, by the terms of the Anglo-French Memorandum, that Britain and France had been disregarding Italy, suspecting also that France and Italy were double-crossing Britain, and believing that a direct two-power treaty between Britain and Germany was now possible—must have been delighted. He must also have considered himself to be the most honest politician in Europe.

Because of the leakages in Rome, Mussolini possibly understood more of the tangled web of deceit than anybody else. Not only was his Intelligence Service keeping him well informed of British attempts to strike a bargain under the counter, Laval was keeping him in touch with the French attitude. Moreover, confirmation of some of the facts was provided by Hitler who, apropos the Anglo-French Memorandum, had suggested to Mussolini that he had "better take serious consideration of our common interests." Whether or not the Duce was better informed or more farsighted, it was largely due to Italian initiative that a conference between Britain, France, and Italy was arranged at Stresa, near the southern end of Lake Maggiore. On April 11, 1935, Mussolini, acting for once as peacemaker, held court on the Isola Bella, chosen because it made security easier than on the mainland. Both Britain and France had insisted on having two representatives at the conference table, and each country sent its Prime Minister and Foreign Secretary.* Mussolini, more than any of the other politicians taking part, would have preferred to have had no witnesses to a strictly three-party discussion, but when Britain and France refused to give way, Fulvio Suvich, his Under-Secretary of State and principal adviser on Foreign Affairs, was deputed to sit at the conference table with him. Accompanying the delegates as advisers went Vansittart for Britain, Leger, his equivalent in France, and Buti, Italy's Director-General for Political Affairs; Vitetti (the Italian chargé d'affaires in London) also attended. For personal reasons the choice of the British delegation might be considered especially unfortunate. Both MacDonald and Simon were elderly politicians who had changed their political views late in life, and neither was fully trusted by either the electorate or Parliament. These limitations inclined them to a cautious policy, and as a result neither had the courage to speak up and break the reticence of their opposite numbers. If Eden had not fallen sick prior to the conference he would almost certainly have gone to Stresa with the British delegation. If that had been so it is more than likely that the delicate question of Ethiopia would have been thrashed out. As it was, Eden urged Simon to warn Mussolini to keep his hands off Ethi-

* Prime Minister Ramsay MacDonald had not intended to go to Stresa. He attended because Eden was ill.

opia and if either MacDonald or Simon had voiced this opinion there might have been a tenuous chance of keeping the West together and preserving peace. But it was not to be.

The two subjects on the Stresa agenda were Germany's unilateral decision to rearm and her threat to Austria. Both the French and the Italian delegations considered that the time for diplomatic niceties with Germany was over—that something positive had to be done before she became any stronger. At the same time, outside the conference and behind the scenes, the Italians were trying to convince the French that it was not vital to have the support of Britain in order to bring Germany to reason; France and Italy, acting together, could do this on their own.

In open discussion, the one question that was studiously avoided was that of Ethiopia. Since African experts from both Britain and Italy had been ordered to attend at Stresa, it appears that there had been some expectation that Ethiopia would be discussed sooner or later. Within six months it would seem almost incredible that what had then become a major issue should have been completely ignored. But in April the majority of people in Britain were little interested in Ethiopia, and both MacDonald and Simon obviously felt that the rights of a "black" country should not be allowed to confuse the more serious considerations of European politics. Neither of the African experts was called to the conference table; they spent their time waiting together in their hotel, talking no doubt about any subject except that with which they were concerned. Mussolini, with the knowledge gleaned from British documents, may not have felt the need to raise the subject himself, but at a subsequent interview he did say he had been ready to discuss the question of Italy's position with regard to Ethiopia at Stresa but neither the British nor the French apparently wished to do so.[10] British avoidance of the growing tension in Africa was established by questions put to Eden by Lloyd George on October 22, 1935:

Mr. Lloyd George: Does that mean that there was no discussion [on Ethiopia] between our Prime Minister and our Foreign Secretary and Signor Mussolini?
Mr. Eden: No official discussions at all.

Mr. Lloyd George: Were there any discussions?
Mr. Eden: Not between heads of delegations.[11]

Eden's reply is sufficiently evasive to admit that unofficial discussions on Ethiopia had taken place. In fact Mussolini had let it be known that he was having difficulties in Africa, where Haile Selassie was "committing daily outrages against Italian nationals." At the same time the Duce reminded the unfortunate British Foreign Secretary of the exchange of notes between himself and Britain's Ambassador in Rome regarding British recognition of Italy's interests in Ethiopia. Simon, worried stiff about Germany, would probably have preferred to have been kept in ignorance, and it is perhaps significant that Vansittart, who was responsible for briefing MacDonald and Simon, "did not press for the subject of Abyssinia to be openly discussed in conference. Nor did Sir Eric [Drummond, later 16th Earl of Perth, British Ambassador in Rome 1933–39] do so." [12] (In fact Drummond had urged that Mussolini should be warned about Abyssinia at the beginning of the conference. Vansittart preferred that he be warned at the end, and he told Italian officials that the agreement on Europe would go for nothing if Mussolini got Italy embroiled in Ethiopia.[13]) Even if the principals kept their mouths tight shut on the subject while in conference, it would be ludicrous to suppose that the lesser fry did not talk, or that the gossip they picked up did not get back to their masters.

Stresa provided a classic example of how leaving unsaid something that should have been said, or alluding to it only by implication, can prejudice the events that follow. When it came to preparing the final communiqué, the agreed text read that "The Three Powers, the object of whose policy is the collective maintenance of peace within the framework of the League of Nations, find themselves in complete agreement in opposing, by all practical means, any unilateral repudiation of treaties which may endanger the peace and will act in close and cordial collaboration for this purpose." As the last clause was read out, Mussolini spoke up: "Let us say, which may endanger the peace of *Europe*." As he spoke with so obvious an emphasis on the word "Europe" and paused for so long before continuing, his meaning was clear. The two words "of Europe" excluded the Three-Power 1906 Treaty of Ethiopia. But nobody spoke up, the communiqué was completed in the form suggested by Mussolini,[14] and the result was that the Duce left Stresa believing that he had gained his point. This point of view was strengthened when the Anglo-German Naval Treaty was signed two months later: Britain, it seemed to him, did not really care what happened in the world so long as her own interests were protected. Everything pointed to Italy being able to go ahead in Ethiopia without fear of ill consequences.

So far as France was concerned, there is little doubt that the agreement which followed the Stresa meeting gave her a greater feeling of security than she had had for nearly a decade. With their Mediterranean back door safe, Frenchmen felt that there would be no need to look over their shoulder if war came on the Rhine. Consequently, when the Ethiopian crisis shattered the idyll, it is little wonder that they should feel both frustrated and exasperated, for what was perhaps not clearly understood outside France at the time was that she was on the horns of exactly the same dilemma as her neighbor across the Channel. Successive French administrators having stated categorically that their country had no thoughts beyond the League of Nations, that war had been renounced as an instrument of policy, and that it was only Germany that prevented all the swords in France from being beaten into plowshares, France was in an uncomfortable position diplomatically. Without an incalculable loss of prestige she could hardly abandon the League; on the other hand, if she abandoned Italy she was in danger of returning to the old nightmare days of the Second Empire, when she was at war in the southeast while her Rhine frontier was open to German attack. Britain was pressing for action against Italy, yet it was by no means certain that the British people really wished to do very much more than make rude gestures at Mussolini. Indeed probably the most difficult facet of the whole business which most Frenchmen—like the majority of Italians—found hard to understand was Britain's pecksniffian attitude toward what, to them, was the cause of all the trouble. Why a barbarous African state enjoying an anachronistic independence should be the object of so much concern was something outside their comprehension. In their view there was very little to be said for preserving Ethiopia's integrity; indeed, she ought to have been taken in hand by a Western nation long before, and it was quite absurd to suppose that the British Government was concerned about the plight of the Ethiopians—if it had been, then surely Britain would have taken them in hand herself. The only apparently valid explanation must be that there was some other dark motive, presumably connected with the well-being of the British Empire.

And, by strange coincidence, evidence suggesting that there might be something in such a theory was not long forthcoming. When the correspondent of the *Daily Telegraph* cabled from Addis Ababa on August 31 that a certain Mr. F. W. Rickett had successfully negotiated an oil concession in Ethiopia, French suspicions seemed to be confirmed. Conferring, as it did, a monopoly over a large tract of what was believed to be the richest part of Ethiopia, Rickett's concession was thought to be an important one, and as such Britain's part in it could be seen as typically perfidious sharp practice. Although the British Government promptly disassociated itself from the deal and advised Haile Selassie to cancel it, the damage was done. Rickett's British nationality temporarily obscured the fact that he was the envoy of an American consortium, the African Exploration and Development Corporation—a subsidiary of the Standard Oil Company— and Haile Selassie was reluctant to cancel the concession because he needed the purchase price to buy arms. (Pressure from Washington ultimately compelled him to do so.) In theory Britain emerged from the affair without a stain on her honor; unfortunately, as always happens in such affairs, some of the mud that had been thrown stuck.

CHAPTER 6

Britain Vacillates

It is not he that begins a war who is blameworthy but he that has given cause for fighting.

MACHIAVELLI

In Britain the results of the Stresa Conference were announced by the Prime Minister in the House of Commons on April 17, 1935. "Without entering into any further commitments," he declared, Britain and France—with Italy as a coguarantor—had "reaffirmed the obligations sketched out in the February Anglo-French Memorandum." The three states had pledged themselves "to keep together to try to find solutions for the present dangers. . . ." They had also discussed ways of "keeping the door open" for Germany to join with them in a collective security agreement, and despite Hitler's recent behavior it was hoped that he could be persuaded to refrain from starting an arms race.

It was not a very impressive speech; in the circumstances it hardly could be. Neither Ramsay MacDonald nor Sir John Simon had any real idea what to do for the best in Europe or Africa, and when they had left Mussolini both had had an uneasy feeling that trouble was in store. But apart from that, MacDonald was a sick man. His health had been failing for some time, his eyesight was troubling him, there was an incredible woolliness in his public utterances; it was daily becoming increasingly evident that the man who, when he became Prime Minister of the National Government, had commented, chuckling, "Tomorrow every duchess in London will be wanting to kiss me," had lost his grip. He was in these unhappy days, according to Winston Churchill, "a boneless wonder" with the gift of "compressing the maximum of words into the minimum of thought."

In Westminster it was clear to all that a change was needed, and in the first week of June the office of Prime Minister was taken over by the ponderous, pipe-smoking, and well-meaning Stanley Baldwin, whose slogan was "safety first." To the British people, Baldwin's public image was the true embodiment of John Bull—solid, dependable, never flustered—and the secret of his power lay in the fact that the electorate trusted him. Not until the pusillanimous line taken by his Government with Mussolini was exposed six months later with the fiasco of the peace plan for Ethiopia was this trust shaken. With Benito Mussolini, Haile Selassie, and Pierre Laval, Stanley Baldwin was to play one of the four major roles in the Italo-Ethiopian drama. Today the man described by one newspaper as the "Methodist Machiavelli" (although he was neither a Methodist nor a Machiavelli) is scarcely less of an enigma than he was to his own generation. He was said to write all his own speeches, never to read the newspapers, and to hate all forms of exercise. Apart from his professed penchant for tripe, the two symbols of his personality—his pig-breeding activities and the pipe he smoked—were designed to create a public image among those who believed that interests in simple matters, like pigs and pipes, were a sound basis for political judgment. Yet there can be no question but that Baldwin was possessed of a vivid political discernment, and in the summer and autumn of 1935 he needed this quality above all else.

Even before Baldwin actually took over the helm, the so-called Stresa front was doomed. *Appeasement* was not a word that was in common usage in the thirties, and probably the first blow that was delivered at the Stresa Agreement within a few weeks of its signature would not have been recognized as such.

Nevertheless, while some of those concerned at the time might have seen the Naval Pact which Britain now entered into with Germany as rather clever diplomacy, the mere fact that it condoned Hitler's violation of the Versailles Treaty condemns it as the first plunge into an appeasement policy. The Pact, which certainly appeared to offer Britain considerable advantages, was negotiated, signed, and sealed with unseemly and undue haste, and it had an inordinate effect on the Italo-Ethiopian dispute. France was not consulted either before or during the negotiations, nor was Italy; nobody in Britain seems to have appreciated the effect the news of the Pact would have until the damage was well and truly done. Sir Samuel Hoare had taken over as Foreign Secretary on June 7, and as the Pact was signed on the eighteenth, it might well seem to have been one of the early effects of the sweep of a new broom. Since most of the negotiations had taken place before Hoare came to office, however, it must be counted the crowning act of Sir John Simon's placatory policy. At a time when everything in Britain's tortuous policy depended on complete and cordial cooperation with France, it was also the most important factor in the subsequent misunderstandings that arose between the two countries.

No doubt the Naval Pact stemmed from the same unease that had led to the formation of the Stresa front, since fear of what the resurgent Germany would do next overawed the whole of Europe. By and large, the British public was hostile to Hitler; reports of the Nazis' anti-Semitic activities were not likely to endear him to a people who are invariably drawn emotionally toward underdogs, minorities, and victims. Nor did the antics of Sir Oswald Mosley's British Blackshirts do much to enhance the appeal of totalitarianism. Yet, despite this there was a sizable influential and articulate section of the British public who were very definitely pro-German. Tories, terrified of Bolshevism, with the 'City' thinking in terms of Britain's investments in Germany, might have been expected to form the majority of such a group. In fact it was a more representative cross-section, and even in the Labour Party there were people harboring the usual odd ideas of chivalry invariably attributed to the British who were reacting against the old hang-the-Kaiser, squeeze-them-till-the-pips-squeak propaganda of 1914–18. Apart from being fellow Anglo-Saxons—and hardworking ones at that—the Germans were considered to have been worthy opponents in the war, and the fact that the French found it impossible to forgive was an added reason why Germany should deserve another chance; in the thirties there were plenty of Francophobes in Britain. And to some extent this pro-German group was supported by the influence of the London *Times*—the one newspaper which claimed to be irrefragably independent. Geoffrey Dawson, its editor, hated Nazis and their ways; but, as he loathed the Communists even more, his articles were often inclined to give Germany the benefit of the doubt in foreign affairs. The net result was that right up to 1939, whenever Hitler appeared to be radiating an air of reasonableness, there were many in Britain who supported a call for compromise.

During May 1935, in one of the Führer's "Let's be friendly" periods, Sir John Simon, assisted by Sir Robert Craigie, the Assistant Under-Secretary at the Foreign Office, decided to set about improving relations with Germany. Von Ribbentrop, head of Hitler's Foreign Political Office—shortly to become Ambassador to Britain and later Foreign Minister of the Reich—was invited to London to discuss "friendship." On May 21, as if in reply, Hitler made a speech in which he said, "The German Government recognizes the overpowering vital importance . . . of a dominating protection for the British Empire on the sea . . . [and] has the straightforward intention to find and maintain a relationship with the British people and State which will prevent for all time a repetition of the only struggle there has been between the two nations. . . . An Anglo-German alliance would hallow the ancient ties of friendship and kinship," and as the price of such friendship all Britain was expected to do was to respect Germany's role in Europe. So far as Germany was concerned the Treaty of Versailles was now dead, but in a new spirit of friendship she was prepared to enter into an agreement which would limit the German navy to a third of that of Britain.

In four weeks the Anglo-German Pact was signed. Both signatories were well satisfied with the deal. Hitler was beginning to believe that if war came in Europe Britain would stay neutral, while the British Government with smug satisfaction felt that it had brought off a true British compromise. By approving Germany's suggestion that she should have a fleet not more than 35 percent of that of Britain, the competition at sea would guarantee the Royal Navy a supremacy that it had not enjoyed even in the Tirpitz era. Ostensibly Vansittart approved of the agreement and his personality dominated the Foreign Office. According to Ribbentrop, "This Foreign Office man . . . advocated the balance of power theory . . . [and] . . . whatever influences he may have been subjected to, the main thing was his basic attitude 'Never with Germany.' There are those who contend that Vansittartism and the hatred of Germany which this word implies were a result of Hitler's policy. To this I reply . . . Hitler's policy was a consequence of Vansittart's policy in 1936." [1]

Unfortunately Samuel Hoare, the incoming Foreign Secretary, was a very tired man when he went to the Foreign Office. A member of a wealthy banking family, bookish, rather delicate, fond of sports like tennis and ice skating, he did not lack experience or aptitude. But long years of strain, first as Secretary of State for Air and then at the India Office piloting through the enormous Government of India Bill, had left him in dire need of a rest. Baldwin had made him Foreign Minister partly because he knew his abilities and partly as a reward for his prodigious labors over India. Hoare accepted the appointment because of a strong sense of public duty combined with a strong public ambition, but as he was subject to recurrent fainting fits he can hardly be regarded as suitable to cope with Britain's foreign affairs in June 1935.

Nor for that matter was he really capable of handling the team he was supposed to captain. Both Vansittart and the pertinaceous Sir Warren Fisher, Permanent Under-Secretary of the Treasury, had strongly recommended Eden to the Prime Minister when Baldwin was making his appointments, and when it was decided that the older man should have the job, Eden was made Minister for League Affairs—supposedly with the same status as that of the Foreign Secretary. Anthony Eden, thirty-eight years old, was still comparatively unknown at this time. He belonged to the generation that had fought the war to end all wars—a war in which two of his brothers had been killed—and nobody could doubt his sincerity in the cause of peace. Of good family, he had studied at Eton and Oxford, had a handsome wife, some private means, conventional good looks, dressed with sartorial elegance, and possessed a Military Cross testifying to his gallantry in action. As a politician he was considered to hold progressive but sound views, broad enough for the Tory left wing but acceptable to the ordinary majority of Conservatives. Skillful and patient in negotiation, he was soon to show that he had a certain flair for diplomacy and an ability to get on with foreign statesmen—with the one exception of Mussolini. But the man whose importance was to rise steeply with the development of the crisis over Ethiopia was ambitious, and his appointment as Hoare's second-in-command with equal rank was bound to create an impossible situation. Doubtless the Prime Minister realized how things were shaping, but beyond sending Hoare a note asking him to settle details of their respective competence "direct with the young man," Stanley Baldwin made no attempt to intervene.[2] The result was that a form of dual ministerial authority sprang up within the Foreign Office and Britain's policy toward Italy pursued two separate lines—one based on established treaties, and the other on the League's Covenant.

The immediate effect of the Anglo-German Naval Pact was to strengthen Italy's link with France and to weaken that of France with Britain. According to Hoare, Laval was consulted about the Pact and did not object. But when it was announced his prompt reaction was to address a protest to the British Ambassador in Paris. "France," he said, "has been betrayed." After all the work at Stresa, Britain had gone behind the back of her allies to bargain with the nation they had lined up against. Public opinion in France backed Laval, and newspapers in Paris were soon pointing out that Hitler had foretold in *Mein Kampf* that a deal with Britain was one of the preliminary phases in a plan for the annihilation of France; great play was also made of the fact that the Pact had been signed on June 18—the anniversary of Waterloo. Britain had broken faith with France, they said, and entered into a new "Belle Alliance" at France's expense; it was typical *perfide Albion* tactics. At this the British Foreign Office, to whom the furore was unseemly if not altogether unexpected, made a lame attempt to denigrate the value of the Pact. Notwithstanding any arrangements with Germany, France could always rely on the support of the British, Whitehall declared. But the damage had been done and on the Paris political market, Britain's prestige sank as Mussolini's stock rose. To the ordinary Frenchman, the Anglo-German agreement had shown just how farsighted their Foreign Minister had been, and approval for the Laval-Mussolini entente was voiced. France must stand by her Latin sister if Britain tried to interfere with Italy's "work of civilization" in Ethiopia, said one newspaper; "Nothing is left of the Franco-British cooperation announced in February and reinforced by Italy at Stresa. Therefore let us have no intervention in the Italo-Abyssinian controversy . . ." said another.

In all the uproar it was Mussolini who made the most cogent appreciation. To him it was evident that the collective superiority which would have enabled Britain and France jointly to coerce Italy into accepting some comparatively mild settlement of the Ethiopian question had been destroyed by Britain's duplicity, and this was a fact which served to give his plans an additional fillip.

Yet in Britain the mood did not seem quite so apprehensive. Hoare had been brooding over the different facets of Europe's problem, and in discussions with Vansittart he had concluded that "the basic facts were stark and ineluctable. Hitler's strength was becoming daily more formidable and his intentions more unabashed. Secondly, Japanese aggression threatened us with war in the Far East. Thirdly, it was essential to Britain to have a friendly Italy in the Mediterranean. . . . Fourthly, Mussolini was at the time on very bad terms with his fellow dictator, Hitler. . . . Perhaps we were too optimistic. . . . Perhaps we did not sufficiently realise the contrast between Mussolini's outlook and ours." [3] In view of this it was decided to send Eden to Rome to see if Mussolini could be bought, bribed, or placated. By telling Mussolini what should have been said about Ethiopia at Stresa, the British Government hoped that the Duce would be prepared to listen to the proposals for a redistribution of territory in East Africa which Eden was now authorized to offer. If Italy was prepared to renounce her claims on Ethiopia, a tripartite territorial settlement would be arranged. In return for a block of desert in the Ogaden which Ethiopia would hand over to Italy, Britain would cede a strip of British Somaliland which would give Ethiopia access to the sea at the little port of Zeila. Once again none of the other interested parties had been consulted prior to the offer being made, and as a concession the offer of Zeila and a corridor across British Somaliland could hardly have been less happily chosen. The strip to be handed over ran across a barren and intractable area. Except as a corridor for camels it was of little use unless a railway was built, and as such a railway would have been a wholly uneconomical proposition it is unlikely that Haile Selassie would have been able to raise sufficient capital for its construction. Apart from this, Ethiopia's natural communications from her fertile areas ran westward toward the Sudan, and the existing French line from Djibuti had never carried much traffic.

If the offer had any meat at all it came too late. The Duce, seeing that Britain had got into a tangle with her new policy of "realism," was not going to be fobbed off with another desert, and on June 24, when Eden submitted his proposals, they were rejected out of hand. Laval had conceded Italy "a free hand in Abyssinia," Mussolini asserted before patiently going on to explain his African ambitions. "I returned to the charge several times," recalled Eden. But Mussolini remained emphatic. He still hoped, he said, to obtain his objectives in Abyssinia without war. "If Abyssinia came to terms without war, he [Mussolini] would be content with the surrender of those parts of Abyssinia which had been conquered by Abyssinia in the last fifty years and which were not inhabited by Abyssinians. In saying this Signor Mussolini made a circular gesture which I took to mean that he regarded such territories as existing on all four sides of Abbysinia. The central plateau could, he continued, remain under Abyssinian sovereignty, but only on condition that it was under Italian control. If, however, Abyssinia could not come to terms with Italy upon these lines, then, if Italy had to fight, her demands would be proportionately greater." He had already sent 150,000 men to East Africa, and if it proved necessary he was ready to send half a million. "Great Britain must realize how serious was the matter for Italy. Some people thought Italy too poor for a great effort. But despite that poverty, Italy had made great sacrifices in the past and could, and would if need be, do so again." [4] He spoke quietly and in a friendly tone; there was no attempt to bluster but it was clear that his mind was made up on the course he intended to take. Clearly there was no more that Eden could do. Twice during the interview the young Minister for League Affairs uttered a solemn warning about the effect on Anglo-Italian relations if Ethiopia were attacked, and this warning was repeated. Finally, after expressing disappointment and anxiety, Eden thanked the Duce for his courtesy in listening to the British propositions and took his leave.

So far as he was concerned the British Cabinet "would now have to determine their course between upholding the League and [so] losing an ally, or undermining the foundation of peace in Europe." [5] And to Eden defying the League of Nations on this issue would weaken its authority and the peace of Europe would be in jeopardy. Vansittart, however, saw the problem differently. He was prepared to concede that the League might be useful against Italy, but in his view the League was no longer an effective weapon against Germany—nor ever likely to be in the future. Unfortunately the effect of the dichotomy was that the Foreign Office was divided and very few people in Britain realized that their Government had embarked on a course of power politics in which it was accepted that the sacrifice of a small and backward country might be necessary. Yet perhaps the strangest aspect of the situation is that far from horrifying Baldwin, the political fiddling engendered by the existence of two diverse groups of policy makers in the Foreign Office seems to have appealed to his subtle mind. He could see nothing odd about Eden trying to rouse interest and belief in the League while Hoare was quietly acquiescing to the virtual decolonization of Ethiopia; to him such a situation made for flexibility.

From this, one is forced to conclude that, up to July 1935, the British Government never had any real intention of trying to stop Mussolini invading Ethiopia, or of allowing the League of Nations to stop him. The essence of Simon's brief to the Maffey Commission was the question of whether British interests would be affected if Mussolini made war in Ethiopia, and when Maffey reported that they would not be affected, there was no case for the Government to exert itself to prevent such a contingency. Furthermore, it must be stressed that although the French and British Foreign Offices might disagree over the handling of Germany, they were still generally in accord over Italian affairs. If Italy behaved properly, protected their interests, and was not too greedy, it might be a good way to let off steam. A successful campaign would bring prestige, justify the regimentation of the Italian nation at the Duce's grandiose claims of a revived Roman imperialism, and serve to reduce her effectiveness to a more controllable level. At the same time it was recognized that the opposition in Ethiopia must not be so strong as to ruin Italy's future effectiveness in Europe in case she was needed against Germany. The official attitude might be summarized as: "We may still need the Italians on the Brenner"—a principle for which the ultimate responsibility lay with Baldwin, Simon, and Hoare, even though it has been attributed to Vansittart.

One of the most ill-judged results of this policy was that, contrary to existing treaty obligations, the two Governments placed an unofficial ban on the import of all armaments into Ethiopia, and warned other countries that it would be an unfriendly act to supply her with munitions. France and Britain controlled the only means of ingress—the French the Djibuti railway, the British the entry point from the Sudan and British Somaliland—and consequently, when the ban came into force in May, it meant that Haile Selassie's efforts to procure weapons for his ill-equipped and untrained troops were abruptly brought to a halt. In July, Hoare announced that licenses for exports of arms to Italy would also be withheld, but he was now prepared to permit the transit of arms to Ethiopia through British territory. Even as late as September, however, a request to send arms through the Sudan was refused by the Foreign Office on the grounds that it was "contrary to the 1925 Agreement with Italy" and in practice very few arms got into Ethiopia except by illicit and extremely difficult channels. The Djibuti–Addis Ababa railway was closed and every possible official difficulty was put in the way of discharging cargoes of munitions at Berbera—an attitude which continued throughout the war, even after Italy had been declared an aggressor.*

With two diverging streams within the British Foreign Office, it was to be expected that the foreign policy emerging from it during the critical months of 1935 would be contradictory. Nor were the two forces described the only ones at work. Those responsible for carrying out the permanent foreign policy of any democratic country invariably come into conflict with members of the Government who seek to impose temporary solutions in order to appease public opinion. In this instance the British public—especially the middle classes, who were very much in control in 1935—was accustomed to having some say in the policy of its Government, and with a general election due in the autumn, Baldwin could not afford to neglect the growing and vociferous section of the electorate which was now clamoring for a solution to an international problem which was of no direct concern to Britain. On other occasions, a similar clamor had been raised in turn for Greeks, Danes, and Armenians when they were threatened with the same fate as that which now hung over the Ethiopians; but in the case of Ethiopia it was not merely the threat of being devoured by Italy, but concern and resent-

---

* A French correspondent eyewitness has related how in June 1935, 225 boxes containing rifles and ammunition deposited on the quay were declared illicit war material and ordered to be locked up in a warehouse. "I believe you overstep your duty," the observer said. "If I am not mistaken we have a Treaty with Ethiopia dating back to August, 1930, which authorizes the entry of arms into Ethiopia." "That's true," said the Customs official, "but such consignments need several licenses and permits and invariably one or the other is missing." In this particular instance the pretext meant that the Ethiopian army was deprived of over 4,000 rifles.

ment over the undermining of the great international structure, which the British public had been educated to believe was the one stabilizing influence for peace in the world.

After World War I the declared basis of British foreign policy was the Covenant of the League of Nations. To a nation exhausted by a four-year struggle in the trenches and lulled by the pacificism which had grown out of it, the ideals propounded in the Covenant had the right sentimental appeal. Unfortunately, few people stopped to consider that the Geneva brand of collective security brought obligations and demanded moral and material resources if it was to remain in being. In the twenties Britain's diplomats, steeped in the Palmerston tradition, might have been embarrassed by the reluctance of the British people to support a Government pursuing an imperialist policy. But as lip service to the Covenant did not necessitate any change in the old order of things, they were able to find ways of reconciling British interests to it. Realism and idealism might be uneasy bedfellows but they could be accommodated in Whitehall as long as nothing arose to bring them into conflict. When Japan's invasion of Manchuria was allowed to pass unchallenged the clash came. Whitehall turned back toward the old policy of power politics, the public began to stir, and by mid-1935, when the British Government had to take a stand on the Italian-Ethiopian issue, there were a number of complicating factors.

Basically the problem was one of League supporters versus those who considered that Britain's adherence to the League was an impracticable, if not highly dangerous, policy. In the main those who advocated faith in the League were left-wing internationalists, and those who opposed it were people who were concerned primarily with the need to preserve Britain from the menace of Germany. But such was the odd complex of motives that the League advocates found themselves allied for diametrically opposed motives with die-hard imperialists who saw in the Italian imperialist threat to Ethiopia a challenge to British interests in Africa and, eventually, the Mediterranean. At the same time, backing for the anti-Leaguers came from Britain's drawing-room Fascists, those who admired the regimes of Mussolini and Hitler and who had little time for the League of "old women" who presumed to oppose the new order in Europe, and also from a new generation of pacifists who disapproved of Mussolini but whose disapproval of war was even stronger.

In the early thirties a good deal of propaganda in favor of the League and collective security was circulating in Britain. Unfortunately much of it was confused by the pacifist section of its supporters who were advocating unilateral disarmament, and others who were convinced that British imperialism had been one of the factors contributing to the First World War. The latter believed that the world would be a safer place if the British Empire was dismantled to become a Commonwealth collection of self-governing states. The general effect of the propaganda was to produce a vague impression that collective security was a good thing and that it involved no risk of war. In this climate the so-called peace campaign was born, and by 1934—despite the failure of the Disarmament Conference and the developing militarism of Germany and Italy—the tide of the pacifist movement was running strongly. In October 1933, when the Conservative candidate was heavily defeated by a Socialist in the traditionally Tory stronghold of East Fulham, the strength of the movement really became apparent.

In January 1934, long before anyone foresaw an Italo-Ethiopian war, a questionnaire circulated by a local newspaper in the Ilford area sought to test public opinion about the League of Nations. In response to the question "Should Great Britain remain in the League of Nations?" 21,532 persons answered Yes and 3,954 answered No. To the question "Do you agree with that part of the Locarno Treaty which binds Great Britain to go to the help of France or Germany if one is attacked by the other?" 5,898 answered Yes, and 18,498 No. Inspired by the enterprise, the League of Nations Union—a nonparty organization but one which had a considerable following among moderate Tories—decided to initiate a national plebiscite. This was the origin of the Peace Ballot and the so-called National Declaration in favor of the League. The theme of the Ballot was peace through collective security, and to increase the chances of a favorable response, the Union decided to appeal in simplified and general terms to the public and eliminate troublesome references to specific treaty obligations. By doing so it was hoped that many of the negative majority who had seen that specific treaty obligations could lead to war would be converted in favor of the idea of collective security and the League.

In a nationwide questionnaire the voter was invited to answer five questions, the last of which was the significant one. It read as follows:

Do you consider that, if a nation insists on attacking another, the other nations should combine to tell it to stop by

    (a) economic and non-military measures?
    (b) if necessary, military measures?

Polling began in November 1934 and continued until June 1935. Of those voting, 10,027,608 said Yes to (a); 635,074 said No; 27,255 were doubtful, and 855,107 abstained. To question (b), 6,784,368 were in favor of military sanctions: 2,351,981 were against; 40,893 were doubtful, and 2,364,441 abstained.

To the Government the Ballot was an embarrassment. Baldwin called it misleading, Sir John Simon deplored it, Neville Chamberlain said it was mischievous. Vansittart declared it was a misfortune, a "free excursion into the inane," [6] and said that the Peace Ballot's formulas were "idealistic frauds." The London *Times* called "the whole business . . . a deplorable waste of time and effort" and said that it was of no importance.[7] And as the voters were not a random sample, representative of all sections of the community, the method of conducting the poll give cause for doubt regarding its impartiality and the validity of the results. Whether or not the poll was a fraud, the results announced in the Albert Hall on June 27, 1935, clearly suggested that an overwhelming proportion of the voters were in favor of Britain remaining inside the League and of using economic pressure to prevent and punish aggression. Such results, claimed the organizers of the poll, were a "victory" giving clear proof of the existence throughout Britain of a fanatical faith in the League.

Despite their disapproval of the Ballot, the Government could not afford to disregard the effects of the National Declaration. Faced with the prospect of a general election and not wishing to cause a split inside his already not very homogeneous party, Baldwin was in a difficult position. The League supporters were becoming increasingly vocal, and by this time their efforts had been reinforced by the growing sentimentality toward Ethiopia as an underdog. From Downing Street the situation presented a dilemma which could only be overcome by a change in foreign policy. Furthermore the change would have to come quickly, for with Mussolini's speeches becoming more and more truculent, public opinion in Britain indicating that it would demand firm action by the League if Italy persisted in her threats, and deadlock at Geneva, it was clear that a crisis was not far away. The unfortunate thing was that apart from the fact that it was rather late in the day for the Government to change what was virtually a policy of acquiescence toward Italy's absorption of Ethiopia, Whitehall could see no good reason for defending Ethiopia's integrity.

Throughout that spring of 1935 the arbitration proceedings over Walwal, under Article 5 of the 1928 Treaty, dragged on, until eventually the Italo-Ethiopian Arbitration Commission had to confess that they could not resolve the dispute. Failure was primarily due to the two sides being unable to agree on their terms of reference. At the outset the two Italian delegates objected to Ethiopia being represented by two foreigners and to a time limit being set for the settlement of the dispute. Largely owing to Eden's initiative this particular deadlock was broken during May, when Italy was induced to waive her objections and agree to a resumption of the talks. At this point, the League Council took a hand in the affair by passing a resolution laying down that unless the Arbitration Commission had reached agreement by July 25, it would appoint a neutral arbitrator; then, if the affair was not settled by August 25, the Council would meet again to reconsider the whole situation. To the Ethiopian representatives' pleas that the Council should insist on the Italian Government abstaining "from sending to East Africa additional troops and munitions or additional specialists," and should not use "for the preparation of an attack on Ethiopia, the troops, munitions and specialists" already sent to East Africa, the Council turned a deaf ear. By resolving to shelve the problem until August the Council had avoided an open discussion, and in this Mussolini could not fail to be encouraged. Nevertheless, by making any resolution on these lines the Council had firmly implicated the League in the quarrel. Unless an arbitration settlement was made by the end of August the Council was committed to take action. At long last, Haile Selassie, knowing that the Italians' procrastination over the arbitration procedure was a deliberate ruse to gain time, had a promise that something would be done. But so, too, had Mussolini, to whom the situation must have looked especially rosy. The Council had given him another couple of months in which to continue his preparations, and its attitude suggested that the League would be prepared to dither again if a suitable excuse could be found. More important still, the British Foreign Office had failed to make it clear that Britain intended to stick by her obligations under the Covenant. It is true that Simon, Vansittart, Hoare, and Eden had all warned him that Anglo-Italian relations would suffer if Italy attacked Ethiopia. But no categorical blunt official warning was ever issued which might have served as a deterrent at the one time when it could have been effective.

It was said then, and with more emphasis when the postmortem came later, that Haile Selassie put too much faith in the League, and that he could have either come to terms with Mussolini or attacked the Italians before they were ready. Certainly if he had chosen to launch an attack on Eritrea or Somaliland before April as some of his chiefs urged him to do, there can be little doubt that the Italians would have been in serious difficulty. But the Emperor knew that the Italians were stronger and that in the long run they were bound to succeed. And once he had given Mussolini the excuse to unleash the dogs of war, it would be Ethiopia that would be branded the aggressor; if this happened she would lose all hope of being succored by the League. In the recriminations period it was also suggested that the British Government, in urging the Emperor to rely on the League, promised help if war came. But for an understanding of this nature, it was

said, the Italians would have got what they wanted by agreement
and without recourse to force of arms. In a sorry tale of international machinations such as this, it is possible to believe that almost any sort of understanding could have existed, *sub rosa*, but
in actual fact, Sir Sidney Barton, the British Minister in Addis
Ababa, never held out hopes, either directly or by implication, of
British military intervention. Indeed, on a number of occasions
he actually warned the Emperor against counting on it.

It was true that Haile Selassie did believe that Britain would
stand by him in the event of war; his encouragement, however,
did not come from official sources in Britain but from the *Times*,
the League of Nations Union, the pacifists, the isolationists, the
British clergy, and the left-wing parties—all the elements of
which Baldwin was now having to take notice. The Emperor's
mistake was to suppose that these elements were the voice of the
British Government and people. Yet even if these influences had
not been present, it is unlikely that he would have behaved any
differently. When Mussolini was enjoying his brief moment of
glory, Haile Selassie was reported to have said bitterly that he
would have reached an agreement with Italy had it not been for
his misplaced trust in the League. Since he made no attempt to do
so, even when the British Government advised him to sue for
peace, it must be assumed that in his stubborn determination to
cede nothing to Italy, he was prepared to risk losing his throne.

When the Walwal Arbitration Commission resumed its negotiations in June, it soon reached another deadlock. With the
Italians persisting that the location of the incident was not relevant to the proceedings and Ethiopia's representatives insisting
that it was, no progress was possible and consequently the Committee adjourned. Until the neutral arbitration recommended by
the League Council at its meeting in May was appointed it could
go no farther toward a solution, and it was July 25—when the
Council met again—before the next move was made in what was
supposed to be the basic dispute between Italy and Ethiopia. In
accordance with Paragraph 2 of Article 15 of the Covenant
(". . . parties to the dispute will communicate to the Secretary-
General, as promptly as possible, statements of their case with all

the relevant facts and papers . . .") Ethiopia's representative
had submitted a statement before the Council actually met, in
which he repeated that the Italian Government had not ceased
"to send to East Africa troops and munitions of war in large
quantities" and that it had accompanied these dispatches with "in-
flammatory harangues and speeches full of threats to Ethiopia's
independence and integrity." Up to the time the Council assembled on July 25, no statement had been received from the Italian
Government, however, and Count Aloisi, the Italian representative, refused pointblank to say anything about the breakdown of
the arbitration negotiations or Ethiopia's other complaints. In view
of this, the Council held only two formal public meetings, on
July 31 and August 3. But, behind the scenes, Eden and Laval
had induced Italy to negotiate under the authority of the
League, and between these dates there was a good deal of to-ing
and fro-ing between the British, French, and Italian delegates. As
the other members of the Council were not told what was happening, not unnaturally this unusual and somewhat high-handed
procedure aroused considerable resentment among them. Ethiopia was not admitted to the negotiations. Initially Eden had
proposed that she should be represented, but Aloisi and Laval
had good reason for not wanting Ethiopia's representative, for
what eventuated was a decision to put pressure on Ethiopia; consequently, at their insistence, Ethiopia was excluded. It was on
August 3 that Eden announced that he would report the results
of the Tripartite talks at the Council's next meeting, which was
fixed for September 4. At the same time an announcement was
made to the effect that the Arbitration Commission would be
resuming its work, and from this it seemed that the negotiations
in camera had already had some little success. In fact, with Italy's
preparations for war nearly complete, there was by this time, no
need to prolong the arbitration over Walwal, and Aloisi had
found it easy to be conciliary. Nikolaos Politis, the Greek Minister to Paris, was appointed as fifth arbitrator on August 20;
within a month the Walwal affair was settled and the verdict of
the arbitrators was published in September. Nobody, according
to the report, was really to blame. Least of all the Italian Gov-

ernment, or the Ethiopian Government, or their agents. So nobody was responsible for what had happened.

Both sides were absolved and in any other circumstances such
a decision could have been satisfactory to everybody. As it was it
passed unnoticed; the incident had served its purpose and Mussolini's readiness to compromise at the eleventh hour had no significance. He had gained the time he needed and at this late stage he
was not going to be balked of the war he had been preparing so
long; glory was what he wanted now, equally as much as Ethiopian territory.

By now it was also clear that if and when war did come, it
would be a much more serious affair than even the most pessimistic had envisaged. The congestion of Italian troopships in the
Suez Canal and the feverish activity at Massawa and Mogadishu,
where tanks, artillery, aircraft, and other war matériel were being unloaded day and night, all testified to preparations on an un-
precedented scale. From Egypt, Kenya, Aden, and even India,
came reports of Italian purchases of everything from fodder for
mules to khaki drill for uniforms. Two regular infantry divisions, the Gavinana and the Peloritana, which had been mobilized in Italy during February together with contingents of native troops from Libya, had all arrived in East Africa by the end
of April.* At the beginning of May another regular division, the
Sabauda, had been mobilized, and two divisions of Blackshirts—
known as the Twenty-third March and the Twenty-eighth October in commemoration of Fascist revolutionary dates—had also
been called to the colors. Later that month, yet another regular
division, the Gran Sasso, and two more Blackshirt divisions, the
Twenty-first April and Third January, were also put on a war
footing, and in July, as events moved remorselessly toward an
attack on Ethiopia, two more divisions—one regular, the Sila, and
the other the Blackshirt First February—were called up. Not

---

* The Gavinana, recruited in Florence, was one of the Italian army's best
divisions. The Peloritana, a Sicilian division, whose troops were accustomed to a
warm climate, was originally intended for Eritrea, but rumors of a secret mobilization in Ethiopia and of an army under the command of Ras Kassa assembling in Central Ankara ready to strike south, led to its being diverted to Somaliland.

counting Eritrean and Libyan colonial troops, the strength of Italy's armed forces was raised to allow for an expeditionary force of five regular and five Blackshirt divisions, and by September 1935, the numbers of troops embarking for East Africa had reached a monthly average of more than twenty-five thousand. If such activity was disturbing to observers of the scene, even more striking than the troops' sailings from Naples were the attendant military measures, such as the calling up of reserves and the stopping of all leave in the Italian forces. No attempt was made to conceal any of the preparations; under the circumstances it would have been impossible to do so anyway, and to do the Duce justice, he spared neither speeches nor interviews to acquaint the world with his intentions of attacking Ethiopia. By letting the world see that he was pointing a loaded gun at Ethiopia he hoped to frighten Haile Selassie and deter others who had any ideas of interfering with his plans.

What worried the world of Europe was not what would happen in Africa when the gun went off but what the effect of the explosion would be in Geneva. When Mussolini pulled the trigger, the members of the League would be called upon to stand by to defend the principles of the Covenant by which they would bound, or to run away. The Duce had a shrewd idea what the decision would be. The key to the situation depended on the attitude adopted by Britain and France, and as he already knew how France would react, everything depended on Britain.

CHAPTER 7

The War Clouds Gather

Italy's gospel must be: better to live for one day like a lion than a hundred years like a sheep.

MUSSOLINI, in an address to Blackshirts, September 1935

The British nation plunged passionately into the controversy over Ethiopia during the summer of 1935. Like the discussion on the King's abdication a year later, Ethiopia was a topic from which people in Britain found it impossible to escape. For the first time since its foundation the League of Nations was faced with a clear issue. Reasons might be found to excuse the League taking action when Manchuria was invaded: that the United States was not a member and without her help the practical difficulties of opposing Japan were insuperable; or that China herself had provided the League with a pretext for evading its obligations. But this time it was different; Ethiopia was a test case, and the man in Britain's streets recognized it as such. The Emperor had done everything to make the provisions of the Covenant applicable, and by virtue of their strength and domination of the Suez Canal the major powers appeared to be in an ideal position to restrain Italy. Yet as time passed, while Italy continued her preparations for a war and Ethiopia reiterated her frantic appeals to a deaf audience in Geneva, public opinion in Britain came to realize two things: first, that as well as Ethiopia the survival of the League itself was in danger; second, that the British Government had not decided to stand up for either. The result was a fanatical campaign on behalf of Ethiopia organized by supporters of the League. Starting in June this was pursued with all religious fervor of a revivalist movement, reaching its first climax in September 1935, before temporarily dying back after the first objective of forcing the application of sanctions had been achieved.

With not only members and supporters of the League of Nations Union, but the Churches, the members of Opposition in Parliament, the academic world, and an extraordinary collection of private individuals all united in a League crusade, the Government could hardly fail to take notice—especially when the London *Times,* after having stigmatized the National Declaration as a "deplorable waste of time, of doubtful assistance to the cause of peace," threw open its columns to the very people whose efforts it had previously castigated, to become the main vehicle for propaganda associated with the campaign. All the old domestic problems, like the atrocious unemployment and the cold-blooded Means Test that went with it—the misery, want, and indifference in the Britain of the thirties—were temporarily forgotten. Articles on the crisis dominated the columns of almost all the newspapers and magazines; messages chalked on walls implored the public to "Support the League"; others more bluntly counseled it to "Mind Britain's Business." In general the clergy confined themselves to the moral issues; the arguments of the rest varied in detail but the main theme was the same—that the British Empire depended for its future safety on the maintenance of the League's authority.

Various proposals to resolve the problem of Ethiopia on these lines were advanced in the London *Times.* One correspondent, after pointing out that the Ethiopians were still slaveholders and barbarians, asked if it was right to suggest that Ethiopia should remain undeveloped, and then went on to suggest that the League should make Ethiopia a protectorate. Under the aegis of the League, he said, the complaints and rights of Italy could be satisfied. Ethiopia would accept—he was sure of that, for the Emperor "must regard Mussolini as irresistible," and Mussolini's agreement "would prove the Duce's strength and mobility of character." [1] Two days later, the suggestion was followed up with a similiar proposal: "There is fairly general recognition that some of the claims of Italy . . . are reasonable in essence, if not at the moment in degree. Any concessions affecting sovereignty should be made through the League of Nations, which might point out to Abyssinia that membership of the League of Nations implies duties as well as rights and that, if she cannot get her house in order, others—not one conquering power but the international body which represents many civilized and civilising powers—must do it for her." [2]

What was being suggested was something approximating to a collective mandate of League Members over Ethiopia, exercised through the League Council. Supervision would be with the League; Italy would gain concessions and Ethiopia would enjoy protection and financial assistance. To the dispassionate compromisers in Britain this was a solution which seemed eminently suited to what by now appeared to be an otherwise intractable problem. In Addis Ababa people were not so sanguine. "The Emperor's policy remains clear. . . . He rejects all suggestions for a mandate or protectorate, national or international . . . it is impossible . . . for the Emperor or a country of such almost vaingloriously independent tradition as Ethiopia to accept them. . . . To resist such suggestions but perhaps to discuss lesser concessions is the task of the Ethiopian delegation at Geneva." [3] From Rome, the Italian view was even more definite: the "dispute must be left to Italy to settle, because nobody . . . can guarantee that Italy can obtain . . . her legitimate rights. . . ." [4] Both sides, it seemed, preferred the arbitrament of war to any solution making Ethiopia a League Protectorate.

With the Pope supporting Mussolini, it was only to be expected that many English Catholics found themselves in a quandary over the matter of divided loyalty. To give their leaders their due, it is fair to say that they probably realized the delicacy of their position and for this reason made no attempt publicly to enter into the controversy over the League's action. But behind the scenes the Roman Catholic Church in Britain identified itself with the support for Italy's case. So far as the Church of England was concerned, the normal line it had taken up to this time had been that political questions were outside its aegis. However, while the established Church had been busy rendering unto Caesar, the Non-Conformists' interest in social and international matters had given them a lead in ecclesiastical matters. Not unnaturally, therefore, the Church of England authorities had begun to ask whether abstention from the political field was altogether a wise policy, and when their congregations began to show intense interest in the Ethiopian affair and the moral issues involved, it seemed clear that the Church could not remain neutral any longer unless it was prepared to renounce completely its already declining spiritual influence. The Church leaders therefore declared for the League and started to preach the gospel of sanctions. In general, the utterances of the Primate, Dr. Lang, were more restrained than those of his colleague the Archbishop of York, Dr. Temple. But Dr. Temple's militancy rapidly led the League opponents to criticize him as an out-and-out holy warmonger. From his pulpit and in *The York Diocesan Leaflet*, he denounced pacifism on theological grounds, and in America he even went as far as to tell reporters that "it might be necessary to have another great and horrible war to establish the efficacy of the League of Nations." The message was taken up by the lesser dignitaries, and from the pulpit on Sundays, mothers' meetings on Wednesdays, and Church bazaar addresses on Saturdays, it thundered out.

The result was that by the time the British Parliament rose for the summer recess, the British people had registered their views, the Government had taken note, and by the middle of August the Cabinet—or at any rate its principal members—had decided on a policy, astute enough in regard to domestic matters but extremely precarious abroad. Baldwin now considered that a strong line on collective security which could rally those who

supported the League to the Government's side might even encourage Mussolini to come to terms in the triangular negotiations
between France, Italy, and Britain that were still continuing. Indeed there was considerable faith in the belief that these negotiations would resolve the dispute. There were good reasons to
suppose that on the basis of the accepted monetary arrangements
Italy was in no position to face the financial burden of a long
colonial campaign, and if this were so, the abortive proposals
which had been made in June had been on the right lines. And as
the French were beginning to show some nervousness, it was assumed that the French Government—Laval in particular—
would be willing to join in a fresh effort to provide a solution.
All that had to be done was to offer Mussolini better terms. But
in satisfying Italy, whatever formula was adopted would not
only have to be acceptable to Ethiopia, it would also have to save
the face of the League of Nations. For this reason it was obvious
that any territorial concessions included as part of the bargain
must not seem to be an offer of Danegeld, with Britain or France
acquiescing in Mussolini's bullying tactics. In short, the solution
had to preserve the League's prestige, reconcile Italy's aspirations, and still offer benefit to Ethiopia.

Since Mussolini had never actually defined Italy's minimum
requirements for a settlement with Ethiopia in so many words,
the task of devising an offer which would both satisfy him and
yet meet the two other requirements was not easy. Within a comparatively short time the experts from the Foreign Office and
Quai d'Orsay had managed to produce a reasonably respectable
plan based on the original Zeila offer. Formulating it had been
made easier by Haile Selassie's accommodating concessions. The
question was whether this limit would satisfy Italy.

On August 15, when the Tripartite Conference arranged at
Geneva opened in Paris, Eden and Laval tried to find out. Aloisi,
the Italian delegate, said smoothly that it was impossible for him
to define precisely what Italy would take to settle the dispute.
The Italian people had been roused to anger, and he did not
think that Italy could be content with anything less than a protectorate over that part of Ethiopia which Britain and France had

recognized as Italy's legitimate sphere of influence in the 1906 Tripartite Treaty. It might be possible to negotiate something on these lines, but Britain and France—and the rest of the world, for that matter—must be clear that the dispute had nothing whatsoever to do with the League of Nations; Italy was going forward "with Geneva, without Geneva." *

Uneasy at this resurrection of a ghost from the past, neither Eden nor Laval could have much faith in the outcome of the discussion. Nevertheless it was decided to submit to the Duce the plan the British and French experts had prepared. The outcome was as they had feared. Reaching Rome on the night of August 16, the plan was formally rejected on the morning of the 18th, although it was apparent on the 17th what the answer was going to be. Mussolini had reviewed some troops before they sailed for East Africa that day and in his address to them he had declared that Italy would attack Ethiopia as soon as sufficient aircraft, bombs, and munitions of war had been amassed to guarantee success. "Our decision is irrevocable," he thundered. "Government and people are now engaged in a fight which we have determined to carry on until the bitter end."

By now the Italians had been conditioned to accept that a war was virtually inevitable, so that neither the Duce's speech nor the rejection of the Anglo-French offer next day had much import. For six months Mussolini had been stamping up and down the length of Italy haranguing and prodding his lethargic countrymen into enthusiasm for a war that few of them really wanted. The main theme was the old chestnut: Italy's greatness. "The stones of the Colosseum and other monuments," he declared at a review of five thousand reservists in Rome, "remind Italians that Rome has been the great mistress of the world and there is nothing to prevent modern Italy from believing that the destiny of yesterday might be that of tomorrow. *We are bent on colonial expansion* [author's italics]." With his journalistic background, the Duce knew the value of propaganda, and there were few aspects which he failed to cover. In the flurry of prepara-

* This phrase appeared in an anonymous article believed to have been written by Mussolini for the *Popolo d'Italia*.

tions there was even a pamphlet distributed to the troops and their families which expressed the view that the coming war would be "without tears." The men bound for East Africa, it assured its readers, need have no fears. "The old terror of an offensive campaign no longer exists, thanks to modern methods. Italy's new army, aircraft, and chemical warfare [will] do the business." This significant reference to aircraft and chemical warfare—probably the first hint that gas would be used in Ethiopia—could hardly fail to be lost on Italy's heroes-to-be.

By the spring of 1935 Mussolini's own concept of the war had undergone a radical change. The original plan, which was supposed to be his brainchild and his alone, envisaged provoking Ethiopia into an attack on the Italian colonies.* By so doing, Ethiopia would be branded as an aggressor; Italy would counterattack, and after a short successful campaign Haile Selassie would sue for peace. Italy would then be in a position to dictate her own terms. However, the whole plan hinged on the initial provocation, and when the Emperor seemed to be determined to remain immune to "incidents" and started to bring in the League, Mussolini saw that Italy would have to start the war. This carried the risk of Italy being condemned as an aggressor, of course, but in the confusion of the time this was a risk on which the Duce was prepared to gamble. In February, therefore, the plan was changed.

Details of the changes in the plan were passed to De Bono in a personal letter from the Duce dated March 8, 1935:

It is my profound conviction that, we being obliged to take the initiative of the operations at the end of October or September, you ought to have a combined force of 300,000 men (including about 100,000 black troops in the two colonies) plus 300–500 aeroplanes and 300 rapid cars—for without these forces to feed the offensive penetration the operations will not have the vigorous rhythm which we desire. You ask for three Divisions by the end of October; I mean to send you 10, I say ten: five Divisions of the Regular Army; five of volunteer formations of Blackshirts, who will be carefully selected

---

* According to De Bono, it was top secret and drawn up during December 1934. Only five copies existed, of which one was held by De Bono.

and trained. These divisions of Blackshirts will be the guarantee that
the undertaking will obtain the popular approbation. . . . Even in
view of possible international controversies (League of Nations, etc.)
it is as well to hasten the tempo. For the lack of a few thousand men
we lost the day at Adowa! We shall never make that mistake. I am
willing to commit a sin of excess but never a sin of deficiency.

Throughout the period of preparation, Mussolini kept De
Bono well informed of the progress of affairs at Geneva, and the
latter records that on May 1 the Duce "gave me details of the
satisfactory result of the negotiations with foreign Powers in respect of the supply of arms to Ethiopia. . . . And in this connection," the Marshal added, "I should say that from Aden to
Djibuti I was accurately informed of the continuous despatch of
arms direct to Addis Ababa; and candidly I must also say that
this disagreeable news had merely the result of making me ex-
claim *transeat a me calix iste!*" [5]

In another letter, dated May 18, the Duce also spoke of diplomatic action:

There has even been talk of taking steps. . . . I have made it understood that we shall not turn back at any price. . . . In the meantime,
with the nomination of the two arbitrators on the Italian side, we
shall get the better of the next Council of the League of Nations, but
in September we shall have to begin all over again. It may be that we
shall then find it necessary to withdraw from Geneva. . . . It is precisely in view of this eventuality that it is absolutely indispensable
not to alter the date—October—which we have fixed for the beginning of the eventual operations. Preliminary to this date you must
have on the spot the whole ten Italian Divisions.

The letter concluded with a warning that De Bono should
accumulate enough supplies and munitions to last three years in
the event of the closing of the Suez Canal. "One must always
make ready for the most pessimistic and difficult eventuality"
Mussolini said. Following a suggestion in Parliament by Major
Attlee, the closure of the Canal had indeed been discussed by the
British Government and the idea of doing so discussed in the
Press. "People," said one columnist, "were glad enough to see the
beginnings of courage and are seldom but anxious as to their ex-

tension of rashness. Major Attlee [has] aroused great wrath in Italy . . . but if agreement were reached as to the application of sanctions there could be no better plan." [6] As may be deduced from his letter to De Bono, Mussolini was not a man to be deterred by what he believed to be empty threats. To him the closure of the Suez Canal was unlikely; in the absence of an official declaration by the British Government that they would debar Italian ships from transit through the Canal he was prepared to brazen out the situation. In this light his rejection of the Tripartite offer is understandable.

By August, Italy was almost all set to attack Ethiopia. In Eritrea and Somaliland new roads led to the Ethiopian frontier, port and base facilities had been developed, hospitals built, and stocks of ammunition, food, gasoline, and the other wherewithal for making war had been amassed. Close to a quarter of a million men, equipped with the most modern weapons of the day, were waiting for the one order, *Avanti*. To get so far had entailed prodigious expenditure of resources, and for the sake of a few economic concessions Mussolini was not prepared to dismantle the vast military machine that was now almost ready to be set in motion. The Tripartite Conference was doomed to failure before it even submitted its proposals for consideration, and all it may be said to have achieved was to give Italy a further breathing space.

On September 4, when the League Council met as arranged to consider the growing tension, Count Aloisi presented a massive memorandum containing Italy's evidence of Ethiopian "aggressions and atrocities." At face value it was a damning document and the conclusions to one chapter, "Barbarism in Ethiopia," which read "by her conduct Ethiopia had openly placed herself outside the Covenant of the League and had rendered herself unworthy of the trust placed in her when she was admitted to membership," amounted to an indirect demand for Ethiopia's expulsion from the League. "Italy's dignity as a civilized nation," said Aloisi during the formal presentation of the memorandum," would be deeply wounded were she to continue a discussion in the League on a footing of equality with Ethiopia." In reply, the

Ethiopian representative called the Council's attentions to "one capital point." "The question," he said before asking the Council to take action under Article 15 of the Covenant,* "is whether a war of extermination will be begun in a few days." By this time there must have been a general realization by the delegates at Geneva that this was exactly what was going to happen—that the situation had reached a pitch which made further diplomatic bargaining futile. However, another attempt was made to effect a peaceful settlement and this time it was the League Council that took the initiative.

On September 6, a committee of five member nations—Britain and France joined by Poland, Spain, and Turkey—was appointed to make a general examination of Italian-Ethiopian relations and suggest ways of bringing about a peaceful solution. The plan that emerged on September 18 was based on the earlier abortive Anglo-French proposals and, in effect, what it amounted to was an international mandate over the whole of Ethiopia. So far as Italy was concerned, the buying-off price had been increased by a proposal to cede the Danakil as well as part of Ogaden, and an arrangement whereby Italians would be permitted to settle in other areas of the country. As a dubious sop to the Emperor it also included the appointment of European experts and technicians, nominated by the League, to help in improving Ethiopian governmental administration. The proponents of the plan claimed that its virtue lay in its flexibility, and it was drawn up in such loosely worded terms that Mr. Rüştü Aras, the Turkish representative on the Committee, had considerable misgivings about its impreciseness. Despite this, it did have some merit, and because it could have satisfied both Italy's aspirations and Ethiopia's basic needs, the scheme might have provided a basis for negotiation in December 1934 or January 1935. The trouble was that it came eight months too late.

In rejecting the new plan as "derisory," Mussolini made his famous remarks about his not being a "collector of deserts."

* Paragraph 3 or Article 15 reads as follows: "The Council shall endeavour to effect a settlement of the dispute and, if such efforts are successful, a statement shall be made public giving such facts and explanations regarding the dispute and terms of settlement thereof as the Council may deem appropriate."

"Apparently the suggestion is that two hundred thousand Italian troops in East Africa should be brought home and told that they have been sent out there on an excursion trip," he said to an English journalist. "That certainly will not be done in any case." With less than a fortnight to go before the date he had set for invasion, the Duce was committed to a shooting war. The whole of Italy was keyed up to expect it, and the only way fighting could have been averted at this time would have been for Ethiopia to have been allotted to Italy as a protectorate—to be disarmed and policed by the Italian army. The Committee of Five had failed, and at a meeting on September 26 the Council was obliged to recognize the fact.

On September 9 and again on the 11th, Laval had had long discussions with Hoare about what sanctions would be applied against Italy when Mussolini made the fateful move which everybody now realized was imminent. Generally it was assumed that economic measures were admissible but not military ones. In particular there would be no naval blockade at the mouth of the Suez Canal under any circumstances. Since reinforcements and supplies for the campaign had to pass down the Canal or take the longer and more expensive route around the Cape, this meant that the teeth were taken out of the policy before it was even applied; it also meant that Mussolini only had to say that he regarded a particular measure as a hostile act to prevent its adoption.

On September 11, Hoare addressed the League Assembly:

In conforming with its precise and explicit obligations, the League stands, and my country stands with it, for the collective maintenance of the Covenant in its entirety, and particularly for steady and collective resistance to all acts of unprovoked aggression.

The last phrase was repeated, with Hoare striking the desk of the rostrum in emphasis.

One thing is certain, if risks for peace are to be run, they must be run by all. The security of the many cannot be assured solely by the efforts of the few, however powerful they may be. I can say that the British Government will be second to none in their intention to fulfill, within the measure of their capacity, the obligation which the Covenant lays upon them.

We believe that small nations are entitled to a life of their own . . . and that backward nations are entitled to expect that assistance will be afforded to them by more advanced peoples in building up their national life. . . . The justice of a claim is not necessarily in proportion to the national passions which are roused in support of it. They may be deliberately roused by what I regard as one of the most pernicious features of modern life—government propaganda.

Since few people knew that Hoare's agreement with Laval had ensured that whatever sanctions were applied would be made ineffective, the firmness of his declaration was a revelation. The speech was in fact part and parcel of the general plan which led up to the infamous Hoare-Laval proposals of the following December. But on September 11 it appeared to be a whole-hearted proclamation of England's loyalty to the idea of collective security and to the League Covenant. Only later, when the news of the agreement with Laval became known, was it apparent that the speech was designed to placate the members of the League and the world at large.

In retrospect Hoare's speech can only be considered a confused exposition of Britain's intentions based on wishful thinking. If, as has been suggested, it contained an element of bluff, the Foreign Secretary sadly misjudged the Duce. The extent of the futility of trying to bluff a gambler like Mussolini (particularly when the latter had access to information in the British Embassy in Rome) is perhaps more apparent now than it was in 1935. Even then it must have been clear that Ethiopia was the real victim of what Professor Arnold Toynbee has suggested was dust throwing, and the conclusion seems to be that the British and French Governments were automatically continuing their procrastination policy of the previous months. Perhaps Hoare's innate fear was that if sanctions succeeded in stopping Italy going to war, the League would be all too ready to apply them against others who might consider they had more legitimate axes to grind in the future. Yet, so far as other members of the League were concerned, this was the very reason for supporting sanctions, and consequently most of them voted with alacrity for their application. If Mussolini could be compelled to abandon his aggression they could hope that if any of them found themselves in a plight similar to that of Ethiopia, the aggressor would be stopped in the same way; if sanctions succeeded against Italy, the great Powers would be morally bound to support them in similar cases in the future. Many of the delegations considered that the Anglo-French program of sanctions did not go far enough, but they hoped that as soon as this was demonstrated, the program would be expanded and its loopholes blocked. Ultimately, a blockade of the Suez Canal would mean that the Italian army in East Africa would be cut off from its source of supplies and Mussolini would be compelled to capitulate.

Two days after Hoare's speech at Geneva, ships of the Home Fleet sailed for the Mediterranean, and in London the League supporters were heartened by what appeared as Britain's forthright stand against the Ethiopian adventure. In his diocesan magazine published on September 24, the Bishop of St. Albans praised the Foreign Secretary in the words of the Fifteenth Psalm.

He that sweareth unto his neighbour and disappointeth him not,
Even though it were to his own hindrance.
Whoso doeth these things shall never fall.

By coincidence, the British Ambassador in Rome handed a message of friendship from Hoare to the Duce on the same day. "Speaking as an old friend," he said, "I desire to eliminate every unnecessary misunderstanding between the two countries." Mussolini's reply was to order more troops to be sent to Libya, while the Italian press let it be known that if Britain was thinking about closing the Suez Canal, she would do well to remember that she had vulnerable positions in the Eastern Mediterranean. Malta was one, Egypt another. If a British fleet blocked Suez, Italian troops would march on Cairo, and journalists attending Italian army maneuvers at Bolzano reported the Governor of Libya, the tall, copper-bearded Marshal Italo Balbo, as saying that he was going back to Libya to get ready for a war.* "With

---

* Balbo was a "Fascist from the first hour" and reputedly the inventor of the

whom?" he was asked. With his Bolognese lisp the Marshal replied *"Gli Inglethi"* and the inference was that he did not altogether intend a jest.

The most generous interpretation of the reasons for the concentration of a British naval force in the Eastern Mediterranean
during September 1935 was that the British Government considered there was the possibility of Mussolini taking a swipe at Britain if there was any interference at Suez. Yet this explanation
seems far-fetched when one considers that with a quarter of a
million men on the far side of the Canal in an area where they
could hardly get enough drinking water and certainly not
enough food, Mussolini had provided a hostage for any maritime
power that chose to attack her. More likely the comings and go-
ings of the British fleet, its concentration at Alexandria, and the
reinforcements sent to Egypt, were deceptive measures designed
to provide the necessary atmosphere at home, where the Conservatives had to be kept quiet, at Geneva, where Britain could pose
as a weary Titan with the world's troubles on her shoulders, and
in Rome, where there was still hope that a show of the might of
the Royal Navy could call the Duce's bluff. In October 1935, De
Bono had supplies for his armies sufficient for six months and
gasoline for only two, and he admitted afterward that if the Suez
Canal had been closed, the Ethiopian adventure would have had
to be abandoned. Subsequently, one of the excuses that was put
forward for not blockading Suez was that to do so could have
resulted in Mussolini linking up with Germany to declare war on
Britain and France—an explanation that in the light of after
events seems pitifully inadequate. It was also suggested that the
Royal Navy was not strong enough to take on the Italian Navy;
Britain could not "hold the Mediterranean route against a hostile
Italy," declared one pessimist in the *Observer* on August 25.
Later it was alleged that the Mediterranean Fleet had only suffi-
cient munitions for twenty-four hours, but if this was true there

---

castor-oil treatment for recalcitrant non-Fascists. Mussolini did not care for
Balbo's popularity as an aviator (which came as a result of a dramatic flight
from Rome to Chicago) or for his close friendship with Umberto, the Crown
Prince, who had anti-Fascist leanings. Balbo was given no part in the Ethiopian
campaign, of which—in its planning stages—he disapproved (like Badoglio and
the General Staff).

must have been gross negligence somewhere and a purge in the Admiralty should have followed.* In fact, man for man, ship for ship, and gun for gun, the Royal Navy was more than a match for the Italians—as was shown five years later at Taranto. Britain had the cards in her hand all right; but courage was lacking in Whitehall, and Mussolini knew it.

By its international consequences Britain's halfhearted attempt at rattling the saber appeared unnecessarily melodramatic. Except to induce Mussolini to reinforce Libya, it had little effect on Italy. To the French it was an unnecessary and unwarranted provocation. They had not been consulted before the Mediterranean Fleet was reinforced, and the idea of the Royal Navy steaming up and down the Mediterranean seemed calculated to increase tension and bring war nearer Europe. Since the League had not asked for such demonstrations there was nothing to justify them, and any idea that the French should join in—either by sending out their own fleet or by permitting Britain the use of French base facilities—was dismissed as ridiculous. Britain, the French decided, had acted on her own, and Laval, looking for the reward for this part in the intrigue by the withdrawal of Italian troops from the French frontier, was not going to jeopardize the French position if he could help it.

Meantime, at Geneva, efforts to effect a peaceful solution continued throughout this final period of growing tension. Recognizing on September 26 that the Committee of Five had failed, the League decided on a new approach, an all-out effort by a Committee of Thirteen, which was to consist of every member of the Council except the two parties to the dispute. Two days later Haile Selassie again drew the Council's attention to the increasing gravity of the situation in Africa and begged it to take some urgent action. He could no longer delay general mobilization, he said. Nevertheless he would keep his troops at a distance of thirty kilometers from the Italian border and he would, as be-

---

* Any lack of munitions cannot have been due to lack of money. During the financial year 1933–34 Britain's expenditure on the Royal Navy was £45,-000,000—a sum which is considerably greater in terms of purchasing power than that which was allocated to the Naval vote during the rearmament period of 1938–39.

fore, continue "to cooperate closely with the League of Nations in all circumstances." Time had run out. The Duce, who had ordered "the general mobilization of all the forces of the regime" on September 10, was now telling his ministers that he was "going to wipe out the defeat which the Ethiopians inflicted on Italy thirty-nine years ago at Adowa and dictate terms of peace to the Emperor." "With the League, without the League, against the League, the problem has only one solution," he declared. "We will shoot straight."

Without the support of France any effective action by the League would have been difficult enough even if the other members had been enthusiastic about vindicating its principles. And, fundamentally, one of the troubles was that the French did not trust the British. In reading their own psychology into others they just could not understand why anybody should want to pursue what to them was a completely unrealistic policy; there must be more to it than they could see. The British Government's twists and turns in its efforts to evolve a policy acceptable to British public opinion while protecting imperial interests were beyond their comprehension. Besides, they had seen Britain apply the old principle of "divide and rule" too often to accept without reservations that there was an idealistic side to Britain's apparent change of heart. In French eyes Britain's aim was the same as it had always been: to maintain a balance of power on the continent while retaining the casting vote for herself, and the sudden concern for the sanctity of treaties—which would have been so welcome a few years before—was suspect. The holier-than-thou's in England—the sort of people who were always a danger to the peace of Europe (France particularly) with their muddled and ill-timed moralization on nonethical problems—had forced the British Government to wave a flag for legality at Geneva. But this was not the real feeling of the British people; there were too many signs that Britain had not changed. What about the isolationists who wanted to steer clear of any continental commitments? The British Empire enthusiasts who thought only in terms of imperial might? The Conservatives who had never been more than lukewarm about the League? The informal plebiscite of the Peace Ballot suggested that some people in Britain believed in the League, but did the League of Nations Union represent Britain? Neither the French nor any other foreigners believed that it did.

As suspicion mounted, an acrimonious controversy developed between the two countries, and for a time British sanctionists diverted their attentions from Mussolini to the person of the French Premier. Needless to say the French gave as good as they got. The sanctionists were described as a "collection of bunglers and half-wits who have transferred a simple colonial expedition into the threat of a world war," and Anglophobia reached its climax on October 11. That day the *Gringoire,* an organ of the French Right, published an article by M. Henri Béraud under the suggestive title "Should England be Reduced to Slavery?" It declared:

England's policy consists of troubling the earth so that she can rule the seas. . . . I think English friendship the most cruel present the gods can give a people. When I see England, the Bible in one hand, the League of Nations Covenant in the other, upholding the cause of the weak or the righteous, I can't but believe she has her own reasons. . . . I have seen His Majesty's police slashing Egyptian students in the streets of Cairo. I saw the Lord Mayor of Cork dying in London in a criminal's cell. I saw convicts, disguised by Lloyd George as soldiers, shooting down the Balbriggan martyrs at their cottage doors. . . . Is it indispensable for human happiness that the route to India be British? . . . In France only hall-porters and M. Flandin are pro-British. . . . I hate England. . . . I say . . . that England must be reduced to slavery. . . .[7]

The unamiable ferocity of this stricture provoked an immediate protest by the British Ambassador in Paris, and Laval himself apologized. But Henri Béraud only said what a great many Frenchmen were thinking.

It was significant that the French Socialists and left-wing parties, who were more committed to support the League of Nations than the French Right, took a strong pacifist line on sanctions. Although they were anxious not to alienate Britain, the Socialists were strongly opposed to any drastic action against

Italy, and their gaunt, elegant leader Léon Blum strongly depre-
cated the application of military sanctions. As a result, on September 29, the Committee of the Popular Front passed a resolution declaring that the Popular Front "which is passionately attached to Peace . . . rejects with horror the idea of a conflict
with Italy or any other country, and is uncompromisingly opposed to any application of armed force." In these circumstances
Laval's efforts to avoid the call to sanctions is understandable.
Not only was it a question of wishing to put obstacles in the way
of the Duce; his own position depended on maintaining a delicate
balance between the right- and left-wing parties.

With an obvious schism between the two nations to whom
the rest of the League members were looking for a lead, it is
hardly surprising that there was confusion at Geneva. The ideas
of individual nations as to the right action to take were bound to
differ, and in the absence of any real leadership some of them
preferred to sit on the fence; the others who did play a part in
the crisis may be divided into three groups. To the so-called neutral nations, like Holland, Denmark, Norway, Sweden, and some
of the South American countries, the rape of Ethiopia was of
little direct concern. On principle they supported the Covenant
because it seemed to be the best umbrella available; as they were
well outside the theater of operations, the consequences of any
sanctions against Italy were unlikely to have any effect on their
own well-being. The second group, consisting of the members of
the Little Entente—Czechoslovakia, Rumania, and Yugoslavia—
and the Balkan countries, Greece and Turkey, had a direct interest in the outcome of Mussolini's adventure. All were on the edge
of the likely zone of hostilities; all had come to be suspicious of
Italy's aspirations, and each was hoping that the League's promised collective security would prove effective if and when they
found themselves in the unhappy position of Ethiopia. The third
group comprised the states which were in Italy's pocket—Austria, Hungary, and Albania. Albania was virtually an Italian de-
pendency, and Hungary had aligned herself with Italy in the
hope of getting the Treaty of Trianon revised.* Austria, bal-

---

* The Treaty of Trianon, concluding peace between the Allied Powers and
Hungary, was a subsidiary of the Treaty of Versailles. Its terms were similar

anced between Germany, the League, and Italy, opted for Italy
because she considered Mussolini would win, although subsequent events were to show that she could still lose to Germany.
Switzerland also was sympathetic toward Italy, but she had no
wish to prejudice her traditional neutrality by taking sides either
by a show of direct support of her Latin neighbor or by applying sanctions against her. In the end she did join the sanctions
camp but very halfheartedly.

Looming over all these little countries was the vast bulk of
Soviet Russia, aloof and watchful. In December 1934 Stalin had
stated the principle of Soviet foreign policy in forthright terms:

Our foreign policy is clear. It is a policy of preserving peace and
strengthening commercial relations with all countries. The U.S.S.R.
does not think of threatening anybody—let alone of attacking anybody. We stand for peace and champion the cause of peace. But we
are not afraid of threats and are prepared to answer blow for blow
against the instigation of war. Those who try to attack our country
will receive a stunning rebuff to teach them not to poke their pig's
snout into our Soviet garden.[8]

What happened to Ethiopia was of no concern to Russia, and she
had nothing to fear from Italy. Her two potential enemies were
Japan and Germany, and Stalin's policy was designed to check
these two countries. On one front, Japanese inroads into China
had been watched apprehensively and had been offset by establishing guarded relations with the United States. But on the other
front, the Soviet Union faced the relentless hostility of a Germany with new dreams of a *Drang nach Osten*. Although their
territories did not adjoin, the buffer state of Poland filling most
of the space between them was a German ally, while the other
buffers, bordering on the Baltic, were all small states. Consequently it suited the U.S.S.R. to maintain that the independence
of small states should be regarded as inviolable. Treaties signed
with France and Czechoslovakia had been designed to create a
ring of steel around Germany, but in October 1935 the Soviet
Union was still prepared to give the League of Nations its sup-

---

to those of the treaty with Austria, and affirmed the separation of Hungary
from Austria. It was signed at the Trianon (Versailles) on June 4, 1920.

port, provided it could offer protection against Germany. If sanctions worked against Italy, there was hope that they might deter Hitler later. Thus, before sanctions had been put to the test and shown to fail, Russia was one of the most ardent supporters of the League. However, as soon as it became clear that sanctions were not going to work the Soviet Union was no longer interested. Like France, her concern for the League was based solely on its potential as a bulwark of use to her. The Soviet Union wanted to forge a weapon for use against Germany, and as soon as she saw that it was not going to be done at Geneva, it was a matter of complete indifference to her what happened to Ethiopia or whether Italy was punished for her misdeeds.

Individual members of the British Commonwealth and Empire who were also members of the League—Australia, Canada, New Zealand, and South Africa—followed the lead of the mother country with varying degrees of enthusiasm. Australia, New Zealand, and Canada all supported the League on principle and out of loyalty to Britain. But their support was not blindly given; none of them wanted to be accessories to the provocation of a war in Europe in which they did not want to become entangled. The one which took the strongest line was South Africa. General Smuts, with whom the future of the League weighed heavily, was quick to point out that a war in Ethiopia might be interpreted in Africa as a racial war. To him the fate of Ethiopia was bound up with the future of Africa, and a victory of the whites over the blacks might have more serious repercussions than would their defeat. Paradoxically English settlers in Kenya —equally concerned with the racial problem—were more afraid of an Italian debacle. In their view this would mean a serious loss of face for all Europeans in Africa.*

Of the countries outside the League the most important were

* This concern for loss of face was still evident in 1941. During the Ethiopian Campaign the author was a junior officer serving with a unit of the King's African Rifles. After one battle a party of Italians were being escorted to the rear under an escort of British Askaris. One of the prisoners lagging behind was brusquely pushed into line by an Askari and the action was seen by a field officer who was an old Kenya settler. Addressing the author, he said, "Don't you let that black man push those white men around; some of us have to live in this country after the war."

the United States, Japan, and Germany, and in their absence the
League's deliberations were haunted by their ghosts. Although
none of them took part in the proceedings, what people believed
to be their outlook undoubtedly influenced the decisions that
were taken. Germany and Japan were kindred spirits of Italy; all
had the same aspirations and believed in the same forceful methods of attaining their ends. Both greeted the Ethiopian affair with
some satisfaction. Although it seems that Hitler did not fully appreciate the point at the time, he stood to gain no matter how it
turned out. If Mussolini won his war, Fascism was vindicated; if
he lost, Germany's rival in Central Europe would be eliminated.
Japan, on the other hand, had nothing to gain if Mussolini won;
nevertheless the League had to ask itself whether she would remain aloof if sanctions against Italy were seen to work. The argument put forward by anti-sanctionists was that Germany and
Japan might well only be waiting for the League to get well and
truly embroiled with Italy to embark on adventures of their own.
What better opportunity than a three-cornered fight between
Britain, France, and Italy, for German troops to march into Austria or Czechoslovakia? What could suit Japan better than an
upheaval in Europe for her to polish off China and possibly expand even further in the Far East? To this the sanctionists replied that only by the League demonstrating its power to curb a
renegade could it hope to maintain its existence. Even if it meant
war with Italy, they insisted, the League would have to act effectively. By doing so it would impress other would-be violators of
international law that it was suicidal to defy the League's authority; with fifty nations ranged against Italy, Germany and Japan
would never dare to move out of step. Whether what the pro-
sanctionists advocated would have been effective is debatable.
Germany herself gave little indication of how she would react in
any given situation, and the Nazi press, apart from evidencing its
natural Fascist affinity, maintained a Prussian correctness
throughout the crisis. Without strengthening Mussolini's hand,
and thereby possibly weakening Germany's position with Austria, Hitler's Government could not support Italy; on the other
hand, Germany had no wish to encourage the League. Conse-

quently Germany remained neutral, taking no part in the sanctions that were eventually applied nor giving any special assistance to Italy.

The indecision of the United States had an altogether different basis. With the states of Europe divided among themselves, she was the only nation strong enough to turn the scales of collective action one way or the other. For this reason her attitude was doubly important to the Italian dictator. If the United States decided that Italy ought to be checked, the fence-sitters in Geneva would undoubtedly come down on the side of sanctions and the cry to halt Italy could swell to a roar; alternatively, even if the League did decide to apply sanctions, it was still possible for the United States to render them futile by ignoring them and supplying Italy with what she was being denied elsewhere. Europe accepted that the United States wanted peace, had no designs on anyone, and made it clear that she wished to avoid entanglements in Europe. At the same time, it was well known that a ruthless commercial instinct invariably prompted American businessmen to seek profit whenever the opportunity arose. Indeed, it was their persistent trading with the belligerents during the First World War that had been partially responsible for the United States being drawn into the conflict. It was difficult to believe that they would now be able to resist the temptation to make money out of someone else's war.

The Rickett oil concession affair suggests that the businessmen had not lost their instinct, and during the summer months of 1935, when Mussolini's intentions had become obvious, the United States was careful not to take any step which could be interpreted as a move which might deter the Duce. Many Americans had an uneasy sensation that a deadly evil was being fostered outside their own world, but they preferred to evade responsibility rather than play any positive part in its suppression. Under President Roosevelt, the Democrats sponsored a new concept of neutrality, and if it had been applied rigidly, Italy would have been unable to obtain from the United States the materials she was denied by the nations applying sanctions. This would have helped the League. Unfortunately when the policy was

translated into action it was restricted to half measures designed
to absolve Americans of the charge of defeating collective action
by the League, while lessening the chances of being drawn into
dispute with the belligerents. Meantime, the State Department,
prompted by an Ethiopian request in July to invoke the Pact of
Paris against Italy, proffered sympathy to the prospective victim
and quietly let Italy know that the United States was disturbed
by the trend of events. At the same time it took care to ensure
that neither Britain nor France should construe this maiden-aunt
type advice as a promise to join the sanctionists at Geneva. On
July 24 the President asked Congress to consider legislation
which would ensure neutrality if hostilities broke out; two days
later he was saying that the Italo-Ethiopian dispute was of no
direct concern to the United States. On August 1 he was piously
expressing the hope that the League would succeed in settling the
affair—an ambiguous wish that could have been satisfied as well
by an arrangement giving Italy what she wanted as by a firm
decision not to do so. In fact, what the President said was typical
of the belief that pervaded the State Department—that the
United States could remain aloof in isolation, no matter what
happened in Europe. Yet it must be recognized that Roosevelt
had a purpose. He did not have a majority in both Houses, and
faced with obstructionism of Congress, and of a large section of
the American public, he was quietly endeavoring to retain control of foreign policy. At that time any overt encouragement of
the League against Italy would almost certainly have strengthened the position of the advocates of isolationism.

During August a Neutrality Resolution, making it manda-
tory on the President to prohibit the sale and export of "arms,
ammunition, and implements of war" to "all belligerents," was
rushed through Congress. The fact that trade in other goods—
including many which were no less essential for waging war—
was not restricted, reflects the feeling that not even the dyed-in-
the-wool isolationist senators were prepared to push peace beyond a point where it might seriously affect America's business.
interests. The Resolution was made effective only until February
20, 1936; nevertheless its advent tended to dampen the enthusi-

asm of those members of the League inclined to support sanctions but chary of finding themselves in economic or military difficulties by so doing. Seen from Europe, what it suggested was that if a country found itself embroiled in a war because it had backed the League against Mussolini, it could not count on the United States to supply arms. Furthermore, if members of the League severed their trade with Italy, it did not follow that the United States would do the same. Under such circumstances economic sanctions would almost certainly prove worthless. The whole conception of substitute warfare where nobody suffered loss of life or limb would go by the board; only a blockade would be effective. Not only did this mean a shooting war, but the United States let it be known that any blockade of Italy would not be tolerated so far as the free passage of American ships was concerned. This, then, was a further cause for hesitation. Nevertheless the Neutrality Resolution was an embarrassment which probably deterred some of the pro-sanctionists and undoubtedly it contributed to the cautiousness of the British Government—especially Baldwin, who had always regarded the application of the Covenant as being totally impracticable unless the League were assured of support from across the Atlantic.

To sum up the various facets of world opinion as they appeared on the eve of the Italian invasion: the majority of nations deplored Mussolini's adventure, but they were reluctant to take a stand against it unless they could be assured that the leaders among them were willing to accept the brunt of any repercussions arising out of their collective action. There was no help forthcoming from the United States or Russia, and everything therefore depended on Britain and France. Regrettably the Governments of both countries were unwilling to accept that responsibility.

The war started on October 2, 1935. During the morning, trumpets, sirens, church bells and loudspeakers in every Italian town and village blared out a call for all citizens to listen to an important announcement, and that afternoon the Duce broadcast the message which everyone was now expecting:

Black Shirts of the Revolution! Men and Women of all Italy! Italians scattered throughout the world, over the hills and beyond the seas: Hear me!

A solemn hour is about to strike in the history of our country. Twenty million people fill, at this moment, all the squares of Italy. The history of man has never known such a sight. Twenty million people, with one heart, one will, one decision alone. This manifestation ought to show the world that Italy and Fascism are a single entity, perfect, absolute, unalterable. Only crass idiots, ignorant of Italy in 1935, the thirteenth year of the Fascist Era, could believe otherwise.

For many months the wheel of destiny, under the impulse of our calm determination, has been moving toward its goal; now its rhythm is faster and can no longer be stopped. Here is not just an army marching toward a military objective, but a whole people, forty-four million souls, against whom the blackest of all injustices has been committed—that of denying them a place in the sun. When in 1915 Italy mixed her fate with that of the Allies—how much praise there was from them, how many promises! But after a common victory, which cost Italy six hundred and seventy thousand dead, four hundred thousand mutilated, and a million wounded, at the peace table these same Allies withheld from Italy all but a few crumbs of the rich colonial loot. We have waited for thirteen years, during which time the egoism of these Allies has only increased and suffocated our vitality. We have waited patiently for redress in Ethiopia for forty years. Now—enough!

At the League of Nations, instead of recognizing this, there is talk of sanctions. Until I am proved wrong, I refuse to believe that France . . . or the people of Great Britain, with whom we have never quarreled, would risk throwing Europe into catastrophe to defend a country in Africa well known to be without the least shade of civilization. To economic sanctions we will reply with our discipline, our sobriety, our spirit of sacrifice!

To military sanctions we shall reply with military measures! To acts of war we shall reply with acts of war!

But let it be said at the start, in the most categorical way, that we will do everything possible to avoid this colonial conflict flaring up into a European war. But never, as in this historical epoch, has the Italian people shown so well the quality of its spirit and the strength of its character. And it is against this people, people of poets, of saints, navigators, that they dare to speak of sanctions. Proletarian and Fascist Italy . . . on your feet!

Italy's day of reckoning had arrived at last; on October 3 Italian troops crossed the Mareb River and started to advance into Ethiopia. "The warlike and aggressive spirit of Ethiopia," Count Aloisi told the Council of the League that afternoon, had succeeded in "imposing war" on Italy.

CHAPTER 8

Puny Power:
Mechanized Might

Better pointed bullets than pointed speeches.

BISMARCK

On the morning of October 3, 1935, Menelek's old war drum thundered out the order for general mobilization which had been signed by Haile Selassie four days earlier. Shortly afterward a royal proclamation was read by the Grand Chamberlain to an assembly of Ethiopian chiefs gathered in the courtyard of the Imperial Palace.

The conflict between Italy and our country, which has now lasted for almost a year, started at Walwal on 5 December 1934. Our soldiers . . . were attacked, in our territory . . . Italy demanded reparations and apologies. . . . When, after much resistance on Italy's part, we were able, thanks to our perseverance and the effects of the League of Nations Council, to bring this difference before the arbitrators, they unanimously recognised that we were guiltless of the fault Italy imputed to us. But Italy, which for a long time has shown an unconcealed desire to acquire our country, now prepares to attack us. . . . The hour is grave. Arise, each of you. Take up arms, and rush to the defence of your country. Rally to your chiefs; obey them with single purpose, and repel the invader. May those who are unable because of weakness and infirmity to take an active part in this sacred quarrel, help us with their prayers. The opinion of the world has been revolted by this aggression against us. God be with us all. All forward for your Emperor and for your country!

The chiefs' response to the proclamation was disciplined, orderly, and methodical. A few seconds of silence were followed by three formal bursts of clapping and some desultory cheers. However, when one of the windows overlooking the courtyard was thrown open and Haile Selassie appeared, the cheering ululations rose to a crescendo and the chiefs surged forward to declare their allegiance. Raising his arm to command silence, the Emperor addressed them as follows:

Do not be afraid. I shall be with you in battle. Do not be afraid of death. You will be dying for your country. March on to death or victory. Let all take up their arms, stand up and move on at the call of your country. *The world is with us, God is on our side. March on for Emperor and country*.[1]

As he spoke the distant beating of the war drums could be heard relaying the mobilization order into the countryside. The die was cast; Ethiopia was now committed to a struggle which she had no hope of winning.

Because it can be argued that mobilization orders are equivalent to a declaration of war, Haile Selassie had deliberately deferred his proclamation until the very last minute. The old Minister for War, Ras Mulugeta, confident that he would be able to inflict another Adowa, had been angrily demanding mobilization since August. But the Emperor, still hoping that the League of Nations would curb the Italians, had refused to sanction the proclamation until the first aggressive act had been committed. To him, Sir Samuel Hoare's speech on September 11 had been a clear indication that Britain would come to the rescue if Ethiopia were attacked, and he was determined that there should be no misunderstanding over mobilization measures which could be deliberately misinterpreted by the Italians as provocation. At a great banquet in the Imperial Palace, where vast quantities of raw meat had been eaten and much *tej* drunk, Ethiopia's attitude had been defined. If a fight was to come, the Emperor had told his besotted chiefs, Ethiopia would put her faith in the support of Britain and France.

But, if the efforts of other nations and our own fail, and devilish violence takes the opportunity to open war, sowing misfortune, shame and misery with the world as its field, Ethiopia will rise up, the Emperor at her head, and follow him in her hundred thousands with the valour and staunchness famous for a thousand years. Leaning on the Divine arm, she will resist the invader to the last drop of her blood, fighting from the natural fortresses of mountain and desert that the Lord has given her.[2]

Since Italy had been mobilizing for months and the Duce's formal mobilization order was merely the excuse for a mass demonstration in Rome, Haile Selassie's delay may appear as an overcautious neglect of a necessary protective measure. But apart from the desire to avoid any accusation of giving provocation, the fact that he had no means of indefinitely supporting large armies in the field was another good reason why the Emperor should hold his hand. Indeed there was some doubt at the time as to when he did actually order the Rases to summon the feudal levies—which is what general mobilization, Ethiopian style, really meant. Some precautionary measures, which included concentrating the Government troops in central Amhara to cover Gondar, the appointment of Ras Kassa as the military commander of the northern zone, and the deployment of a covering force under Ras Seyoum in Tigre during April 1935, were interpreted by the Italians as a secret mobilization. As a result, Mussolini subsequently argued that Haile Selassie's order to mobilize was issued before his own. What really happened was that the call to the feudal levies was prepared but withheld, and an exuberant journalist, wishing to be first with the news, cabled from Addis Ababa that the proclamation had been made a few days prior to October 5. By the evidence of George Steer, "The Ethiopian mobilisation was not ordered until five hours after the Italian bombardment of Adowa [October 3]."[3]

Before the war drums beat out their message, the Ethiopians had boasted that they could call up over a million men. It is impossible to estimate the numbers in the field at any given time, but it appears that less than half that number were actually mobilized, and the number of effectives was approximately 300,000. Although the Ethiopians had encouraged an exaggerated estimate, the Italian assessment was close to this figure since their Intelligence reckoned that De Bono's armies would be opposed by about 200,000 men in the north and 100,000 in the south. Ill-equipped and psychologically ill-prepared for the sort of war with which they were faced, most of the Emperor's men were untrained and a few were wholly unreliable. Despite his efforts at modernization, Haile Selassie's ideas had sunk deeper into the minds of his civil rather than military advisers, and a century of difference lay between men like Bilatengeta Herrouy, the Foreign Minister, or Dr. Martin, the Ethiopian Minister in London, with their sons at public schools in England, and the older generation of military chiefs like Ras Mulugeta and Ras Kassa. His Imperial Majesty might be able to call a million men to the colors to meet a life-or-death emergency, but while Haile Selassie had some appreciation of the shortcomings of the ragged army that would emerge from such a call-up, his chiefs were still debating whether men would fight better wearing their lion skins when they went into battle.

Military incompetence was part of the price that the Ethiopians were to pay for their backwardness, and more especially for their distrust of Europeans. There were plenty of the latter to give advice, but Ethiopian conceit precluded them taking it from foreigners. Adowa had provided the culminating proof of their invulnerability, and as the sons of Solomon they considered themselves invincible. Nobody bothered to analyze why they had been successful at Adowa—the numerical inferiority of the Italians and Baratieri's heinous strategic error. Considerations of firepower, mobility, and aircraft just did not interest them; they were unaware of the effect of massed machine guns; tanks and armored cars, and above all aircraft, were factors of which they had no comprehension. Victories over the Italians, Egyptians, Mahdists, the Mad Mullah, and the peoples of the "colonial provinces" had established Ethiopian bravery in battle; that was good enough. Even the traditional titles of their senior officers reflected this attitude. The Fitorari—"Front of the Rhinoceros"— was the general who would lead the vanguard and establish contact with the enemy; the Kenyazmatch—"Leader of the Right Wing"—and the Gerazmatch—"Leader of the Left Wing"— would envelop him. Then, under the Dejazmatch—"Commander of the Threshold"—the reserves would be thrown in to the battle at the enemy's weakest point and annihilate him. It was all a matter of getting to grips, for at close quarters the Ethiopian long-sword would prove who was the best soldier in the stern realities of battle. Hand-to-hand fighting; cold steel, no quarter asked or given—this was how the issue would be decided. Or so the Ethiopians thought. But an army needs more than brave men. Against the overwhelming firepower of the Italians, and their superior generalship, the Ethiopians had no hope of survival. Obsolete rifles, a few hundred machine guns, a couple of hundred miscellaneous artillery pieces—none of which had more than three hundred rounds per gun—and an air force of fifteen aircraft, of which only three were fit for combat, were no match for the Fascist juggernaut.

The Ethiopian regular army was about 100,000 strong. The *corps d'élite*, the Imperial Guard, was armed with modern Mausers and dressed in khaki uniforms. But the remainder consisted of men armed with a miscellaneous collection of weapons, requiring a variety of ammunition, and dressed at the opening of hostilities in conventional white shirtlike *shammas*. Their rifles were honorable ornaments but seldom weapons of precision, and many of them had seen service at Königgrätz, Sedan, Ladysmith, and Liaoyang. More often than not the ammunition carried by its owner bore no relationship to the weapon. The feudal levies were in an even worse plight. When, in response to the Emperor's mobilization summons, the "chiefs of fifty" and "chiefs of a hundred" paraded their lithe warriors for war, the best of these men were equipped in the same fashion as the bulk of the regular Government Army. But many had no rifle—only a sword or a spear. On the whole, they were tough, courageous and unambitious, simple and decent individuals, wholly unaware of what civilization had prepared for them. They expected the war to last only a few weeks at the outside, and when they reported for duty each man brought his own bundle containing a few days' supply of grain, which he thought would see him through to the end of hostilities. They had no transport, no organized supply service, no medical arrangements, and when their own paltry rations ran out they had to depend on local supplies, or, like the Boer commandos, they had to return home.

For this reason alone, if Ethiopia stood any chance of winning the war it had to be a quick campaign. And the Italians were thinking on totally different lines. When De Bono's vanguard deployed in Eritrea and Somaliland in May 1935, it was reckoned that it would take three years to conquer Ethiopia. Nobody expected to reach Addis Ababa in one campaign; nobody thought in terms of a reckless dash across country. Cautious progress followed by systematic consolidation, rather than a mad effort to swallow the country in one gulp, was the plan. Even this might not be necessary, for an internal revolt which would give Italy her Empire without a casualty list was considered to be a realistic possibility. As it turned out, the imposition of sanctions brought a change of tactics, but the slow progress and apparent lack of enterprise shown in the opening phases of the campaign is explained as the unraveling of the original plan.

Haile Selassie did not share the conviction of his warlords that Italy would be driven out of Ethiopia as they had been driven out in 1896. He foresaw a long war and favored guerrilla tactics as a means of holding the Italians at bay. When the guns spoke on October 3, both he and his Foreign Minister were still clinging to the idea that the League would save Ethiopia, and that it only needed a month or two before Britain stepped in to bring Italy to heel. Knowing that his troops with their puny weapons and superlative arrogance would be no match for the Italians in a set-piece battle, the Emperor's plan was to harrass the Italian outposts and communications. By refusing a pitched battle and falling slowly back before the Italian advance, he hoped to keep most of his levies and his regular army intact until the rains set in about April; this should provide further respite for the League to act and it might even make the Italian position untenable. But the pursuance of this plan would have required a far more disciplined nation as well as more loyal and understanding subordinates than Haile Selassie had at his command. A planned retreat demands the highest standard of training in a regular army, and guerrilla warfare requires coordination of movement. With no General Staff and the minimum of communications, the latter would have been difficult enough. Add to this the consideration that, when the Emperor's orders did eventually reach their destination, they were either too late, too vague to be acted upon, or the recipient unwilling to take any notice of them, the situation will be seen to have been well nigh impossible. Haile Selassie was an admirable bridge between his people and Europe, and he had plenty of physical and moral courage. But he had none of the stern toughness of Menelek, and the qualities he lacked were precisely those which would have kept his chiefs working independently and obediently in a guerrilla campaign.

In many ways the people and the terrain were admirably suited to guerrilla tactics. The Ethiopian irregulars could march great distances and needed very little food, so there was no transport problem. But not having any supply services meant that they were dependent on the readiness of the civilian population to support, feed, and hide them, and although the Tigre population was ready to do so at first, a taste of aerial retribution loosed by the Italians on the villages believed to be cooperating with guerrillas soon brought the population to the realization that they would be annihilated if they continued to support Haile Selassie's cause. The result was that when there was cooperation with the guerrillas it was usually short-lived. Guerrilla warfare also depends on freedom of movement out of contact with the enemy, and such movement was impossible by day because of the Italian Air Force. With four hundred bombers and the "pursuit" planes which had nothing to pursue, the Regia Aeronautica kept up a droning survey of the battle area which tied the Ethiopian formations to the ground from dawn to dusk. It should have been possible to move at night, but as most of the troops were

strangers to the area in which they were committed to battle, control—already a major problem—became impossible. Apart from
this, the Amharan tribesmen had neither the training in mountain
warfare, nor the incentive to the sort of independent fighting
developed by the Pathans on the North-West Frontier of India,
nor the African equivalent of the rifle factories of Kabul to assure their supplies of ammunition. During the last couple of
months of the war they learned more about guerrilla fighting
than they had learned in the previous century, but it was only
after the fall of Addis Ababa that they began to put this learning
into practice. By that time it was too late; the world had lost
interest and cared as little for what was going on in the mountain
vastness of Mussolini's *Africa Orientale* as it did about the contemporary campaigning in Waziristan.

In three decades, the Ethiopian feudal system had degener-
ated. Such a system rallies round a dominant character, and Haile
Selassie never pretended to be a soldier. Undisturbed by any
foreign menace until 1930, the struggle in Ethiopia had been between the Emperor and his chiefs, between modernization and
suspicion of foreign influence. To get to power, Haile Selassie
had had to play one chief off against another; the result was jeal-
ousy and suspicion, and those who were not jealous were often
too proud to ask for help. As the Ethiopian Army was organized
in 1935, there was a lack of centralized control and lack of cooperation between formations. Thus, on one occasion, Ras Kassa,
having asked in vain for reinforcements from Ras Mulugeta, subsequently ignored the Emperor's order to go to his rival's assistance when he was later in danger.

By September the Emperor was making frantic efforts to put
his regular army on a war footing and to collect rifles and ammunition. How his efforts to procure arms were hampered, and the
effects of the extension of the Foreign Enlistment Act in Britain,
have already been referred to briefly. The latter precluded the
raising of a foreign legion which might have helped to block the
road to Addis Ababa as effectively as French volunteers and British Communists were to hold up Italians, Moors, and Spaniards a
year later outside Madrid. By mid-September a large number of

men had offered their services to Dr. Martin in London, and it ought to have been possible to have collected a force of about five thousand men. Pressure brought to bear by the Foreign Office was the primary cause which led to the abandonment of this idea. Nevertheless Dr. Martin cannot wholly escape blame on this score. An Anglo-Indian, not only did he have a great affection for Britain, a country he had served for many years before entering Haile Selassie's employment, and a peculiarly bigoted faith in her omnipotence abroad, he also believed in the probity of her foreign policy. This made him an easy victim to the cheery exhortations of people who assured him that Britain would "see him through." Consequently, at a time when Ethiopia might have been raising loans, buying arms, and recruiting mercenaries, her minister in London was being urged not to do anything which might complicate the international situation or make the Foreign Office task more difficult. Since they were thus denied of political support and practical aid, it is probably just as well that the Ethiopians who rallied to the Emperor's call had such pathetic confidence in their own prowess and were ignorant of what awaited them.

The Italians could invade Ethiopia from one of two directions, or both. They could advance south from Eritrea, north and west from Italian Somaliland, or attack simultaneously from both directions. Choosing the latter course offered two important advantages: first, the Ethiopians would be compelled to fight on several fronts and so be unable to concentrate their enormous manpower in one sector; secondly, the conjunction of two Italian armies advancing toward each other would establish a land link between the two Italian colonies. In the original plan for a long campaign the second objective was extremely important, but with the increase in the tempo of operations and the early collapse of organized Ethiopian resistance, it was subordinated to the swift occupation of Addis Ababa and the total annexation of Ethiopia. Nevertheless, if the campaign had taken longer or had proved more difficult, occupying the Ogaden in order to extend the Italian foothold in Africa from the Red Sea to the Indian Ocean could have become the paramount strategic consideration.

Because the strength of the Italian forces employed far exceeded that of any previous colonial expedition, and the difficulties associated with the terrain and climate of Ethiopia—as well as geographical and strategical considerations—were exceptional, the logistic problems are of considerable interest. At the beginning of 1935 there were no base facilities in either Eritrea or Italian Somaliland which were anywhere near capable of supporting operations on the scale which Mussolini was planning. Over two thousand miles of sea separates Naples from Massawa, the main port for Eritrea, and Mogadishu in Somaliland lies sixteen hundred miles beyond that; at that time, neither of the ports had the facilities to cope with the volume of seaborne traffic needed to land and maintain a large expeditionary force. Massawa was the better of the two, but it is noted for an exceptionally hot climate even for the Red Sea, and its sole merit was a harbor with deepwater inshore; otherwise heat, dirt, dust, and flies made it particularly unsuited as a base for military operations. Prior to 1935, the normal traffic of the port had been confined to coastal shipping, occasional British tramp steamers, and a few Japanese ships loading salt for India; consequently the facilities associated with modern ports—mechanical means of loading and unloading, warehouses, and railways—were sadly lacking. What was sufficient for a capacity of four or five ships discharging an average monthly traffic of 2,000 tons was clearly inadequate for fifty ships a week unloading about 2,500 tons daily. Obviously these would have to be built up. Similarly, up to this time very few passengers had chosen to disembark at a port of call in which there were few amenities of the type to which most travelers in the tropics are accustomed. But now arrangements had to be made to put whole divisions ashore and provide accommodation for them. To do so would entail a lot of work, which—if it was to be accomplished within Mussolini's timetable—would necessitate a vast labor force. In turn this would bring subsidiary problems which had to be overcome before the real work on the base could be started. Water was one such. Prior to the sudden influx of soldiers and civilians the fresh water supply in Massawa was barely sufficient for the pre-emergency population of 600-odd whites and 3,500 Eritreans. Before the labor force could be assembled additional sources had to be provided.

In this and other problems, the Italians' earlier experiences in Libya stood them in good stead. As the work progressed and the volume of traffic increased, the congestion in Massawa grew to almost unmanageable proportions. Yet despite its clogged state, the organization not only remained operative, it operated effectively. In conditions of squalor and confusion, wharves were extended; new jetties built; basins dredged to take larger ships; large areas of wasteland were cleared; warehouses erected, and a complete new railway system established. The Italians have an amazing capability for road and bridge building but no feat they have ever performed can be considered more prodigious than their achievement in these preparations for the landing of their enormous expeditionary force in East Africa, and it is hard to imagine any other European nation performing such a task so quickly with comparable efficiency. Shortage of native labor—which was anyway loath to undertake the work because of the conditions—meant that the task had to be done by Italians specially imported for the purpose.* Stripped to the waist, their bodies covered with an ugly heat rash, and lacking the most elementary amenities, in six months these men performed wonders, and their work is more deserving of recognition than that of the soldiers for whom they paved the way. Pay was high but every lira was hard-earned.

At Mogadishu, there were even greater difficulties to overcome. While a port of sorts did exist at Massawa, Mogadishu was simply an open roadstead in a monsoon area, and ships anchoring in the open bay had to ferry their cargoes of men and materials ashore in tenders. Consequently considerable effort was needed to install facilities for the amount of traffic it would have to bear. Not that Mogadishu was ever intended to be any more than a secondary base for operations. Massawa was a better port to begin with—closer to Naples and a place which would lend itself more readily to the development of its facilities and the hinterland was healthier and more inviting. Half an hour by road or rail, and one was out of the sweltering low-lying coastal re-

---

* The shortage was aggravated by the regulations prohibiting migration from Egypt, the Sudan, and other British territories in which native labor might have been recruited.

gion, climbing up the escarpment to the plateau where Asmara lies, 7,700 feet above sea level and with a climate well suited to Europeans. Behind Mogadishu was nearly three hundred miles of low-lying scrubland, tropical in the most unhealthy sense. From Asmara the northern Ethiopian border was only another thirty miles farther on, and there were three good roads to it, while only a few tracks ran from Mogadishu to the eastern frontier.

Leaving aside any question of base facilities and roads, the climate alone was sufficient reason for deciding whether the decisive Italian effort should be made in the northern or southern zone. Add to this the fact that an advance southward from Eritrea led straight to the heart of Ethiopia, while any advance from Italian Somaliland necessitated negotiating vast tracts of semidesert even before the Ethiopian border was reached, and there would seem to be every reason for the main effort to be concentrated in the north. But what clinched the decision was not a practical consideration but a psychological one. Most of the Duce's generals were old men, men molded by the past, whose personal recollections included Adowa and the tragic fate of Baratieri. To them Adowa was an obsession, a smirch on Italy's escutcheon which had to be wiped off by blood and glory; Adowa had to be avenged. Once that was done, they could look forward to the reacquisition of the rich regions of Ethiopia which their predecessors had been forced to abandon in 1896. Everything therefore pointed to the northern front as the principal zone of operations.

Despite the inertia which had pervaded Italy right up to the beginning of 1935, Mussolini had managed to stir up a warlike spirit, and to most of the Italian soldiers the forthcoming campaign was a gay enterprise. Certainly by the reports of the enthusiasm said to have been shown by Italians ordered to East Africa, the Fascist brainwashing process must have been very efficient. During the spring and summer of 1935, five regular and five Blackshirt divisions sailed for East Africa, where they were joined by other ancillary formations from Italy and a brigade of native troops raised in Libya.* Of all these formations only one division, the Sicilian Peloritana, disembarked at Mogadishu; the

* See Appendix 4 for details of the formations concerned.

rest were concentrated in Eritrea. Unless one is traveling in air-conditioned luxury, a journey down the Red Sea in the summer months is a hideous enough experience in itself, and Massawa—Mogadishu even more so—is even today hardly calculated to impress one as an example of the potential benefits to be derived from that corner of Africa. Consequently it is hard to believe that the first impressions of the Italian troops, packed like sardines into liners hastily converted as troopships, arriving at what they had been told was one of the gateways to the Second Roman Empire, were altogether favorable. As their ships steamed in to the harbor, the flat and barren coast baking under a blazing sun must have seemed a particularly unappetizing Eldorado. To the early arrivals, first experiences ashore could only be calculated to make the promised land seem even less promising, and it is surprising that the ardor survived. The experience of those who arrived after June 1935 was less difficult than of those who came in April and May, since sufficient transport had been collected by that time to enable a fleet of vehicles to carry those landed at Massawa straight up to the plateau. Fortunately for Fascism, once the troops had left the hothouse of Massawa and got over the interminable days cooped up at sea, the champagne atmosphere of the highlands provided a much needed boost to morale.

Those who had to stay in Massawa to operate the base and the contingent concentrated in Italian Somaliland were the real martyrs to patriotism, as they had to endure the full rigors of the inferno which the climate and terrain of the region combine to produce. However, as the months of 1935 slipped by, conditions did improve. The shortage of water was gradually overcome by the sinking of wells, and by concentrating all the available Italian water tankers in the Red Sea; and two hospital ships, with a couple of other vessels equipped with refrigerating plants to provide ice, were sent out to Massawa and Mogadishu in June.* These provided welcome relief to those who fell sick in the stifling heat.

Luckily few, if any, of the Italian soldiers were in a critical

* Before the end of the campaign, eight hospital ships—the *Urania, Tevere, California, Vienna, Helouan, Cesarea, Aquilea,* and *Gradisca*—were operating in East African waters, air-conditioned and providing 5,000–6,000 beds.

frame of mind for they had gone to Africa believing that they would win riches as well as glory. Mussolini's propaganda had painted a picture of an Ethiopia that was a land flowing with milk and honey, and with the prospect of a higher standard of living many of the Blackshirts were hoping to stay and profit from a successful campaign. A lot of them came from the ranks of the unemployed, others from areas where grinding poverty had compelled them to work for very little gain, and Mussolini had imbued them with the spirit of the American pioneers setting out to seek fortunes in the West.

As soldiers, however, the men who waited in East Africa during September 1935 were a motley collection. Little thought had gone into planning for the sort of fighting in which they were to be engaged, and the army that had been collected together was more suited to a Fascist demonstration than mountain and desert warfare. To give the expeditionary force the political symbolism of a united Fascist Italy, every conceivable unit and detachment had to be represented, and the tactical value of many such units appears to have been of secondary consideration. The supporting arms included a preponderance of heavy artillery, but its usefulness was limited by its lack of mobility in the mountainous terrain of Ethiopia. On the other hand some of the troops who ought to have been included—like the mountain-trained Alpini —were conspicuous by their absence. (Until the end of 1935, there was only one Alpini battalion in Tigre, and its object was not so much to fight as to represent the Alpinis in Africa.) Five distinct categories made up the force: regular Italian soldiers; the regular native troops; native levies; Blackshirt militia; and the laborers. Since the war turned out to be a campaign of communications it was these sturdy peasant laborers who constituted its real strength, the most valuable tail that any army has ever had. Burned black by the sun, swept unceasingly by clouds of dust, living on a handful of macaroni each day, they worked incessantly with picks and shovels in little groups on the mountainsides and in the sweltering heat of the plains, to build the roads without which Mussolini's overencumbered army could never have moved.

The native levies, the irregular Banda—their work as *agents provocateurs* finished when the campaign started—were employed mainly as scouts. Most of them were no more than armed riffraff and had little military worth. Their brothers, the black Eritrean Askaris of the regular Colonial Infantry, were very different, however. For the most part these men who provided the army's spearpoint belonged to the same race and had the same religions and customs as their Abyssinian brothers. They were dressed in baggy khaki trousers terminating in puttees above bare feet, and wore on their heads tall red fezzes with dangling tassels. Colorful cummerbunds wound tightly around their waists denoted their different regiments. Tall, slender, flat-bellied and spindle-shanked, without an ounce of superfluous flesh, they were disciplined men of marked endurance, and in the campaign which was to follow they not only showed themselves to be absolutely trustworthy, but proved savage and pitiless fighters. Because they were better trained, needed less in the way of supplies, and were altogether more suited to a war of mobility than their European counterparts, the Askaris bore the brunt of every action. And because the Askaris' battle casualties were higher than those of the white troops, Mussolini's critics—including some of his black Eritrean subjects—observed that the Italians had built the roads while the fighting had been left to the natives. The fact that the casualties among the Italian officers serving with the Colonial regiments was proportionately greater than those of their counterparts in the regular army and Blackshirt militia lends credence to this criticism, and in many of the actions the white troops would seem to have been little more than spectators of the Askaris' gallantry.

To suggest that the white troops were less courageous than the Askaris, or indeed less capable of standing up to the rigors of the campaign, would be to do the Italians an injustice. What both the regular conscripts and the Blackshirt militia lacked was training. Enthusiasm was not wanting; everybody had an almost fanatic confidence in their leaders and in the Duce's ability to see them through to victory. But with the exception of the Alpini, who considered themselves the elite, and the Bersaglieri, who looked down on the line regiments, even the regular soldiers dis-

played a contempt for smartness or appearance that would be
regarded with horror in most armies. So long as such disdain is
confined to uniform and personal equipment, this is not a matter
of great concern in the field. But when weapons are not looked
after, it becomes a matter of extreme importance, and according
to foreign eyewitnesses the Italians paid scant attention to this
aspect of soldiering. "The rifle is the soldier's best friend" does
not appear to have been one of the apothegms in the Italian military vocabulary. In their efforts to assert individuality, the
Blackshirts went out of their way to pursue unorthodoxy; of
their beards and carbines, a Polish war correspondent is said to
have commented: "If the first were shorter and the second
longer, they would be better fitted for war." With their death's-
head-and-thunderbolt badges; their knives, war cries, and violent
mottoes, and their propensity for singing paeans to themselves
and Il Duce, they behaved more like troubadours than soldiers.

The one major asset that this army did possess was its overwhelming preponderance of arms. To be superior to the Ethiopians, they would not have needed much equipment. But so great
was the Italians' firepower that practically any Ethiopian assault
was doomed before it started. Time and again Ethiopian units in
defense dissolved into mobs of panic-stricken refugees; with no
antitank and no antiaircraft guns the bewildered Ethiopians just
could not hope to compete. On the other side of the hill, the
tactics of the elderly Italian commanders were strictly conventional, based on experience twenty years out of date and gained
in the static warfare conditions of the 1914–18 war; none of
them had appreciated the potentialities of the tank and the airplane—they were too set in their ways for innovations anyway.
Consequently the Italian army went to war in Ethiopia relying
solely on superiority in numbers and firepower. Furthermore,
De Bono, the first Commander in Chief, was more of a politician
than a soldier, and he did little to encourage initiative. "Little
Beard," as he was known, was more concerned about his popular
image than professionalism, and if he could not give orders with
a smile he did not give orders at all. Officers were addressed as
Caro, soldiers as *Bambino*, and the corps and divisional com-

manders were allowed to do almost as they pleased. When the Duce decided the war needed to be speeded up, De Bono was relieved by Marshal Badoglio—a soldier's general, but a cautious one. How these influences affected the campaign will be seen in the following chapters.

CHAPTER 9

"Avanti": *Adowa and Makale*

There is no such conquering weapon as the necessity of conquering.

English Proverb

Toward the end of August 1935, General Dall'Orra, the Quartermaster-General of the Eritrean Expeditionary Force, who had been on leave in Rome, flew back to Asmara with a confidential package for De Bono from Mussolini.

This is the last letter I shall write to you before the action. . . . After September 10th, when you receive a telegram from me with the words "Received your Report" with my signature, you will give the order to advance. . . . You will celebrate Mascal [a Coptic religious festival celebrated on September 27 and 28] in conquered territory.

By bringing forward the date on which operations against Ethiopia were to begin, Mussolini was hoping to take the League by surprise, and with a quick military success confound those at Geneva who were now openly clamoring for sanctions. The greater part of De Bono's preparations had been completed, and a large number of troops was now concentrated close to the Eritrean and Somaliland borders. As it was highly unlikely that Haile Selassie would provide an excuse for invasion at this late stage, Italy was bound to be branded an aggressor, and so it seemed to the Duce that the sooner the campaign got under way the better. But as two of the Blackshirt divisions* which Mussolini had promised would be included in the order of battle had not yet arrived in East Africa, De Bono asked and got the Duce's permission to adhere to the original date of October 1.

By the beginning of September three army corps had been organized in Eritrea: the First and Second, each comprising one regular and one Blackshirt division; and the Third "Native" Corps, of two colonial divisions and one Blackshirt division. Each corps was allotted a sector behind the Mareb River, immediately facing its intended zone of operations. Army headquarters was set up in Asmara which, despite the fact that it was a colonial capital, was still only a heterogeneous collection of a few brick houses, shops, and dirty restaurants surrounded by the larger mass of squalid mud and wattle, corrugated-iron-roofed dwellings of the native population. Lacking both the exotic charm of a tropical city and the amenities of a European civilization, Asmara was neither African nor European. A church dominated the European quarter, and there was one second-rate hotel and two movie houses to provide distractions for the permanent residents; beyond that little else. After fifty impoverished years Asmara suddenly found itself shaken out of its somnolence by the influx of thousands of troops, and by August 1935 it was wearing the look of a frontier town, with shacks and tents being run up and trucks bumping through the potholed streets. It did not take long for the shops to be cleaned out, and it goes without saying that 200,000 lusty young men passing through on their way to the assembly areas near the frontier were bound to create social problems. As in other campaigns the time-honored solution was to establish a house of prostitution; this was set up, opposite the church, and a certain Signora Mira installed as *grande madame*. Under her management, the Casino, as it was called, flourished and the hostesses were never idle for long. Regulations

* Third January & First February Divisions.

provided for the use of the Casino by the rank and file during the mornings at ten lire a session (ten lire was then worth about fifty cents), by the noncommissioned officers at twenty lire in the afternoon, and officers in the evening at thirty lire. If the fees were small, the clientele was large and the Casino enjoyed a monopoly. Few of the girls who went out to Asmara on a six months' contract had the stamina to sign for another tour. But few of them wanted to do so, for by then they had amassed sufficient capital to ensure a less strenuous occupation in Italy. To the Italian troops, Signora Mira's establishment was a haven of refuge in an otherwise drab existence.

Many of the troops were in position several months before the order to advance was given, and the long wait under canvas was a trying period which the white Italian troops came through better than many observers had anticipated. Morale was good; everybody realized that a pause was necessary until the army had been assembled, and the fact that everybody knew the general plan also helped. On the northern front the first main objective would obviously be Adowa; and in the south it was equally obvious that it would be the wells of Gerlogubi, thirty miles southeast of where the incident triggering the war had taken place. With the Italian First East African Corps facing toward Adigrat, the Second straddling the main track leading to Adowa, and the Third deployed between them, the only question was which route De Bono would select for his main thrust. Not without good reason, the Ethiopians assumed that it would be the same as that which the Italians had used in 1896, and that the Second Corps would spearhead the advance. Contrary to their expectations, De Bono had decided to rely on an advance by the central column. This had a number of advantages. Not only did the main track down the Adowa valley run through some difficult and intricate terrain suited to ambushes, but it was to be expected that resistance would be strongest here. Furthermore, although national prestige demanded that Adowa should appear to be avenged by *white* Italian troops, by letting the native Eritreans bear the brunt of the actual fighting Italian casualties would be reduced. Another consideration was that the existing organization did not allow any army reserve. As all the units of the Twenty-first April Blackshirt Division allotted to the Second Corps had not yet arrived in Eritrea, it seemed logical to pull that back into reserve rather than take a battle-ready formation.

All the information collected by De Bono's Intelligence suggested that there was unlikely to be much opposition to the advance. Italian sentries staring across the Mareb from vantage points on the high cliffs overlooking the river reported no visible signs of Ethiopian activity which could be interpreted as having a military connotation. Indeed, in the area of the low foothills stretching up from the river to the jagged mountains which screened Adowa, there was little sign of any life at all. Smoke could sometimes be seen rising from one of the tiny villages and sometimes a caravan of camels or mules winding down one of the trails to the river. But that was all. Haile Selassie's men were not there. In accordance with the Emperor's orders, Ras Seyoum— the Governor of Western Tigre—had withdrawn his forces thirty kilometers from the frontier. Only a few scouts had been left to watch the Mareb, and the local population had made itself scarce. Thus, in contrast with the Eritrean side of the border, Ethiopia presented a vista of emptiness.

This might have been regarded as ominous but for the ample evidence from inside Ethiopia confirming the absence of troops. Native spies, Italian consuls, and Italian merchants were all agreed that little resistance would be offered in the first stages of the campaign. Rumors of a secret Ethiopian mobilization persisted throughout September and there were positive indications that the chiefs were beginning to collect their levies together. But nowhere were any large troop concentrations reported. It was said that Haile Selassie favored guerrilla warfare, that he wanted to lure the Italians on until they outran their supplies before bringing them to battle and that Tigre had been evacuated as part of this plan. On the other hand a rumor that Ras Seyoum had announced he was not going to surrender any of his territory without a fight ran counter to such strategy. Adowa was Ras Seyoum's capital and if he intended to fight, then it was a certainty that the main Italian objective would not be taken without some bloodletting. In theory, Ras Seyoum could expect the support of his neighbor, the Governor of Eastern Tigre, Haile Selassie Gugsa, whose capital of Makale lay sixty miles southwest of Adowa. But Gugsa was already in the Italians' pay and they knew that he would defect when the opportune moment presented itself.*

On September 28 the Mascal celebrations in Asmara, marking the end of the rainy season, included a great banquet and military tattoo. De Bono, the guest of honor at the banquet, made it an occasion to deliver a bellicose speech. According to his own account, when he got up to speak there was "an aspect of exceptional solemnity," while he "delivered a brief admonitory discourse, warlike in tone and phrasing. . . ." What he said in his concluding comments is sufficient to illustrate the gist of his speech to the vast assembly outside the banqueting tent: "You must seize Italy's enemies by the throat," he declared dramatically as he vehemently executed the throat-cutting gesture on himself. Three thousand Askaris fired salvos into the air, waved banners inscribed "For Italy—for Death and Glory," and through their teeth trilled the high-pitched ululations which substitute for cheers.

On September 29, the long-expected order fixing the day and hour for the advance to begin arrived from Rome. There was to be no formal declaration of war; so far as the Duce was concerned, the Ethiopian statement at Geneva that general mobilization in Ethiopia could no longer be delayed had provided the

* Haile Selassie Gugsa, a soft, bloated, effeminate creature, was the Emperor's son-in-law. In order to offset the power of Ras Seyoum he had been given the governorship of Eastern Tigre and his marriage to the Emperor's 13-year-old daughter was part of a package deal to effect the unification of the rival Shoa and Tigre dynasties. (The other part was the marriage of the Crown Prince to Seyoum's daughter.) The arrangement, like Gugsa himself, turned out to be a ghastly failure. The Emperor's daughter died—reputedly of pneumonia because their "palace" had no glass in the windows, but more probably because she was treated by a witch doctor—and Gugsa's taste for soft living turned him into a confirmed alcoholic and a libertine. How much the Italians paid for Gugsa's defection will probably never be known. A million lire has been quoted, and if this was the amount it was grossly in excess of his worth. The Italians hoped to manipulate Gugsa, as an Italian puppet, for propaganda purposes, within and without Ethiopia. Gugsa's subsequent contribution to their objectives was a disappointment.

ultimate *casus belli*. Everything was ready. The troops were standing by; all the Italian consuls in Ethiopia were on their way to Eritrea, except the consul in Adowa, who had been told to hang on until the last minute; all that remained was to give the order *"Avanti."* "I order you to begin advance early on the third. I say the third of October . . ." the Duce signaled, and on the evening of October 2 De Bono issued a proclamation:

HIGH COMMAND, EAST AFRICA

Officers and noncommissioned officers, soldiers of the land, the sea, and the air, Blackshirts, Askaris!

You have waited until this day with firm discipline and exemplary patience. The day has come. His Majesty the King desires and Benito Mussolini, Minister for the Armed Forces, orders, that you shall cross the frontier. Proud and honoured to lead you, I know I can count on the experience of the Commanders and on the discipline and courage of the soldiers. You will have to endure fatigues and sacrifices and confront a strong and warlike enemy. The greater will be the merit of the victory for which we are striving, which will be the clean victory of the new Fascist Italy.

East Africa, 3rd October, 1935. A.XIII.
General Emilio de Bono.

According to one of the host of foreign journalists that had assembled in Asmara to report the war from the Italian side, the news was a signal for great jubilation:

About nine o'clock on the night of October 2nd . . . Church bells start ringing wildly . . . Governor's residence and Fascist Club floodlighted by searchlights. Impromptu band marches up the street playing "Giovinezza," the Fascist song. Hundreds of men in ferment of emotion follow shouting, singing, chanting "Il Duce, Il Duce" . . .[1]

By 2:00 A.M. on the morning of October 3, 1935, Eritrean patrols crossed the Mareb to attack the little frontier posts on the Ethiopian border, and three hours later, as nine Capronis of the Disperata Squadron took off with nine tons of bombs to be dropped on Adowa, the vanguards of the three Italian army corps waded across the shallow river. There was no opposition at any of the crossing places, and the Italians were subsequently reported to have sung and cheered Mussolini as they scrambled across to Ethiopia. So started the war whose echoes have not yet died down.

De Bono's first objective, the line running east and west from Adigrat to Adowa, was less than thirty miles from the border. As only a few scattered bands of Ethiopians occupied the intervening territory, the enormous tactical power represented by De Bono's three columns was a sledgehammer to crack a nut, and the extravagant use of Italian manpower gave De Bono's operations the appearance of enormous peacetime maneuvers against a skeleton enemy, mounted perhaps as a demonstration to terrify the Emperor.* When the ponderous machine rolled forward, everything went more or less according to plan. With so many aircraft flying overhead, there was little risk of the marching columns being surprised even if there had been enough Ethiopian troops in the area to offer any worthwhile resistance. Adowa, which Ras Seyoum was preparing to evacuate, was bombed. The casualties came to one woman, one child, and a few cows killed, but it was not the lethal effect of the bombs that mattered: on a population many of whom had never seen an airplane or heard an explosion louder than the discharge of a firearm, it was the noise and their own imagination which created panic. Most of the four or five thousand inhabitants of Adowa fled to the hills after the first sortie, and reports went back to Addis Ababa of Adowa being bombed to the ground and swimming in blood. More leaflets than bombs were dropped on the town, in fact. Printed in Amharic, they appealed to the local population to "remain calmly at work" and to pray "that the war we are waging for the triumph of justice may be quickly victorious." Italian soldiers, the people were told, were coming "to bring peace, to defend

* In 1868 Napier's dash to Magdala was accomplished with a force of 50,000 men; the British expedition penetrated 300 miles toward the center of Ethiopia and returned safely, having accomplished its object of releasing the English prisoners and punishing the Emperor. It is true that there were special circumstances attending Napier's operation: the chiefs in territory through which the column passed were friendly, disposed toward the British, and the mission was a sally not intended to remain on Ethiopian territory a moment longer than necessary.

them against molestation, to punish those guilty of provocation, and to assure their tranquility" and they were warned not to create trouble or spread false information. When the time came and the Italian soldiers approached, most of the wretched peasants took the line of least resistance and made the appropriate acts of submission.

Progress on the ground was sure although extremely slow. On the left, Santini's First Army Corps, following the main track southward toward Adigrat, met no resistance and had a comparatively easy passage. In the center, Pirzio-Biroli's Eritrean Third Corps also made rapid progress until it arrived near Amba Augher, a tiny village under the great mountain mass of Dejiak Gebriet. The lightly equipped Askaris leading the column, who marched barefoot at a sort of trot, tended to leave the slower-moving, scarcely acclimatized Blackshirts of the Twenty-third March Division behind, which meant that the vanguard had to be constantly checked in order to allow the white troops to catch up. Amber Augher, where five hundred Ethiopians were esconced in caves in the side of the mountain, was the first enforced halt. If the advance was to continue toward Enticcio there was no option but to attack, and so, as low-flying aircraft machine-gunned the summit and rear slopes of the mountain, two of the Eritrean brigades were thrown against the Ethiopian positions. Outnumbered, outgunned, with their morale sadly shaken, the Ethiopians fled in disorder as soon as the attack got under way, and the column was able to reform and resume its advance.

It was on the right that the advance was the slowest. The objective of Maravigna's Second Corps was Adowa, and every Italian from Mussolini downward was watching its progress with some trepidation. Since the Ethiopians were fully alive to the historical reasons motivating the choice of Adowa as the column's objective, it was taken for granted that they would put up a stubborn defense. Apart from this probability, the Second Corps had conventional difficulties to contend with. Not only had Maravigna's 22,000 men farther to go than the other two columns, but the ground along the line of advance was thickly

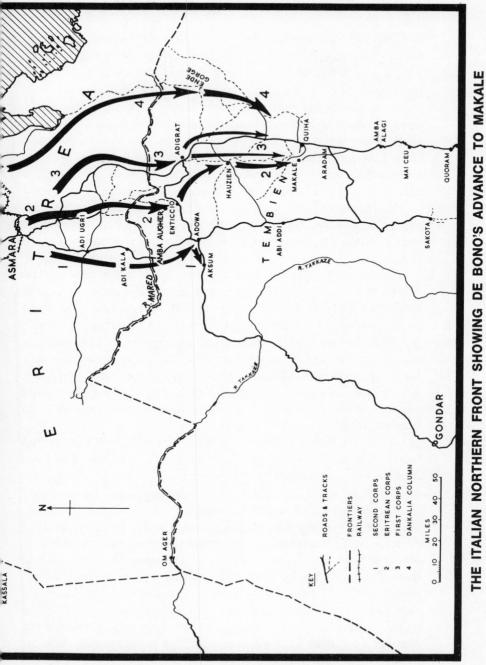

THE ITALIAN NORTHERN FRONT SHOWING DE BONO'S ADVANCE TO MAKALE

wooded and broken by deep ravines. Under the circumstances, the advance might have been expected to have been organized in such a way as to permit the main body to move securely between protective columns or pickets operating on parallel routes well away on the flanks in the style of North-West Frontier operations. Instead the Italian columns moved solidly down the central track. Fortunately for them the Ethiopians were not of the same caliber as the fierce hillmen of India and they made no attempt to swoop down on the massed formation. A group of irregulars commanded by a Lieutenant Morgantini acted as the vanguard of the Italian column. Behind them came a detachment of the "Duca degli Abruzzi's" light tanks, and then the first battalion of the Gavinana Division—the First Battalion of the Eighty-fourth Regiment.

Contact with the Ethiopians came shortly after crossing the Mareb, but the action was short and sharp. Within an hour the Ethiopian force had been dispersed and Morgantini's vanguard pushed on toward Adowa. Soon afterward Morgantini himself was shot down in a skirmish with another group of Ethiopians— becoming the first white officer killed in Mussolini's war—and his troops, demoralized by the loss of their leader, broke and ran. The Third Eritrean Battalion was rushed up to take their place and by dawn on October 4 the Ethiopian patrols had been brushed aside.

After the actions described, little of consequence occurred before the Italians completed the opening phase of the campaign. The center column reached its objective of Enticcio during the morning of October 5, and by noon the same day the vanguard of the eastern column had occupied its objective of Adigrat. Nearly forty years had elapsed since Italian troops evacuated Adigrat, and by a strange turn of the wheel of fortune it fell to General Santini to rehoist the flag which, as a subaltern, he had seen hauled down in 1896. Meanwhile the western column, which had been delayed by a sharp encounter at the Gashorki Pass a few miles short of Adowa, was laboring on toward its objective, and in the late afternoon its advance guard reached the ramshackle Italian Consulate a couple of miles outside Adowa.

(The Consul, who had remained at his post until the evening of October 2, had burned his files and contrived to get across country to join the column during the advance.)

At dawn on the sixth, patrols reported Adowa to be clear of Ethiopian troops; Ras Seyoum had pulled out. With the way clear for a triumphant entry, Maravigna ordered General Villa Santa, the Gavinana divisional commander, to take possession, and at 10:00 A.M. on October 6 the Second Battalion of the Eighty-fourth Regiment marched up the steep rocky streets with band playing and colors flying. Villa Santa rode behind with his staff and a posse of eager journalists. As the party clattered up toward the Coptic Church, which stood close by Ras Seyoum's so-called palace in the center of the town, people who had not fled when the bombing started humbly bowed their foreheads to the ground. At the church—a circular, corrugated-iron-roofed structure standing in a mud-walled compound—priests were waiting dressed in the gaudy robes and loaflike headdress worn by the Coptic clergy. Villa Santa inclined his lips to the grimy gilt cross tendered to him to kiss, saluted, and then addressed the little gathering from his saddle. An interpreter translated: "Your religion," he said, "will be respected. There will be no more bombing; all who have fled should return; Italy will respect their property." As he concluded, the group emitted the usual shrill ululation and Villa Santa's entourage rode on to inspect Ras Seyoum's old residence. Although this was the most elaborate structure in the town, it consisted of just half a dozen low, iron-roofed, whitewashed stone buildings, surrounded by a stockade. In the courtyard Italian soldiers were digging a grave for the corpse of an Ethiopian. Five men had fired at one of the patrols preceding the ceremonial entry, and in the subsequent exchange of shots one had been killed; the other four escaped. The "palace," which swarmed with flies, proved to be as crude in its furnishings as it was in its construction. Straw covered the floors; three or four rickety chairs, a rough, wooden canopied throne, and an old brass bedstead were all the furniture. A cheap print of Haile Selassie, a colored chromo of the Crucifixion, and some crude native paintings of African animals hung on the walls; empty wine bottles and documents strewn around testified to a hasty departure. (One of these documents—a gilt-edged parchment, dated July 8, 1924, and bearing the signature of King George V—conferred "the dignity of an Honorary Knight Commander of the Civil Division of the Order of the British Empire" on Ras Seyoum.)

According to De Bono, the news that Adowa had been captured reached him at 10:30 A.M. from General Ranza, commanding the Third Air Brigade.[2] When confirmation came from Maravigna half an hour later, the news was telephoned to Rome, where it was received with boisterous rejoicing. "Announcement reconquest of Adowa fills the soul of the Italians with pride," the Duce wired to De Bono. "To you and all the troops my highest praise and the gratitude of the nation." "This," said De Bono "was a great reward for us. We had not had the good fortune to meet the enemy in force." However, such encounters as had taken place would no doubt have convinced the Ethiopians of "the solidarity of our detachments and the valor, discipline and impetuosity of our soldiers." The main point was that Italy had avenged Adowa. Losses had been small, those of the Ethiopians "considerable." *

Meanwhile in the south, General Graziani had started operations in Somalia. At the beginning of October his troops occupied the village of Dolo, close to the border of Kenya, while farther north others attacked and occupied Gerlogubi, thirty miles southeast of Walwal. Graziani's ultimate aim was to capture Harar and Diredawa on the Djibuti–Addis Ababa railway with the idea that as he advanced northeast, the lateral routes between Ethiopia and British Somaliland, along which supplies of arms and ammunition were now passing, would be cut. He was limited, however, by the need to protect Italian Somaliland from invasion by Ethiopian forces sent in that direction. Since this meant looking after a five-hundred-mile frontier, and with

---

* Italian losses were 30 killed, 70 wounded, 33 missing. There are no figures of Ethiopian casualties, but De Bono claimed "some five hundred prisoners." Prisoners were put to work on the roads or unloading vehicles, and the Italian troops amused themselves trying to teach the new laborers the Fascist salute and to shout "Il Duce."

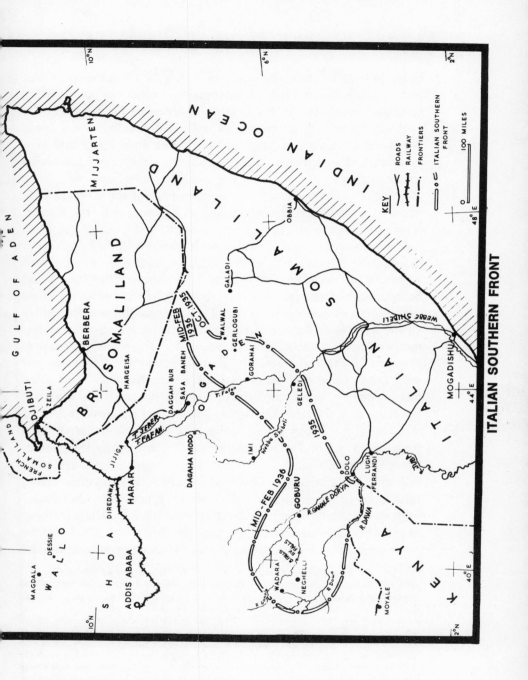

ITALIAN SOUTHERN FRONT

only about sixty thousand troops for all his commitments, it was to be expected that Graziani's operations could not be either on the same time scale or so extensive as those of De Bono on the northern front. Apart from this, rain and flooded rivers hampered the campaign on the southern front during the first two months, and so Graziani's contribution to the first phase is of minor importance.

One of the first acts of the conquerors after the second battle of Adowa was to erect a monument as a memorial to the Italians who had fallen in the first. (A few weeks later one of the giant sandstone needles, which had stood in the sacred city of Aksum since time immemorial, was shipped back to Rome, where it still stands.*) De Bono himself unveiled the marble pillar which had been brought from Italy by the engineers of the Gavinana Division in anticipation of the event. The ceremony was attended by all the local notables and it was made the occasion for other announcements. A proclamation annexing Tigre had been prepared before the war actually started, but its issue was delayed until De Bono staged his official entry into Adowa. Then, with due ceremony, it was announced "in the name of His Majesty, the King of Italy" that De Bono had assumed the government of the country. "From today," the proclamation declared, "the people of Tigre and Agame are subject to, and under the protection of, the Italian flag. . . . tribute . . . the market dues, tolls, and customs duties are abolished. Traders, continue to trade, husbandmen, continue to till the soil." The ceremony concluded with the applause which De Bono later admitted, with refreshing candor, had been organized.

Another proclamation issued about the same time announced

* In 1966 the Ethiopian Government asked for the return of the obelisk, together with the larger-than-life lion statue which once stood at the gate of the Imperial Palace of Addis Ababa. Italy agreed to return the obelisk but the soft sandstone has crumbled so badly that it cannot be moved. The lion was made of sterner stuff but the Italian Government said it did not know where the statue was now. With due Fascist ceremonial it was set up in front of the railway station in Rome in 1937, but when Italy changed sides during the war, either the Germans or the Italians themselves hauled the statue away, and the Italian Foreign Ministry said that it had no idea where it was taken. Resurgent postwar Fascists are inclined to hint that they could find the statue but have no intention of seeing it returned to Ethiopia.

the suppression of slavery: "People of Tigre: HEAR: You know that where the flag of Italy flies, there is liberty! Therefore in your country, slavery under whatever form is suppressed. The slaves in Tigre are free and the sale or purchase of slaves is prohibited. . . ." Nobody knew quite how many slaves there were in Tigre, and to what extent the abolition of slavery made the Italians more acceptable to the population is difficult to say. Not that this really mattered. Mussolini was more concerned with impressing the world outside Ethiopia with the benevolence of Italy's civilizing mission than with the benefits such gestures brought to the Ethiopians. The benefits were limited. Those slaves who were set free had little cause for jubilation since their problem now was who would be responsible for feeding them. As slaves the men had been employed as servants or serfs, and the women were for the most part their masters' mistresses and well cared for. With the new decree their masters were not only freed from any obligation to their former servants, but under compulsion *not* to retain them, and in the disturbances that the war had brought to Tigre, most of the slave owners were only too willing to comply with an order that relieved them of the responsibility for useless mouths. On the Emperor's orders many thousands of their cattle had been driven south to feed the gathering armies, and the prospects of harvesting their crops seemed remote. Not unnaturally, the slaves who were deprived of their means of livelihood were far from appreciative of Italian magnanimity, and De Bono was compelled to explain to their former owners that discharge did not mean abandonment. What he had really meant was that the slaves could change their employer and choose another—work, or starve, as they pleased; the choice was that of the individual.

Arrangements for the administration of the occupied territory had been completed before the invaders crossed the Mareb, and within a few days of the capture of Adowa and Adigrat it was functioning efficiently. Civil bureaus under the control of colonial officials from Eritrea and Somaliland were opened and these were soon besieged by applicants demanding compensation for damage caused by the troops, by people wanting work, and by beggars. "We had to appear wealthy," said De Bono "if only to disperse rumours to the effect that we should bleed the people white in order to continue this war. England had made abundant use of this slander." [3] Demonstrating wealth needed money, and the basic unit of the Ethiopian currency was the thaler, a heavy silver coin stamped with the head of the Austrian Empress Maria Theresa. As the Italians had had an unfortunate experience in 1890 when they found that their own version of the coin was unacceptable to the Ethiopians, they had acquired from Vienna the original press for minting these thalers, and a million glittering new coins were sent out to De Bono to be distributed as largesse to the local population. The effect was soon apparent: it was not long before the local clergy—who only a short time before had been praying for the defeat of the Italians—were preaching to the returning inhabitants of the villages that submission to the new regime was their duty.

Because of its important military consequences, something further must now be said about Haile Selassie Gugsa's defection. That he would defect to the Italians was known to both sides before the war actually started. The Emperor knew because the Ethiopian Consul in Asmara, Wodaju Ali, had produced proof to him of Gugsa's double dealings. For three years Gugsa had been making trips to Asmara, and his imagined slights at the Emperor's court made him an easy prey to the Italians' promises of high reward for his cooperation.* The upshot was that two weeks before the invasion, Wodaju Ali flew to Addis Ababa with copies of bank receipts for money paid into Gugsa's account by the Italians. Despite this damning evidence, Haile Selassie stubbornly refused to believe that Gugsa would actually betray him. "Most of my chiefs take money from the Italians," he told Wodaju Ali. "It is bribery without corruption. They pocket Italian money and remain steadfast to Ethiopia." Having decided that Gugsa had been good enough to be made a Dejaz-

---

* He found it more convient to travel to Addis Ababa via Asmara. By arrangement with the Italian Consul at Makale he would be met at the Eritrean frontier and then taken by car to Asmara, where he was treated as an honored guest. From there he would go by rail to Massawa, by steamer to Djibuti, and then by rail to Addis.

match and marry his own daughter, the Emperor would not let doubts be cast on his judgment. Gugsa was not to know this, and when he heard of Wodaju Ali's visit to Addis Ababa, he assumed that his days were numbered. The original plan for his defection had been that he would feign loyalty to the Emperor and make no move until the Italians attacked his capital of Makale, by which time his troops would have been joined by those of Ras Seyoum. In the middle of a battle a sudden transference of Ethiopian allegiance could then have been expected to spread chaos and confusion along the whole Ethiopian front. Not only could the Italians hope to take Makale without a blow, but there was a good chance that Ras Seyoum's resistance would also collapse. Because Gugsa feared arrest and acted prematurely, this plot miscarried. On October 8, after cutting the telephone line providing the only link between Ras Seyoum and Addis Ababa, he marched his army north to meet the Italians. Ultimately, only twelve hundred of his ragged force of ten thousand men entered Adigrat with their chief, and the Italians had reason to feel disappointed. However, as he brought with him the Swiss engineer Fernand Bietry, who had been designing an extension of the road from Addis Ababa to Dessie, he did provide one invaluable aid to future operations. The road was not on any map, and as those charts which the Swiss brought with him contained a detailed survey of the whole route, the Italians were relieved of engineering problems in their subsequent advance.

In Rome, Gugsa's defection was hailed as an event of great significance, auguring the dissolution of Haile Selassie's empire. This was an exaggerated view; nevertheless it was undoubtedly a serious blow to the Emperor. The vacuum created behind Ras Seyoum's army by Gugsa's treachery compelled the former to fall back, and this was one reason why no real resistance was offered at Adowa. Gugsa's action gave Mussolini a virtually bloodless propaganda victory, and its moral effect, though less than had been hoped for, was to cause several of the minor chiefs in Tigre to submit without a fight. At the same time, because Gugsa had acted prematurely, the overall damage was probably less than it might have been. Ras Seyoum had been able to withdraw with his army intact and De Bono's overcautious attitude precluded any rapid follow up. The way to Makale was open but reports that the Ethiopian clans were gathering led to the decision to play safe. "The first thing to do . . . was to put ourselves in a position to resist any enemy attack; it was necessary to fortify [our positions] and make sure of our lateral communications," De Bono wrote. Gugsa was rewarded with a taste of European civilization in Asmara, and an appointment as Governor of the whole of Tigre. In Asmara—where he was fitted out with a khaki uniform, red striped trousers, high laced boots, and a Sam Browne belt—most of his purchases were reported to be limited to perfume, gold-plated safety razors, and bottles of champagne. Speaking in his native Tigrean, he explained to journalists that he had joined the Italians because he was "a partisan of European civilization."

De Bono's preoccupation with consolidating his position along the Adigrat-Enticcio-Adowa line kept the troops fully occupied for the next few weeks. Digging, wiring, building new roads and bridges, organizing and establishing supply and ammunition dumps, took precedence over everything else. Thousands of soldiers, sunburned to the color of old leather, were put to turning the tracks from the Eritrean border into roads which would stand up to the constant procession of vehicles ferrying stores to the forward area. Stripped to the waist, long lines of men tossed stones from hand to hand to lay the foundation; every now and again they had to stop to let a convoy bump past —many of its trucks chalked with the inscription "Rome to Addis Ababa." Such activity was to become the regular feature of a campaign in which the troops spent more time handling shovels than they did their rifles. Nevertheless, morale was excellent. Nobody worried very much about reports that Ras Seyoum with about twenty thousand men was forty or fifty miles away to the south, or that Ras Kassa was supposed to be moving north with another forty thousand. It was known that a small force of about five thousand men under one of Ethiopia's better generals, Ayelu Burru, was threatening the Italian right flank. But the possibility of Burru being able to outflank Maravigna's corps and invade Eritrea was discounted; even if he managed to slip past Maravigna, few of the Italians had any doubts that he would be smashed when he was eventually brought to battle.

So far as the Ethiopians were concerned the war might have got off to a bad start, but it had hardly begun. The postponement of mobilization deliberately imposed by the Emperor —together with the inefficiency of the administration and inherent leisureliness of the Ethiopians themselves—delayed any positive action in the field. With the possible exception of the foreign population, who stared apprehensively at the skies, few people in Addis Ababa behaved as if there was a war on. The Emperor was still hoping for a miracle to be enacted at Geneva which would stop Mussolini, and no one else was imbued with any urgent desire to strike back at the Italians. Confident in the military prowess of their followers, and believing themselves safe in their mountain retreat, the Rases saw no reason for haste; when the time came they would smash De Bono's army just as their fathers had smashed that of Baratieri. And so it was not until October 17 that Ras Mulugeta, the elderly War Minister who had been designated Commander of the main body of the Ethiopian Army, was ready to move north against the enemy.

His Force, the Yamahal Sarawit, or Army of the Middle, was numbered at 80,000. . . . His chest blazing with decorations, he paraded his troops before Haile Selassie and himself passed the throne about noon, preceded by hornblowers dressed in European clothes, their gigantic antlers lifted high. Halting in front of the Emperor he drew his sword, saluted, and proceeded to give the Emperor a few blunt words of advice. "Your Imperial Majesty, do not interest yourself too much in politics. Your weakness is that you trust the foreigner too much: kick him out. . . . I am ready to die for my country, and you are too. War is now the thing and to conduct it you had better remain in the city of Addis Ababa. Send all the foreigners packing. I swear undying loyalty to you." Mulugeta's army drifted off. . . . We watched the curious procession pass the British Legation gates by twos and threes. What could they do? They thought that they could do everything. Bare-footed, in their ragged dirty jodhpurs, their swords sticking far behind them, they moved along with a steady stride. [Most of the men took their wives and some had mules.] The

men went ahead carrying the tent-poles, from the ends of which
dangled sandals and a few pouches of calabashes; more pouches holding food hung around their persons. The woman leaning forward in
her long broad skirts to haul the mule, brought up in the rear the
tent and sacks of mashila and dried peas.[4]

Mulugeta followed behind his straggling army and

. . . in spite of his age (he was well over seventy) and his confirmed
alcoholism, he proved himself an indefatigable marcher. Leaving at
dawn, he would do twenty-five miles a day until four o'clock, when
he encamped. Behind him followed his seven secretaries and their
servants. . . . His military adviser was a Cuban machine-gunner,
Delvalle, education in Texas, and for some time a member of A.B.C.,
the secret Cuban revolutionary organisation.[5]

Slowly the War Minister's army marched toward the front. The
Emperor had ordered that it should respect the property of the
inhabitants of the country through which it passed and that the
troops' behavior should be beyond reproach. There was to be no
pillaging, no raping, no settling of old scores. But "when they
saw a field of beans, corn or maize," wrote Steer, "they were
down on it like a troop of monkeys; it was stripped and eaten
raw; to hell with this new fangled commissariat, thought Mulugeta as he trudged along." [6]

Fearing an attack from the air, Mulugeta sent scouts ahead
with horns to sound the alarm if they saw aircraft approaching.
In the Galla country he paused to organize the flogging and hang-
ing of dilatory characters unwilling to join the army the Crown
Prince was trying to raise, and when he came to Gugsa's province there was another halt while he exacted revenge from the
populace in respect of their former Governor's treachery. Altogether it took two months for Mulugeta to get his army to Tigre
and by that time his men were beginning to desert. In a message
to the Emperor he complained that his painfully slow progress
was due to the Italian Air Force. "They chain us up like prisoners," he said. But Mulugeta's habit of marching by night, scattering and lying up while keeping clear of the villages during the
day, had been more effective than he knew. The Italians were

aware that both he and Ras Kassa were marching armies up to the front, but they had no accurate information as to their location or strength.

To an exponent of the *blitzkrieg*, the two months the Italians waited while the Ethiopian armies marched up to the front will seem to be a waste of a golden opportunity—an accusation which, no doubt, De Bono would have countered by saying that it was his duty to consolidate his position before embarking on a further advance. There was another reason for delay. Events had been moving swiftly at Geneva, and the very day Mulugeta started out from Addis Ababa Mussolini himself had instructed De Bono to call a halt. Until "the European situation has cleared up in respect of sanctions," and above all, Anglo-Italian relations were settled, it would be better to mark time. The Duce was by no means certain that the British were going to refrain from active interference in his adventure and he was wondering how he would be able to deal with it. If Britain had decided on some form of military action it seems certain that the campaign in Ethiopia would have to be abandoned there and then, and De Bono's army might have been swung west for an attack on the Sudan.

Judging by the lack of initiative shown by the Italian High Command in East Africa four and a half years later, a threat to the Sudan may well have been illusory. Nevertheless, with only two battalions of the Sudanese Defense Force to defend twelve hundred miles of frontier, De Bono, by striking boldly, should have been able to overrun Khartoum before his two months' reserve supplies ran out. Combined with an attack on Egypt by Marshal Balbo's army in Libya, and possibly a bombardment of Alexandria if the Italian fleet had been able to get past the Royal Navy, Britain's position in the Mediterranean might have been very uncomfortable. Whether the Italians would have been prepared to embark on what eventually would have proved a suicidal war is another matter. The feasibility of such operations would almost certainly have been discussed in Rome and contingent plans drawn up in case they were needed. (Copies of such plans were supposed to have been found in the wreck of an Italian aircraft which crashed in Egypt during August 1935.) Badoglio also flew to East Africa to consult De Bono on "the possibility of undertaking operations toward the Sudanese front." Both men, it seems, were strongly opposed to any move which would mean a conflict with Britain, and advised Mussolini against extending the war. Faced with the possibility of a fight with Britain, Badoglio—who had been against the adventure in the first place—might have been prepared to come to terms with Ethiopia; indeed, rather than imperil Italy for the sake of prestige, he might even have been prepared to call off the whole campaign. This is not to suggest that the Duce would necessarily have listened to the Chief of the Italian General Staff. More often than not dictators are unpredictable, their decisions being influenced as much by emotional factors as by the cold logic of their experts. Yet Mussolini was no Hitler, and in 1935, if faced with a decision which meant a shooting war with Britain, he might well have decided to back down in Ethiopia. It was a point when a political solution could have been imposed. As things turned out it was to be the last, and because the League was unwilling to force a conclusion, Mussolini did not have to make a choice.

Telegrams passing between Mussolini and De Bono at about this time seem to illustrate the underlying concern for the outcome of the talks regarding the imposition of the sanctions. On October 12 De Bono had signaled the Duce suggesting that it might be possible to "make a lunge" at Makale. "The Head of the Government," he said, "would be glad to have another pawn in hand so promptly." However, after discussing the mechanics of such a lunge with General Santini and his own Chief of Staff, General Gabba, De Bono was inclined to second thoughts, and a later telegram suggested the operation be deferred. Mussolini replied promptly: ". . . you must not march on Makale before organizing your rear and before receiving my orders. My orders will reach you when the European situation has cleared up in respect of sanctions. . . ."

The next development came on October 18, when De Bono, Badoglio, and Signor Lessona, the Italian Minister of Colonies (who was visiting East Africa with the Chief of Staff), drafted a joint message to Rome. ". . . given the defensive attitude now to be assumed, it is expedient and necessary to delay the departure of the two Divisions of Blackshirts [the Third January and First February, which were intended as further reinforcements]. This would enable the stores which had not been cleared from Massawa to be transferred to the front." It also stated that there was a chronic shortage of gasoline. Everything, it seemed on October 18, pointed toward caution.

Two days later, the Duce was urging enterprise. The situation at Geneva had eased, and he was able to assure De Bono that "there would be no complications for us in Europe before the English election fixed for the middle of November . . . by that date, all Tigre to Makale and beyond ought to be ours . . . you asked for a month and a month is at your disposal . . . in waiting for my order, which may reach you between the 1 and 5 November, push forward the occupation like the spreading of a spot of oil. . . ." With the lifting of the arms embargo on Ethiopia, weapons would shortly be reaching Haile Selassie's troops, he reminded De Bono; furthermore, too prolonged a halt might "embolden our enemies and cause perplexity among our friends." To this De Bono replied that while the Duce "must be confident that your programme is mine and that substantially progressive advance is *modestly* proceeding . . ." the possibility of further actions was "in dependence on logistic preparations." De Bono assured his master that he was following his wishes with "the utmost activity and pertinacity." [7] Yet the message was clear; the Commander in Chief of Italian East Africa was not going to take any positive step forward for the time being.

Following this interchange, there began a tussle of wills across two thousand miles of telephone cable, with Mussolini trying to prod his reluctant Army Commander into action while De Bono procrastinated. Messages passed between Rome and Coatit, the Expeditionary Force headquarters, thick and fast; typically those of De Bono usually ended with a profession of loyalty and invariably with "affectionate regards." Eventually, before Badoglio left for Rome, De Bono agreed to an advance on Makale on

November 10. The Duce's reaction to this was an order to start five days earlier. De Bono said he could not do so without prejudicing the success of the operation, and "those who declare it to be possible without more ado, are speaking without positive authentication of the possibilities of the moment. Affectionate regards." A few days later this cable was followed up with another expatiating on the logistic difficulties De Bono was facing. Theoretically, he had enough mules, but he did not have enough drivers; because there had been insufficient saddlers the animals' packs did not fit, as a result of which a third of the mules were "lying brutally exhausted in the animals' hospital." His men were working all out to extend the roads; once the road was built, he would need more trucks and that would mean more gasoline. So the catalogue went on: ". . . it is a task which would make even a bald-headed man's hair stand on end. . . . This, my dear Head of Government, I feel it my duty to tell you . . . to put you on your guard against any frivolous statements . . . made by Lessona and even Badoglio. . . ." Since Mussolini's reply was a peremptory command—"I order you to resume action objectives Makale and Takkaze [River] on the morning of the 3rd November"—the only effect of the General's self-exculpatory efforts seems to have been the exhaustion of the Duce's patience. When De Bono replied, "Action will be resumed 3rd November with objective Makale," it seemed the argument was over. But he followed up with another telegram saying that while he agreed to occupy Makale with a strong column, as far as the Takkaze was concerned he would only promise that "the other troops would follow methodically—working at the same time on the road, a matter of prime necessity to feed troops, especially Italian, and for advance of armoured cars and motorised artillery." (On this occasion there were no "affectionate regards.") This elicited the reply that the advance must continue beyond Makale. ". . . Forward then. Cordial greetings."

By this time a host of individuals anxious to have a share in the glory were descending on De Bono's headquarters. These included the Duke of Bergamo to take over as second-in-command of the Gran Sasso Division, the Duke of Pistoria to take over command of the Twenty-third March Blackshirts, and numerous Fascist dignitaries, poets, and artists of the Revolution, journalists, and officials. "Such cooperation," commented De Bono wryly, "pleased the soldiers and was a great testimony to the fact that the enterprise had found an echo in every heart!"

The track from Adigrat winding precipitously down to Dessie was known by the Ethiopians as the "Imperial Road," and Makale's importance stemmed from the fact that it was a nodal point on this route, at the junction of a caravan route running south and southeast from Adowa and Hauzien. To the Italians the territorial gain that the capture of Makale would bring was less important than the possibility of being able to bring to battle and destroy the Ethiopian army which lay astride the Imperial Road. It was now known for certain that Ras Seyoum with some thirty thousand warriors was somewhere in the rocky Tembien plain forty miles west-northwest of Makale, and other smaller concentrations of Ethiopian troops were reported to be in the area between Adigrat and Makale; still others were reported to be marching toward it from the south. Clearly the longer the operation was delayed the stronger the opposition would grow.

The advance began on the morning of November 3, as Mussolini had stipulated. Maravigna's Second Corps was given the task of garrisoning the existing line, while the First and Third Eritrean Corps advanced. Santini's First Corps, flanked by Eritrean battalions and irregulars, was to advance down the main track leading south from Adigrat to Makale, while Pirzio-Biroli, starting farther west, advanced across the vast rugged tableland toward Hauzien; from Hauzien, Pirzio-Biroli would then converge on Makale and link up with Santini. Meanwhile, on Santini's left, a flying column—the Dankalia column—starting from Massawa and crossing the Danakil desert, would cover the left flank of the main column to link up with it on the eastern edge of the plateau thirty miles from Makale.

By the evening of the third all three columns had covered a distance of about thirty miles, unopposed except by a few Ethiopian outposts, who fell back after firing a few rounds. However, air reconnaissance had reported that Makale was still occupied, and that groups of Ethiopians had been seen moving up toward the battle area. Heavy rain tended to delay the columns on the fourth, but by the evening both columns were twenty-five miles nearer their objectives, and next day the Eritrean Corps halted just outside Hauzien to comb the broken ground southwest of the town.* The approach of the Italians was greeted by a deputation of the local notables, headed as usual by the Coptic clergy, who came to surrender the town and make their act of submission, and the only action that took place was against three hundred Ethiopians holding a covering position on the approach road. Two Italian officers were wounded here—Lieutenant Aldo Lusardi mortally. The Italian press made a good deal out of this individual's reputed last words: ". . . please tell the Duce that I die with his name on my lips. Long live the King, long live the Duce, long live Italy."

Both columns resumed the advance on November 7, and in the early hours of the following morning their advance guards reached the Makale basin. Aircraft had reported that the town appeared to have been evacuated and all that was left to do now was to make a ceremonial entry. A column which included the puppet Gugsa and his followers was drawn up on the plain, and on the morning of November 8 the Italians marched in to the town with bands playing and colors flying. There was no resistance, no casualties; the Ethiopian garrison had fled, and when Eritrean patrols probed south it was found that the district was clear for at least another twenty-five miles.

Only the Dankalia column saw any real fighting, and its experiences were instructive.† The column was commanded by Brigadier General Oreste Marriotti, a hard-bitten professional

* The troops marched in what was described as "regular march formation": an advanced guard, usually a native unit, followed by the main body of infantry in three columns, flanked by more native troops. Two batteries or artillery, ready to deploy, followed immediately behind the infantry; in the rear followed the pack animals with an infantry guard.

† An excellent account written by an American journalist who accompanied the column is to be found in Herbert Matthews, *Eyewitness in Abyssinia*. Luigi Barzini, better known for his recent book *The Italians*, also made this journey. Lieutenant-Colonel (later General) Raimondo Lorenzini, a gallant soldier who was killed at Keren five and a half years later, commanded one of the Eritrean battalions in this column.

soldier who had seen considerable colonial service—a fact which made him an ideal choice for the operation. When its units had concentrated fifty miles northeast of Makale on the fifth, the total strength amounted to about twenty-five hundred Askaris and Banda, officered by about thirty Italians. Across an unexplored, hostile, lunar landscape, in a roasting temperature with little water, the operation would have been difficult enough without any enemy, and the fact that the population of Danakil was noted for its bloodthirsty habits made it even more hazardous. Success depended on the negotiations of Italian political agents whose bribes had induced the tribal chiefs to promise that ten thousand men would be put at Marriotti's disposal, but because conditions turned out to be worse than expected, the approach march took considerably longer than had been anticipated, and less than a day's march from its objective the force ran into trouble. As the straggling column entered the steep Ende Gorge leading up to the plateau it was fired on from the heights on both sides; it had walked straight into an ambush in a position where the Ethiopians had an overwhelming advantage.

Unable to contain their impatience, the Ethiopians opened fire prematurely, and the vanguard of Eritrean irregulars and the two hundred Danakil tribesmen—all under command of another colonial veteran, Colonel Vittorio Belly*—took the brunt of the first tremendous crash of musketry. Belly was among the first casualties. Scattering, the column took up such cover as was available and fired back while the four 70-millimeter mountain guns carried on camels at the rear were hastily brought into action. In an exposed position, dominated by heights held by the Ethiopians, Marriotti's troops were in a desperate position. They had no means of calling for assistance and little hope of being able to withdraw without suffering severe losses; all they could do was to fire in the general direction of the Ethiopian positions. Darkness provided a brief respite, but as they fully expected the Ethiopians would administer the *coup de grâce* next morning, it was a night of anguish for the Italians. However, when dawn

* A curiously un-Italian name which the contemporary foreign press decorously changed to "Belli."

broke it appeared that the Ethiopians had pulled out and left the field to Marriotti. Scarcely able to believe their luck, the column formed up and resumed its march toward the plateau, struggling up a precipitous path where a handful of men could have annihilated them. But not a single Ethiopian appeared and the column reached the plateau without another shot being fired.

These experiences of the Dankalia column typified the Ethiopian methods of waging war. On this occasion both sides were fairly evenly matched numerically. The Italians had no tanks or aircraft to support them, and the Ethiopians had the advantage of superior prepared positions. If they had chosen to fight the battle of Ende Gorge to its limit, the outcome should have been the massacre of Marriotti's column. While it is possible that they were short of ammunition and that there was bad leadership, probably the real explanation was that the Ethiopians did not relish a prolonged battle. Their mentality was conditioned to quick shock actions and they were incapable of sustained effort. Subsequent experience was to confirm that whenever an attack failed, an Ethiopian formation would disappear into thin air and there was rarely a second assault. The Ethiopian warrior might be courageous but he lacked the patience and stamina for the sort of warfare which might have brought success in this campaign. In the past his victories had been won in a few hours, and the idea of hiding and waiting for days, if not weeks, for the right opportunity was not his idea of fighting.

After the occupation of Makale, there is every reason to suppose that a further Italian thrust southward would have met little opposition. But De Bono was obsessed with his line of communications. Makale had added another fifty-six miles of track to what he considered was already a tenuous thread. To him the town was a pumpkin at the end of a long slender stem, and until he had built a proper road from Adigrat and made sure that the ground west of this road was clear, he was not prepared to move any farther. "The situation," he wrote "recalled to mind the old adage that the cat that would hurry made blind kittens." Mussolini thought otherwise; the Duce needed a series of demonstrable successes to counteract the effect of the sanctions which were soon to come into effect. It was patently clear that De Bono was not going to give them to him, and so on November 11, he peremptorily ordered De Bono to resume the advance: "On the right bring the Maravigna Army Corps to front on the river Takkaze and with the native divisions march *without hesitation* on Amba Alagi while the national divisions remain at Makale. Reply to me." To this De Bono sent a long and involved answer which amounted to a refusal to comply. Explaining that a third of his line of communications, extending over three hundred miles, was a mere track through the bush, he reminded the Duce of "painful historical memory." For the Second Corps to advance another sixty miles would be to court disaster; the terrain favored an ambush; there were no heavy guns in position; he had no reserves because every available man was building roads. As for the other objective: Amba Alagi, which had no strategic importance, was "tactically defective because it could be surrounded." Finally he suggested that, being on the spot, he was better apprised of the military situation than anyone in Rome, and he believed "at this moment the military situation should have precedence over any other consideration whatsoever."

This was not the kind of response to please Mussolini. A telegram on the sixteenth sanctioning a "reasonable" halt on the Makale line was followed up next day with another terminating De Bono's appointment and announcing his replacement by Badoglio. "With the reconquest of Makale," the Duce said, "I consider your mission in East Africa is completed. . . ." The blow was softened with some flowery phrases conveying the usual conventional bouquets. The mission had had to be undertaken "in difficult circumstances": De Bono had earned "the gratitude of the Nation" and his "incontestable and universally recognized merits . . . were . . . explicitly consecrated" with his deeds, etc. The announcement of his promotion to Marshal provided a further sop.

Because De Bono accepted his recall with resignation, there were rumors that he was not displeased. Probably this was so. He must have realized by this time that he was unfitted to undertake the large-scale operations that were now clearly pending, and so he was probably secretly relieved that he would not have responsibility for them. He was over seventy years of age; a political soldier rather than a field commander, he had been appointed in recognition for his work in the Fascist cause. Yet it would be unfair to conclude without adding that it was De Bono who had made the campaign possible. Under his direction, an army of over a quarter of a million had been assembled, and its administrative services organized; in one month he had also avenged Adowa and occupied a strip of Ethiopia seventy-five miles deep. The capture of Makale ended the first phase of the war, and there was to be an interval of nearly a month before the next; decisions at Geneva had metamorphosed the character of the whole campaign, and a different kind of soldier was now needed to direct it.

CHAPTER 10

Sanctions

God save us from the lie of an honest man.
Neapolitan Proverb

On October 5, 1935, two days after the Italian invasion of Ethiopia was launched, the Committee of Thirteen, set up on September 26, presented its report to the League Council. Since the war had already begun, any recommendations it might have made to avert the conflict were already out of date. Pointing this out in the discussion which followed, the representative of Ethiopia demanded the application of Article 16 of the Covenant without further ado. Since Italy had clearly resorted to war in disregard of the Covenant, he said, not only should she be expelled from the League, but its other members should initiate punitive measures. Such an exhortation was bound to cause some tooth-sucking among the delegates; this was not how the League worked. Some idealistic speeches were made—the general tone of which was that the dispute should be regarded as a test case—but the only action that was taken was to appoint yet another committee: the Committee of Six, consisting of the representatives of Britain, Chile, Denmark, France, Portugal, and Rumania. This committee was instructed to bring the record up to date and report to the League Council not later than the October 7, so that the latter might "take decisions with a full knowledge of the facts."

Italian reaction to the Council's decision came by way of an extraordinary but characteristic public announcement. The operations in Ethiopia, Count Aloisi declared, were "quite legitimate and *even within the framework of the League* [author's italics]." They were, he continued, "an immediate and necessary reply to an act of provocation." This was a reference to the mobilization orders which had been signed by Haile Selassie on September 30—although, as has already been recorded, they did not become effective until October 3. Ethiopian troops had certainly been withdrawn well away from the Italian colonial frontiers, Aloisi conceded, but this was only a subterfuge. Haile Selassie was continuing aggressive preparations and the Italians had been compelled to undertake what would now be called a preemptive strike. As one British journalist ironically interpreted the Italian argument: the Emperor, "by ordering the withdrawal of his own troops in his own territory had committed a provocative act." "The responsibility [for Italy's action]," Aloisi continued, "must be attributed to the encouragement which Ethiopia thought she could find in the discussions at Geneva. . . ."

In fact, the issues were too clear to allow of any doubt, and the findings of the Committee of Six were a foregone conclusion. After specifying the events subsequent to October 2, their report, presented to the Council on the seventh, concluded by damning Italy:

After an examination of the facts. . . the Committee have come to the conclusion that the Italian Government has resorted to war in disregard of its Covenants under Article 12 of the Covenant of the League of Nations.

When votes on the two reports—that of the Committee of Thirteen and the one of the Committee of Six—were counted in the Council chamber, the only dissentient was that of Count Aloisi. The President solemnly declared: "Fourteen members of the League of Nations, represented on the Council, consider that we are in presence of a war begun in disregard of the obligations of the Covenant." On October 11, when the Assembly which had adjourned on September 28 met, the Council's decision was endorsed by an overwhelming majority. Of the 54 members present, 50 accepted the condemnation of Italy; only 4—Austria, Hungary, Italy, and Albania—were against. All that remained now was to decide what measures were going to be taken to stop Italy, and to translate them into effective action. For the first time in history an International Court had declared a Great Power guilty of causing a breach of the peace, and was deliberating on how the punishment was to be meted out.

Italy, meantime, had been warned of the possible consequences of the condemnation. Laval, fearing the worst, tried to cushion the blow by cautioning Mussolini. Telephoning Count Charles de Chambrun, the French Ambassador in Rome, he said over an open line: "England fears a conflict with Italy, a conflict that Sir Samuel Hoare and I have done everything to avoid. We have failed and I deeply regret it. Call on the Head of the Italian Government. Tell him that, to my great regret, *I have been obliged to consent to sanctions and that, in the event of war I shall be obliged to take sides with the United Kingdom* [author's italics]. . . ." That the line was tapped and the Duce's men had recorded the conversation was evident next day when De Chambrun called to deliver his message. The news that France would stand by Britain if it came to war in Europe might not have been to the Duce's liking, but by the morning of October 8 he had got over it. From the way Laval had spoken, it was clear that Mussolini could still count on his support, provided the situation was not allowed to deteriorate into actual hostilities involving Britain. The fact that he was careful not to allow it to do so may be taken as a measure of his bluff.

The decision of the League that the Italian Government had resorted to war in disregard of its Covenants under Article 12 automatically brought Article 16 into operation, and every individual member state of the League was duty-bound to see that the penalties specified in it were applied. The word *sanctions*, which has become all too familiar in our vocabulary, was coined to cover the penalties that were adopted at this time. Originally, its meaning extended to exacting punishment by measures which barely stopped short of war. During the wrangling at Geneva, the fact that the second paragraph of Article 16 specifically provided for *military* action was glossed over, and as military measures (which in this case meant closing the Suez Canal, and possibly using the British Fleet) were never contemplated, *sanctions* have come to be regarded as the application of economic measures—the cutting off of all financial aid and the raw materials on which a country is dependent for its economic survival.

To any country dependent on unhampered imports from overseas, economic sanctions must present a formidable deterrent. It is because they have never been rigidly applied that they have failed. Italy, in 1935, was able to hold out because the more important commodities were never included in the embargo, and because international entrepreneurs could always be found to supply any real deficiency. With every concern for the proprieties, the Assembly passed a resolution acknowledging the obligations of its members and the desirability of coordinating the measures that they might severally contemplate. Much more could have been done if the determination had been there—but it was not. And there was a loophole. In 1921 a resolution adopted by the Assembly had conferred on the Council discretionary power in the matter of economic sanctions. Instead of member states being obliged to sever their connections with an aggressor immediately, this ruling allowed a Coordination Committee to be set up to recommend what measures should be adopted and when they should come into force. Consequently yet another committee was brought into being in order to consider the framing of those sanctions which would end the war to everyone's satisfaction without anybody being hurt by them.

In effect, the new Coordination Committee was a diplomatic conference, legally distinct from the League itself, but made up of the delegates of the fifty Governments which had voted for the October 11 declaration. As its name implies, it had no authority to take any decisions; it was only empowered to list the measures to be submitted to each member Government for approval.

Moreover, although the constitution of the Committee was virtually the same as that of the Assembly, according to the strict letter of the law whatever it decided as a committee could only be held to be recommendations. On the other hand, when the occasion arose, such recommendations could be cited as League decisions and hence sacrosanct. Thus, at a later date when protests were raised in Britain regarding the ineffectiveness of sanctions, Eden was able to silence his critics by saying that the Coordination Committee had decided on what had had to be done, and that anyone devoted to the principle of collective action was bound to obey the League.

Meeting for the first time on October 11, the first task of this massive gathering was to elect a more manageable Subcommittee of Eighteen, and these eighteen subsequently split up into three sub-subcommittees.* By now it was already clear that few of the members relished the idea of any positive action, and the general attitude of the Coordination Committee was ably summed up by the French delegation as one of "collective enthusiasm and individual coolness." (Low, in one of his famous cartoons at this time, depicted Laval asking Sir Samuel Hoare and Eden "It is time to padlock the stable door, n'est-ce pas?" to which the answer was "But no, the horse is not yet quite flown.") It was not long before it was apparent that the Committee of Eighteen were concerned about not merely coordinating the application of sanctions but deciding which sanctions were to be applied. In this it ignored the categorical terminology of Article 16, ruling that *all* members of the League were pledged *immediately* to sever *all* trade and financial relations and to prohibit *all* intercourse between their nationals and the nations of the Covenant-breaking state. Dominating the Committee's deliberations was the fearful thought that too harsh a treatment of Italy might well lead to reprisals and so precipitate a general war, and although the words "immediately" and "all" did not allow any evasion, it was to the discovery of loopholes that the experts employed by the Com-

---

* The eighteen nations concerned were: South Africa, Argentina, Belgium, Britain, Canada, France, Greece, Mexico, Netherlands, Poland, Portugal, Rumania, Spain, Sweden, Switzerland, Turkey, U.S.S.R., Yugoslavia.

mittee of Eighteen primarily devoted their energies. Fear of how the Duce would react was the main reason for not considering the closing of the Suez Canal—although this particular sanction had been ruled out on September 10 when the president of the commission in charge of the Canal Company's finances had assured the world at large—and Italy in particular—that nothing short of force on the part of Britain would prevent Italy from using the Canal.

Another of the Coordination Committee's major concerns was the fact that several Great Powers who were not members of the League would be able to render ineffective any of the economic sanctions imposed by a ruling at Geneva. For instance, unless she agreed to cooperate, or the League was prepared to go to the very brink of an all-out war, the United States could pour unrestricted quantities of sanctioned material into Italy and so nullify the whole program. No positive indication of the American attitude had been forthcoming, and although President Roosevelt seemed to be taking a benevolent interest, there was good reason to suppose that there would be an outcry if United States merchantmen were stopped by warships of League states blockading Italian ports. Germany posed a similar problem, and stopping supplies to Italy implied also stopping them to Germany. This was quickly resolved by Germany herself. Mussolini had not yet joined hands with Hitler. Austria was still a bone of contention, and the Nazi Government saw no justification for getting embroiled in Italy's difficulties. Germany, the League Secretariat was told, would continue to export to Italy only "normal supplies" of goods. In other words, she was not prepared to help, but she would not hinder the League's punitive measures. Since this decision deprived the Committee of an alibi for the ineffectiveness of some of the measures they were then contemplating, it was not altogether welcome news.

In view of the reticence shown by some of the delegates, the Committee of Eighteen completed its task with surprising promptness. By October 19, four proposals had been drafted and approved by the full Coordination Committee. Proposal 1, which lifted the arms embargo against Ethiopia, was suggested by Eden and unanimously adopted by the Committee on the very first day of its sitting. In theory the "exportation, re-exportation or transit of arms, munitions, and implements of war" in force, had applied equally to both parties. But industrial Italy imported very few weapons as such, and it was Ethiopia, who depended exclusively on imports of arms, that had suffered. Eden's first proposal may therefore be regarded as retrospective corrective justice. Proposal 2, which called for the prohibition of loans and credits to or for the Italian Government, and for the cancellation of any financial transactions in which Italy was involved, was adopted on October 16. Three days later Proposals 3 and 4, for which Britain and France were jointly responsible, were also adopted. Proposal 3 prohibited the members of the League from importing all goods consigned from Italy, other than gold, silver bullion, and coin, and Proposal 4 called for an embargo on certain goods normally exported by member states to Italy. This was the most important proposal, and an imposing schedule of articles of general utility was embodied in it. But the real sinews of war—raw materials such as coal, oil, iron, and steel —were deliberately excluded. On the other hand, the export to Italy of aluminium, for example, was strictly forbidden. But aluminium was the one metal which Italy produced beyond her own needs. Scrap iron and iron ores were similarly vetoed; but as the Italian steel industry normally imported neither, using steel billets and pig iron, production was not interfered with.

On the day that Proposal 4 was adopted (October 19), the Coordination Committee also came up with a fifth proposal. This dealt with the economic support of those states which would suffer as a result of their applying the sanctions covered by the four previous proposals. It was necessary because some of the smaller countries, who would be hard hit if they stopped trading with Italy, were determined to make their participation in the sanctions program contingent on their being compensated. Not unnaturally, it was Britain—ostensibly the richest country concerned and, judging by Eden's attitude, the one that was most concerned in the application of sanctions—to whom the smaller countries looked for their dole. Nor was their attitude unrealistic. By abandoning Italy, countries like Rumania and Yugoslavia would lose the greater part of their overseas trade and it stood to reason that they should want something more substantial than mere assurances of moral support. As Eden learned in the course of the negotiations on Proposal 5, not all the fifty nations who had aligned themselves against Italy were prepared to make sacrifices for the League's ideal without counting the cost.

Four countries refused to participate in the sanctions: Albania, Austria, Hungary, and Paraguay, who had already said that she intended to withdraw from the League. Proposals 1 and 2 were agreed to by fifty-two Governments; Proposal 3 by fifty; Proposal 4 by fifty-one; Proposal 5 by forty-nine. November 18 was fixed as the date when the first four proposals should come into force. Details of what had been decided were communicated to all nonmembers of the League, and as a result of this, the Egyptian Government decided to enforce Proposals 1 to 4; Liechtenstein announced that it would follow Switzerland in applying only Proposals 1 and 2; and Brazil declined to undertake to adopt any of them. In fact, what Egypt, Liechtenstein, and Brazil did was really of little consequence; what counted was the reaction of the two Great Powers outside the League, the United States and Germany, and to the implied invitation to join in the sanctions, both countries answered evasively. Before any action was taken by other Governments, replied the U.S. State Department, the United States Government had prohibited the export of arms and munitions of war to both belligerents and had warned American citizens of the dangers of traveling on Italian ships and against any dealing with Italy and Ethiopia. From the German Government came a brief statement to the effect that it would take steps to ensure that German nationals did not realize exceptional profit from the war.

In formulating the sanctions policy the League worked with a speed which can hardly be said to be characteristic of its other actions during the crisis. Within sixteen days of the outbreak of hostilities a series of penalties had been drawn up which—even though they were to prove inadequate to deter Italy—were mildly repressive. Their failure was due to a variety of reasons.

Clearly, their content—or what their content lacked—was one. But the inefficacy of the action taken by those who were ostensibly applying the sanctions, the noncooperation of the nations outside the League, and the unexpected capacity of Italy's own resources, were contributory factors. The relatively modest economic restrictions recommended by the Coordination Committee strictly followed the lines of the agreement reached by Sir Samuel Hoare and Laval between September 9 and 11, and because the League tailored its action to the Assembly Resolution of 1921, Article 16 of the Covenant was never properly applied. (Article 16 stipulated, among other points, that diplomatic relations should be severed, which meant that diplomatic missions should have been withdrawn immediately. Eden wanted the British Ambassador in Rome to be recalled, but the Foreign Office objected on the grounds that the arrangements agreed by Hoare for Britain and Laval for France during September specifically excluded diplomatic and political sanctions).[1]

The initiative for deferring the prohibition on coal, oil, iron, and steel exports to Italy came not from France but from Britain. When the Committee of Eighteen drafted Proposal 4, the French proposal was that all Italian exports should be prohibited in order to stop Italy getting foreign currency, and that other countries exporting goods to Italy should refrain from supplying armaments and any material necessary for the prosecution of the war. The key products which the French representative specifically referred to included coal, oil, iron, and steel. At that time Mussolini had not stipulated the extent of the prohibitions he would regard as a declaration of war, and whether Laval was more sincere in his desire to stop the war than he has been given credit for, or whether it had just not occurred to the French that any exceptions regarding these materials was necessary, France was ready to include them in the sanctions at this particular time. Consequently it was Britain who came to the Duce's rescue when Eden's counterproposal that an embargo on exports of coal, oil, iron, and steel should be postponed, was adopted.

The sanctions excluded any real measures that might have paralyzed Italy, and even the mild measures introduced were only partially applied. Apart from the four countries which had refused to participate at the outset, seven members of the League failed to apply the arms embargo (Proposal 1); eight failed to apply the financial embargo (Proposal 2); thirteen the imports embargo (Proposal 3); and ten the exports embargo (Proposal 4). In other words, when it came to a showdown, more than a quarter of the League members—including Switzerland, who as Italy's neighbor held a key position economically, and most of the Latin American States*—were unwilling to stand by principles they had agreed to support when they signed the League Covenant.

Of those outside the League, the United States put an embargo on arms which Italy did not need. Like other countries, however, she continued to provide the commodities that really mattered. In October, American businessmen unwilling to let profitable opportunities slip away flocked across to Rome to solicit Italian orders. As a consequence, by November 18, when the sanctions came into force, the volume of American exports had risen so steeply that Mr. Cordell Hull was hinting that if the developing commercial interest in Italy was not kept within reasonable limits, the United States Government might publish the names of the firms engaged. Despite the protests of the exporters and the fury of the Italian-American community, this threat had its effect, and according to the figures that were published, the increase in trade during the last three months of 1935 was only 20 percent above the corresponding period in 1934. Needless to say Italy did not go short of any vital commodity. What could not be supplied by the Americans, Germany was happy to provide. And while the Americans demanded payment in gold, the Germans were more accommodating as they were prepared to accept fruit, olive oil, silks, and sulphur.

So far as Europe was concerned, the most significant effect of the sanctions was the very one which Laval and Vansittart had feared, for it was during this period that the seeds of a new Italo-

---

* "It is a well-known fact that when sanctions were imposed, the Pope's envoys in South America used all their influence with the South American Governments to induce the latter to vote in Geneva to have sanctions raised." W. Teeling, *The Pope in Politics* (see Bibliography), p. 253.

German friendship began to sprout. Hitler forgot that the Duce had referred to him as "that mad little clown"; the Duce stopped declaiming the inherent antipathy of the Latin for the Teuton, and in both countries articles in the controlled press began to talk about the common aims, common culture, and common systems of the two countries. Out of this grew the Rome-Berlin Axis.

Mussolini was probably as much surprised as annoyed at the official condemnation of his Ethiopian adventure. But it did not take him long to realize that sanctions could be a means of bringing home to the Italians the cruelty of an unjust and misunderstanding world. For at that moment the Ethiopian venture was in need of a boost. Despite the Duce's exhortations, appeals to patriotic duty, and assurances of riches to come, some Italians had shown considerably less ardor than the Duce had thought proper. In the south, where economic conditions were harder, the promise of new land to cultivate had been fairly convincing. But in the healthy and prosperous Tyrolean districts the population had shown remarkably little enthusiasm for leaving their homes in order to fight in some uninviting tropical region. Sanctions brought grist to the propaganda mill and presented Mussolini with a glorious opportunity to pose as Ajax defying the Geneva lightning. By employing all the stock heroics, he was able to build up a picture of Italy against the world, and the nation rallied behind him. Very few people in Italy actually felt any effect from what was supposed to be economic ostracism.* Some luxury articles such as English woolens, French perfumes, and Dutch cheeses were missing from the shops for a few months, but these were things which most people could do without, and where the pinch should have been felt sanctions had no effect.

As Churchill wrote later, the Duce showed a deep shrewdness in turning the situation to his advantage. "Instead of saying, 'Italy will meet sanctions with war' he said: 'Italy will meet them with discipline, with frugality, and with sacrifice.'" And she did. Where there had been grumbles before, the voice of criticism

---

* An account of Italy's internal reactions to sanctions is given in Beatrice Baskerville's *What Next, O Duce* (see Bibliography).

was silent. Women donated their jewelry to the war effort; November 18 was marked on Italian calendars as a black day—sanctified as a "Lest we forget" occasion. It was also posted on public placards and billboards as the day when Italy stood against the world. Italians came to believe that they were fighting not merely for an Empire but to preserve their very existence, and they were imbued with a new determination to resist the men at Geneva and win Ethiopia come what may. Doubts were swept away, sacrifices demanded in the name of what now assumed the nature of a jihad were accepted without question, the political hand of Fascism was immeasurably strengthened, and one of the jokes of the period ascribed the making of United Italy to Cavour, Mussolini, and Eden.

In theory, the sanctions that were approved on October 19 were an introduction to progressively more drastic measures, of course. The Committee of Eighteen remained in being, and its task was to watch the effects and recommend more sanctions which would tighten the screw if Italy persisted in defying the League. Oil was really the crucial commodity because this was the one thing which Italy really lacked. One of the reasons put forward for not including it in the original list of banned products was that the League could only legislate for goods controlled by its members, and as the United States produced over 59 percent of the world's supply, the practical difficulties in enforcing an embargo on it would render it inoperative.* Nevertheless there was a strong feeling among some of the members of the Committee of Eighteen that an attempt should be made to deprive Italy of her oil supply, and on November 2 the Canadian delegate, Mr. Riddell, submitted a proposal for the extension of Proposal 4 to include petroleum and its derivatives, by-products,

---

* The United States normally supplied only about 6 percent of Italy's oil; 20 percent came from her own resources, the rest from Rumania (46.5 percent), Russia (13 percent), the Netherlands (12.5 percent), and Iraq (2 percent). If these countries had cut off supplies and the United States had not increased her quota, Italy would have faced a serious shortage. In fact, imports of American oil amounted to nearly 18 percent of Italy's total requirements in the last three months of 1935, and unless President Roosevelt had been able to bring in legislation to stop the traffic, no doubt they would have risen further when a League boycott was declared.

and residues; pig iron; iron and steel, case, forged, or rolled; coal, coke, "and the agglomerates, as well as fuel derived therefrom." Consideration of the proposal was deftly deferred. Mussolini had stated quite emphatically that if his Ethiopian enterprise was endangered he would go to war with whoever stood in his path, and the British and French Governments wanted to avoid the risk of calling his bluff. If it was bluff. While the Duce did not actually want a war in Europe, he knew that Britain and France wanted one even less, and his veiled threats—whose efficacy was the greater because they were never defined—were a powerful deterrent.

In Britain, the possibility that the proper application of sanctions might lead to an open war had not been grasped by the public, which clamored for them in the belief that they were a sure way of bringing the operations in Ethiopia to a stop. Baldwin, with the General Election pending, could not afford to flout the electorate; at the same time he was determined not to be drawn into war on any account. Whether, if he had taken a bold decision to back an oil boycott, and even cut Italy's communications at Suez—thereby risking a fleet action—it would ever have come to war is a matter for conjecture. Different writers have put forward different theories in an attempt to explain the British Prime Minister's actions at this time. Of these the most charitable, propounded by his supporters, was that it was his sincere love of peace that prompted the British Government to prevaricate. Other explanations range from bald indictments of faintheartedness to the dark inference of a desire on the part of a capitalistic imperialist to see Fascism maintained as a bulwark against international communism.

One certain fact is that Mussolini was a better psychologist and bolder gambler than Baldwin, another that France was lukewarm as to the application of even limited sanctions. To Laval, Germany remained the key menace, and as he saw it, if the sanctions policy led to Italian retaliation, Germany might be induced to attack France. In such circumstances he wanted to be quite sure that Britain would spring to France's aid immediately, and in the absence of a specific guarantee to this effect he was quite

determined that his excellent relationship with Italy was not going to be jeopardized by any definite step being taken on an oil
embargo. The result was that by October, Mussolini's astute
brinkmanship had succeeded in cowing public opinion in France,
and it would be less than fair not to say that irrespective of his
partiality for Italy, Laval's attitude was conditioned by this. By
threatening war and capitalizing on the fact that many people
believed him capable of setting Europe on fire if it suited his
ends, the Duce had terrified the French people. Economic sanctions were a dangerous enough precedent, and military sanctions
were completely out of the question unless France was prepared
to fight; with or without Britain, this was too appalling to think
about. If proof of this feeling were needed, it was provided at a
meeting of the Confédération Générale du Travail in Paris on
September 23, when the Secretary-General of the Confédération was cheered after saying that "whilst French workers urge
their Government to remain faithful to the League Covenant in
order to maintain peace . . . they do not agree with their British comrades in demanding military sanctions." In reporting this
scene, which concluded with a peroration "We not only hate
war; we hate all wars" and an uproarious ovation, the *Manchester Guardian* commented somberly that ". . . it must be admitted that public opinion in France—even on the Left—is for
the present strongly against the application of naval sanctions
against Italy."

Against this background Laval had been seeking a compromise solution which would bring about a cessation of hostilities.
He had, in fact, never relaxed his efforts to find a conciliatory
formula, and when Italy was condemned as an aggressor his
efforts were redoubled. By October 15 he thought a way out
had been found. Sending for Signor Cerruti, the Italian Ambassador in Paris, he suggested that it might be possible to "arrange"
for Tigre and Ogaden to be conceded to Italy if the Duce would
stop the fighting. The message was duly relayed back to Rome,
where Mussolini's reaction was to express his readiness to negotiate; for an "honorable" peace, he said, Italy had always been willing to compromise. By honorable peace, he meant, of course, a
settlement which would give Italy what he had wanted for her

all along. The outlook was definitely brighter. With France trying to reduce the tension and Britain clearly nervous at his
threats, Mussolini held the initiative. Even if his secret service
had not been able to keep the Duce informed of what passed
between London and the British Embassy in Rome, Ambassador
Drummond's formal representations were evidence of the British
Government's apprehensions.*

As a result of Laval's tentative promise of further concessions
to Italy, Sir Maurice Peterson, head of the Ethiopian department
of the Foreign Office, went across to Paris for talks with his
counterpart in the Quai d'Orsay, the Count de St. Quentin. British ideas for a settlement were compared with the Italian claims
submitted to the French, and the fruits of their labors eventually
matured in the ill-famed "Hoare-Laval" proposals for a settlement of the dispute. When the talks opened toward the end of
October the ideas of the would-be peacemakers were separated
by a gulf. Over the weeks—as lines were drawn across the map
of Ethiopia, dividing tribes and territories with little thought of
ethnic and physical barriers—this gulf narrowed. But while Britain was initially prepared to back a settlement which ceded the
eastern half of Tigre to Italy, there was hesitation about giving
away the other half of the province. With short intervals to enable Peterson to renew his instructions in London, and a long
break over the period of the General Election in Britain, the talks
continued throughout November.

Ethiopia was not asked for her views. Haile Selassie could
hardly be expected to take kindly to giving away territory that
eventually would total a third of his empire, and so there was no
point in consulting him. Yet, as the formula the mediators were
seeking would have to be accepted by the Emperor eventually, it
was clearly desirable to whittle Italy's claim down to its bones.
For this reason alone formulating a plan would have been difficult enough; the task was made harder by Mussolini's vacillations. In the first two weeks of November the occupation of
Makale stiffened the Duce's attitude, and he let it be known that

* In difficult circumstances Sir Eric Drummond tried to keep the Duce
sweet. Mussolini did not abandon his purpose because he bargained on Britain
not stopping him.

there were no more concessions coming from him. Later in the month, De Bono's gloomy predictions from the field, coupled with second thoughts about the possible repercussions of sanctions, may have accounted for the Duce seeming to be willing to accept less. Clearly, whatever plan was devised would have to cede large slices of Ethiopia to Italy, or Mussolini would reject it out of hand. The conclusion of the British and French War Offices had been that it might well take Italy several years to conquer Ethiopia. But by this time it was beginning to look as if they had overestimated. Clearly Ethiopia had no chance of winning, and there was a distinct possibility that unless the League quickly took more drastic action, she might even be beaten before sanctions became effective. For this reason, in the hope of preserving at least a fragment of his kingdom, it was presumed that the Emperor would come to terms quickly. Some cajolery might be necessary but that was not the problem. The limiting factor was what would satisfy Mussolini, and to make sure of a deal, generous concessions seemed to be indicated. In drawing them up, it turned out that the geographical location of Greenwich and the idiosyncrasies of the Foreign Office and Quai d'Orsay officials seemed more likely to decide the future of the Ethiopian people than any consideration of their religions, tribes, and loyalties.

Apart from Aksum—which Ethiopia was to be allowed to retain because of its historic and religious significance—Italy was to be granted almost the whole of Tigre in the north, and most of Ogaden in the southeast. In return Italy would be persuaded to cede to Ethiopia a strip of land stretching to the Red Sea at Assab. Because this strip lay to the north of the existing railway line and farther from the Harar district—the only productive region east of the Hawash River—it appeared even more uneconomic than the earlier offer of Zeila. However, the most important and fatal component of the plan was undoubtedly the proposal to constitute a high area in the south as a "zone of economic expansion and settlement reserved to Italy." As its boundary some of the experts airly suggested the 40th degree of longitude; others opted for the 38th. Both arbitrary limits ran through

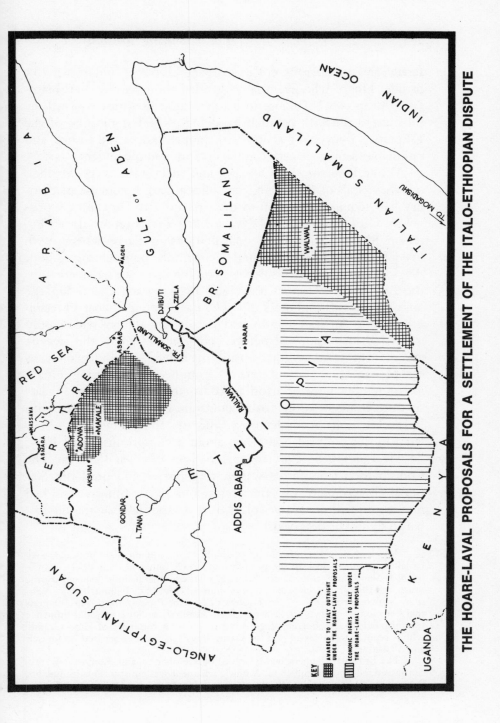

THE HOARE-LAVAL PROPOSALS FOR A SETTLEMENT OF THE ITALO-ETHIOPIAN DISPUTE

fertile and prosperous coffee-growing districts, and it was Sir Samuel Hoare who eventually decided the issues in the Hoare-Laval proposals.* Taking up his pen like the unjust steward, he substituted the 35th parallel; by doing so he left nothing of the Emperor's domain of southern Ethiopia except the dismal and uninhabited swamps between the uplands and the Sudan.

While Peterson, St. Quentin, and their staffs were working out the details of their plan, the political and diplomatic machinery had swung into action to prepare the way for the new proposals. On October 30, *The New York Times* reported that Peterson had returned from consultations in Paris, where, with French experts, he had found "a formula representing a joint Anglo-French effort to solve the trouble in a way satisfactory to the League of Nations, Italy, and Ethiopia together." On the same day the (London) *Daily Herald* announced that Peterson and Count de St. Quentin had drawn up a plan which only needed British approval before being submitted to the League and that this plan met the demands made by Mussolini two weeks earlier. Meantime, taking time off from his electioneering, Hoare instructed Sir Sidney Barton in Addis Ababa to urge Haile Selassie to open negotiations for a compromise peace settlement with Italy. Then, after condemning whispers and innuendoes circulated by his political opponents about a compromise with Italy, he left London on November 1 to join Eden at Geneva. The Coordination Committee was getting restive and until the National Government was safely reinstated in Westminster and had nothing to fear from the voters, it was essential that the oil embargo should be deferred.†

* At whose door the ultimate responsibility for evolving these proposals may be laid is problematical. In the postmortem which followed their disclosure the hand of Vansittart—with whom Peterson worked—was plainly detected by the press, and the *News Chronicle* pilloried him as "The Man Behind It All." Vansittart's own version of the negotiations (*The Mist Procession*, p. 538) suggests that Peterson was given a free hand. That Vansittart undoubtedly did influence the proposals in the drafting stage is borne out by a comment of Dino Grandi, who is reputed to have said that the Hoare-Laval plan was concocted by himself and Vansittart.

† The British Parliament was dissolved on October 25, and the General Election was fixed for November 14. A new Parliament was constitutionally due, but Baldwin's sudden decision brought accusations from the Opposition that he

On the evening of November 1, following his arrival in Geneva, Hoare had a private meeting with Laval, Count Aloisi, and the Belgian Prime Minister, Paul van Zeeland. The latter, because of his cooperation with the British Government on other occasions, had been selected as the man to fulfill the role of a catalytic agent; with his help the League would be made responsible for what was being concocted behind the scenes, and on November 2 the part he had to play was finalized at lunch with Eden and Laval. The idea was that at the meeting of the Coordination Committee the following afternoon, Van Zeeland would invite the Committee to give the British and French Governments a "mission" to try to find a solution to the Italo-Ethiopian dispute. At the end of the meeting, in accordance with this arrangement, the Belgian Prime Minister rose from his seat and addressed the delegates who were just about to disperse. "I propose," he said, "that the British and French Governments should be entrusted with the mission of seeking—under the League's auspices and control, and in the spirit of the Covenant—the elements of a solution acceptable to the League of Nations, Italy, and Ethiopia." As the Coordination Committee had no authority to give any such instructions to Britain, France, or any other Government, the proposal was quite irregular, and M. Komarnicki, the Polish delegate, was quick to point out that the Coordination Committee had been set up to study the enactment of sanctions, not to promote conciliation; the place to discuss Van Zeeland's proposal, he said, was a meeting of the Council or the Assembly of the League. Consequently, the proposal was only recorded in the minutes of the meeting; that was all. And, as the three instigators had anticipated a vote being taken, this ruined their arrangements, although it did not stop the British and French Governments subsequently alluding to the "moral mandate" entrusted to them by the League when trying to pin some of the responsibility for the Hoare-Laval plan on the Coordination Committee.

---

had staged a "snap" election—which was true. It was a particularly favorable moment for the Conservatives since the popular reaction to Hoare's apparently firm stand at Geneva had been very favorable, and before the storm broke Baldwin was anxious to obtain a new five-year mandate.

One result of this maneuver was the postponement of the proposed extension of the sanctions, and although four days later the Committee of Eighteen submitted a proposal for an embargo of oil to the Governments of the League members, it carried a proviso that it would not come into operation "until the conditions necessary for the efficacy of the measures had been realized." The British and French Governments were reluctant to introduce an oil ban if it could possibly be avoided. Nevertheless the proposal was so well received that Señor de Vasconcellos, the Chairman of the Coordination Committee, decided to convene the Committee of Eighteen on November 29. But when the French said that this date would be inconvenient for Laval, there was further postponement until December 12. When the time eventually did come for the Committee to consider introducing the oil boycott, not only was it too late, the bottom had been knocked out of the whole sanctions policy.

CHAPTER 11

The Betrayal

If two men ride on a horse, one must ride behind.
SHAKESPEARE, *Much Ado About Nothing*, iii, 5

If Baldwin's Government was to be returned to power it was essential that the peace plan should not be revealed until after the election. Great play had been made in the campaign of the Conservatives' record in support of the League: "The League of Nations will remain, as heretofore, the keystone of British foreign policy" ran their manifesto.

The prevention of war and the promotion of peace in the world must always be the most vital interest of the British people, and the League is the instrument *which has been framed* and to which we look for the attainment of these objects. We shall therefore continue to do all in our power to uphold the Covenant and to maintain and increase the efficiency of the League. *In the present unhappy dispute between Italy and Abyssinia there will be no wavering in this policy we have hitherto pursued.* [Author's italics.]

The success of the appeal obviously depended entirely on the Conservatives being able to convince the electorate that they were indeed pursuing an unswerving policy in support of the

League. If it leaked out that they were considering cajoling Haile Selassie into handing over large slices of Ethiopian territory to Italy in order to purchase peace, they were lost. Hoare's speech to the Assembly in September had left the impression that the League as a whole, and Britain in particular, was resolved to stop Italy from profiting by her aggression. For the time being nothing must be done to destroy that impression. Once the election was over and Baldwin's party was safely back in office, the Government could afford to take a more realistic point of view. But not until then.

Because its members were divided among themselves, the Labour party was unable to compete with the Tories. Probably they had a shrewd idea of what was going on, but they were a mixed bag and spoke in different tongues. George Lansbury had been succeeded by Attlee as party leader, but a large section of the Labour voters were still strong pacifists; on the other hand, the Trade Unionists—among whom Mr. Ernest Bevin, a future Foreign Secretary, was outstanding—were by no means pacifist in temperament. To them, hatred of Fascism and a sincere belief in the efficacy of the League of Nations bred a strong desire to stop the Italians at all costs—by force if need be. At the Labour Party national conference on October 20 it was the nonpacifists who carried the day. By 2,136,000 votes to 102,000, a resolution declaring support for military sanctions was passed, and two days later Attlee voiced his party's demand for decisive action in the House of Commons. "We want effective sanctions, effectively applied," he said. This was clear enough. Unfortunately the effect was lessened when he went on in the same speech to say: "We are not persuaded that the way to safety is by piling up armaments. We do not believe that in this [time] there is such a thing as national defense. We think that you have to go forward to disarmament and not to the piling up of armaments." If the "effective application of effective sanctions" the Labour party advocated were to result in a League war, it was obvious that Britain would have to take the brunt so far as naval operations were concerned. Yet, here was the Labour party advocating decisive action on the one hand, and denouncing the means with which to carry it out on the other.

Rumors that the Cabinet was considering a dubious deal with Italy circulated freely throughout the electioneering campaign, and even though the Labour party was not able to make much of them, they were assiduously cultivated by all the non-Tory candidates. Equally energetically, the Tories denied that there was any truth in them. Never, said Sir Samuel Hoare and his colleagues piously when they addressed their constituents, would the Tories sabotage the League; the rumors were false. So too, was the suggestion that the new Government would embark on an enormous rearmament program. It was true that there was need for *some* rearmament, but Baldwin's reference to the unsatisfactory state of the Royal Navy did not mean that the peace-lovers had anything to fear. To emphasize the point, the Prime Minister himself made a speech to the Peace Society at the Guildhall two weeks before the poll: "I give you my word there will be no great armaments race," he declared. In view of other speeches he and every other member of his Cabinet had made during the election campaign, this was an extraordinary promise. But it must have had the right effect since a large number of uncommitted voters who had drifted along with the vast current of public opinion that had manifested itself in the Peace Ballot was captured, and the National Government was returned to power by 431 seats to 184.

As soon as the election was over, Sir Samuel Hoare picked up the threads of the "moral mandate" which he had dropped in order to campaign in Chelsea. By mid-November, Peterson's and St. Quentin's studies were well advanced, and everything seemed well set for the diplomatic masterstroke which was to settle the Italo-Ethiopian affair once and for all. Starting with the proposals presented by Eden to Mussolini five months before, the plan produced by the Foreign Office and Quai d'Orsay had run through a succession of drafts, each of which had consistently conceded more and more to Italy at Ethiopia's expense. The basic problem was unchanged from what it had been when Eden had tried to negotiate direct with the Duce: how little would Italy take; how much would Ethiopia yield; how far could a solution be imposed without incurring an outcry. To the French Government the prime requirement was to satisfy Italy; on the other side of the Channel the newly returned British Government, apprehensive about reaction in Britain once the public saw that it had turned aside from its declared resolve, was more reluctant to grant concessions. Nevertheless Stanley Baldwin was quite ready to sacrifice Ethiopia to preserve the shreds of the Stresa front. It was just that he wanted it done in a nice sort of way. And according to Vansittart there was little alternative to sacrificing Ethiopia: "We were making the best of a very bad job. Our Chiefs of Staff insisted we were in no position to wage war. Nor were the French—a revealing admission from an army supposed by wishful experts to be the shield of Europe. . . ." [1]

To finalize the sellout scheme before it was referred to the British Cabinet and to the League for rubber-stamping, Laval announced his intention of visiting London at the beginning of December. At Geneva, a breathing space had been obtained, but something had to be settled before the postponed discussion on the oil embargo on December 12. Fortuitously, or by intent, the visit to London was canceled and it was arranged that Sir Samuel Hoare should call on Laval to examine the fruits of Peterson's and St. Quentin's labors.* Hoare had been a sick man for some time, and on his doctors' advice—and with Baldwin's concurrence—he had decided to take a recuperative holiday in the Engadine, where he would be able to enjoy some skating, at which activity he held a high regard for his abilities. As he had to go through Paris it seemed quite logical that he should stop off to see the French Premier. Equally fortuitously, or equally by intent, Vansittart happened to be vacationing in Paris at the same time. In consequence he "was roped in" for the discussions which started on the Saturday evening and continued throughout Sunday, December 8. Vansittart wrote later that there was little time to find out what the Cabinet's brief to the sick and overtired Foreign Secretary had been before both of them were ushered in to Laval's ornate office:

I did not know Sam's instructions. John Simon thought him only authorised to take soundings, in which case the visit was superfluous

---

* Judging by Vansittart's account, the British Government disapproved of Laval coming to London. The French Premier was "fobbed off," he said.

seeing that we already had Clerk [Sir George Clerk, the British Ambassador in Paris] and Peterson there for the purpose. Sam understood that he was authorised and expected to do more. I warned him
that the way of the peacemaker would be hard, and asked whether
the Government meant to fight. He replied that neither Cabinet nor
nation had any such intention. "Then you will have to compromise,"
I said, "that will be unpopular, but there is no third way." [2]

On the face of it, this version of the preliminaries suggests
that either the Foreign Secretary was incredibly naïve, wholly
uninformed, or totally unfit to confer with Laval. Many writers
have represented that the latter was the more credible explanation—that the hard-bargaining Laval got the better of his opponent because Hoare was too sick to argue coherently. Others
have suggested that Hoare acted on his own responsibility, and
that had Baldwin only known what was going on, the affair
would have been better managed. Both conceptions can be dismissed. That Hoare was a sick man in sore need of a long rest is
not in doubt. But as there was no question of "bargaining," and
the discussions—in which he had the support of Vansittart,
Clerk, and Peterson—were concerned only with putting the fin-
ishing touches to a prepared draft, the relative states of health
of Laval and Hoare are of minor importance. Hoare knew well
enough what he was in Paris for on December 7, and although
they had not reached any conclusions on the terms of a settlement at this stage, to suppose that his Cabinet colleagues, Baldwin in particular, were unaware of what he was up to stretches
the imagination.

What has already been said about the contents of the Hoare-
Laval plan is sufficient to show that what was proposed entailed
the bloodless transfer to Italy of about half the Ethiopian Empire. As only a fraction of the territory in question had been
occupied by the Italians up to that time, such proposals were extremely generous. That the Duce had had a hand in drafting
them seemed obvious to Vansittart from the way Laval spoke at
the discussions on December 8. "Once, when alone with me in
his room, he offered to ring up Mussolini [to confirm that the
latter would insist on an Italian monopoly south of Addis

Ababa] . . . I was sure, anyhow, that he was in daily communication with Rome and that the French terms were therefore the
only ones that Italy would accept. . . ." [3] In a memorandum
written in the prison of Fresnes on September 11, 1945, Laval
made no mention of any collaboration he might have had with
the Duce:

All the attempts at Geneva to solve the Ethiopia crisis by friendly
means had successively failed. It was clear that a peaceful solution of
the crisis hinged exclusively on complete agreement between France
and Great Britain. Neither Italy nor Ethiopia would have been able
to oppose a compromise imposed by our two countries. Sir Samuel
Hoare understood this and, with an acute sense of realities and a desire to put an end to an adventure which threatened the gravest consequences . . . agreed to discuss . . . a formula, which I was certain
Italy would accept, and which he was certain the Negus would accept, and which we were both sure Geneva would not oppose.[4]

The plan which was evolved was a great triumph for the Duce.
Not only did it present him with more territory than he had won
by the sword so far, it also gave him virtual control of, amounting to a right to annex, almost half Ethiopia. Moreover it upset
the sanction timetable, and—most important of all in the eyes of
the world—it exonerated Italy as the aggressor in the dispute. As
the Italian Fascist newspaper in France, *La Nuova Italia*, said on
December 12, the proposals "proved that the two Great Powers
knew that Italy was not the aggressor. We have never heard that
conciliatory proposals are made to aggressor nations. . . ." Such
an assertion, logical in itself, put the British Government in a
decidedly awkward position. However reluctantly, Britain had
gone too far along the path of sanctions to be able suddenly to
turn aside. To do so would have required an explanation which
subsequent events showed the British public would not easily
have accepted. Having said this, it must be remembered that if
Mussolini had accepted the plan, the same British public would
have been confronted with a *fait accompli*. The war in Ethiopia
would have ended the tumult of shouting and would probably
have soon given way to a general feeling of relief that peace,
even if it was a bad peace, was preferable to war—especially as
people in Britain were not called upon to pay any price for it.

One of the most extraordinary features of the Hoare-Laval proposals was that Ethiopia's acceptance and the League's concurrence were taken for granted during the drafting stages. How the plan could be reconciled with the terms of the League Covenant is difficult enough to understand, but the idea that Haile Selassie would tamely accept the dismemberment of his country and win over his chiefs to such a policy is incredible. If he refused, presumably it would have been made clear that he could expect no further help from the League. On the other hand, once he accepted the proposals, Ethiopia would be regarded by the League of Nations as a protected state under Italy's wing—at the mercy of further aggression and penetration. As it turned out, the Emperor rejected the plan even before he had official cognizance of it.

On the Sunday evening (December 8) when the details of the plan were finalized, Hoare caught the Paris night express to Switzerland while Peterson returned to London with the draft plan. "I did not see Hoare before leaving," Peterson recorded, "but Vansittart urged me in his name to emphasize in London the pressing need for closing the ranks against the oncoming rush of Germany." [5] Vansittart, with his eyes constantly fixed on Hitler, was both loath to lose Italy as an ally and concerned with keeping France sweet.

Peterson and I thought that there was a chance of bringing the League to supervise those bare non-Amharic areas which had never been under effective Abyssinian control. . . . We also tried to comfort ourselves with hope that the slave-trade might at last be checked, by extending the Proposals of the League's Committee. We were unhappy, but George Clerk, scrutinising France, never thought that we could wring more out of her. . . .[6]

A short and guarded Anglo-French communiqué noting progress toward a settlement of the Italo-Ethiopian affair was issued to the press on December 8. The understanding was that the plan itself should remain a profound secret until the British Cabinet had had time to consider it; "There could be no question at present of publicising these formulas," it said. Next morning, however, authoritative details of the proposals appeared in the *Echo de Paris* and *Oeuvre*, and the news reached London that afternoon. How the Paris newspapers got hold of the story has never been fully explained. At one time Vansittart suspected Laval, who "began talking and talked quite a lot" at lunch on December 8. Mussolini believed that the disclosure was one of Laval's tricks designed to force his hand. Hoare thought that it might have been himself who unwittingly gave away something when he briefed several newspaper correspondents at the British Embassy before catching his train. (Rather ingenuously he asked them not to comment in any detail on the "very general idea" he gave them, and added that "they appeared ready to fall in with my request.") Laval thought M. Herriot, French Minister of State, might have had a hand in it.* Others suspected that someone unfriendly toward Laval in the French Foreign Office saw a chance to embarrass the French Premier and took it.

Whatever the reason, the leak created a furore to which the British Government could not shut its eyes. On December 9, hurriedly abandoning the inaugural session of the London Naval Conference, Baldwin rushed to a Cabinet meeting called to decide whether to accept the Hoare-Laval plan or repudiate the Foreign Secretary. With the storm of public opinion about to break, a quick decision was imperative, and matters were so rushed that it was said that there were no maps of Ethiopia in the Cabinet Room. Consequently ministers had to consider the plan without any real idea of how much Ethiopian territory had been ceded to Italy. A reluctant assent was given to the project, and from that moment a fantastic political tornado struck Britain. Had Mussolini seized the opportunity to accept the proposals while it was raging, all the elements of a tragicomedy would have been present.

By the morning of December 10 it was becoming clear that the British public was not prepared to stomach the Hoare-Laval plan, no matter how it was presented. Indignant letters poured into the newspapers, and the newly elected rank and file of Government supporters were beset by wrathful constituents claiming

---

* In his Fresnes memorandum written while awaiting trial, he made no mention of this notion. All he said about the incident was that "At this critical juncture there was a leak to the Press, and market-place polemics immediately ensued. . . ." (*The Unpublished Diary of Pierre Laval*, p. 31.)

that the Tories had won the election under false pretences. During the electoral campaign a pamphlet, hastily published by a party of students of international affairs opposed to the Government, had aroused considerable attention: "They reckon on the General Election definitely giving them the upper hand in the Conservative Party, with a blank cheque to arm to the teeth as well as freeing them from the fear of public opinion. *Then they will do a deal with their friend Mussolini* [author's italics], and after that launch out on the 'new foreign policy' about which the Government Press have been hinting for some time . . ." it had said. That this warning should be shown to be an accurate forecast of Government intentions so soon after its earnest repudiation by the Tory candidates exacerbated public feeling. The people in Britain felt they had been bamboozled because their idea of public morality was outraged. In retrospect it is easy to pass judgment and say that within two years they would become conditioned to the acceptance of almost any redistribution of territory under threats of war, and to consider the partition of countries as one of the normal methods of resolving an international problem; that in twenty years they would even welcome such a solution. But at that time, Spain and Austria were still free, India was still the Empire's brightest jewel, and any wind of change in Africa was a mere zephyr.

It was some days before Sir Samuel Hoare heard of the leakages. On his first venture out on to the ice near St. Moritz, a sudden attack of vertigo caused him to fall in the middle of a turn, knocking him unconscious and leaving him with a badly fractured nose. He was ordered to rest by his Swiss doctor, and it was some days before he was able to fly back to England. There, as the clamor mounted, the Cabinet's brave resolve to stand by the Foreign Secretary, accept collective responsibility for the peace plan, and face the music together was already weakening. After two damaging debates in the House of Commons, by the time Hoare got back to London on December 16 they were losing their nerve. Baldwin called to see him in bed at his house in Cadogan Gardens on December 17 with an assurance that "We all stand together." But after a Cabinet meeting that evening,

Neville Chamberlain was sent to Cadogan Gardens with a message instructing Sir Samuel that he must publicly recant on the Hoare-Laval proposals—admit that they were bad, and withdraw them. The Cabinet had decided that the Foreign Minister should be made the scapegoat; someone had to be sacrificed, and Hoare seemed best suited to the role.

The first signs of trouble, suggesting that a sacrificial lamb would be necessary, had come during the afternoon of December 10. Rising at the end of a debate, during which the Government had been accused of selling the Ethiopians down the river, Baldwin gave his version of what had happened. The British Government, he said, had first learned of the Hoare-Laval plan on the night of December 8. He had not yet had time to read the newspapers, but "he had been told by those who had studied the original proposals and the Press reports that there were considerable differences in the matter of substance." This was indeed true, although not in the way Baldwin implied. For once, the newspapers erred on the side of moderation and their version of the plan actually underestimated the extent of the concessions to Italy. Not that this was important; what most people resented was the fact that Italy had been given anything at all. In the words of the *Manchester Guardian* of December 12, the Prime Minister "knew nothing, had heard nothing, had read nothing and said nothing." It was in this speech that the historic statement which has since been associated with Baldwin's name was uttered. "My lips," he said, "are sealed." * If, he continued, he were able to confess the secrets in his breast, he could make such a case that "not a man would go into the Lobby against us." Such a piquant observation was bound to lead to speculation, and the consensus has been that what Baldwin had in mind was the opinion of the Chiefs of Staff that Britain's armed services were in no fit state to go to war. Although Baldwin himself never unsealed his lips in public, one explanation which was recorded in 1948 has been reproduced by his son:

* After this, David Low invariably portrayed Baldwin without the cherry-wood pipe but with sticking plaster across his mouth. The most famous caricature is that which shows him standing in front of the League's corpse, muttering through the plaster, "You know you can trust me!"

. . . This remark brought a quick smile; he remembered the context of that immediately and said: "Ah yes, that was another stupid thing to say. I have said many stupid things. But what of course I meant was that I was morally sure that Laval had been bought by Mussolini, and I could not very well say that to the House. After all, we had to remain on good terms with the French. . . ."[7]

Whatever lay behind his words does not disguise the fact that Baldwin's image as the honest, well-intentioned, pipe-smoking squire received a dent from which it never really recovered. Try as he might to plead for the benefit of the doubt, or to pretend that the newspapers had got the story all wrong, or were a trifle inaccurate, the public was not prepared to listen. Somebody had to go and many Conservatives thought that it should have been the Prime Minister.

Prior to Baldwin's explanation to Parliament, Eden had spoken at some length in the debate. In defending the Government's support of the Hoare-Laval plan as the least bad of several alternatives, he attempted to shift some of the responsibility on the League. "The Coordination Committee," he said, "had specifically approved of attempts to find a basis of discussion between the two parties." Consequently, "with the knowledge and approval of our fellow-members of the League . . . negotiations were started"; "clearly that [the formulation of the plan] was the course which the League approved; that was the course which we followed." [8] This was true; both Hoare and Eden had been told in private of approval at Geneva for attempts to find a settlement. Furthermore, at a meeting of the Coordination Committee, Chairman Vasconcellos said—after other delegates had expressed views in this sense—that he felt he was speaking for the Committee when he said that members of the League hoped that a basis for a just settlement would be found. However, "I am bound to say," Eden continued, "that to me that [a search for conciliation] seems an eminently wise and reasonable course." Switching his line of argument, the Minister for League of Nations Affairs continued, "If the plan is contrary to the principles of the Covenant, then it is for the League to say so. . . ." The plan was only a "basis for negotiation"; if the League expressed disapproval, "we shall make no complaint. We shall be ready to accept their judgement, just as we have been ready to accept our part in this very unwelcome task." On the face of it, the statement was all very plausible. But underlying its logic was a desire to gain time—a few days, during which it was hoped the parties to the dispute might accept the proposals.

As the League's popular champion in Britain, Eden was in a delicate position, to say the least. He did not expect the proposals to be accepted and if they failed—as indeed they did—someone would have to be offered up as the sacrificial lamb. Baldwin cut the sorriest figure and would have made the better meal. But it was easier to throw out a Foreign Secretary than a Prime Minister. However, if Hoare went, his replacement would have to be acceptable to the British public, and Eden's much publicized personality and popularity—deriving principally from his previous activities at Geneva—made him an ideal choice. Moreover it could be argued that Eden was less involved in the intrigues over Italy than any other member of the Cabinet. It was true that as a member of the Cabinet he had his share of responsibility. But illness had prevented him from going to Stresa, where there had been so much left unspoken which he might have said; he had not wanted to go to the Foreign Office to serve as a second-in-command, he had not relished his mission to Rome, and he had been uneasy about Hoare's September speech at Geneva. Viewed in this light, Eden was merely the victim of the circumstances in which he came to power.

Hopes that the situation might be saved by Ethiopia's acceptance of the Hoare-Laval plan were quickly dissipated. On the evening of December 10, after Baldwin had sealed his lips, he opened them again sufficiently to utter what was a half-truth. *So far as he knew*, no communication of any kind had gone to Rome or Addis Ababa. At the time his assurance was given— 9:47 P.M.—it was indeed true that the official telegrams had not actually been dispatched. But a little over an hour later two identical telegrams conveying the terms of the plan were sent from the Foreign Office to Sir Eric Drummond in Rome and Sir Sidney Barton in Addis Ababa.* An hour later, a third telegram in-

* According to Robert Dell (*The Geneva Racket 1920-1939* [see Bibliog-

structed Sir Sidney Barton to try to persuade Haile Selassie to bow to the inevitable.

> London, 10th December 1935.
>
> My immediately preceding telegram. You should use your utmost influence to induce the Emperor to give careful and favourable consideration to these proposals and on no account lightly to reject them. On the contrary I feel sure that he will give further proof of his statesmanship by realising the advantage of the opportunity of negotiation which they afford, and will avail himself thereof.[9]

Whether Barton's influence would have made any difference to what happened is extremely doubtful. A report of the plan cabled from Paris had reached Addis Ababa even before the details had been published in Europe. On the morning of December 10, this was in the hands of Mr. Colson, the Emperor's American adviser, and no doubt it was Colson's advice to the Emperor that largely contributed to Ethiopia's prompt rejection of the plan. Although he shared the Emperor's faith in the League, Colson was an honest, hardheaded American, possessing a full measure of his countrymen's distrust in British imperialism, and he saw the plan as a delaying tactic designed to avert the oil embargo. Even if this were discounted, the terms of .the proposals were completely unacceptable, and a statement was drafted in the Emperor's name:

> We desire to state, with all the solemnity and firmness which the situation demands today, that our willingness to facilitate any pacific solution to this conflict has not changed, but that the act by us of accepting even in principle the Franco-British proposals would be not only a cowardice towards our people, but a betrayal of the League of Nations and of all the States which have shown that they could have confidence up to now in the system of collective security. These proposals are in the negation and abandonment of the principles upon which the League of Nations is founded. For Ethiopia this would consecrate the amputation of her territory and the disappearance of her independence for the benefit of the State which has attacked her. . . .

---

raphy], p. 130), these telegrams were drafted on December 6/7 and initialed by Eden in Hoare's absence on the 8th or 9th.

The vital interest of Ethiopia is in question and for us this takes precedence over every other consideration: but in reaching our decision we are not unmindful that the security of other peaceful, weak, or small States will be made doubtful if such a recompense should be accorded to a State already condemned as the aggressor, and at the expense of the State victim of its aggression.

Probably the Ethiopian refusal made no practical difference, for it was already clear that the Hoare-Laval plan had been stillborn. But as the meeting to discuss the oil embargo had been fixed for December 12 and the proposals were not officially rejected until the tenth, the former was bound to be affected by the latter. Thus, when the Committee of Eighteen assembled at Geneva, the Hoare-Laval plan inhibited the adoption of any boycott on oil. After Laval had proposed that the Anglo-French proposals—which were described as "suggestions of a preliminary nature"—should be examined by the League Council, and Eden had expressed a hope that it would make negotiations possible, the Committee agreed to adjourn. The result was that the oil embargo was deferred yet again—this time indefinitely.

The adjournment put an end to any effective action against Italy. The scheme of sanctions, recommended by the Coordination Committee and adopted or partially adopted by the countries who believed or half-believed in them, lingered on nominally for several months. But with the one sanction that might have embarrassed Italy deferred, the Duce was left with a free hand to advance in Ethiopia. With the adjournment in December, the Hoare-Laval plan really was dead, and when the League Council met again on the 12th, its corpse was quietly interred. Eden, representing Britain, opened the ceremony by saying that the proposals of December 8 had been made solely to ascertain the views of the two parties to the dispute and the League. If they did not fulfill that purpose, then Britain wanted to have nothing more to do with them. Laval, for France—after reminding the Council that they had a duty to go on trying to find a means of conciliation—said that his country also wanted to drop the plan. Everything was conducted with the utmost decorum and only the Ethiopian representative introduced a controversial note with a violent denunciation of the plan as a "complete and flagrant negation" of the proposals made by the Committee of Five on September 18. Finally, the doleful proceedings concluded with the adoption of a resolution thanking the representatives of Britain and France for their efforts on behalf of peace, and a polite intimation that the matter could now be dropped.

Italy was not present at the session, but the silence the Duce had maintained for over a week was broken that day. In the hope that the plan might have been accepted as a basis of discussion, he had waited. But as soon as he appreciated that there was no chance of this materializing he too denounced it. Mussolini was not going to lose face by allowing it to be thought that he was disappointed at their failure, and—according to Aloisi—he did not like proposals anyway. For this reason his belated response was couched in vitriolic terms. ". . . The war which we have begun on African soil," he thundered in a speech on December 18, "is a war of civilization and liberation. It is the war of the poor, of the disinherited, of the proletariat. Against it is ranged the front of conservatism, of selfishness, of hypocrisy. Against this front also we have engaged in our stern struggle and we will carry it through to the end." [10]

The Duce's speech sealed the tomb, and Baldwin told Parliament the following day that the Hoare-Laval plan was dead and buried. Public opinion in Britain had condemned it, Ethiopia had sentenced it, and the men at Geneva had executed it. Nevertheless the plan may be considered to have served a purpose, for although war in Ethiopia had not been brought to an end, the threat to peace in Europe appeared to have diminished.

The result was not accomplished without casualties, however. In France, Laval—whom his critics were now openly called "Lavalini"—had suffered a crippling blow. His policy of trying to pursue a middle course that would alienate neither Britain nor Italy had failed, and his descent from power was inevitable. Criticism over the way he was handling matters had been mounting in the Chamber for some time. His "poverty decrees," his failure to have the Franco-Russian Pact ratified, and now his surrender to the aggressor, encouraged the Radical Socialists to join forces with the extreme Left, before the elections, due in May, were upon them. Paul Reynaud from the Right and Léon Blum from the Left both resigned in December, and when five Radical-Socialist ministers followed a month later, the Ninety-ninth Government of the Third Republic was at an end. Laval retired to sulk in the French political wilderness for four years, and was seldom seen in the Senate. He was not finished; French politicians rarely are finished until they are dead. But when he returned to power, the Germans he feared were in Paris and the Italians he favored were in Provence.

Meanwhile in Britain the furore had risen to such a pitch by December 15 that it was clear someone would have to be thrown overboard quickly if the Government was to survive. The responsibility was clearly that of the Cabinet as a whole and the Prime Minister in particular. But to Baldwin the National Government had a divine mission, and his prime duty was to remain in office. Although he might be reluctant to throw over a loyal colleague, if the only way of redeeming the Government's sins was by sacrificing the Foreign Secretary, then he was prepared to do so. Personal loyalties do not count for much in political life, and as long as there was a public bloodletting it could be arranged for the victim to be quietly reinstated in some other post when the tumult and the shouting had ceased.*

The final debate, when the dismal explanations were made and the scapegoat exposed to the House of Commons, took place on December 19. Of the two chief culprits in the Government, the apologia of the resigning Foreign Secretary was reckoned to be more dignified and more acceptable than that of the Prime Minister. In one of those scenes which are so dear to the hearts of journalists, Hoare attempted to explain the circumstances of his resignation. He had acted as he thought for the best; it had been his lifelong ambition to be Foreign Secretary and when it was realized, disappointment had followed. He had tried to do his

---

* Which is what happened. After six months of martyrdom and a recuperative trip to Switzerland, Sir Samuel reappeared in the Cabinet as First Lord of the Admiralty—his health, broken heart, and career apparently mended.

duty, and it was for posterity to judge whether he had been wise or not; if his career was finished, he had no regrets. It was an emotional address, restrained at first but ending in tears. Because of this, perhaps, his sincerity seemed more striking. Cromwell is said to have been given to weeping: Churchill was also prepared to shed tears if need be, and on the right occasions tearfulness can be remarkably effective. This was one such occasion.

Yet the emotional atmosphere did not detract from the importance of what the Foreign Secretary had to say, and the central theme of his discourse shed a great deal of light on the attitude of Baldwin's Government. After referring to the League's responsibilities in regard to sanctions, he said:

It seemed clear that, supposing an oil embargo were to be imposed and that the non-member States took an effective part in it, the oil embargo might have such an effect on the hostilities as to force their termination. Just because of the effectiveness of the oil sanction, provided that the non-member States took an effective part in it, the situation immediately became more dangerous from the point of view of Italian resistance. *From all sides we received reports that no responsible Government could disregard that Italy would regard the oil embargo as a military sanction or an act involving war against her.* [Author's italics.]

After defending the Hoare-Laval proposals he went on to speak about the possible annihilation of Ethiopia as a sovereign state.

I have been terrified with the thought . . . that we might lead Abyssinia to think that the League could do more than it can do, that in the end we should find a terrible moment of disillusionment in which it might be that Abyssinia would be destroyed altogether as an independent State. I have been terrified at that position, and I could not help thinking of the past, in which, more than once in our history, we have given—and rightly given—all our sympathy to some down-trodden race, but because we had been unable to implement and give effect to those sympathies, all that we had done was to encourage them, with the result in the end their fate was worse than it would have been without our sympathy.

In the light of what was to happen—first in Ethiopia, later in Poland—these words were more prophetic than could have been

realized at the time. It was not that Haile Selassie might have
been better off in a position analogous to that of the Khedive of
Egypt under Britain or of the Bey of Tunis under France, Hoare
could have argued. The real question was whether the Ethiopian
people would have been spared the horrors of war and derived
benefits from peaceful Italian economic activity in their country.
One thing is certain: if Ethiopia had been partitioned in accordance with the Hoare-Laval plan, it would not have been long
before Italy gobbled up the whole country. In a speech at Ponti-
nia—before Baldwin had announced his intention of withdrawing the proposals—Mussolini had declared that "we shall not
send the flower of our manhood to distant lands if we are not
sure that they will be protected by the Tricolor." Once the Italian flag was flying over Tigre and Ogaden the Emperor would
have been in no position to resist further incursions. Having accepted partition he would have had little hope of refusing Italian
demands on his greatly diminished kingdom. By accepting the
Hoare-Laval proposals he would have gained a brief respite, but
the "moment of disillusionment" to which Hoare had referred
was inevitable. If he wanted to retain his throne and defend a
principle, Haile Selassie had no option but to reject them.

Hoare's excuse for postponing the oil embargo was an interesting sidelight on his defense of the peace plan. If Italy retaliated
—as Mussolini had said she would—and Britain were attacked,
he reasoned, the inevitable result would be the breakup of the
League of Nations. Even if Britain came off best, it was hardly
likely that its members would be willing to champion the
League's cause once they had seen the risk they ran in doing so.
This was a novel way of looking at the principle of collective
security, and presupposed that Britain would have been left to
face the music on her own. This was obviously what was in
Hoare's mind when he said, "There is the British Fleet in the
Mediterranean, there are the British reinforcements in Egypt, in
Malta and Aden. *Not a ship, not a machine, not a man has been
moved by any other member State* [author's italics]." Obviously
there was a risk of this nature, and it disclosed a fundamental
weakness of the League. The States who were members of the

League were, politically and economically, nationalist entities. When confronted with a challenge to League authority, it was natural that each Government should weigh the risks of war to its sectional and national interests before considering its obligation to international responsibilities. Such considerations—not the spirit of collective security—were the main factors influencing their outlook, according to Hoare's theory. But events were to show that the League failed because it remained passive when faced with a crucial issue, and the consequences spelled out by Hoare never came about because no action was taken. The smaller Powers lost faith in the League because Britain and France failed them. After being cajoled into sacrificing their own interests in order to follow an Anglo-French policy, they suddenly found that they had been left in the lurch because it suited Britain and France to give way to Italy.*

In the United States, where the Roosevelt administration had been working for American cooperation with the League, there was a feeling of revulsion against the whole business. The Hoare-Laval plan was seen as evidence of duplicity—a sure sign that Britain and France were concerned more with their own interests and the preservation of the balance of power in Europe than with international justice—and a discordant chorus of objections rose to thwart the State Department bill dealing with neutrality. Congress denied Roosevelt the powers to restrain American trade and the only thing the President could do was to continue to appeal to American businessmen to limit their trade with Italy and Ethiopia. Under the circumstances this proved to be of little value.

Thus, at the beginning of 1936, the outlook for Italy's venture was distinctly promising. An objection had been recorded at

---

* The correspondent of *The New York Times,* Clarence Streit, reported from Geneva that the British Government, after getting the Governments of some of the smaller States to promise their support, had asked them to declare their view to Mussolini. The news of the Hoare-Laval plan "astounded them and stopped them in their tracks." At the same time they also learned that the British Government had already revealed their intent to Mussolini. "This greatly increased their bitterness for it seemed to them that Britain had dangerously exposed the weak States to Italy's future wrath and had then deserted them." (*The New York Times,* December 22, 1935.)

Geneva but it was clear that nobody was going to take any drastic action. The countries to whom the League looked for leadership—Britain and France—were obviously not going to do anything effective, and after the sound and fury of protestations in December, public opinion in both countries returned to its concern with domestic issues. The wave of feeling against the Hoare-Laval plan gradually receded, and although the Italian war was no less unpopular, people in Europe were growing tired of it. Feelings of disgust mingled with cynicism bred indifference, and barely six months were to pass before it was seen that all the agitation in 1935 had not saved a single yard of Ethiopian territory. By then the issue of the war—like most wars—had been decided in the field.

CHAPTER 12

War in Earnest

There is only one form of war; to wit, the attack of the enemy . . . The combat is the single activity in war.

CLAUSEWITZ

One direct effect of sanctions was to precipitate a change in the character of the war in Ethiopia. In November 1935 Mussolini was uncertain of what would happen if the campaign was allowed to drag on. To get it over and done with, the tactically unenterprising De Bono had to make way for the professionally competent Badoglio. Administratively De Bono had accomplished a good deal, but strategically very little. The retiring Commander in Chief was a humane individual who believed the Italians had gone to Ethiopia not merely to conquer the country but to civilize its savages, and he would have preferred to dispense with the fighting. But if De Bono, the political soldier, did not want battle, his successor, the professional soldier, did.

Like most of the Italian generals, Pietro Badoglio had been trained in traditional methods. War to him was smashing the enemy, and that was why he had been sent to replace De Bono. Badoglio, sixty-five years old, had taken part in the last phase of the Adowa campaign, though not in the actual battle; he had

fought in Libya, at Caporetto, and had worked out the plan for
the battle at Vittorio Veneto. (Had he been given his head, he
would even have fought the Fascists in 1922.)* With such a
background it is all the more to his credit that he was able to
adapt his ideas to the modern techniques of war which the airplane, the tank, and mustard gas put into his hands—although he
was helped by the fact that his opponents were also traditional-
ists and were thinking in terms of spear-power long after Badoglio had ceased to assess a situation in numbers of bayonets. But
this does not detract from the fact that he learned quickly, and
because he was a man of decision, a man who preferred action to
routine, the reputation Badoglio already enjoyed was consolidated by his success in this campaign.

Arriving in Eritrea toward the end of November 1935, Badoglio was not impressed with what he saw. The Italian army in the
north was strung out across the front; a guerrilla war had started
in the Tembien massif—the great bastion stretching between
Aksum and Adigrat—and the Regia Aeronautica was busy
bombing Ethiopian troop concentrations wherever they appeared. With a third of the campaigning season already spent,
changes would have to be made if he was to annihilate the Ethiopian forces and bring the war to a speedy conclusion. And so,
after publicly proclaiming his entire agreement with his predecessor's plans, Badoglio set about transforming them.

That changes were in the air quickly became apparent to the
host of foreign journalists haunting his headquarters. Summoned
to a conference on November 29, they were told that a rigid
censorship would be established forthwith. Because the war was

---

* As Chief of Staff in 1922, Badoglio was sent for by Signor Facta, the Prime
Minister. Mussolini had sworn to seize power and Facta wanted his advice. Badoglio assured the Italian Cabinet that he could settle the Fascists' hash very
quickly. "After five minutes of firing," he told Facta, "the whole of Fascism will
collapse." This drew a vehement response from Mussolini: "We do not believe
that the vile intentions of General Badoglio will materialize," he wrote. When
the March on Rome was actually being organized Badoglio was sent for by the
King and asked for his advice on the maintenance of public order. "Sir," said
Badoglio, "give me a single battalion of the Royal Carabineers and I will drive
these upstarts into the sea." Mussolini never forgave the man who held him in
such disdain. But because of Badoglio's reputation he could not eliminate him.
And in 1935 the Duce needed his military skill.

a national war, units would not be mentioned by name; in fact no names—not even that of Badoglio himself—were to appear in any messages. Moreover no journalist would leave the precincts of Asmara without special permission. Such action precluded any wind of Badoglio's intentions reaching the outside world, but it also lessened the news value of the journalists' dispatches from the front, and from then on the newspaper contingent with the Italian Northern Army steadily dwindled. Strict censorship also imposed a serious delay on word of Badoglio's reorganization and redeployment getting out of the theater. Starved of news from Italian sources, the foreign newspapers culled most of their information from reports written by their correspondents on the Ethiopian side, and many people were misled into thinking Ethiopia was fighting back more successfully than was actually the case. Only one or two of the hundred or so journalists who had rushed out to Ethiopia at the beginning of the war ever caught more than a glimpse of the actual fighting. Few got any farther north than Dessie or east of Jijiga, and many of them returned home after a few months. As with their colleagues on the Italian side, the official press releases in Addis Ababa were the principal source of information for those who remained. More often than not these were completely farfetched—exaggerated not because they were necessarily intended to boost Ethiopia's cause but simply because lack of communications often made it impossible for the Emperor's Government to know what was happening four hundred miles away. (Although it must be added that where facts were lacking, the Ethiopian officials tended to use their imagination, while the curt Italian communiqués, although they sometimes omitted unpleasant news, appear to have been accurate as far as they went.)

Badoglio's innovations took the war into a completely new key. In the first phase of the campaign, which lasted until December 15, there was practically no fighting. After that the war can be divided into two periods, each of which roughly corresponded to a third of the campaigning season. During the second phase, from mid-December until March, Badoglio moved comparatively slowly, taking care to avoid Italian casualties. The

final phase, which brought the campaign to its inevitable conclusion in May, was fought under the realization that there was
really nothing to stop the war being finished quickly provided
the risk of a few Italian casualties was accepted.

During the first two weeks of December there was a lull in
the operations along the whole of the front. The Italians were
busy reorganizing before embarking on the second phase of the
war, while the Ethiopians were not yet in a position to give battle. It was in this period that Badoglio, who had moved his headquarters forward to Adigrat, decided on two important changes
of policy: first, the Regia Aeronautica, whose missions up to that
time had been confined to reconnaissance flights and close cooperation with the troops, was ordered to extend the scope of its
targets. From then on the bombers would strike at "strategic
centers" as well as tactical targets, in order to deter the Ethiopians from mobilizing and simultaneously to produce a state of
panic among the civilian population. Since "strategic centers"
sounds a somewhat pompous way of describing towns, it must be
added that Ethiopia offered few choice objectives. The country
had no industrial centers, no important road or railway junc-
tions, and no arsenals, the destruction of which would have im-
peded Haile Selassie's war effort. Because of this the Italians
elected a wholesale bombing of everything Ethiopian and in the
process bombs fell on open towns and hospitals. Such tactics
were bound to be denounced as diabolical; they were not unexpected, but because they were new they were especially ugly.*
Moreover Italian attempts to popularize war by publicizing the
exultations of some of the pilots engaged in these activities did
not exactly promote the Duce's boast of a cultural responsibility
in Ethiopia.†

* In the days of Rhodes and Jameson, aircraft and mustard gas were unknown. But in the conquest of Rhodesia what was a new weapon then, the
machine gun, was equally denounced as diabolical.

† In 1936 Vittorio Mussolini, the twenty-year-old son of the Duce, published
a book *Voli sulle Ambe* (*Flights over the Amba Mountains*) which he hoped
would "serve as a handbook for future efforts." There was one occasion, he said,
when "closed in a circle of fire, about 5,000 Ethiopians suffered a bad end. It
was hellish; the smoke rose to spectacular heights," and "I still remember the
effect I produced on a small group of Galla tribesmen massed around a man in

Badoglio's second policy change was to disarm the civilian population and to impose new and stringent restrictions on the activities of Eritreans and Ethiopians alike. While he was preparing for what he hoped would be a second battle of Vittorio Veneto, it was natural that he should resent any need to look over his shoulder. But by this time distinct rumblings were coming from behind the line. The pre-1935 population of Eritrea was estimated to be about 600,000 and of this nearly a third were non-Italian Tigreans; as Eritreans and Tigreans were of the same ethnic stock, even the other 400,000 had much in common with the subjects of the invaded territory. Furthermore, until Italian troops had started to pour into Eritrea, there were only about 5,000 Italian settlers and there was virtually no racial problem. The population was predominantly black, the Italian Government tolerant, the administration easygoing. Only when the war came did racial differences and sympathy toward Ethiopia start to grow.

The confiscation of the rifles, themselves a status symbol to the tribesmen, was bound to be unpopular. Badoglio considered it necessary because some of the Eritreans were reported to have slipped over to join up with Ras Seyoum. How much substance the rumors contained was difficult to assess. Undoubtedly discontent abounded, and apart from the resentment over the disarmament decrees this may be attributed to a number of causes. First of all, reports of Tigrean villages being bombed and burned, in accordance with Badoglio's new edict, had begun to filter back; as some of the Eritreans had relatives in the region the news was bound to shock them. Secondly, reports of Ethiopian successes also provoked a certain amount of uneasiness. By December, as a result of this measure combined with the slowness of the Italian advance, an increase in banditry, and a few Ethiopian raids into the conquered parts of Tigre, many Eritreans were beginning to wonder if they were on the right side. Thirdly, there was the

---

black clothes. I dropped an aerial torpedo right in the center, and the group opened up just like a flowering rose. It was most entertaining." Vittorio's conclusion was that "War certainly educates and ripens, and I recommend it to everybody because I believe it to be the real duty of every man to take part in at least one war."

justifiable belief that the Askaris were being employed as the shock troops, and that their casualties were out of proportion to those suffered by the Italians. Such conjecture led to the bulk of Ras Gugsa's followers deserting and to rumors of thousands of armed Eritreans getting ready to go over to Haile Selassie when his armies started to advance. When the conscription laws were tightened, the women naturally asked why more and more Askaris were wanted. Finally, there was the matter of civil restrictions which increased in severity as the war continued. The Eritreans did not understand the curfew and several were shot for not answering a sentry's challenge. Nor did they appreciate the rising prices resulting from the ever-increasing shortage of supplies, or the restrictions on gathering fuel imposed to keep people from wandering. (As no fuel could be bought, and a permit was needed to collect brushwood on the mountains, this measure led to considerable hardship.)

At the front, Badoglio's appreciation of the military situation in December was that an advance to Makale at that particular time was strategically unsound, as his predecessor had warned the Duce it would be. South of the town, eighty miles from its supply base and at the end of a track which had not yet been converted into a road, Santini's First Army Corps was out on a limb. Sixty miles northwest of Santini, Maravigna's Second Corps, dug in around Adowa, was out on another limb. Between the two main Italian concentrations Pirzio-Biroli's Eritreans sketchily patrolled the broken country of the Tembien, maintaining a tenuous link. No continuous front of the kind which the Italian generals were accustomed to was possible; huge unoccupied gaps existed between the two forward corps, and on their flanks. Through these gaps or around the western flank, it was possible for a daring enemy to strike toward the base and even invade Eritrea itself. And, if the Ethiopians had been able to take advantage of this—either by marching around Santini and cutting the road between Makale and Adigrat, or alternatively by slipping around the western flank and crossing into Eritrea— they would have created chaos. Eventually both operations were attempted but by then the initiative had passed to Badoglio.

January 1935. The British Prime Minister, Ramsay MacDonald, with Sir John Simon (left). *Fox Photos*

Pierre Laval signing the Franco-Italian agreement in Rome—January 7, 1935. *Associated Press*

The British delegation to Stresa. Sir Robert Vansittart is second from the left. *Associated Press*

Mussolini leaving Stresa at the end of the Conference. *Associated Press*

Emperor Menelek II (1844–1913), creator of the modern state of Ethiopia. *Underwood & Underwood, N.Y.*

His Imperial Highness, Haile Selassie I, Emperor of Ethiopia. *Ethiopia Ministry of Information*

Benito Mussolini. *Fox Photos*

Fresh Italian troops depart for Ethiopia. *Brown Brothers*

Massawa, 1935—one of the busiest and filthiest ports in the world. *Underwood & Underwood, N.Y.*

Fascist *Balilla* training for chemical warfare. From the age of six, the Italian male child underwent military training. The *Balilla* program was for ages eight to fourteen. *Underwood & Underwood, N.Y.*

Haile Selassie Gugsa (right hand extended to rifle), photographed in Adigrat wearing Italian-style uniform. *Wide World Photos*

General De Bono, Commander
in Chief of the Italian forces and
Governor of Italian East Africa,
1935. *Fox Photos*

Pietro Badoglio, Marshal of Italy. *Underwood & Underwood,
N.Y.*

An Italian troopship leaving Naples for East Africa—October 20, 1935.
Wide World Photos

Smoke from burning native huts screening Italian soldiers during an attack on the northern front. *Keystone Photos*

An Italian outpost near Makale—November 1935. *Wide World Photos*

ABOVE: Capronis of the *Regia Aeronautica*. *Wide World Photos.* BELOW LEFT: Ethiopian aircraft defense. With no antiaircraft guns, the Ethiopian Army relied on small arms to deter the *Regia Aeronautica*. *Wide World Photos.* BELOW RIGHT: The bombing of Dessie—January 1936. *Underwood & Underwood, N.Y.*

The Imperial Guard, cream of the Ethiopian Army, leaving for the northern front. *Keystone Photos*

Gojjamese chiefs in Addis Ababa. Barefoot, most of them are armed with old French rifles. *Keystone Photos*

One of the military roads which the Italians had to build from Eritrea into the interior of Ethiopia. *Brown Brothers*

Mussolini and the crowds below the Palazzo Venezia on
the night Il Duce announced
the annexation of Ethiopia—
May 10, 1936. ABOVE: *Associated Press* BELOW: *Paul
Popper*

Haile Selassie in exile: ABOVE arriving at Southampton June 3, 1936. *Fox Photos;* BELOW at a garden party arranged by "The Friends of Ethiopia" later that summer. *Underwood & Underwood, N.Y.*

Italian troops marching into the outskirts of Addis Ababa—May 5, 1936.
Underwood & Underwood, N.Y.

Marshal Graziani, Viceroy of Ethiopia, at the Mascal celebrations in
Addis Ababa in November 1936. *Associated Press*

Stanley Baldwin, the British Prime Minister. *Associated Press*

Anthony Eden at Geneva, addressing the League of Nations Assembly. *Associated Press*

At the beginning of December the Emperor's armies were still moving up to the front, while Haile Selassie himself, after a flying visit to Jijiga to "encourage" the Ethiopian troops on the southern front, had established his headquarters in full state at Dessie.* With him were his European chef, his cellar, his Arab horses, and the collection of walking sticks from which he selected a different one daily when he went to church. "At his table four courses of well-cooked food were served," reported the London *Times* correspondent, George Steer. "The Emperor," he continued, "had the gift of appearing at all times, even in the middle of war, completely detached and poised above the melee, pursuing his quiet, rather delicate and well-dressed life, without noting overmuch the noise that surrounded him." And soon the noise was to rise in a crescendo.

On December 6 three squadrons of Italian planes bombed Dessie. According to the Italian reports, the aircraft flew in through heavy antiaircraft fire, and bombs were dropped on buildings clearly used for military purposes, and on large camps outside the town. From Addis Ababa the Ethiopian communiqué asserted that Dessie was undefended and that Red Cross hospitals were among the objectives that had been attacked. (The account in the Ethiopian *Official Liberation Jubilee* booklet contradicts the report issued at the time. The Emperor, it declares "spent a full day with his valiant defenders, operating his anti-aircraft gun, which was a great source of encouragement to the Ethiopian Army.") Whether it was known that the Emperor's headquarters had been established at Dessie or whether reconnaissance merely suggested unusual activity, Dessie invariably figured in the daily target list of the Regia Aeronautica from that date on.

The largest of the Ethiopian armies, that under command of

* He is reported to have "decorated the valiant . . . visited the wounded and comforted them." He also doled out punishments. Dejiak Nasibu, the commander of the Ogaden operations, had sentenced three officers and some of his men to be shot for cowardice in one of the first engagements with the Italians. Haile Selassie commuted the sentences to public flogging. Stripped, the other ranks were given thirty lashes across the back, the officers were flogged across the stomach. Reminiscent of the discipline in Ghengis Khan's armies, such measures were in keeping with the Ethiopian way of life. The Emperor had, after all, shown his humanity by commuting the death sentences.

Ras Mulugeta, had been marching northward and by the second week in December it had reached a point about thirty miles off Makale. There Ras Mulugeta halted and took up a defensive position on the mountain plateau of Amba Aradam, which, with considerable satisfaction, he appears to have regarded as an impregnable stronghold. To get there had taken a long slow march, beset with problems. Apart from the Regia Aeronautica and the natural dilatoriness of the Ethiopians themselves, other problems had delayed the straggling column. Desertions and resistance to the passage of an Amhara army through the Galla country had all added to Mulugeta's difficulties. The Gallas were a warlike and primitive race, antipathetic toward their overlords and sympathetic toward Ras Gugsa. Many of them were more than willing to throw in their lot with the Italians even without the Maria Theresa thalers which the Italians offered as inducement, and old Mulugeta, knowing that they were only awaiting an opportunity to attack his column—and probably not unwilling to settle a few old scores of his own—systematically dealt with each Galla village as he came to it.

In Gojjam, Ras Imru was also having to lash enthusiasm into his vassals, and the fact that he had been able to raise an army of only twelve thousand men from this well-populated area was a measure of local reluctance to obey the Emperor's call to arms. Like the Gallas, the people of this province harbored a grudge and felt that they had ample justification for feeling hostile toward Haile Selassie and the Government in Addis Ababa. Their hereditary chief, Ras Hailu, one of the best fighting chiefs in Ethiopia, had been deposed and sentenced to life imprisonment on suspicion of plotting against the Emperor, and his possessions had been seized for the benefit of the Imperial Court. Ras Imru and his alien officials had been sent to govern the province in Ras Hailu's place, and the consequence had been oppression, rebellions, and impoverishment. In such circumstances it was hardly to be expected that there should be much enthusiasm for the Emperor's cause in Gojjam.

All these troubles, delaying the concentration of the Ethiopian armies against the invaders, gave Badoglio the time he needed to consolidate his position, prepare for the Ethiopian attack he expected, and resume the offensive after it had been repulsed. The new Commander in Chief set about the task with vigor, and by the middle of December he had strengthened his position and done something toward closing the gap between Adowa and Makale. Reinforcements and fresh formations from Italy enabled him to redeploy the three existing corps and form a substantial reserve. When this was effected the situation was much improved—although Badoglio still had cause for anxiety. Air reconnaissance kept him informed of the progress of the Ethiopian armies toward the front, but their exact intention remained hidden and he was as yet unable to assess their military worth.

The second phase of the war opened on December 15 when, at the head of about three thousand warriors, Ras Imru crossed the Takkaze river at a ford about thirty miles southwest of Adowa. From the ford, a track to Adowa ran back through a deep gorge, and about a mile from the river an Italian outpost of an irregular Eritrean battalion barred the approach to the town. Ras Imru attacked and after a token fight the Italian troops retreated up the gorge, along which a squadron of light tanks was trundling up to their assistance. However, during the Italian withdrawal another of Ras Imru's columns had crossed the Takkaze farther down the river and had made a wide detour to cut in behind the Italians at the far end of the gorge. Sandwiched between two Ethiopian forces in country admirably suited to the Ethiopians' ideas of warfare, the Italians extricated themselves only with great difficulty. Unable to maneuver in the narrow gorge, the tanks were either captured or put out of action. Warriors, brandishing their swords, rushed up to them from behind, and either scrambled on top to prise open the turrets or levered off the rubber-shod steel tracks with metal bars. The crew of one tank was captured, and the men concerned probably owed their lives to the startled enthusiasm of the deliriously triumphant Ethiopians at the Italian commander's shout in Amharic: "Long Live Haile Selassie. Christ is risen!" With three others, they were the only Italians taken prisoner by the Ethiopians in the whole campaign. (Lodged in the civil jail in Addis Ababa, all five were released to the custody of the French Ambassador when the Emperor fled from the capital.)

Tactically this was a minor action; although Italian casualties were relatively heavy, only a handful of Italian troops had been engaged.* But strategically it was of marked importance, since Ras Imru had shown for the first time that the Italians, for all their modern equipment, were not invincible. In Addis Ababa the battle was hailed as a decisive victory, and from Dessie the Emperor signaled his other commanders, suggesting that they might well take a lesson from Ras Imru's book. Spurred on by this admonition, Ras Seyoum now decided to take the offensive, and twenty-four hours after the news of the success at the gorge Italian air reconnaissance reported about five thousand Ethiopians† advancing toward Abi Addi, the chief town of the Tembien and the junction of four caravan routes—running north to the heart of the Tembien, west to the Takkaze, south through the vast region of Saloa, and east toward Gheralta. Four Eritrean battalions supported by several batteries of guns and a squadron of tanks were defending Abi Addi, and when Ras Seyoum's men launched a frontal attack in traditional style on the evening of December 18 they were hurled back. While the Ethiopians licked their wounds and prepared for another assault, reinforcements consisting of four Eritrean battalions were rushed up to the Italians, and a vigorous counterattack supported by aircraft and artillery was made on the twenty-second. Fighting con-

---

* Italian casualties were 9 officers, 22 Italians, and 370 Askaris killed. The Italian estimate of Ethiopians killed in the same action was 500; this was probably grossly exaggerated.

† In the Italian accounts of the campaign the figure of 5,000 appears with monotonous regularity. By inference it can be taken that the Ethiopian strength was unknown but that a large number of warriors were involved. Unfortunately no information from Ethiopian sources exists. The Ethiopian forces were not organized on orthodox lines; no war diaries were kept; there were no casualty returns in the accepted sense. Ethiopia was inarticulate enough before the Italians conquered the country, and after that many witnesses who might have provided useful information were, at best, prevented from expressing their opinion, at worst, exterminated. Knowledge of the conditions under which the Ethiopians fought has had to be acquired from secondhand accounts. Of the foreigners serving in Haile Selassie's army only a few—like Colonel Konovaloff, Wahib Pasha, and Farouk Bey—were reliable soldiers.

tinued throughout the day, with fierce hand-to-hand struggles taking place—both sides often being so closely locked in combat that the low-flying aircraft were unable to give any close coop-eration to the Italians. Italians and Ethiopians alike suffered heavy casualties and toward the evening Ras Seyoum's troops retired from the field. For some curious reason—perhaps because he had not realized that he had had a success—the Italian com-mander also decided to withdraw, and to Badoglio's annoyance, the Italians evacuated Abi Addi and retired to a position about fifteen miles north of the town. (Badoglio explained his subordi-nate's decision as being "an entirely personal appreciation of the local situation.")[1] By doing so Ras Seyoum's troops were left in possession of an important strategical center, in a position which threatened the lateral communications between Santini in Makale and Maravigna in Adowa.

The Italian war communiqué issued at the time made no mention of the state of affairs, but Badoglio regarded it as a se-vere setback. "This," he wrote, "created a particularly delicate situation of which the enemy might well have taken advantage, had he profited by his greater mobility and his facility for quickly varying his own lines of operation. These aptitudes of his, I may well say at once frankly, were still at this period over-estimated by us, and on them, to a great extent, were based our calculations when attempting to forecast his possible courses of action."[2] Later, when further experience had revealed the weakness of Ethiopian leadership, the incompetence of their higher command, and—most important of all—the lack of coor-dination between the armies, Badoglio was prepared to accept greater risks. For the moment caution ruled his plans, and he re-mained on the defensive to await the arrival of more troops from Italy. Two divisions had been asked for; three were sent, and when these started to arrive at about the end of December, a fourth Army Corps was formed, its mission to protect the right flank from any incursions into Eritrea.

Gas seems to have been used for the first time during Decem-ber, when tear-gas grenades were dropped from bombers on concentrations of Ras Imru's men south of the Takkaze. The

fact that the Hoare-Laval plan collapsed about that time may be
a coincidence, and possibly what motivated Badoglio's decision
to employ it was his determination to use every means at his disposal to smash the Ethiopians. As soon as it was appreciated that
tear gas was ineffective, its use was discontinued and the barrels
of mustard gas that had been shipped into Massawa were
brought up to the airfields. At first the barrels were merely
dropped like bombs; later, to distribute the gas more evenly, and
presumably more economically, sprays were fitted to the aircraft. By spraying the mountainsides flanking his advancing columns with a corrosive dew, Badoglio was able to seal off an avenue and there was no need to picket the heights. In this way gas
substituted for the mountain warfare in which his troops lacked
training, and so may be said to have effected a saving in manpower. Then, by spraying the Ethiopians' avenues of retreat, he
was able to add to the demoralization of the barefoot warriors, to
whom the mystic rain from heaven was appalling evidence of the
overwhelming strength of their enemies.

How much this sensational weapon contributed to the ulti-
mate success of the Italians is difficult to assess. *Gas*, like *napalm*, is
an emotive word; when soldiers are killed and maimed by high-
explosive shells, bombs, or bullets, there is rarely any adverse
comment regarding the weapons used. But the mere mention of
gas invariably creates a public outcry. This is not to suggest that
the use of mustard gas is to be condoned, but few realize that it
does not ordinarily kill. It burns, and only in the unusual cases
when the burns are extremely severe does it cause death. In
Ethiopia the effect on morale was undoubtedly far greater than
the physical damage caused, and this was an important factor
contributing to Badoglio's victory. In the field, Haile Selassie's
troops endured wounds from shell fragmentation, bullets, and
cold steel with a stoicism which few Europeans could equal.
Heavy artillery fire, and being bombed and machine-gunned
from the air they could understand. But mustard gas was different. Barefoot, the Ethiopians were pathetically vulnerable, and
through areas that were thought to have been contaminated by
the dreaded rain from heaven they dared not even run away.

The employment of gas in Ethiopia was roundly condemned and the world recoiled with horror when reports of systematic attacks on Red Cross units by Italian aircraft began to reach Europe. On December 30, 1935, a Swedish Red Cross unit was bombed at Dolo on the south; on the same day an Egyptian ambulance was bombed near Bulale, and five days later an Ethiopian medical unit was destroyed at Daggah Bur. Further attacks were reported during January and February, but the bombing of the British Red Cross camp outside Quoram, a few miles south of Lake Ashangi, on March 4, 1936, appeared to be the most deliberate of all. Red Cross signs were conspicuous, and as the aircraft flew in to make a low-level attack there should have been little doubt in identifying the hospital area.* Not that the Italians ever made a secret of the attack; the contention was that what they had bombed was a false Red Cross unit. As explained † by General Aimone-Cat, the commander of the Italian Air Force in East Africa, a reconnaissance of the Quoram area had been greeted with heavy antiaircraft fire from the Red Cross camp. No action was taken at the time, but when another aircraft returned next day and was fired on again, the Italians were convinced that this was no genuine hospital unit. The result was the bombing attack a few days later by a single aircraft believed to have been piloted by Lieutenant Bruno Mussolini, the elder of the Duce's two sons.

It seems difficult to believe that the Italians should be either so inhuman or so foolish. Probably the explanation is simply that hospital tents were placed so close to legitimate objectives that when these were bombed it was difficult to distinguish between them. Nevertheless it is interesting to quote the opinion of George Martelli, the Rome correspondent of the (London) *Morning Post.*

It is generally assumed that the Italian motive in destroying the unit was to eliminate European witnesses in the use of poison gas. Dr. Melly and his companions had been treating gas cases at the rate of a

---

* John Melly, a young British doctor, had raised the volunteer unit concerned. His account is contained in *John Melly of Ethiopia* (see Bibliography, Nelson and Sullivan).

† To Herbert Matthews, the correspondent of *The New York Times.*

hundred a day, and it was evidently undesirable from the Italian point
of view that they should continue to accumulate such damaging evidence. And yet short of killing every white member of the unit,
which was unlikely, it was impossible to prevent the truth from coming out, so that the commonly accepted explanation is not really very
plausible. It seems more probable that the raid was just a sheer piece
of "frightfulness" with the hatred of the British as an additional incentive.[3]

Various excuses and explanations for these breaches of the rules
of war were subsequently advanced both by the Italians themselves and their apologists. The Ethiopians were accused of various atrocities including the use of dumdum bullets and the mutilation of the wounded, and the Red Cross emblem was said to
have been used to protect military stores. In support of this thesis
Evelyn Waugh pointed out that a red cross was a common sign
in Ethiopia, denoting among other things a brothel.[4] Without
question the Italians meant to appear ruthless, for they wanted to
finish the campaign quickly before sanctions could make themselves felt. So perhaps after all it may be significant that the terrorization policy only started after the rejection of the Hoare-
Laval proposals. Militarily Badoglio would wish to employ every
means to his hand; politically some of these means might not
have been acceptable before the issue was forced at Geneva.

CHAPTER 13

The Decisive Battles

The fighting forces of Italy, whose valour was proved in the Great War and proved again in this great enterprise, are today second to none. With such soldiers Italy can dare anything.

BADOGLIO

As long as the Ethiopians held the wild and mountainous Tembien region, Badoglio was not prepared to undertake any further advance. Before the march south could be resumed, the forces of Ras Seyoum and Ras Kassa now ensconced in this thickly wooded region would have to be evicted; while they remained, there was always the danger of their cutting his lines of communication between Makale and Hauzien. Reports that reinforcements had been filtering through to the region seemed authentic, and by the middle of January Italian Intelligence estimated that there were about thirty thousand warriors in and around Abi Addi. If they moved north it was possible that they might be able to force a wedge between Adowa and Makale; alternatively, if they moved eastward, Makale might be surrounded, and as it was known that the Ethiopians attached great importance to the recapture of Seyoum's old capital, it was thought that they would opt for this course. Before they could act Badoglio decided to seize the initiative.

The operation which followed was conducted in two successive phases. On January 19, 1935, the Third Corps* moved down into the zone between Mulugeta's army in front of Makale and that of Ras Kassa centered on Abi Addi. The intention was to block the routes by which Mulugeta could reinforce Kassa, and to cover the deployment of the Italian troops used in the second phase of the operation. This began on the twentieth, when the Eritrean Army Corps advanced to attack Kassa's flank along the high east-west ridge; as usual the Askaris had been selected to carry out the most dangerous part of the operation. Concurrent with the Third Corps attack, the reinforced Blackshirt garrison that had retired from Abi Addi was to "demonstrate" on Ras Kassa's front. The action which followed, which was to become known as the First Battle of Tembien, lasted four days and was not conclusive. The Askaris advanced along the ridge and attacked according to plan. But after two days of bitter fighting they fell back to their original positions northeast of Abi Addi. Meanwhile the Blackshirts' demonstration had fizzled out; driven back into their trenches they had to fight hard to hold their positions as Ras Kassa's men repeatedly counterattacked. Another division was hurriedly sent up from Makale, and the situation was so serious on the twenty-second that Badoglio was actually considering evacuating Makale and pulling back his main force down the Adigrat road to the Hauzien track junction. However, after another twenty-four hours of heavy fighting the Blackshirts managed to drive off the Ethiopians and on the evening of the twenty-third the action was broken off. But it was a close call, and the end came none too soon for the worn-out men of the Twenty-eighth October Division. Italian losses in killed and wounded—60 officers, 605 Italians, and 417 Eritreans—reflect the bitterness of the conflict, as does the Ethiopian wireless message to Addis Ababa intercepted by the Ital-

---

* Now comprising the Sila and Twenty-third March Blackshirt divisions.

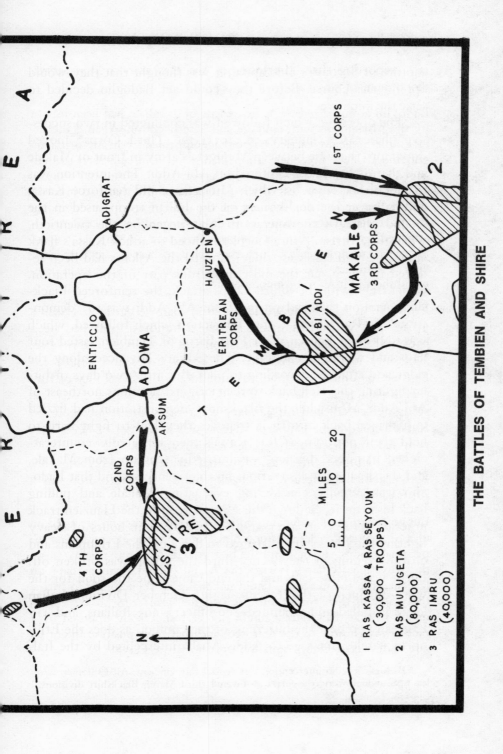

THE BATTLES OF TEMBIEN AND SHIRE

MILES

5 0   5   10   20

1 RAS KASSA & RAS SEYOUM
  (30,000 TROOPS)

2 RAS MULUGETA
  (80,000)

3 RAS IMRU
  (40,000)

ians, reporting that "the losses of the Ras amounted to about 8,000 men." *

Badoglio commented: The first battle of Tembien had been fought by the Abyssinians with courage and determination. Against our attacks, methodically carried out and accompanied by heavy machine-gun and artillery fire, their troops had stood firm, and then had engaged in furious hand-to-hand fighting; or they had moved boldly to counter-attack, regardless of the avalanche of fire that had immediately fallen upon them. Against the organised fire of our defending troops, their soldiers—many of them armed only with cold steel—attacked again and again, in compact phalanxes, pushing right up to our wire entanglements, which they tried to beat down with their curved scimitars. In contrast to so much valour, the Abyssinian command showed itself to be incompetent.[1]

From Addis Ababa the world was told that the battle had been a great victory for Ethiopia, and that a hundred guns had been captured. In actual fact the situation was completely the reverse. Not only had Ras Kassa suffered heavy losses and almost exhausted his ammunition, he was now facing the possibility of further Italian attacks before he could reorganize. At least this was what he feared, and on January 21 a radio intercept reported Kassa as telling the Emperor that he was in danger of being surrounded, and desperately needed reinforcements.

To Badoglio this was additional evidence confirming that Kassa lacked the ability, the background, and the training of a professional soldier:

But no function of command did he [Kassa] exercise; no gleam of an idea of manoeuvre flashed upon him; not even that of employing his personal troops, the best and the best armed. As in the past, so now: the Abyssinian chiefs—fearing the friend behind them perhaps no less than the foe in front—could not make up their minds to throw the whole of their forces into the struggle, preferring to keep them intact, so that their retreat might not be too actively opposed by a race always hostile to the defeated, and that their position might be safe in districts which, originally, were not always loyal.[2]

* Badoglio's radio interception was remarkably efficient. All Ethiopian wireless nets—which were few—were monitored.

Haile Selassie's oft repeated contention that he was "no soldier" was borne out by his performance as Supreme Commander. Shortly after arriving at Dessie one of his first actions had been to replace Ras Mulugeta as Commander of the North Armies with his old favorite, Ras Kassa. War Minister Mulugeta was a brave old man, respected as a leader in battle—a "soldier's soldier." But Ras Kassa, though totally ignorant of the arts of war, was of royal blood and politically sound, so he must command. Not unnaturally Mulugeta was furious, just as Badoglio, hearing the news from a deserter, was delighted. To the Italian Commander in Chief, the Ethiopian Army "whilst revealing greater courage in its individual soldier, displayed great deficiencies in its commander. Most deficient of them all was the Negus—presumptuous but of very modest parts, utterly inept as a commander-in-chief from lack both of culture and character. . . . Ras Seyoum, had personal interests at stake; Ras Kassa was a mere 'churchman'; Mulugeta 'a warrior' but lacking subtlety and skill: such was the Abyssinian High Command." [3]

To Kassa's appeal for reinforcements, both Mulugeta at Amba Aradam and Imru in Gondar turned a deaf ear. The Minister of War said afterward that he never received his superior's message; Imru pleaded that he had to deal with an incipient rebellion. But the real reason why both failed to respond was probably that in their hearts they were hoping Kassa would be defeated and his prestige lowered in the eyes of the Emperor. Meanwhile, Haile Selassie, unable to compel either of his subordinates to go to Kassa's aid, signaled that he had arranged for reinforcements to be sent up "from the troops in the rear"; this meant a six-day march from Quoram, when men from Amba Aradam could have reached Abi Addi in a few hours. Ras Kassa was already concerned at his position and unable to do anything about it, but in the same signal the Emperor warned him to be on his guard "lest the Italians do as they have already been doing in Ogaden, that is, pretend that they have employed all their forces in your direction and then surround Ras Mulugeta's troops from the rear, causing them to lose their positions." [4] This was exactly what Badoglio was planning to do. On January 31, having decided the moment was ripe to take the offensive, Badoglio issued orders for the first phase of what he called "The Great Strategical Battle of the Tigre." His aim was to destroy Ras Mulugeta on Amba Aradam, and in a telegraph to Mussolini he commented:

Ras Mulugeta will either accept battle, or will have to retire south— thus uncovering Ras Kassa's lines of communications and abandoning his strong position. I hope he will decide to fight, in which case it will be an important battle.[5]

It was, in fact, to be the vital battle of the war.

The great mountain mass of Amba Aradam, between the Gabat River in the north and the Maara Plain in the south, is about twelve miles south of Makale. Six miles long and three miles wide, it lies 9,000 feet above sea level athwart the road running south through the great barrier of Amba Alagi to Quoram and Dessie. On the north and east a few mule tracks led to its flat top which was broken and fissured, covered with scrub, and riddled with caves—features which served to provide the Ethiopians with excellent cover from artillery and air attack. To the Italians, the near-vertical cliffs on these sites of the massif seemed incapable of being scaled, and only by an approach up the more gentle slopes on the southern and western faces of the mountain did it seem possible that the stronghold might be breached. From what had been learned during the first battle of the Tembien and his own experience at Adowa, Badoglio reckoned that the fighting qualities of the Ethiopian troops on Amba Aradam and the belligerent character of the stubborn old man who commanded them were such that a tough battle could be expected. However, although he expected the Ethiopians to fight bravely, he guessed that Mulugeta would have organized his defenses to meet a frontal attack, rather than an assault from the flanks and rear; this was the traditional Ethiopian practice. Badoglio also calculated that under artillery fire and air attack the Ethiopians would go to ground; in such circumstances they would not be likely to detect the preparations for an assault from the sides and rear. Experience against Ras Kassa had also shown that by prolonging the battle there was every likelihood that the Ethiopians would exhaust their supplies of ammunition. "For the execution of the operation, the last of which was particularly delicate, I relied above all on the aggressive qualities of our troops," Badoglio reported, "on the employment in manoeuvre of the powerful body of artillery at my disposal, and on the continuous activity of aircraft in successive waves, with bombing and machine-gun fire from a low altitude." *

The battle opened on February 10, 1936, when the First and Third Corps deployed for an assault against the eastern and westerly edges of the plateau. Six Italian divisions in two columns were to encircle the Ethiopian position. The aim of the easterly column—the First Corps (Sabauda and Third January divisions with the Montagna Blackshirt Group)—was to create a diversion which would cause Mulugeta to move the bulk of his troops across to that side of the mountain. When the feint was seen to be working, the Third Corps (Sila and Twenty-third March divisions) was to attack up the western slopes, and while all this was going on the Italian flanks would be guarded on the east by Ras Gugsa's renegade militia (now called the Enderta Bands) and on the west by Eritrean cavalry. In reserve there were three other divisions—the newly arrived Val Pusteria Alpini, the Assietta, and the well-tried First Eritrean Division. As the troops moved up to their starting lines, aircraft and artillery plastered the mountain. The bombardment was so effective that Mulugeta knew nothing about the mass of men moving out to encompass his stronghold. His men "sat in their caves and clefts in the giant's castle, or lay in the trenches which the Italians supposed were constructed for battle. Their whole war life had been one of subjection to the aeroplane. Every cave, hole and trench was there to shelter them from bombs. If one lay very quiet, covered in one's dirty earth-covered shamma, the 'aeroplan' would at last go away and the 'pomps' would cease to fall." ⁶ But the airplanes did not go away and the bombing continued, and at 7:00 A.M. on the morning of February 11, Mulugeta "was pulling on his field boots and wondering how long the Galla would stick these air

* The plateau was raided 546 times in five days. The Italians dropped 396 tons of high explosive and fired 30,000 shells at it.

bombardments, when the whole mountain thundered about his ears. He retired deeper into his cave. Amba Aradam from one end to the other was a cloud of dust. . . . Not a shot was fired from the tremendous Amba. Not a man remained on sentinel. They lay, wrapped head and body . . . like immobilised pools of mercury. . . ." [7]

Unaware of the pincers closing in on them, Mulugeta's men were taken completely by surprise when the Italians launched the feint frontal attack. Rallying, the Ethiopians beat off the attack and sallied out to meet the threat on the eastern flank. When they were beaten back by a hail of artillery fire, Badoglio gave the order for the general assault. By now the two wings of the encircling columns had made contact to the south of the mountain, and the nimble Alpinis were soon scaling the cliffs.

Mulugeta raised a terrible din, all his horn blowers blew and the War Minister himself drew his sword from his side. Messengers ran here and there to set the pools of dirty mercury unrolling. Through the Amba the Ethiopians jumped to their feet, too late, for the first defences were taken. There was no barbed wire for the Italians to pass. After the first trenches there were no second trenches. Rocks and holes everywhere, steep precipices, twisted channels that once carried water, but little deliberately placed to oppose an enemy. It was child's play for the machine gun which rattled merrily into knots of black men, just awakened, and for the hand grenade which cleaned the caves. [8]

As dusk cloaked the scene on the Saturday evening of February 19, 1936, men of the Twenty-third March Division planted the Italian flag on the summit of Amba Aradam. Ras Mulugeta was grateful for the darkness which followed: "Abandoning all his equipment, his uniforms, medals, books, papers, his ceremonial dress, his glory of the civil wars," he fled south before the Italians could close the last avenue of escape. [9] Six thousand Ethiopians lay dead on the battlefield; thousands more were to perish in flight, as aircraft of the Regia Aeronautica harried them with bombs, mustard gas, and machine-gun bullets. Others died from attacks by the savage Azebu Gallas who had been lurking in the

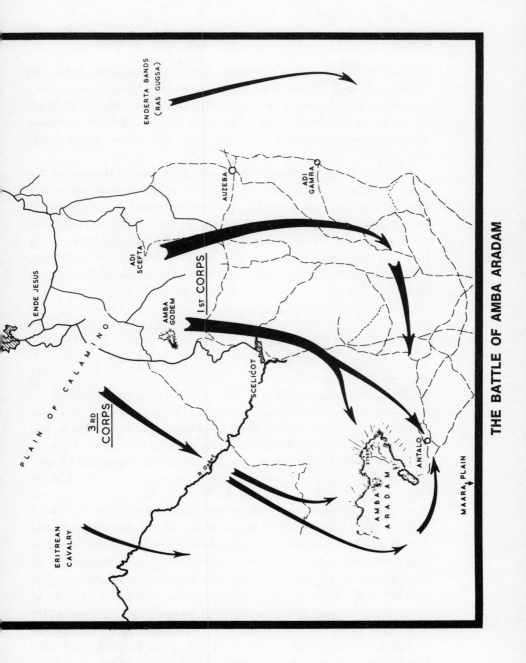

THE BATTLE OF AMBA ARADAM

hills ready to pounce on the beaten and demoralized remnants of Mulugeta's army. The young men of this tribe were not considered warriors or fit to marry until they were able to produce another man's testicles as proof of their valor, and they had been paid, equipped, and encouraged by the Italians to prove their manhood.

The Minister of War, almost exhausted, was struggling on past Amba Alagi with his bodyguard of Shoans, hoping that aircraft would not spot his party; Major Burgoyne, a British officer in charge of a Red Cross unit, was with him. Mulugeta had lost track of his son, and when one of the scouts he had sent out to look for him returned with the news that the boy had been murdered and mutilated by the Galla, the old warrior turned back with vengeance in his heart. It was his last act. The Galla surrounded the little party, and aircraft spotting khaki uniforms in the middle of their allies flew in to machine-gun Shoans and Gallas alike. So Ras Mulugeta, the last of Menelek's commanders and the man who had killed more men with the sword than anyone else in Ethiopia, died. Burgoyne died with him and the Galla stripped and mutilated his body. The battle for Amba Aradam, or Enderta, as it was called, was over. Neither Ras Kassa, Ras Seyoum, nor Ras Imru had done anything to help Mulugeta, and in remaining idle they had sealed their own fate.

According to Badoglio, Italian casualties incurred in the fighting for Amba Aradam amounted to 36 officers, 631 Italians of other ranks, and 145 Askaris. As for the other side, he reported that: "The enemy's losses were enormous—they may be reckoned as amounting in all to about 20,000 men. These losses were due in a large measure to the heavy concentration of artillery fire, and as we were able to prove later, to the relentless action of the air arm in pursuit. The determined guerrilla warfare waged by the local inhabitants against the fugitives during the whole of their retreat also contributed very materially to their casualties." [10] Thus, at a comparatively small cost, the largest of the Ethiopian armies had been destroyed or dispersed beyond recovery. Mulugeta had played directly into Badoglio's hands. Instead of extending the guerrilla war in order to delay the Italian advance until the rains came, he had presented the Italians with an opportunity to stage a set-piece battle which they could not fail to win. The monsoon was the Ethiopian's one true ally, and in failing to recognize this they suffered defeat, for Amba Aradam was soon to be folowed by equally crushing blows in the Tembien, and at the battle of Shire (the western province of Tigre). In flight Mulugeta's levies melted away back to their own villages and homes, every man hoping to save what he could. Mulugeta's army was no longer an organized fighting force, and it never played any further part in future operations.

Meantime, in the Tembien, desertion was beginning to take its toll, and by the middle of February the forces of Ras Kassa and Ras Seyoum grouped around Abi Addi had been reduced from an estimated 200,000 men to about 40,000. During the battle for Amba Aradam the two chiefs appeared to be completely ignorant of what was happening, and an intercepted wireless message from Ras Kassa to the Emperor throws a pathetic light on the Ethiopian Commander's military conceptions. He wanted, he said, a cannon—a single cannon—to blast the Italian position in front of him in order to open the way to a successful offensive. Before the cannon could arrive, his army was following that of Mulugeta in flight to the south.

On February 17, while the Italians were still pursuing the rabble retreating from Amba Aradam, Badoglio initiated the next phase of his offensive. After occupying the dominating position of Amba Alagi,* twenty miles south of Aradam, he was in a position to turn back to deal with the Tembien. Once Kassa and Seyoum were moved, there was nothing to restrain the Italians, and reports that Haile Selassie's empire was beginning to disintegrate were already coming in to Badoglio's headquarters thick and fast. Italian bombs, Italian gas, Italian Maria Theresa thalers, and Italian propaganda were beginning to take effect. In the province of Wallo, adjoining Tigre, bandits roamed the countryside, murdering and pillaging, and government troops sent out to quell their activities had either been defeated or had thrown in their lot with the troublemakers. Gojjam, where a riot

* Where Toselli had fought his last battle forty years before.

had only just been put down, was also seething with discontent. An Italian victory was clearly only a matter of time, but if its fruits were to be garnered before the rains came it was vital that Badoglio should move quickly.

Marching northwest from Amba Aradam across country, the Third Corps reached the ford on the Gheva River, almost due south of Abi Addi, by February 20. Considering that the troops concerned had just taken part in a six-days' battle and the going was extremely difficult, this was a notable feat. During the whole of the march food was supplied to the corps by airdrop in one of the first large-scale air-supply operations. The two Rases were now in an unenviable position, with the Eritrean Army Corps, which had blocked their progress in the first battle of the Tembien, facing them in the north, and the Third Corps cutting off the escape route to the south. As Badoglio deployed his forces for the *coup de grâce*, neither of them relished the prospect of the fight that lay ahead. Ras Kassa had little idea of what to do; Seyoum had never had the stomach for fighting, and as Colonel Konovaloff, who was with them, said: "They [Kassa and Seyoum] knew nothing about modern warfare, nothing at all." [11]

In the early hours of February 27, Pirzio-Biroli's men of the Eritrean Corps started to converge on Abi Addi. On the northern edge of the Ethiopian defense perimeter, Eritrean Askaris and a platoon of Alpini scaled the hill of Work Amba (Golden Mountain), took the garrison by surprise, and slaughtered it to a man. Furious at the loss of what was a key position, the Ethiopians counterattacked again and again. But by the time the first attack was launched the Italians were solidly entrenched behind machine guns, and in each successive attack wave after wave of Kassa's men were mowed down. Meanwhile, on the other side of Abi Addi, the Third Corps was moving slowly forward against negligible resistance. Outnumbered, outmaneuvered, and out of ammunition, the Ethiopians gave up the fight on the third day of the battle; leaving thousands of dead and wounded, they fled westward, pursued as usual by strafing aircraft. At a cost of 34 Italian officers, 359 Italians, and 188 Askaris, all that remained of the armies of Ras Kassa and Ras Seyoum by the end of the first week in March were a few organized detachments and a large disorganized rabble. Discipline broke down; there was no food, and to buy some many of the fugitives bartered their last remaining rounds of ammunition with the Gallas, who promptly used them to shoot other fugitives. Nearly three weeks elapsed before Kassa and Seyoum got back to safety, and it was March 20 before the organized remnants of their depleted force limped back into Aia, about 110 miles north of Dessie, where Haile Selassie was getting ready to make a desperate gamble to save his empire. Prostrating themselves before him, the two chiefs begged the Emperor's forgiveness; they had failed him, they said. "Ras Kassa and Ras Seyoum are with us, but have not a single armed man with them," wrote Haile Selassie to Ras Imru. "An army . . . went to pieces without having suffered serious losses and without any attempt whatever at resistance. This is a grievous matter. Our army, famous throughout Europe for its valour, has lost its name. Brought to ruin by a few traitors, to this it is reduced." * [12]

With the Tembien in their hands, only the army of Ras Imru —the last of the Ethiopian commanders in the north—remained to threaten the swoop of Addis Ababa which Badoglio was now planning. One of Haile Selassie's "new" Ethiopians, whom the Emperor had singled out for his ability as an administrator, Imru was the only one of the Ethiopian generals who showed any tactical ability. Only he had attempted to wage a guerrilla war, and his army had given the Italians more trouble than all the others put together. Imru's men were more reliable than the troops of the other Rases, primarily because he paid them regularly and had some regard for their welfare. As they were probably the most ill-equipped troops in the whole ramshackle Ethiopian army, the credit for their successes must go entirely to their leader. Having established himself in a position near Aksum, dug trenches, and issued standing orders—covering the action to be taken in air raids and crude precautions against mustard gas ("You soldiers must be always washing")—Imru set about har-

---

* This letter is one that fell into the hands of the Italians when the courier taking it to Ras Imru was captured.

rying the Italians. Commando-type patrols, raiding deep into Italian-held territory, created havoc on the roads leading to the front and fanned the smoldering mutinous spirit in Eritrea proper. Convoys were harried and the massacre and mutilation of parties of Italian laborers making up the roads not only created alarm, despondence, and insubordination among their colleagues but raised an outcry in Rome denouncing Ethiopian barbarism. However, so far as Ras Imru was concerned, it was not terrorism but the successful ambush of an Italian ammunition convoy which brought the greatest dividend. One hundred thousand precious rounds of ammunition for the Italian rifles his men had captured in earlier raids came into his possession, and he was going to need them all.

By this time further reinforcements had arrived from Italy. Two divisions had been mobilized on the frontier of the Alps— the Cosseria Division raised in the Italian Riviera district and the Assietta Division, which was usually stationed near Mondane— and shipped to East Africa in the latter half of November. They were followed by the Tevere (First February) Blackshirt Division* in December and another Alpini division, the Val Pusteria, in January 1936. From these reinforcements Badoglio formed a Fourth Army Corps† which was concentrated northwest of Aksum. At the end of February he decided to strike, and during the early hours of the twenty-ninth, troops of the Second Corps began to advance on Ras Imru's positions from the east. At the same time the Fourth Corps began to move down from the north. From his operation orders it is apparent Badoglio anticipated strong and prolonged resistance by Ras Imru's men. It was expected that there would be two phases in the battle since the Second Corps was only nineteen miles from its first objectives while the Fourth Corps, which was to attack Imru's left flank, had over sixty miles to march. Thus the first phase would be an encounter battle when the Second Corps clashed with the Ethiopians, followed by what Badoglio called a "development battle" after the arrival of the Fourth Corps. In the event, the attack by

* Made up of Italian volunteers from abroad, and university students.
† Comprising the Cosseria and First February Blackshirt Division.

Maravigna's Second Corps was sufficient to ensure victory, and when the Fourth Corps reached the scene the Ethiopians were already streaming away southwest.

The first real resistance came soon after midday on March 1, and the Italians halted, brought up their artillery, and started to shell the Ethiopians' positions. The battering which followed came as a surprise to Ras Imru, who had not realized that his enemies had so many guns. (On the morning of March 2, the artillery was brought back from Makale, where it had been used for the assault on Amba Aradam.) Nevertheless some of the bitterest fighting the Italians had experienced in the whole campaign took place next day. "He [Ras Imru] now launched all his men in a series of diabolical attacks upon the field guns and machine-guns of the enemy. Often, the Italians reported, their artillery had to fire at pointblank range. Machine-guns were seized by the dark hands of Imru's soldiers, as they fell sawn in half with bullets. The contempt for death that the Sudanese showed at Omdurman was nothing to this: The Ethiopians knew what machine-guns were." [13] But this tenacious resistance could not continue for long; by the evening the Ethiopians' morale was beginning to crack, and next morning they abandoned the action and started to withdraw, through the Dembeguina Pass toward one of the fords across the Takkaze. There, at the crossing place, the congestion caused by the rabble of refugees and disorganized troops provided the Regia Aeronautica with an ideal target, and the battle of Shire, as it has been called, ended with the complete rout of Ras Imru's force. The last Ethiopian army on the northern front had been wiped out and the whole of Tigre was now in Italian hands. In the three battles of Amba Aradam, the Tembien, and the Shire, the Ethiopians had lost over 15,000 men killed and wounded, the Italians just under 2,600.*

With the defeat of Ras Imru, the way was now open for a general advance along the whole front. There was no question of the three defeated armies being reformed and refurbished; most

---

* According to Badoglio the Italians lost in the battle of Shire 63 officers, 894 Italians, 12 Eritreans. The estimate of 15,000 Ethiopian casualties is believed to be a realistic assessment.

of the levies either returned to their homes or crept away to hide, and the Ethiopian chiefs were lucky if a handful of men remained to them as bodyguards. But for Haile Selassie's army barring the way to the capital, there was nothing to stop the Italians overrunning the whole country. Nor was there any reason to suppose that the Emperor's army would behave differently from those of his Rases. It was inevitable that against superior manpower, superior equipment, superior firepower, and superior tactics the Ethiopians stood no chance. This was the best reason why Haile Selassie should never have risked a *personal* defeat. In the eyes of his chiefs, his people—and above all in the eyes of the superstitious priesthood who really controlled them—the Emperor's status was the linchpin of his power. So long as it held firm, the war would continue after a fashion. But just as the Persian Empire was lost when Darius fled the field of Arbela, the fate of Haile Selassie's Ethiopia was sealed when the Emperor's image was shattered.

Yet, from Haile Selassie's point of view he had little option but to follow the course he took. By mid-March he had come to realize that little help could be expected from the world outside; nobody was coming to his rescue, and even those European countries who had ostensibly appeared friendly now seemed anxious to disassociate themselves from his impending downfall. Among his people the bombing and the gassing had had their effect; his armies were rabble and as bombs fell on the hospitals the foreign medical missions were withdrawing from the forward areas.* With their medical supplies, gasoline, and food stocks running down and the chaotic state of the country making replenishment impossible, and their native staffs deserting, there was little they could do. "This isn't war—it isn't even slaughter," Dr. John Melly wrote at the beginning of March. "It's the torture of tens of thousands of defenceless women and children with bombs and poison gas. . . . And the world looks on and passes by on the other side. . . ." [14] In such circum-

---

* The Kenya medical orderlies serving with the British Red Cross unit demanded repatriation on the grounds that their terms of employment did not include being bombed and gassed.

stances the Emperor had three courses open to him: something unthinkable—to give up the struggle and surrender to the Italians; to fall back before the Italian onslaught and pray for some act of God to save his country; or with the remaining troops to dare all in one last battle. In electing the last alternative he has been criticized for throwing away his last chance of winning the war. The rains were due, and in a few weeks Badoglio's army might have bogged down in a slough of Ethiopian mud at the end of its tenuous line of communications. Guerrilla warfare, which Ras Imru had shown could be surprisingly effective, could have perpetuated the stalemate; during that time the men in Geneva might have been jolted into action and help might have come. But such arguments are riddled with "ifs" and "mights," and time had run out. Tradition demanded that Haile Selassie should do what an Emperor of Ethiopia was expected to do. If he could not win the war then it was his duty to go down fighting. The people expected it, the Emperor knew it; there must be a final full-scale attack, an Armageddon, in which he must personally lead his army to victory or death.

Whatever the Emperor was thinking when he marched out of Dessie at the head of his Imperial Guard, Badoglio must have felt that final victory was within his grasp. A week after the battle of Shire he ordered every available vehicle to be concentrated, ready for an advance on Addis Ababa. While the Italian engineers and road gangs worked feverishly to build new roads, supplies of food and ammunition were rushed up to establish fresh dumps in the forward area. By March 10 a bridge had been thrown across the Takkaze, and the Italian columns were pushing forward on every section of the front. With less need now to concentrate on tactical objectives, strategic bombing raids by the Regia Aeronautica were stepped up, and by the beginning of April the Ethiopian Air Force had virtually ceased to exist. Preparation for an advance across the Danakil from the Red Sea coast to Aussa had begun in December, and by March 11 a band of irregulars had installed themselves in Sardo, the capital of the Sultanate. To get there the Aussa force had to cross 120 miles of inhospitable stony desert covered with basaltic slabs and broken by mounds and craters of lava. Twenty-five aircraft acted as escort to the column, dropping supplies, scouting ahead for ambushes and machine-gunning parties of Danakils and Ethiopians unwise enough to expose their presence.

The capture of Sardo, little more than 150 miles from Diredawa and 120 miles from Dessie, marked the end of another phase, and an airfield was built there to facilitate easier air communication between Badoglio and Graziani. Meanwhile other Italian columns were marching south from the Setit and the Takkaze, and on March 28 troops of the Second Corps reached Sakota, an important market town and the center of communications with Lake Tana and the Gojjam.* Simultaneously, other troops of the Second Corps operating farther west had occupied Debarek (Devark) and Dabat, and were joined at Dabat by a motorized column. This column, comprising the Second Bersaglieri Regiment, the Benito Mussolini Blackshirt Battalion, two batteries of mechanized artillery, a battalion of mechanized machine guns, and the usual ancillary services, was under command of General Achille Starace, the Secretary-General of the Fascist Party, and organized as a self-supporting brigade group with thirty days' supplies. Setting out from Asmara on March 15 it had moved to Om Ager, near the Sudan frontier, and from there it had followed a caravan route never previously used by wheeled traffic. Having covered 220 miles in twelve days, it occupied Gondar on April 1, and after hoisting the Italian flag in Ethiopia's ancient capital, continued on to perform a similar ceremony on the shores of Lake Tana. (Throughout all these operations the population was said to have received the Italians "with equanimity," and the people of Gojjam and Wallo were said to have turned on the survivors of Ras Imru's army fleeing through their territory.) Thus, within a few weeks and almost without having to fire a shot, the Italians had taken possession of the whole of northern Ethiopia down to the 12th parallel.

On the southern front the Italians were having equal success.

---

* To get to Sakota involved a long exhausting march up a track unfit for vehicles. There were insufficient mules to move both food and ammunition so the troops had to carry an extra 66 pounds per man.

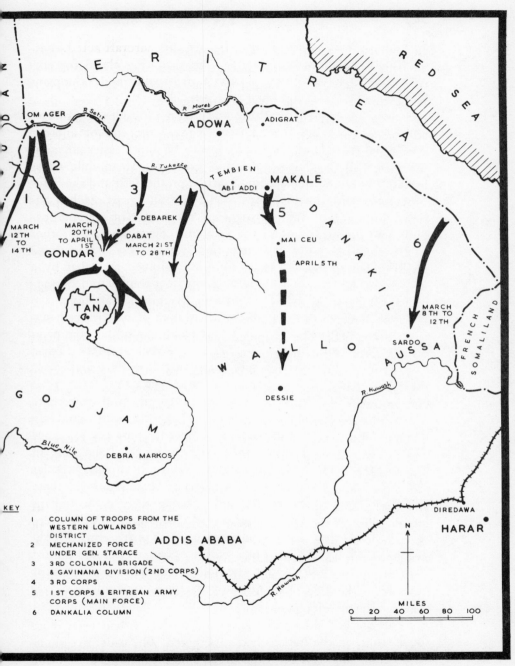

KEY

1   COLUMN OF TROOPS FROM THE
        WESTERN LOWLANDS
        DISTRICT
2   MECHANIZED FORCE
        UNDER GEN. STARACE
3   3RD COLONIAL BRIGADE
        & GAVINANA DIVISION (2ND CORPS)
4   3RD CORPS
5   1ST CORPS & ERITREAN ARMY
        CORPS (MAIN FORCE)
6   DANKALIA COLUMN

THE ADVANCE TO GONDAR AND LAKE TANA

In January, Graziani had taken the offensive in order to destroy an army of between 30,000 and 40,000 men under the command of a son-in-law of the Emperor—the bellicose Ras Desta, who had sworn to drive the Italians into the sea. Until Desta's army had been rendered innocuous, Graziani was uneasy about any advance toward his main objective of Harar and the Djibuti railway. Like Badoglio in the north he was unwilling to move until his flank had been secured and proper communications established. Consequently, the two months in Somalia from mid-November 1935 until mid-January 1936 were a period of operational immobility and stalemate while new roads were being built, and offensive action was limited to bombing and strafing. In December aerial reports of large numbers of cattle near Neghelli suggested that Ras Desta was collecting rations on the hoof as part of his preparations for an offensive. Before he could move, Graziani forestalled him by launching his own offensive, when on January 12 the Italian war machine started to roll down toward Neghelli. The advance began in two columns—the force on the right following the course of the Ganale Dorya River toward Amino and Malka Dida, while that on the left moved up the Dawa River, about fifty miles west. When the right-hand column reached Goburu on January 13, it split into two groups —a mechanized column of tanks, armored cars and motorized machine-gun detachments, which headed straight for Neghelli, and a slower moving force which continued up the course of the Ganale Dorya. Of the three columns, the center, mechanized and moving ahead of the others, first clashed with the Ethiopians, and after a brisk action Ras Desta's men fled. Soon afterward the left column on the Dawa also made contact and three days of sharp fighting delayed its progress. But in that time the mechanized column had resumed the advance, and on January 19 Graziani's vanguard reached its objective of Neghelli, three hundred miles from the base of Dolo. Two days later they were joined there by the marching columns.

This marked the end of an operation which had been more successful than the Italians had anticipated. The usual five thousand Ethiopians were reported to have been killed in the fighting and another five thousand were said to have died of thirst during the retreat; hundreds of others were taken prisoner and a considerable quantity of arms and ammunition abandoned in Neghelli fell into the hands of the Italians. Ras Desta himself escaped with his Belgian adviser, Lieutenant Frère, but his personal luggage, the precious radio which was his only link with the Emperor, and even the insignia of his command,* were left behind.

Italian columns were sent out from Neghelli to patrol north and west, and during the ensuing weeks there were some minor skirmishes with scattered parties of Ethiopian troops still at large. But the main resistance had been broken; Ras Desta's army of the southwest no longer existed as a fighting force and Desta himself was not seen or heard of again until the end of the war. Numerous tribal chiefs and notables of the Galla Borana reported to the Italian authorities in Neghelli to make their formal act of submission, and by mid-February Graziani was confident that he could turn to his real objective.

For Haile Selassie, Ras Desta's defeat was but one more catastrophe. By ordering a total mobilization and appointing a new commander to take the place of his son-in-law, he tried to stabilize the situation. But it was too late; his Empire had already started to disintegrate.

* The *negarit*, the drums which every high-ranking Ethiopian chief carried to war.

CHAPTER 14

Exploitation and Success

A chi la vittoria? A noi!—*"To whom belongs the victory?
To us!"*

Fascist cry, often following or preceding the singing of "Giovinezza"

"Everything," declared Haile Selassie at dinner on March 20,
1935, "is going normally. . . . We have resisted . . . and kept
them back. I see nothing dangerous in the situation." This extraordinary statement—made to Colonel Konovaloff, his sole remaining European adviser—was not a true expression of the Emperor's thoughts. But he and Konovaloff were well aware of the
hopelessness of the position. The Emperor was too proud to
admit his inner fears to a European subordinate, and the Russian
colonel "did not want to sadden the Emperor with the revealing
details" of the facts, ". . . the ineptitude of the chiefs, the complete disorganisation and demoralisation of their forces . . . to
tell him how we, once tens of thousands against only thousands
of Italians, used to abandon our positions at the first caprice of
the chiefs or their soldiers, to hide in our distant camps, in caves
and huts scattered mile over mile, until our armies became a
chaos beyond my power to paint." That Haile Selassie was

equally aware of the situation may be deduced from what he wrote to Ras Imru: "For yourself, if you think that with your troops and with such local inhabitants as you can collect together you can do anything where you are, do it. If on the other hand your position is difficult, and you are convinced of the impossibility of fighting, having lost all hope on your front, and *if you think it is better to come here and die with us, let us know your decision* [author's italics]."

Thirty-one thousand men had been concentrated near Quoram under the Emperor's standard. Of this force only the five-thousand-strong well-equipped Imperial Guard (organized into six battalions of infantry and one regiment of artillery) could be considered reliable; the rest were Gallas, whose prime concern was profit by loot irrespective of which side provided it. All the Europeans except Konovaloff had departed; military advisers, doctors, Red Cross volunteers, and war correspondents were all making their way back to Addis Ababa—fed up, and finished with the war.

On March 20, even the Russian colonel was about to take off for the comforts of Adis, when Haile Selassie sent for him. "I have decided to attack the Italians at their camp near Mai Ceu," he said, and then told Konovaloff that he wanted him to reconnoiter the front and advise him on a plan of attack.

Watching the Ethiopians assembling in the valley below the heights of Mai Ceu, Badoglio, who had already deduced the Emperor's intention, was delighted that Haile Selassie was apparently going to risk a final gamble and not withdraw as he had feared. On March 21 confirmation came by way of an intercepted radio message sent by the Emperor to his consort in Addis Ababa. "We are drawn up opposite the enemy," the message read, "observing each other through field glasses. We are informed that the enemy troops assembled against us number, up to now, not more than approximately 10,000 men. Our troops amount to exactly 31,000. Since our trust is in our Creator and in the hope of His help, and as we have decided to advance and enter the fortifications, and since God is our only help, confide this decision of ours in secret to the Abuna [the Patriarch of the

Ethiopian Church], to the ministers and dignitaries, and offer unto God your fervent prayers."

With this confirmation of the Emperor's intentions, all Badoglio needed to know was when the attack would take place. Evidence from intelligence sources seemed to indicate some time during the fourth week of March, and a soldier's instinct told Badoglio that it would be about the twenty-fourth. This was indeed the date which the Emperor had set in his own mind, but it turned out to be impossible. However, the afternoon of that day, the Emperor gave a great feast for his chiefs:

Konovaloff wrote: ". . . A cave about forty feet long, which looked as if carved in rectangular form, was covered in soft carpets, while at its entrance employees of the Ministry of Public Works raised a wall of middling height with a door veiled by white silk . . . the Emperor, seated on an improvised throne, had on either side the two Rases, Kassa and Seyoum. To the side, but sitting lower were the other chiefs. . . . As I entered, the banqueters were eating their favourite dish, raw meat, offered at each table by a young man who was a servant of the Imperial household. Others offered tej in little cups. . . ." [1]

When the eating and drinking were over, the Emperor addressed the gathering. He was ready to give battle, he said; the attack would begin that night. But with their bellies full of meat and *tej*, few of the chiefs relished the idea of being flung into battle at such short notice, and their objections led to a good deal of wrangling. Their men had not all reached Aia, they complained to the Emperor; some of the equipment was missing, the troops were not ready. Far from showing their enthusiasm for Haile Selassie's last venture, some were even for postponing the attack indefinitely.

Meanwhile the Emperor's staff had attempted to negotiate with the Azebu Gallas—"the same Azebu who had killed Ras Mulugeta, his elder son and his soldiers during their retreat from Makale. Their corpses now littered the road between Mai Ceu and Lake Ashangi." [2] Now, the same pariahs were being bribed to fight for the Emperor with "long striped silk shirts and black satin capes, the complete outfit that is given to petty

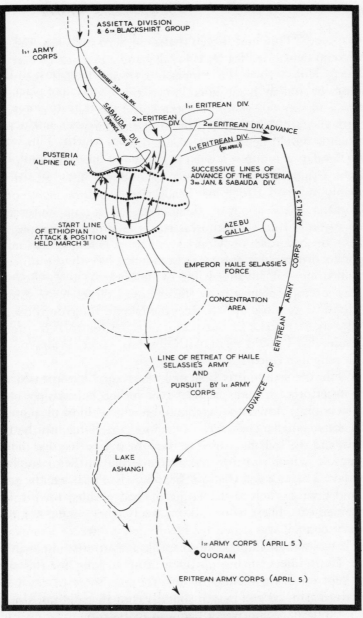

THE BATTLE OF MAI CEU
AND ADVANCE TO LAKE ASHANGI

chiefs. . . ." This, and fifteen thalers in hard cash, was the price
the Azebu demanded for their loyalty and a promise to harry the
Italians' flanks when the Emperor's troops hurled themselves
against the Italian front line. When the Gallas had given this
promise all seemed set for the attack and the date was fixed for
Saturday, March 28, with a proviso that if things were not ready
by then it would definitely be launched on Monday, the thirti-
eth. (Sunday was out; not even in the worst moments of the war
did the Ethiopians ever fight on a Sunday.) This information
probably reached Badoglio's headquarters before many of the
Ethiopians knew about it themselves, as another intercepted
radio message told the Empress that the Emperor proposed to
attack "on Saturday or Monday." This was ample notice, and
Badoglio ordered his troops to stand by. "With the object of
consolidating our advanced line of defence, so as to break any
further attempts against it by the enemy, I directed the supporting divisions to close up," he recorded, "and the troops occupying the western flank of our positions to be reinforced—thus on
that side also I could resist with absolute security any possible
enveloping movement. . . ." [3]

While the Ethiopians hesitated the Regia Aeronautica dou-
bled its efforts, droning ceaselessly overhead, dropping bombs
and swooping down to machine-gun the Ethiopian positions.
Such activity had a considerable demoralizing effect on the Ethiopians, and the Italians probably thought it was this that delayed
the attack, which did not materialize either on Saturday or on
Monday. The fact was that on Saturday the Shoan chiefs, parad-
ing and fawning before the Emperor, had pleaded for a further
postponement. They were still not ready, they said. "A kind of
military council was called by His Majesty," wrote Konovaloff,
"but it was almost impossible to speak and utterly impossible to
hear. The soldiers, strung up by waiting so long for the offensive, kept on firing their guns into the air. Some of the nearer
ones were arrested and beaten soundly, but that did not stop the
row." [4] The outcome was a decision to postpone the operation
until Tuesday.

All this time, secure in their mountaintop trenches behind

masses of barbed wire, the Italians quietly waited. Two corps (the First and the Eritrean) were drawn up obliquely on the heights of Mai Ceu. On the right, the Pusteria Alpini Division and three Eritrean battalions looked down on what would be the Ethiopian line of advance; behind them lay the Sabauda and Third January divisions. To the left, but slightly withdrawn, the Second Eritrean Division held the heights of Mai Ceu; farther to the left rear, the First Eritrean Division occupied another range of hills. With the Assietta Division in reserve, the overall deployment gave the Italian dispositions the approximate shape of a broad arrow pointing down toward Lake Ashangi. As the Emperor was expected to try to outflank the Italian positions, the arrow was an ideal defensive formation and was well placed.

On the Monday afternoon as his troops moved up to their start lines, ready to advance at dawn next day, Haile Selassie climbed to his tactical headquarters on the hill overlooking Mai Ceu. Gazing across the valley he could see the wire entanglements of the Italian positions in front of which the broken glass, thrown down to lacerate the naked feet of his warriors, glittered in the late afternoon sun. The plan was for a three-pronged attack, and that evening the Emperor summoned his chiefs to announce that the columns would be led by Ras Kassa, Ras Seyoum, and Ras Getachu. All three were old men who had demonstrated their ineptitude in war, but under the feudal system they were seigneurs and as such had the right to lead; there were other, younger and more capable officers, but for the Emperor to use them would be to dishonor his princes. The battle plan had been worked out by the Emperor himself. What he hoped to do was to engage the Italians' attention by a feint frontal attack against the positions occupied by the Pusteria Division, and then throw the main part of his force against the Italian flanks. Because the plan was based on traditional Ethiopian tactics its simplicity appealed to the chiefs. For once, they would have a chance to put the old Adowa methods into operation—close with the enemy and use cold steel; Ethiopian bravery and sheer weight of numbers should do the rest.

It was wishful thinking. Not only did Badoglio know when

the attack would take place, he also knew how it would be organized. Despite their promises and arrangements with the Emperor, the treacherous Gallas had decided to renege. Having seen
Ras Mulugeta's men pulverized by Italian bombs and shells and
concluded that the same fate awaited Haile Selassie's army, they
had no wish to be included among the victims. So, after reporting the details of the Emperor's plan to the Italians—who also
made a cash payment for their services—the Gallas retired to the
mountains to watch and wait.

According to Badoglio, "the night of March 30th–31st
passed quietly." Then, "at 5:45 A.M., almost simultaneously on
the front of both the Pusteria Division and of the 2nd Eritrean
Division, the alarm was given: the first hostile patrols had come
in contact with our advanced posts." This, of course, was Haile
Selassie's feint—directed against the right wing of the Italian line
held by the Alpini of the Pusteria Division—meant to cover the
first major assault on the positions held by the Eritrean Division.
Under cover of a barrage from all their available artillery, the
Ethiopians gallantly charged up the slope of Mai Ceu, but
decimated by withering machine-gun fire, they faltered and the
assault quickly lost its impetus. Some progress was made on the
Eritrean divisional front, but elsewhere Haile Selassie's men were
pinned down on the hillside and were being systematically cut to
pieces by artillery.* From their strongly entrenched positions the
Italians had complete control of the situation, and the minor
gains which seemed to indicate some signs of Ethiopian success
were wholly illusory. Pirzio-Biroli, the Eritrean Corps Commander, had selected a killing ground into which Haile Selassie's
men were deliberately lured as the Eritreans fell slowly back.
From his observation post above the valley, Haile Selassie could
see the battle spread out before him like a diorama, but even if he
realized that little groups of *shamma'd* warriors were heading toward a trap he had had no means of stopping them. Forced eventually to take cover, the infiltrators lay down and blazed away

* Not all of it Italian. Konovaloff said that "Our [Ethiopian] gunners had
no idea of the objectives they were supposed to bombard. They shot at random
and sometimes hit their own men. . . . The Emperor had said 'Our men must
hear the artillery shooting. It will give them courage and improve their morale.' "

the remainder of their ammunition. This was exactly what Pirzio-Biroli had hoped would happen, for when their ammunition was gone the Ethiopians would have no alternative but to withdraw and they would be completely at his mercy. "The bravest," wrote Konovaloff, "some 900 men, struck at the redoubts. But the rest lacked courage to advance and crown their efforts with the capture of the Italian works. Under cover, they preferred to blaze away until their cartridge belts were empty. Then they withdrew."

It was some time before the final scene was enacted, and it was preceded by a supreme effort to break through the Italian lines. At 9:00 A.M. the Imperial Guard moved forward, "supported by a lively fire . . . advancing in rushes and making good use of the ground, giving proof of a solidity and a remarkable degree of training combined with a superb contempt of danger." [5] Having got to within a couple of hundred yards of the Italian fortifications the Guards then charged across the open ground. It was a magnificent demonstration of useless courage; they were met by a "veritable avalanche of fire" and those who did manage to reach the Italian trenches were "thrust back with the bayonet and grenades." [6] By noon the battle was over, and although another desperate assault was mounted at about 4:00 P.M., nothing came of it. The "concerted action of the two Eritrean Divisions and the firm stand of the 'Intra' battalion of Alpini on the right, supported by detachments of Blackshirts, decided the day." [7] "It was clear that the offensive had failed," commented Konovaloff, and Badoglio wrote: "This was the last action launched by the enemy in a final effort."

Haile Selassie's plan had failed; the attacks on the Italian flanks had been foiled; the Italians were still holding their ground, and Badoglio had not even had to call on his reserves. By 5:00 P.M., under heavy artillery, small-arms fire, and constant aerial bombardment, the Ethiopians began to fall back all along the line. In a wireless message to the Empress that evening the Emperor summarized the situation:

From 5 in the morning until 7 in the evening our troops attacked the enemy's strong positions, fighting without pause. We also took part in the action, and by the Grace of God remained unharmed.* Our chiefs and trusted soldiers are dead or wounded. Although our losses are heavy, the enemy too has been injured. The Imperial Guard fought magnificently and deserve every praise. The Amhara troops also did their best. Our troops, even though they are not adapted for fighting of the European type, were able to bear comparison throughout the day with the Italian troops.

Significantly he ended with the comment: "The Gallas helped us only with shouts, not with their strong right arms." At that very moment the Gallas were flexing their muscles, ready to pounce on the Emperor's stragglers.

At dawn on April 1, the Ethiopians were back in the positions they had occupied before the attack. The rain which had started to fall heavily during the night shrouded the battlefield with a sullen gray mist and added to the general atmosphere of depression which pervaded the Emperor's camp. Haile Selassie knew that there was little hope of holding the Italians; his troops had made their effort and it was useless expecting them to do more. Even if he had wished to renew the attack—and he told Konovaloff that it was his intention to do so—a glance down the valley was enough to convince him that another assault was impossible. Already what remained of his army was beginning to break up; even the Imperial Guard was drifting back, and the heavy equipment procured at such cost had been abandoned. The Emperor had played his card and lost; now it was Badoglio's turn.

The next day (April 2), the Italians attacked. As Badoglio's reserve division moved up to the front, the Eritrean Corps left its trenches and moved down the hill into the valley. The Ethiopians had already started to retreat, and as the Italians pushed swiftly forward, their withdrawal rapidly deteriorated into a panic-stricken pell-mell rush down the tracks toward Dessie.

Konovaloff wrote: "Men . . . tried to shove the crowd back and keep them from coming near the Imperial cave, with blows of sticks to left and right. 'What a disgraceful disorder,' said the Emperor,

---

* During some of the action Haile Selassie manned a machine gun. He did not—as some contemporary accounts allege—lead a charge.

'when we ought to be ready to stop the Italians from turning our flank. Fitorari Taferi! Where is he? Bring him here!' A stocky Ethiopian chief with a sword scar across his forehead came forward. 'You see that mountain covered with bush?' The Emperor pointed. 'You must occupy it with your men and stop the *ferengi* from taking it.' The Fitorari hesitated, then went away. Two hours later he was still to be seen around the camp, chatting to his underlings. He had sent fifty soldiers forward, the only ones he could find, and had stayed behind himself to be near the Emperor." [8]

With the dawn of April 3 came the Regia Aeronautica to bomb and strafe, and Konovaloff recorded a vivid description of the scene:

"Along the road the weary people dragged themselves, scattering for a moment in panic, or massing together in groups. Four, six, eight bombs burst one after the other . . . the people quicken pace. Here is another aeroplane which seems to be chosing its victims as it flies just over their heads. One explosion . . . then another which raises a jet of earth, clods, sand and stones." [9]

Along the shores of the lake there was little cover, and the frantic fugitives could not take to the hills because there the Gallas were waiting. "These irregular units," Badoglio dryly declared, "deserve special mention. Warriors by instinct,* particularly adept at surprise action, under the orders of their own chiefs and animated by a deep hatred of their Shoan rulers, they rendered signal service to our cause throughout the whole campaign." [10] Indeed they did. Activated by Italian bribes, the Gallas wreaked their vengeance on the human debris of Haile Selassie's army for past grievances under the Ethiopian system. By the evening of April 3 all semblance of order had gone, and the only way the Emperor could find to save his remaining stores and supplies from capture was to make a free distribution to the rabble streaming past his cave. Clothing, canned food, liquor, weapons, and ammunition were handed out to the men jostling through Aia. Everything else, including the radio, had to be abandoned when the Emperor's party left. Joining the mob streaming south, the royal bodyguard often had to force a passage for His Impe-

* Hereditary bandits would have been a more appropriate description.

rial Majesty by beating the hysterical fugitives with the butts of
their rifles. "Every inch of the road was jammed," said Konovaloff. "When the Ethiopians march, the main object of each man
is to pass all others. The mob of people trying to thread its way
through donkeys, mules and hundreds of other Ethiopians created an incredible disorder." [11] It is only about twelve miles from
Aia to Lake Ashangi but to get there in the dark took the Emperor's party nearly twelve hours.

Having to run the gauntlet of two enemies, the Ethiopians
suffered far more casualties during the pursuit than in the battle.
Littered with corpses and the bodies of the dying emasculated
victims of the Gallas, the road back to Dessie became a veritable
Via Dolorosa, and according to an Italian estimate, of the 31,000
Ethiopian warriors who had seen the dawn rise over Mai Ceu,
8,000 perished. (Their own losses totaled 68 officers, 332 Italians,
and 874 Askaris.) Haile Selassie had intended to try to rally his
troops and stand again south of Lake Ashangi. But it was a for-
lorn hope; his men had had enough of fighting, and all they could
think about was getting away from the aircraft. Admitting that
he had virtually given up all hope of saving his country from the
Italians, he said to Konovaloff, "I do not know what to do. My
chiefs will do nothing. . . . It is beyond our power to hold
them [the Italians]." This statement was made on April 11, 1936
—the day that Badoglio laconically reported to the Duce, "The
battle upon which the fate of the Empire depends is over. Of the
Ethiopian army which fought at Mai Ceu, nothing remains but a
few groups of armed men, terror-stricken by the losses they have
suffered, scattered over a wide area, and for the most part heading for their own villages."

Within four days Pirzio-Biroli's Askaris had raced down the
road to occupy Dessie, 150 miles from the scene of the Emper-
or's last stand; occupying it so soon after the battle was no mean
feat. To get there most of the troops had to march, covering an
average of thirty miles a day. During the whole of the march and
the first week in Dessie, they were supplied by air. Fourteen
hundred dead mules marked the route from Lake Ashangi. Many
of the corpses were simply left in the middle of the track where

they fell, and the trucks that followed drove over them. In time the bodies were flattened, the bones became dust, and the road was built over them.

The situation was ripe now for the push toward the capital, the arrangements for which Badoglio's staff were hurriedly completing. Meanwhile, as the tentacles of the Italian octopus probed farther into Ethiopian territory and tightened their grip on the occupied provinces, the Emperor was seeking divine guidance at the sacred town of Lalibela, ninety miles northwest of Dessie. Turning off the main track, the royal party had halted here on April 11, and for two days the Emperor stayed to pray. Meantime Italian columns were overrunning Gojjam, Italian engineers were working like demons to turn the track south from Makale into a road which would carry vehicular traffic, and Graziani in the south was preparing for his final drive on Jijiga, Harar, and Diredawa.

It was April 14 before the Imperial entourage, escorted by what was left of the Imperial Guard, left Lalibela for Dessie. When the column entered the town they found it practically deserted. The last of the garrison had departed when the Crown Prince returned to Addis Ababa after the Wallo army, to whose command he had been appointed, had gone over to the Italians. Following a hurried conference, Haile Selassie decided to press on south, down the track strewn with all the debris and discarded impedimenta of his retreating troops. Discipline was disintegrating even among the elite bodyguard traveling with him, and the smoking villages looted by the main body of raping, pillaging fugitives who had gone before provided ample evidence of the fact that it was nonexistent ahead. Lawlessness and anarchy were spreading throughout the country, and even among his entourage the Emperor was losing his authority. "It was death," wrote Konovaloff, "who followed us everywhere, and seemed to be stronger than the aristocratic power of the Emperor and his chiefs: he made us all equal, and it was he who drove us from the places where he was able to reign." The Emperor ordered the looting to stop and those caught at it to be punished. But it was too late. "Soldiers?" one chief replied when asked where his men

were. "Today there are no more soldiers, they are all brig-
ands." [12] However, four more days brought the royal party
to Fiche, 125 miles from Addis Ababa, where at the end of a
passable road a car was waiting. Physically, mentally, and emotionally exhausted, the Emperor drove back to his capital.

Meanwhile, Badoglio's men had almost finished making up
the road from Makale to the end of the so-called Imperial Highway at Quoram, which ran to Addis Ababa.* Engineers and
labor gangs, who had been working on the stretch running back
from Makale since the town was occupied, were brought up to
continue the road forward from Makale to Amba Alagi; from
there on to Quoram the First Corps was set to work. Laying
aside their rifles, all available men were put to hewing and digging; infantrymen, gunners, "employed" personnel, officers and
soldiers alike—all were diverted to the battle of the road. The
work went on day and night, rain or shine, and the east section
was open by April 17. Simultaneously an interminable crocodile
of vehicles began to wind its way forward from Asmara, and by
the time the Emperor reached his capital, 1,725 trucks had been
collected at Dessie to carry Badoglio's army on the last stage of
its journey. Concurrent with these preparations the Regia Aeronautica was busy softening up the population of the Ethiopian
capital. Squadrons of Capronis and Savoia-Marchetti bombers
regularly flew over the city on leaflet raids from April 13, often
performing pointless heroics in the absence of an effective opposition.†

Badoglio's decision to undertake as quickly as possible the
four-hundred-mile sortie to capture Addis Ababa was based on
the assumption that no organized resistance was to be expected
between Dessie and the capital. As he saw the situation, the Emperor had no army; according to Intelligence the Rases were mu-
tinying and his priests were whispering defeat. Haile Selassie's

---

* The grandiose title belies its state. It was a mere track built under Haile
Selassie's orders, but at the time one of the best roads in Ethiopia.

† Count Ciano, the Duce's son-in-law, commander of the Disperata Squadron,
was given to such antics. On one occasion he is reported to have flown low in
order to drop a Disperata pennant on the principal marketplaces. Badoglio
frowned on such games, and had little patience with the flamboyant Ciano.

power was almost dead; to oppose the invaders there was nothing except nature. Yet nature was a formidable opponent whose strength was growing with the passage of time. Mountains were still mountains, the gorges and ravines remained, and the monsoon was approaching. The campaign had already taken six months, and only six weeks of dry weather now remained; if Addis Ababa was to be occupied before the country became impassable it was vital for the advance to be pushed on at top speed. There was little risk, and Badoglio correctly calculated that the moral effect of getting even a small force to the capital far outweighed the dangers of its isolation. Everything, he decided, should be sacrificed to speed, and the force assembled for the final dash was cut to the minimum consistent with the logistical assets. About 20,000 men, half of whom were Italians, deployed in three columns. The motorized column, under Badoglio's personal command, consisted of the Sabauda Division (which for this operation included a battalion of Blackshirts for prestige reasons), the Second Eritrean Brigade, motorized artillery, and some tanks. This column was to follow the Imperial Highway. The second column—moving on foot and composed of the First Eritrean Brigade and several squadrons of cavalry—was to take a more direct route running southwest across the hills, while the third column, also of Askaris on foot, was to follow the route of the mechanized column but setting off two days before it. According to the timetable, the motorized column would reach Addis Ababa on May 1, and be joined by the marching columns four days later.

As planned, the two marching columns left Dessie on April 24 and 25 respectively, and were followed on April 26 by the motorized force. All went as anticipated, except that the Imperial Highway proved to be even less negotiable than had been expected. The track crossed rivers which flowed between deep banks or lost themselves in bogs, climbed precipitous mountain slopes, and traversed passes well over a mile above sea level; where bridges existed, often they consisted only of tree trunks thrown across chasms. Never intended for heavy traffic, its surface had been softened by rain, and under the weight of the

heavy trucks it soon gave way. The worst stretch was south of
Makjud, where the column had to negotiate the 8,000-feet-high
Termaber Pass. There, in teeming rain, the soldiers toiled and
sweated for thirty-six hours, cutting a new road out of the side
of the hill before they were able to push and drag the vehicles up
the pass. However, after almost superhuman efforts, the column
reached the top and was able to creep slowly down the far side.

Two days had been lost, and subsequently the armchair
strategists in Europe attributed the delay to a deliberate pause,
which would enable the Italians to claim that they brought law,
order, and civilization to a city that was being torn apart by its
inhabitants. For by now disaster had overtaken the capital. The
Emperor had left on May 2, and in the interregnum the city was
being sacked and looted by the riffraff of its population and by
the fleeing soldiers who had lost their leaders.

Exhausted and unattended, Haile Selassie had arrived back in
his capital on the last day of April. In an "all is lost save honor"
speech he had declared "I must still hold on until my tardy allies
appear, and if they never come, then I say, prophetically and
without bitterness, the West will perish." The Emperor's decision to fight on was a difficult one. Colson—the one foreigner in
whom he had implicit confidence—had had a heart attack and
was not available to counsel him, and the Empress, the retinue of
priests attached to the Court, and Ras Kassa, all pleaded with him
to leave the country. Like Napoleon III, who had hoped after
the battle of Sedan to meet a Prussian bullet, Haile Selassie
wanted to go down fighting. It was not to be.

Initially, his plan was to send the Royal Family out of the
country, transfer the Government to Gore—a remote and
inaccessible town in western Ethiopia—where he would set up
his standard, and reassemble his army in the less accessible mountain districts. With this end in view, a few truckloads of files and
papers were sent off to Gore, and a short-lived provisional Government under Ras Imru was eventually set up. But to gain time
for the plan to be put into effect, it was necessary to delay the
approach of the Italians, so for two hours on May 1 the great
drum of Menelek boomed out a summons to the chiefs and any

officers remaining in Adis Ababa. When they gathered in the palace courtyard, the Emperor addressed them. The fight would go on, he said; Ethiopia was not yet lost. He would go west, rally the people, collect a new army, and continue the struggle. But a respite was needed, and they must march out and hold up Badoglio's advance on the capital. Ras Getachu would command this force, and five thousand volunteers were needed for it. It was not a soul-stirring exhortation—the Emperor was too depressed and too tired to make it so. Nevertheless, judging by the demonstration which followed, it seemed that there was no lack of volunteers for what would clearly be a suicidal mission.

But when the Emperor went into the palace, where Ras Getachu awaited him, it was a different story. When battle was joined, the hesitant nominee for command asserted, the volunteers would not stand up to the Italians. The war was over, he declared; Ethiopia was finished; the Emperor's position was hopeless. The Empress and Ras Kassa gave their opinions. Better to get out; go to Geneva and make a final appeal to the League, they pleaded. Even at this late hour, the Emperor's eloquence and his appearance in person might induce the League to take some positive action to save the country. The fighting might be over, but Haile Selassie could still carry on a diplomatic war; this was Ethiopia's only hope. "It must have been then that the Emperor decided to go," wrote George Steer. "Reason, the appeal to the League, allied itself to the instinct of flight. . . . Ato Wolde Gioghis was sent to the British Legation. Ras Kassa stopped talking. Imru, who had arrived in Debra Markos, was informed by telephone of his sovereign's decision." [13]

Throughout the night a chain of vehicles, carrying boxes of silver thalers and luggage, shuttled between the palace and the railway station in Addis Ababa. A special train had been drawn up, and at 4:00 A.M. on the morning of May 2, 1936, the Imperial Family—the Empress, the Crown Prince, the Duke of Harar, Prince Sahle Selassie, Princess Tananiye Work Desta (Ras Desta's wife), Princess Tsahai—arrived. Most of the senior Rases were there, including Kassa and Seyoum, as well as "the relatives, the palace servants, some of the ministers and directors of some of the ministries, and the Emperor's dogs. One got lost and was recovered later by a French station employee who did not like men who were not white and treated the little dog badly because it had been the domestic pet of one of them." [14] There was even a political prisoner, Ras Hailu, who had been fetched out of his dungeon to accompany the party in order that he should not fall into the hands of the Italians and be used as a puppet.* Haile Selassie himself boarded the train at Akaki, ten miles outside the capital, and got away only just in time, for when the train crossed the Danakil desert it was but a couple of hours ahead of the Italian patrols from Graziani's army moving up to cut the line to Djibuti.

In Addis Ababa, news that the Emperor had gone spread like wildfire. All civil and military authority collapsed, and until the Italians arrived there was chaos. Breaking into the government arsenal, looters quickly distributed the arms, which the Emperor had bought to be used against the Italians, and soon every male Amhara in the city had a rifle and ammunition to spare. Stocks of liquor from the shops were handed out in the same way as the rifles, and by the evening of May 3 the city was filled with drunken, trigger-happy Ethiopians looking for trouble. Having sacked the European shops, ripped the Emperor's palace to pieces, and shot the royal lions, the rioters turned on the Europeans.† The police were powerless; indeed many of them had joined in the license. Most of the European residents had collected in the compounds of their respective legations, or at the railway station, the Imperial Hotel or in the Bank of Ethiopia, while the Arab and Indian shopkeepers took refuge in the compounds of the major trading companies. At the British Legation no less than 1,650 refugees had congregated by the morning of May 4, and the Embassy guard (an Indian Army detachment of the 4th/14th Punjab Regiment and the Eighth Light Cavalry) was involved in some brisk actions which included a rescue oper-

---

* He escaped during the journey and joined the Italians.

† About 30 were killed and 300 wounded; some 700 Ethiopians are also believed to have lost their lives. Dr. John Melly, the Red Cross missionary, was among the casualties. Shot in the chest by a wounded rioter he had tried to help, Melly died in the British Legation a few days later.

ation to extricate the United States Minister and his staff. It was not that Europeans were specifically singled out for attack; the dominating incentive was loot, and the European property was the most valuable. Most of the victims were among the looters themselves and they died as a result of brawls over the division of the spoils.

In the early hours of May 4 Badoglio's long column of vehicles halted about thirty miles outside the capital; by evening the first Eritrean Brigade, which had moved on foot, was camped on the hills outside the city. And because no attempt was made to enter Addis Ababa until the fifth, Badoglio was accused of purposely dawdling so that the world could see what a barbarous people the Ethiopians were. No doubt the Italians did experience a feeling of quiet satisfaction—perhaps even of sardonic joy— out of the situation. But Badoglio's troops had had a trying time on a difficult march and the straggling columns had to be properly organized before they entered and took over the city. Badoglio could not be sure that the drink-maddened Ethiopians would not attempt a last savage attack when his troops marched in. His entry into Addis Ababa was to be the crowning achievement to the campaign, and the Italian Commander was determined that it should be done properly even if it meant that the foreigners inside the city had to undergo some extra hours of terror.

At 4:00 P.M. on Tuesday, May 5, 1936, the Italian Commander in Chief drove into Addis Ababa. There was nothing spectacular about his entry—no excitement, no shouting, no cheering crowds, no ceremony. Badoglio led the long column of 1,600 trucks in a plain Model T Ford car, and while the Italian flag was raised over the Imperial Palace Italian troops quietly occupied the important points in the city, and patrols of Carabinieri, infantry, and tanks set about restoring order. There was no formal surrender—just the passive occupation of a prostrate city. The imperial capital was in ruins and buildings were burning; gutted houses, gaping shops, and corpses in the gutters testified to four days of disorder. The local population was sullenly apathetic, and only the foreigners were happy as the tired, dusty, unshaven Italian soldiers plodded past the legations. Badoglio's goal and his new headquarters was the attractive house, set in a sheltered spot, which had been the former Italian Embassy. Significantly, although it had been undefended, this was one place which had escaped pillage. As the Italian Commander in Chief's column passed the British Legation, where the Union Jack fluttered over the gate, some of the Italians put out their tongues and a few jeered. It was a mild demonstration, and did not draw a response from the occupants of the British compound.

While Badoglio's troops had been sweeping down through the Wallo country in Shoa, Graziani had been preparing an offensive in the Ogaden. After the successful sortie against Ras Desta at Neghelli, activity in Graziani's sector had been confined to bombing operations and the administrative buildup for a drive north to open the route from Mogadishu to Jijiga. Only one coherent Ethiopian formation—an army of thirty thousand men under command of Dejiak Nasibu—stood between the Italians and their ultimate objective of Diredawa, and Graziani's aim was its total destruction. Resistance elsewhere was thought to be negligible, although shortly before the offensive got under way a sharp engagement in the Neghelli area suggested that it could not be dismissed entirely. Patrolling near Wadara, about fifty miles northwest of Neghelli, a motorized detachment of Aosta Lancers encountered a strong force of Ethiopians. Both sides fought with considerable courage and determination, and in the end the Ethiopians were forced to retreat. The fact that forty-six Italians were killed or wounded in the action was significant, indicating as it did that the Ethiopians still had the ability to strike back when circumstances favored their tactics.

The battle of Ogaden opened on April 14, when the Libya Division started to advance northwest from the caravan junction of Danane toward Birkut. With Nasibu was the sixty-year-old Turkish ex-general Wahib Pasha, and under the latter's directions a defensive line had been established in the Upper Ogaden, between Sasa Baneh and Daggah Bur. A long line of trenches had been dug, and caves, with which this region abounds, had been adapted as shelters and machine-gun emplacements. To back it up a strong force, under command of Dejiak Abbebe Damteu, Ras Desta's brother, was poised on the right flank. As this force was reputedly preparing to attack the opposing Italian left flank at Danane, and with events moving so rapidly and favorably in the north, Graziani decided to strike before his arrangements were perfected. In three columns his troops advanced along toward the Ethiopians' fortified region; as the distance between the opposing forces closed, the three columns converged and the front narrowed.*

When the Italians arrived at the fortifications, which Wahib Pasha had boasted would witness a *"deuxième Verdun,"* they found them to be less formidable than Graziani had feared. In three months, fifteen miles of entrenchments had been dug to block the Jijiga road, but the trenches had no parapets, no fire steps, and no water. Barbed wire had been sent up to Jijiga but little of it reached Wahib's Maginot line, and the men in the trenches had less than sixty rounds apiece for their rifles. When the battle opened on the left of the line at dawn on April 16, the Ethiopians fought bravely enough, but after three hours they broke and ran, leaving all their heavy equipment and the customary five thousand dead on the battlefield. After that, it was merely a matter of rolling up the line. Daggah Bur, the pivot of the fortified system, fell on April 30. By then the rains had started, and Graziani—like Badoglio in the north—faced greater problems with nature than with resistance from the Ethiopians. To get from Daggah Bur to Jijiga, the flooded Jerer River had to be crossed, and this entailed building a sixty-foot-long bridge. With this completed, the march was resumed, and Graziani entered Jijiga on May 5, only a few hours after Badoglio's occupation of Addis Ababa. Detachments of Dubats, sent ahead to occupy the Marda Pass on the Jijiga–Harar road, were followed by the Libya Division, and this virtually brought the campaign in the south to a close. Ethiopian resistance had completely col-

* *The left column*, made up of the Libya Division, tanks and ancillary troops and commanded by General Nasi, constituted the main force. *The center column*, commanded by General Frusci, was a motorized column. *The right column*, commanded by the Blackshirt General Agostini, was also motorized.

It is interesting to note that only 25 field guns were deployed on the Ogaden front during these operations. Most of the support given to the ground troops was supplied by the Regia Aeronautica.

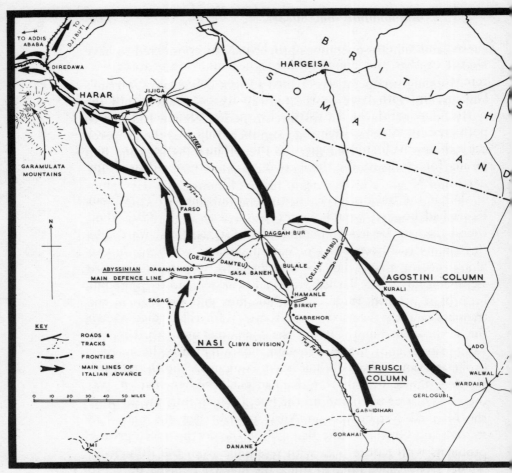

GRAZIANI'S OPERATIONS IN THE OGADEN

lapsed and military operations proper may be considered to have ended.

Mopping-up operations created a slight delay, and Graziani's objective of Diredawa on the railway was not taken until the early hours of May 9. In the interim period Nasibu had fled to Djibuti with Wahib Pasha, and from there followed the Emperor to Palestine. Wahib, told that the French intended to hand him over to the Italians, took a taxi to Zeila and a boat to Aden. Behind him Nasibu's broken army had a glorious three days plundering and sacking in Harar before the Italians arrived to put a stop to their activities. Then, as Graziani's men approached, the disorganized rabble streamed out southwest to the mountains of Garamulata to become *banda,* described either as "patriots," by those of the Emperor's cause, or as "bandits" by the Italians and their sympathizers. At noon on May 9, the forces of Badoglio and Graziani symbolically joined hands at Diredawa; according to Italian journalists the junction of the two armies was effected at an "impressive" ceremony. A battalion of the 46th Infantry Regiment—regular soldiers from the Sabauda Division—traveled down the railway from Addis Ababa to be greeted on the Diredawa station platform by a battalion of the 221st Legion of "Fascists Abroad." * So the war ended. Ethiopia still had to be pacified, but the campaign proper was finished and the customary honors were handed out. By royal decree Graziani was promoted to Marshal of Italy, and Badoglio was created Duke of Addis Ababa and appointed Ethiopia's first Viceroy.

News of Badoglio's victory had been eagerly awaited in Rome, and as soon as the laconic message announcing his arrival in Addis Ababa came through, Mussolini ordered a national rally, for which all the necessary preparations had already been made. At 6:00 P.M., to the wailing of sirens and a clamor of church bells, the people of Italy poured out of their homes, shops, and offices to gather in the squares where loudspeakers had been set up; flags, bands, and uniforms abounded. In Rome, the Piazza Venezia was packed with a multitude which overflowed down the Via del Impero as far as the broken ruins of the

* From the Tevere Division.

Colosseum. As the minutes ticked past, the excitement grew, until promptly at 7:30 P.M., with Mussolini's appearance on the floodlit balcony of the Palazzo, it was released in a roar like a volcanic eruption. Dressed in the gray uniform and round black cap of the Fascist Militia, the Duce struck one of his characteristic poses and held up his hand imperiously. "Today at four o'clock," he shouted in the strained silence, "our victorious troops entered Addis Ababa. I announce to the Italian people and to the world that the war is over. Ethiopia is Italian!"

A storm of jubilation drowned his voice, and the Duce leaned on the parapet staring down on the tumultuous scene with a look of supercilious arrogance on his face. Raising his hand again to silence the tempestuous chants of *"Duce! Duce!"* he continued:

. . . Italian in fact, because occupied by our victorious armies; Italian by right, because with the sword of Rome it is civilization which triumphs over barbarism, justice which triumphs over cruel arbitrariness, the redemption of the miserable which triumphs over the slavery of a thousand years.

A spontaneous outburst of cheering enforced another pause before he went on:

At the rally of October 2nd, I solemnly promised that I would do everything possible in order to prevent an African conflict from developing into a European war. I have maintained that pledge, and I am more than ever convinced that to disturb the peace of Europe means to bring about the collapse of Europe. But I must immediately add that we are ready to defend our brilliant victory with the same intrepid and inexorable decision with which we have gained it. We feel that in this way we are interpreting the will of the combatants in Africa, of those who are dead, who have gloriously fallen in battle and whose memory will be treasured for generations and generations in the hearts of the whole Italian people.[15]

Italy had won her war; Italy had her Empire; the vitality of Fascism was vindicated. Mussolini had set the Italian people on new paths and every Italian rejoiced. Italy would go to take her place as one of the dynamic nations in a new world community; May 5, 1936, was a great day in Italian history.

CHAPTER 15

The Occupation

Italy finally has her Empire. . . . Will you be worthy of it?
MUSSOLINI, May 9, 1936

In Rome it had been decided that the official victory celebration
would be staged on May 9, and at 7:00 P.M. Mussolini delivered
another histrionic performance on the balcony of the Palazzo
Venezia. It was the Duce's formal declaration of the conquest of
Ethiopia, and it was received with wild approval by the thousands of Italians gathered in the Piazza, and the tens of thousands
more congregated in the squares of the towns outside Rome.

Two new but long-prepared decrees were issued in Rome
that night. The first of them placed the territories and peoples of
the "former" Ethiopian Empire under the sovereignty of the
Kingdom of Italy; the second announced Marshal Badoglio's appointment as Governor-General and Viceroy of Ethiopia.
Copies of the first decree were handed to the Secretary-General
of the League of Nations and to the respective Foreign Ministers
of Britain and France next day. The intention was to document
and seal a *fait accompli,* and to pave the way for a return to
normality. The war had been inevitable—a clash of historic
forces; now that it was over he could see no reason why Italy

should not resume her rightful place in the councils of Europe.

At home the attitude of the Vatican was seen to be enthusiastic. In Rome priests blessed the taxis being exported to Addis Ababa, and even the Pope went out of his way to allude to his pleasure "in the triumphal happiness of a great and good people in a peace which it [the Roman Catholic Church] hopes and confidently expects will be a prelude to that new and European world peace. . . ." [1] And when the Queen of Italy became the Empress of Ethiopia the Pope presented her with his Golden Rose. It would be unreasonable to suppose that Pius XI approved of every aspect of the Fascist regime, and according to Sir Luke Teeling, Catholic opinion in Britain excused the Pope's apparent enthusiasm for Mussolini's venture on the grounds that he was "a poor old man sitting in the Vatican, surrounded by Italians, and in a sense this was true. . . . He could not have wanted war. . . . It is true that he kept silent—many people think for too long a time. It is equally true that he wanted to see the spread of Catholicism in Abyssinia, and he felt that would only be possible with the support of Italy. It is equally true that he has thrown his weight on the side of the totalitarian leaders, and he has felt that the imperial policy of Italy must mean an advance for his own Church in the conquered countries. But he did not altogether satisfy Mussolini, since the latter brought all possible pressure to bear on the Pope to induce him to bless the Italian armies and come out wholeheartedly for Italy. The Pope did not do this himself, but he raised no finger to stop Italian bishops up and down the country from going on Fascist platforms and doing everything possible to support the Italian armies." [2]

The announcement of the Italian victory had one important outcome: it brought an end to the dilemma of Britain and France. For over six months the Governments of both countries had lived under the shadow of war; for more than a year they had trod a path between the Scylla of Italian reprisals if they attempted too much, and the Charybdis of repudiation by their own peoples if they did too little. Always there had been a crisis hovering in the background. Even if Mussolini had won a diplomatic victory more striking than the achievements of his soldiers, even if Britain and France had lost face, better to have done with the dangerous game, forget Ethiopia, and get Italy back into the fold.

Such a process, they were to find, was more easily said than done. Mussolini had got what he wanted and in his newfound greatness saw no reason for gratitude to either Britain or France. In both countries changes in attitude toward foreign affairs after the fall of Addis Ababa did not promise much material reward, and as the Government of France moved to the Left and that of Britain to the Right, the Duce looked for a more enterprising ally and other fields to conquer. Hitler was the obvious partner, and Spain the key to the Western outlet of the Mediterranean.* Germany's professional soldiers, amused by the enormous force Badoglio had found necessary for the campaign, were openly skeptical of Italy's military worth. But, as plans for an invasion of Spain were being completed in Berlin and Rome, the Führer found it expedient to demonstrate his support for Mussolini. Consequently a few months later, Germany became the first country to recognize the annexation; Austria and Hungary followed suit shortly afterward.

Haile Selassie the First, Lion of Judah, Elect of God, Emperor of Ethiopia, remained the one major embarrassment to a quiet settlement at Geneva. The League Council had been doing its best to mark time until faced with the inevitable *fait accompli*, but the Emperor—or *ex*-Emperor, as many people were already beginning to think of him—had other ideas. He had left Ethiopia to continue the fight for his throne, determined to carry the dispute to the bitter end before his cause was forgotten. But before he had traveled very far it was clear that the intention was to direct him to obscurity. Aboard the British cruiser H.M.S. *Enterprise* he had sailed from Djibuti for Haifa, and from there gone on to Jerusalem. No official welcome awaited him at either place, and "urgent business" in Sinai kept the British High Com-

---

* At the time, it was contended that the need to check the "Bolshevik danger" motivated Italian (and German) aggression in Spain. But a scheme for hegemony in the Mediterranean based on Italo-Spanish cooperation had existed even during the earlier period of the Spanish Monarchy.

missioner out of Jerusalem throughout the Emperor's sojourn. Lesser officials took their cue from the High Commissioner and studiously avoided the Ethiopian party. Yet this was not a situation which could continue indefinitely, and a telegram to the League Secretariat on May 10 eventually brought it to an end. "We now demand," cabled the Emperor, "that the League of Nations should pursue its efforts to ensure the respect of the Covenant, and that it should decide not to recognize territorial extensions on the exercise of an alleged sovereignty resulting from illegal recourse to armed force and many other violations of international obligations."

The next day, when the League Council met in Geneva, Mr. Wolde Mariam, the Ethiopian delegate to the League, followed up the telegram with a plea of his own.* After declaring passionately that "The Covenant has been torn up," he concluded by asking if the League of Nations—which was also the victim of Italian aggression—would bow its head to violence. This was a decidedly awkward question. Most of the delegates had in fact resigned themselves to accepting just that; and they were only awaiting a lead from Britain to terminate sanctions. But Britain was not yet ready for this step, and it seemed desirable in the meantime to propitiate those who clamored for justice for Haile Selassie by offering him sanctuary in Britain. The offer would not please Italy, and Baldwin was not prepared to permit the Emperor to be more of an embarrassment than his mere presence would make him. And so Eden announced that the Emperor would be expected "not to participate in any way in the furtherance of hostilities" while he partook of British hospitality.

Having decided to provide refuge, the next problem was to get the exile to it. Rumor had it that if the Emperor and his party were to travel through the Mediterranean on an ordinary passen-

---

* Count Aloisi objected to the presence of Wolde Mariam at the meeting. His delegation, he said, could not agree to the "self-styled Ethiopian representative" being present. "The only sovereignty in Ethiopia," he said, "is Italian sovereignty." Next morning (May 12) Aloisi and his delegation were recalled to Rome and on December 11, 1937, the Italian Government gave notice of its intention to withdraw from the League. As a consequence no Italian delegation was sent to any session of the Assembly or Council or to any meeting in Geneva after May 11, 1936.

ger liner, Mussolini planned to kidnap him and whisk him off to some place of exile in Italy. To thwart any plot of this nature it was decided that the cruiser H.M.S. *Capetown*, on her way from South Africa to Devonport for a refit, should be diverted to Haifa to pick up the Ethiopian entourage and provide a safe passage. According to one of the cruiser's officers, "the jetty was deserted, except for a few Palestine policemen stationed at intervals along it. The Emperor and his party walked slowly towards us down the whole length. To me he seemed a most impressive and dignified figure . . . the scene seemed to have an element of drama which has stuck in my mind. . . ." [3]

The ship's company remained at defense stations throughout the voyage. But the Italian fleet made no attempt to intercept the *Capetown*, and four days after leaving Haifa Haile Selassie disembarked at Gibraltar to finish his journey on the liner S.S. *Orford*. It has been suggested that the original intention of the British Government was to convey the Emperor and his entourage all the way to the United Kingdom in a British warship, but that second thoughts—prompted by Vansittart—resulted in the government ordering the captain of the *Capetown* (Captain D. Budgeon) to stage a diplomatic breakdown necessitating repairs at Gibraltar. [4] It is certainly true that the *Capetown* was on her way home to "pay off" after a long Far Eastern Commission, and the members of the ship's crew were wholly concerned with getting home. With the fallen Emperor aboard, a reception at Devonport by the men's wives and a band playing "All the nice girls love a sailor" would hardly have been appropriate. And the fact remains that the government's mission was nothing more than a safe passage of the Emperor's entourage through the Italian sphere of influence.

The S.S. *Orford* arrived at Southampton on June 3, 1936, and the Emperor traveled to London the same day. At Waterloo Station he was given a warm welcome by the "Friends of Abyssinia," members of the League of Nations Union, and similar organizations. A crowd had gathered along the route he was expected to take to the Ethiopian Embassy in Prince's Gate, but the police diverted his car, and the people waited in vain for a glimpse of the man whom the British Government would continue, for three years, to treat as a hot chestnut.

A detailed account of Haile Selassie's years of exile has no place in this story; it is sufficient to say that they were a period of frustration and humiliation. In the first few months there was still an opportunity to continue the struggle against Italy by diplomatic means. But as the months slipped by, the Emperor's cause steadily lost ground. Sanctions were raised and one by one the nations began to recognize the Italian regime in Ethiopia. From London, the Emperor and his entourage were shifted to Bath where after a few weeks in the Spa Hotel, "Fairfield," an unpretentious house on the outskirts of the city, was bought out of the proceeds of the sale of the royal banqueting plate to accommodate him and his retinue. Here, with the passage of time, the aura of regal distinction began to lose its charm, and sympathy for what was increasingly regarded as a lost cause steadily evaporated.

When the League Assembly met in Geneva on June 30, 1936, the decision to close the unhappy episode of Ethiopia had virtually been agreed. The first hint that Britain wanted the whole affair neatly finished had come by way of a calculated indiscretion three weeks previously when Mr. Neville Chamberlain described the continuance of a policy of sanctions as the "very midsummer of madness." [5] This had been followed on June 18 by a statement from Eden confirming the Cabinet's decision to propose to the League that sanctions should be abandoned. "It cannot be expected by anyone," the Foreign Secretary declared, "that the continuance of existing sanctions will restore in Abyssinia the position which has been destroyed; nobody expects that. That position can only be restored by military action. So far as I am aware no other Government—certainly not this Government —is prepared to take such military action." Five days later the Home Secretary, Sir John Simon, hammered the realism of the proposal: "The point is that, with the present situation in Europe and the great dangers surrounding us here at home, I am not prepared to see a single ship sunk even in a successful naval battle in the cause of Abyssinian independence."

Once Britain had pointed the way, other countries took up the cry. The French Government announced that in its view "consideration of fact" demanded the abolition of sanctions. Austria and Canada had already come to the conclusion that perpetuating them was useless; Belgium fell into line on June 22, as did Haiti, Honduras, Uruguay and, three days later, the "neutral" group—Sweden, Norway, Denmark, Holland, Finland, Switzerland, and Spain. And impetus to the movement was given by a proclamation issued under President Roosevelt's authority on June 20, which canceled the restrictive measures adopted by the United States and thereby gave a clear indication that the State Department regarded the war as being over.

The floor and galleries of the Assembly Hall in Geneva were packed on June 30; news that Haile Selassie was to plead his cause in person had filled the house with uneasy delegates and eager journalists. No matter how his listeners might feel at the appearance of this spectre from an Ethiopian grave of their digging, the League could hardly deny the Emperor his right to address the Assembly, and his performance has deservedly won its place in history.

After the formal business of electing the President, the Assembly got down to its deliberations, and Haile Selassie was called to the rostrum. As the small, dignified figure of the deposed Emperor rose and stood calmly by the microphone, Italian correspondents in the press gallery produced whistles from their pockets and blew them while others hooted and screamed insults. Still shouting epithets, the miscreants were hurriedly ejected by ushers and police, assisted none too gently by other foreign journalists.* When the hullabaloo subsided, Haile Selassie started to speak.

I, Haile Selassie I, Emperor of Ethiopia, am here today to claim that justice which is due to my people, and the assistance promised to it

---

* Subsequently the demonstrators were deprived of their cards of admission to the Assembly and expelled from Geneva. The Executive Committee of the International Association of Journalists publicly protested against their conduct and privately urged that they should be excluded from meetings of the League for a long period—if not permanently. Two months later, however, the Secretary-General, M. Avenol, reissued the admission cards to the culprits.

eight months ago, when fifty nations asserted that aggression had been committed in violation of international treaties. There is no precedent for a head of State speaking in this Assembly. But there is no precedent for a people being a victim of such injustice. . . .

After describing the horrors of war and attributing the Italians' success to their terrorization tactics—especially the "death-dealing rain" of mustard gas—he traced the diplomatic negotiations before and after the invasion, and Ethiopia's betrayal by the League. What assistance had its members—who had undertaken to prevent aggression—given to Ethiopia? he asked.

. . . It is not merely a question of the settlement of Italian aggression. It is collective security: it is the very existence of the League of Nations. It is the confidence that each State is to place in international treaties. It is the value of promises made to small States that the integrity and independence shall be respected and ensured. . . . In a word it is international morality that is at stake. . . . Representatives of the World I have come to Geneva to discharge in your midst the most painful of the duties of the head of a State. What reply shall I have to take back to my people? [6]

He concluded:

"God and history will remember your judgement."

It was an astonishing and polished oration for the head of what Italian spokesmen had persistently referred to as a "barbarous" state. The translation from the Amharic, in which it was spoken, dulled its vibrancy, but the words that came through were enough to cause the audience unease. Haile Selassie spoke prophetically; it would be presumptuous to pronounce on God's judgment but history has certainly had good reason to remember what happened. As he stepped down from the rostrum to a sheepish scatter of applause, the deposed Emperor was heard to murmur, "It is us today; it will be you tomorrow!"

If the lesson of the League's failure to assert the rule of law and the validity of the Covenant had the greatest impact on German policy, it was not altogether lost on France, Britain, or Soviet Russia.* With their eyes on the growing German threat,

* The reoccupation of the Rhineland had already produced a tragicomic

these countries appreciated that even if it had not been convenient for the Covenant to operate in the case of Ethiopia, it would
be extremely inconvenient should it fail to operate in Europe.
There was no hope for Ethiopia; but it was essential to ensure
that the sun rising over the new Italian Empire should also shine
over Europe, and to this end the League now vainly devoted its
efforts. It was left to Eden—regarded by the world as the man
who had forced the League to go as far as it had gone—to deliver
the obituary address and declare the Ethiopian affair over. After
reiterating what had been said about the desirability of canceling
the sanctions, he gave his opinion of why the League had failed:

. . . failure [was] due to the fact that there are certain risks which
nations are not prepared to run, save where there own interests are
more directly at stake than they were in this case. Clearly the ideal
system of collective security is one in which all nations are prepared
to go to all lengths—military lengths—to deal with the aggressor. . . .

Nobody held out any hopes for the Emperor; it was more
convenient to concentrate attention on the future. M. Blum for
France and M. Litvinov for the U.S.S.R. both echoed Eden's
sentiments. However, the cause of the trouble did not lie so
much in the Covenant as in its uncertain application, they said;
the sanctions against Italy had been too few, too late, and too
weakly enforced. Nevertheless sanctions were a powerful
weapon which could be, and should be, made an effective deterrent to other international lawbreakers. There was no point in
harping on the past; what was wanted now was a fresh start.

Only one voice—that of South Africa—was raised in support
of the continuance of sanctions; South Africa could see farther
into the future of Africa than the mother country, and she had
been set against the Italian adventure from the very beginning.
But her objections to the raising of sanctions had no effect, for
the minds of the rest of the Assembly were already made up.

Realizing that the Geneva flag was about to be hauled down,

situation at Geneva. Italy, indicted for her action in Ethiopia, was one who
was then in the seat of judgment on Hitler's move.

the Emperor made a last desperate attempt to stem the tide of events and rally support to his cause. On July 2, two Ethiopian resolutions were submitted to the Assembly, with the request that the vote on them should be decided by a roll call in the Assembly. The first declared that the League would not recognize "annexation obtained by force," the second recommended a £10,000,000 loan to enable Ethiopia to "defend her integrity and political independence." What they amounted to was a request that the League should agree to Ethiopia's fight continuing, and provide the wherewithal for it to do so; those members who did not agree were to declare themselves publicly. In the circumstances this was not an unreasonable demand—despite the fact that Haile Selassie no longer had any real authority in his country and no army to do any fighting.

Before the Ethiopian resolutions could be put to the Assembly, however, the President, M. van Zeeland of Belgium, introduced one of his own which, because it had been approved by the General Committee, was given priority. Following a long dissertation recording that "various circumstances have prevented the full application of the Covenant," that the Assembly remained "firmly attached to the principles of the Covenant" and was "desirous of strengthening the authority of the League," and so on, the resolution concluded quite briefly by recommending that the "measures taken in execution of Article 16 [i.e., sanctions against Italy] should be lifted." On July 4, M. van Zeeland's resolution was put to the vote. Being a recommendation, it was not necessary that it should be carried unanimously, but 44 delegations voted for it, only one (Ethiopia) against, and there were four abstentions. Then by 23 votes to one (Ethiopia), Haile Selassie's second resolution concerning the £10,000,000 loan was rejected. No vote was taken on the first of the Ethiopian resolutions, as the President ruled that it was covered by the adoption of his own. Two days later the Coordinating Committee decided that sanctions would be brought to an end, and on July 15, the day they were officially lifted, the event was celebrated in Italy in characteristic fashion. "Today," declared the Duce ebulliently, "on July fifteenth in the fourteenth year of the

Fascist era, a white flag has been hoisted in the ranks of world 'sanctionism.' "

This was not the end of Haile Selassie's struggle; nevertheless with the July decision at Geneva he suffered as crushing a defeat in the diplomatic campaign as he had suffered on the field of battle at Amba Aradam. Time would show that with the sunset on his empire the light was beginning to fade elsewhere; in 1936 the world reverted to 1914 and there was no turning back.

CHAPTER 16

Aftermath

Wars and rumours of wars are occupying the attention of Governments and peoples, but the world is thirsting more than ever for peace and justice. . . .

EMPEROR HAILE SELASSIE I,
London, September 8, 1936

With the departure of Haile Selassie from Addis Ababa a curtain was drawn between Ethiopia and the rest of the world. A strict Italian censorship ensured that little information got out of the country, and only from accounts of returning travelers was it possible to get any idea of what was happening. Foreign newspaper correspondents who had accompanied Badoglio's column to Addis Ababa linked up with those who had been reporting on the Emperor's side from capital. From them it was learned that the reactions of Badoglio's triumphant troops on entering the gaunt and debris-strewn capital which had been their goal for so many months, were disappointment and disillusionment. The town was but a burned-out shell, and the things the troops had anticipated would be the reward of their martial valor had all been looted. There were no cigarettes, no wine, and not much food, and for some weeks they were compelled to exist on a reduced ration scale. The capacity of the single-track railway bringing supplies from the coast was not enough to maintain the enormous army to European standards, and the five-hundred-mile track along which they had advanced from Massawa was the only other communication with the base area. Restraining nature in order to keep this road open during the rains was a gargantuan task, especially as the road gangs were constantly harassed by roaming bands of "patriots," and many of the garrisons holding isolated posts along this line saw more active service in the rainy season of 1936 than they had during the period of active campaigning.

The campaign was over but hostilities did not end with the occupation of Addis Ababa. Mussolini's jubilant proclamation announcing the founding of an Italian East African Empire ushered in little more than five years of incomplete military occupation. For four months the rainy season restricted serious military operations, and to ease the supply problem many of the white troops were withdrawn. The rest had to settle down under canvas, waiting behind their barbed wire entanglements for the weather to clear. Within three days of the occupation of the capital the death penalty was instituted for looting and possession of firearms, and during the following week eighty-five Ethiopians accused of breaking these laws were tried and sentenced by a Summary Court. Many more were executed on the spot by the Carabinieri, treatment hardly calculated to induce those Ethiopians who had fled to the hills* to return to their homes. Armed parties roamed around the vicinity of the town, and it was not safe for the Italians to venture far unless they were in strength. Farther afield, the country was in an even greater turmoil. The Emperor's provisional Government at Gore continued to function under Ras Imru, but its authority was confined to a limited zone in the western provinces, and Ras Desta, with the remnants of his army, exercised a certain amount of control in Galla Sidamo. Elsewhere, other than in the immediate vicinity of the strategic points garrisoned by Italian troops, the only authorities

---

* French sources estimated that a minimum of 1,500 Ethiopians left the capital before it was occupied by the Italians.

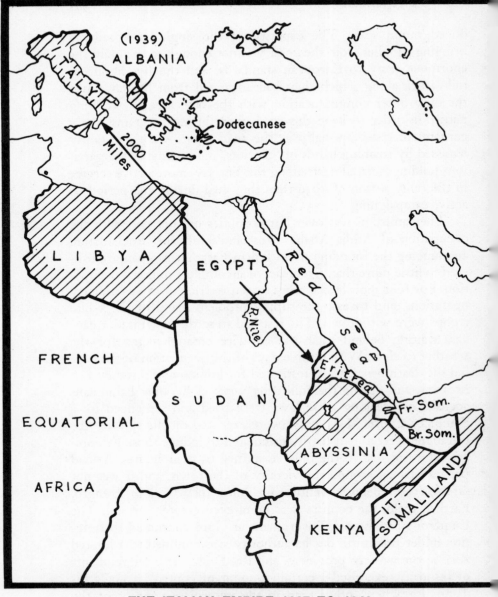

THE ITALIAN EMPIRE 1937 TO 1940

were the local chiefs who ruled according to the age-old feudalistic tradition. Well-armed parties of tribesmen roamed these regions, and as time passed these parties became increasingly daring. Toward the end of June 1936, all but one of a party of Italian airmen (including General Magliocco, Second-in-Command of the Regia Auronautica in Italian East Africa) that had made a forced landing at Lehemti in Jimma, were massacred. A week later a stretch of the railway track was torn up by another party of Ethiopians, and three weeks after that an organized attack on Italian outposts guarding the southern approach to Addis Ababa was repulsed only after heavy fighting.

Pending the arrival of the dry season, the Italians concentrated their efforts on organizing the civil administration in the regions they had occupied. Marshal Graziani superceded Badoglio as Viceroy in August, and the pacification policy laid down by Rome followed the pattern of that which he had masterminded in Libya. Mussolini's intention was that Ethiopia should be governed for the benefit of Italy and that those parts of the country suited to the settlement of Italians should be colonized. To provide Italy with more foreign exchange, Ethiopia's export trade was to be developed, and her imports were to be exclusively Italian. Racial segregation was to be enforced and strict regulations were laid down to ensure the separation of European and Ethiopian quarters in the towns; taxi and bus services provided solely for the use of Italians imposed another measure of apartheid. Employment would be found for 100,000 soldiers who would be given indefinite leave in Ethiopia, it was announced. District Commissioners were appointed; Italian law courts established; new schools and hospitals opened; the finances of the country were taken over by the Bank of Italy; the Fascist salute became obligatory.

Implementing this colonial policy in the larger towns—Addis Ababa, Harar, Diredawa, Jimma, and Gondar—was relatively easy as the people were not in a position to argue with Italian bayonets. But in the country districts it was a different matter. The western region centered on Gore clearly had to be brought to heel by a military operation, and before this could be achieved

Ras Imru had written to the League suggesting that his territory should become a British mandate, excluded from the Italian Empire, and left in peace to continue its coffee trade with the Sudan.* The attitude of the population of Gojjam was surprising, since this was one area in which the Italians had had considerable propaganda success before and during the campaign. However, a short spell of Italian administration had soon convinced the Gojjams that the new masters were little or no improvement on the Emperor. Fostered and directed by a group of young educated Ethiopians who had escaped massacre in Addis Ababa and called themselves the Committee of Union and Collaboration,† the Gojjams rebelled in 1938. In order to terrorize the population, Graziani initiated a policy of iniquitous reprisals and his minions added another series of crimes to those which so disgraced Italian rule in Ethiopia. All Ethiopians who had occupied administrative posts were systematically and ruthlessly liquidated. Some were bundled into aircraft, ostensibly to visit the King of Italy in Rome; later, when their broken bodies were found in the hills, the expression "He went to Rome" became synonymous with one-way air passages to eternity.

Military operations were resumed as soon as the rains abated, and an Italian column starting out from Addis Ababa in September occupied Gore just over a month later. The provisional Government had fled, but Ras Imru, hemmed in between the Italians and the Sudanese border, gave himself up on December 17. Subsequently he was taken to Italy and sent to a penitentiary island. Meanwhile, another Italian column assembled in the capital had set off southwest, in order to deal with Ras Desta and Dejazmatch Gabre Mariam, who were reputed to have mobilized a considerable force of "patriots" in the Great Lake District. First contact was made in the foothills of Galla Sidamo on December 16, and the Ethiopians lost the battle. The Italians followed up, and by the end of the month the provinces of Jimma, Kafa, and Arusi were all under tenuous Italian control. But it was another

---

* Hardly a practical proposition, although the territory did adjoin the Sudan. Britain continued to forbid the passage of arms and ammunition into the region on the grounds that it might encourage war between the tribes!

† It was an offshoot of this movement that welcomed the advent of the British Mission to Ethiopia in 1940.

eight weeks before the remnant of Ras Desta's army was surrounded. Gabre Mariam and Desta were ordered to surrender.
They elected to fight it out, and Gabre Mariam was killed in the
action which followed. Perhaps it was better that he did die in
battle, for Desta was captured and immediately executed and his
severed head paraded through the streets of Jimma for all to see,
"in order to liquidate the situation once and for all." * With the
capture of Imru and the demise of Desta, the major trouble spots
had been dealt with, and Graziani, whose Libyan nickname "The
Butcher" was shown to be not without foundation, signaled
Rome. "I am proud to place in the Duce's hands," he said,
"the clear-cut totalitarian victory that will allow us to devote
ourselves without anxiety to the civil development of the Empire."

By February 1937, it appeared that the situation had not in
fact been liquidated once and for all. Graziani's terrorist methods
had had considerable effect, but the Ethiopians were a tough and
resilient race. To many of them cruelty was a mere mode of expression, but even the most hardened of them had been shaken
by the savage reprisals which followed an incident in Addis
Ababa on February 19, 1937; indeed the atrocities which were
perpetrated then are still regarded by the Ethiopians as the apo-
gee of Fascist barbarity. On this date, it had been customary for
the Emperor to make an annual distribution of alms to the poor
of Addis Ababa, and the Italian Viceroy had decided to ape the
Emperor. During the ceremony, grenades were thrown at the
table where Graziani and members of his staff were sitting, and
although nobody was killed, Graziani and several other officers
were wounded. General Liotta, the Commander of the Regia
Aeronautica in East Africa, who had to have his leg amputated as
a result of the explosions, was the most severely injured.

In the confusion, who actually threw the bombs was not
quite clear; some accounts say that one of the assailants was a
disgruntled Eritrean interpreter employed by the Italians. The
Italians themselves believed that the attempted assassination was
the work of Ras Desta's agents, who had gone to the ceremony

---

* This was how Graziani explained his methods to the Duce in a telegram
of March 1, 1937.

concealing grenades in the voluminous folds of their *shammas*. Whoever was responsible, retaliation was swift and ferocious. No sooner had the bombs exploded than the Italian guards at the ceremony panicked and emptied their rifles into the crowd. Ethiopian observers subsequently claimed that more than three hundred dead were counted in the palace courtyard. This was only a beginning. As soon as darkness fell, groups of Blackshirts, flaming with blood-lust, went through the native quarter exacting savage reprisals with sword, dagger, rifle, bomb, and torch. All that night, and again on two following nights, the Italians searched, herded, killed, and burned, and by the morning of February 22, 1937, thousands of the city's inhabitants had been slain. What part the Italian administration played in the massacre is difficult to assess. Graziani is reported to have stood at the window of the Italian hospital to which he had been taken after the incident, gazing over the burning city like a second Nero; Italian officers are said to have driven around the town admiring the orgiastic scenes but making no attempt to stop them. The most charitable explanation must be to attribute the tragedy to the excitable Latin temperament of officers who lost their heads, and troops who got out of hand. But the fact that the Addis Ababa massacre followed the slaughter of priests in the monastery at Debra Libranos, and similar treatment was meted out at several of the smaller towns, tends to devalue this view.

It was General Douhet of the Regia Aeronautica who conceived the tactics of the *Guerra Fulmine*—the lightning air war which the Germans really put into practice in 1940. From his theory of mass air attacks to break the morale of a civilian population, it was a short cry to other terrorist methods. "First it must be the victory of one country," said Douhet, "then humanity." This might have been Graziani's text in Ethiopia. However, when his blood-and-iron policy failed—and there is little doubt that the attempt on his life in February was symptomatic of its failure—he was replaced in December 1937 by the humane and worthy Duke of Aosta, who introduced a policy of greater cooperation with the Ethiopians.*

* Graziani's career was not finished, but a few years later, when he failed to lead an Italian army to victory in Egypt, he had to resign in disgrace.

With the demise of Ras Desta, there was no more serious opposition to the Italian regime in Ethiopia until after the outbreak of the war in Europe. An ill-organized resistance movement continued until 1938, when the efforts of the Committee of Union and Collaboration fostering the spirit of nationalism began to gain ground. Guerrilla operations against Italian columns and isolated outposts were waged throughout the period, but jealousies between the chiefs and their retainers led to the spilling of as much Ethiopian as Italian blood. With the gradual development of the Italian administrative machine and the disarmament of the Ethiopians, conditions started to settle down. Appreciating that the key to the progress which had evaded the Emperor lay in development of adequate communications, the Italians devoted considerable resources to the construction of a network of new roads linking the main centers and designed to open up the interior. Am ambitious scheme of public works, including the development of Assab as a port, a hydroelectric works on the Juba River, land reclamation, town planning, housing, hygienic measures, and other projects were also launched. Unfortunately for the Ethiopians, who would have benefited most in the long run, developing a virgin country takes both time and money, and although Italy expected to have plenty of time, the Duce's "fatherland" certainly did not have plenty of money. The war had cost four billion lire—$200,000,000—and the Fascist treasury was empty. The new colony undoubtedly had resources, but as it became clear that they were not as extensive as the glowing reports submitted by the Consuls had predicted, the business of empire building began to lose its charm.

"This is not a country where one can win wealth easily, but a land of hard toil," said Graziani at the end of his term as Viceroy, and Badoglio voiced the opinion that at least thirty years would be needed before Ethiopia began to show any return for the money that had already been spent. Mussolini had talked of settling a million peasants in the country, but only a few agricultural colonies were actually set up and none of these was particularly successful. Conditions for growing rubber and cotton were favorable, and it was hoped to expand the coffee and citrus cultivation around Harar. But willing emigrants were slow in coming

forward; there was, in the words of the Minister for Italian East
Africa, "a certain luxury mentality which is in opposition to the
discipline of Fascism, which might threaten to compromise colonization." Meanwhile the thousands of Italians who had gone to
Ethiopia as soldiers or laborers and elected the Duce's offer of
indefinite "leave" resisted the efforts to be settled on the land.
Preferring to settle in the towns as shopkeepers and artisans,
many of them fell on hard times and by 1939 a growing "poor
white" problem in Ethiopia exposed the hollowness of the new
Roman Empire.

By the time the Duke of Aosta succeeded Graziani, Italy was
embroiled elsewhere and the Duce's spotlight was no longer fo-
cused on Ethiopia. Appetite, it is said, comes with eating, and
although Italy had not digested the Ethiopian meal, she was looking for another dish and the pressure in Ethiopia diminished.
Under Aosta's direction efforts were made to substitute the military with a colonial administration. Police took over from troops
in the towns; Ethiopians were elected to minor administrative
appointments, and the terms of the Constitution promulgated in
1936, designed to destroy the last vestiges of the feudal power of
the great Rases, were quietly applied. *Africa Orientale* was divided into five provinces, each ruled by an Italian governor with
the assistance of an executive council, a secretariat, and an advisory body of administrative and technical advisers. The military
tribunals were closed down, and for civil cases a system of native
courts presided over by Italian officials was introduced. By 1939
the enlightened policy was beginning to show positive results,
especially in the old provinces of Harar and Jimma, where the
population was predominantly Muhammadan. During the campaign the Italians had tried to establish good relations with the
Coptic Church, whose titular head, the foreign-born Abuna
Kyril, declared when Addis Ababa was occupied that it was the
duty of the Ethiopian clergy to obey Italy.* (Those of the Cop-

---

* Kyril was on the dais with Graziani on February 19, 1937, and was
wounded during the attempt to assassinate the Viceroy. From Cairo, where he
went to recuperate, he denounced the Italians and refused to return to Ethiopia.
An old, half-blind priest, Abraham, was appointed as Abuna by the Italians,
but he did not enjoy the respect of the Ethiopians and was excommunicated by
the synod of Alexandria.

tic prelates who failed in this duty were liquidated.) But good relations were not confined to those of the Christian faith, and although officially the Italian administration afforded complete religious toleration to all *loyal* subjects, it was to Islam that Mussolini biased his friendship and support. By posing as the champion of Catholicism and of Islam at the same time, the Duce hoped to drive a wedge between the Muhammadans and Christians of Ethiopia,* by cutting back the authority of the Christian Amhara—the former rulers—in favor of the Hararis, Somalis, and Moslim Gallas. But the policy was not particularly successful. During the latter half of 1938 the Ethiopian nationalist movement began to gain ground, and early in 1939 a link was established with the Emperor in exile. To consolidate this link, Haile Selassie dispatched one of his officials, Mr. Lorenzo Taezaz, on a secret mission to Ethiopia, and the fact that Taezaz was able to wander about Ethiopia—in uniform and with an escort, it was said—is an indication of the state of affairs prevalent in Ethiopia just before the Restoration. Italy had not had sufficient time to organize and develop the Empire of which she had expected and on which she had squandered so much. When the time came it was to collapse like a pack of cards.

Even before Badoglio had brought the Ethiopian campaign to its conclusion, Mussolini had been planning to use the diplomatic victory it would bring to start upon new adventures nearer home. To retain its mystique the Fascist system had to continue to look efficient and powerful. The appearance of power was the important thing; even if it meant chasing an imperial phantom, the Roman Eagle must spread its wings over greater tracts of territory and dominate more souls. Ethiopia was not the only pebble on the beach; for fifteen years the Duce had dreamed of Italian domination of the Mediterranean and of pursuing "civilizing missions" south and east from its seaboard. To this objective he now devoted his efforts. Italian agents and fifth columns in Syria, Palestine, Afghanistan, and even India and Turkey, were set to work exploiting every international event which

---

* During 1935, on a visit to North Africa, Mussolini proclaimed himself "Protector of Islam." It was a gesture that did not go unreproved. "A Catholic Power" said Pius XI, "should not be the protector of the infidel."

showed up the "weakness" and "perfidy" of the British and French, as contrasted with the "power" and "magnanimity" of Italy. Other covert activities which were pursued included intrigues inside metropolitan France and the British Isles; at the same time the Italian press and the Italian radio drew themselves into a violent polemical campaign against the two "decadent" Powers.* In the case of France, this was a poor return for Laval's contribution to the Duce's success in Ethiopia. But things were changing in France, and the Popular Front Government of M. Blum did not promise the easy bargaining which had obtained in the days of Laval.

At this juncture, partnership was as advantageous to Hitler as it was to Mussolini. The Führer had two alternatives: either he could take advantage of the fact that the Ethiopian venture had alienated Italy from Britain and France and brought condemnation by the League to try to smash Italian influence in Central Europe, or he could ally himself with Mussolini and exploit Britain's fear of Italian encroachments in the Mediterranean, in order to bargain for a free hand for himself in Central and Southeast Europe. When he decided to opt for the latter, war in Europe was inevitable. Up to this moment a German-Italian alliance had been virtually unthinkable; German occupation of Austria would bring the frontier of Germany right up to the Brenner Pass, beyond which a German minority was under Italian rule. Austria had remained a bone of contention between the two countries. But when this bone was eliminated and Mussolini's suspicions lulled, the Duce's face turned irrevocably toward Germany. An agreement was signed in the summer of 1936, and so the Rome-Berlin Axis was created.† Shortly after ratifying the

* While planning aggression in Spain, Mussolini was backing the Cagoulards and other French terrorist organizations. In Ireland there was a deliberate attempt to establish a Fascist nucleus with Irish-born boys of Italian parentage. During the summers of 1937 and 1938 a number of these children (Irish citizens, not Italian subjects) had a free holiday in Italy; there they were taught that their first loyalty was to the Fascism Mussolini had once said was "not for export."

† This phrase was remembered from a somewhat muddled speech at Milan by the Duce: "This Berlin-Rome line is not a diaphragm but rather an axis, around which can revolve all those European states with a will to collaboration and peace."

agreement, Mussolini was given a private view of the new Austro-German Treaty, published in July, which recognized the "full sovereignty of Austria." Each party to the treaty—the wolf and the lamb—pledged itself to refrain from interfering in the "internal affairs" of the other; if this meant anything, it could only be that the lamb was no longer in danger of becoming part of the prey of the wolf, and almost a year later Hitler showed his junior partner a map of Europe with Austria under the German colors. A few months later this situation was realized. Italians were concerned but they could offer no resistance; Austria under German domination was part of the price they had to pay for the new partnership. Britain and France protested, and when he was sure the Duce was going to make no move, the German Dictator sent a telegram: *Benito*, it read, *Ich werde es Ihnen nie vergessen* ("Benito, I'll never forget it"). Benito could hardly have forgotten that only two years previously he had mobilized an army corps on the Brenner for the express purpose of keeping Germany out of Austria. But thoughts of rebuilding the Stresa front had been lost in the excitement of the Ethiopian success. A new adventure loomed in Spain; "the Italian character had to be formed through fighting," and there was a chance for military glory, for the superman to create himself greater than Caesar.

Except as a consequence of what happened in Ethiopia, what happened in Spain forms no part of this story. Foreign intervention in the Civil War was supposed to be motivated by ideological reasons, although from Italy's point of view there were material considerations.* What mattered most was Spain's strategic position, for a friendly Spain could seriously embarrass British naval power in Mussolini's *mare nostrum*, and in his endeavors to secure a speedy victory the Duce was drawn even more deeply into the struggle. However, but for his embroilment in Spain, it is possible that a new and lasting Anglo-Italian understanding might have been reached in the autumn of 1936. Yet it is doubtful whether any such understanding would have made any dif-

---

* Both Germany and Italy had their eyes on the wolfram deposits on the Spanish side of the Pyrenees, and Spain's copper—two important commodities lacking in both countries.

ference in the long run. Ostensibly, both sides attempted to bury
the hatchet, return to the pre-Walwal era, and reestablish the old
Anglo-Italian friendship. In pronouncements intended for domestic consumption the Duce tended to crow over Italy's achievements, diplomatic and military. But in private, and in statements
meant for British ears and eyes, more conciliatory language was
used. Speaking in Milan on November 1, he declared that it was
never Italy's intention to threaten British sea routes across the
Mediterranean. Two days later Lord Halifax informed the House
of Commons that Britain and Italy both had vital interests in the
Mediterranean and that there was no question of which country
had the greater interest. Next day, Eden voiced his concern. He
did not challenge Mussolini's assertion that the Mediterranean
was, for Italy, "her very life," he said. But freedom of communication in those waters was "vital in a full sense of the word"
to the British Commonwealth of Nations.[1]

A Franco-Italian commercial agreement was signed on November 6—about the same time as the Duce was telling Mr.
Ward Price that he would welcome a "gentlemen's agreement"
with Britain, protecting the interests of both sides, and "reassur-
ing all other Mediterranean States." [2] The outcome was a joint
declaration, issued in Rome on January 2, 1937, in which both
countries agreed to respect each other's rights to the Mediterranean and guarantee the maintenance of the territorial *status quo*.
In this way the Duce disclaimed Italy's intention to establish
bases in the Balearic Islands, Andalusia, and Spanish Morocco—
from which Italy hoped to control the western entrance to the
Mediterranean. The idea of Britain and Italy establishing a
friendly relationship once more was regarded favorably in Britain. And if the Gentlemen's Agreement failed to produce the results expected of it, it was not the fault of the British Government. As a token of goodwill the British Legation at Addis
Ababa was closed and replaced by a Consulate. Three weeks
later the gesture was supplemented with an agreement with Italy
which permitted the Somalis under British rule to continue to use
the grazing areas and water holes in the frontier region that had
been their right for generations. (As these rights had been guar-

anteed by previous treaties, Britain gained nothing.) Friendly relations between the Italian administration in Ethiopia and the British authorities in Kenya and the Sudan were also established, and from these developments it was clear that the British Government was doing its best to let bygones be bygones.

Despite these efforts, Anglo-Italian relations on the public level were anything but cordial. Before the ink of the Gentlemen's Agreement had had time to dry, a verbal war broke out between the two countries. Every incident which presented an opportunity to criticize Italian policy was seized upon avidly by some British newspapers, and their Italian counterparts replied in kind. In March 1937, when a division of Italian "volunteers" was routed by the International Brigade at Guadalajara on the road to Madrid, British journalists coupled the defeat with Caporetto. Reaction in Rome to the outburst of scorn and sarcasm showed that the Italians were as sensitive of their military prowess in Spain as they had been about Adowa. Two months later, news that Haile Selassie had been invited to attend the Coronation of King George VI became another provocative issue, and the attendance of the Prince of Piedmont (as the representative of King Victor Emmanuel) was canceled.*

On May 28, 1937, Stanley Baldwin resigned and his place was taken by Neville Chamberlain. Throwing himself enthusiastically into Vansittart's policy of detaching Mussolini from Hitler, Chamberlain let it be known that Italy's conquest of Ethiopia would be recognized, and Italian intervention in Spain condoned. Only if Italian troops were withdrawn, Eden insisted, and when it was clear that Chamberlain was set on his policy, Eden resigned—his place being taken by Lord Halifax. For the time being Eden left the stage, to return later with his wagon hitched to the star of a greater and more worthy Prime Minister than the man whose indecisive foreign policy he had endeavored so earnestly to promote.

On November 3, 1938, Lord Halifax announced a *de jure* recognition of Italy's regime in Ethiopia. Chamberlain settled down to an openly pro-Italian policy and in January 1939 he and

* Italy was represented at the ceremony by her Ambassador, Count Grandi.

Halifax visited Rome to confer with the Duce and meet the new Emperor of Ethiopia. The flags waved, salutes were fired, the two British ministers were wined and dined, toasts were drunk to an Anglo-Italian *rapprochement*, and in the midst of the ceremonial goodwill, Haile Selassie, bitterly eking out his time in Bath, was forgotten. For trusting the League of Nations, and having faith in its two most influential members, Britain and France, the Emperor had paid a heavy price. Little wonder therefore that he is supposed to have sent a telegram to the President of the Polish Republic when he learned of the British guarantee to Poland: "Learn that you have received the promise of British support. You have my warmest sympathy."

Epilogue and Epitaph

It is not the part of a wise physician to croon incantations over a disease that needs the knife.

SOPHOCLES

The campaign in Ethiopia has been aptly described as a colonial war of European proportions. Except for some administrative pointers which were soon forgotten, few lessons of any military importance emerged from it. David's trial of strength with Goliath is interesting only because of David's success, and no doubt if the Ethiopians with their 1874 Etienne rifles had been able to stem the advance of the Fascist Juggernaut with its Fiat machine guns, how they did so would have revealed either some startling application of the principles of war or alternatively incredible stupidity on the part of the Italians. The extensive use of motorized columns made possible the rapid advance into the heart of Ethiopia; the use of mustard gas and vast numbers of aircraft simplified ground tactics and helped to compensate for the lack of training of the Italian troops and some of the amateurish mistakes of their commanders. One thing that can be said is that the Italian High Command did learn as the campaign progressed, and it is greatly to Badoglio's credit as a soldier that he was able to readjust his ideas to take account of the power which aircraft and gas put in his hands. On the other hand, the inability of the Ethiopians to appreciate that their only hope lay in guerrilla warfare cost the Emperor his crown.

With De Bono in command, the war started like an eighteenth century colonial operation, and not until sanctions were called for at Geneva was it precipitated into the twentieth century. To pay off the moral debt of Adowa and as a contribution to the ideal of making Italy "great, respected and feared," Mussolini wanted some Italian blood to be spilled. De Bono, more of a Latin than the Duce, put caution before glory, and his bloodless tactics might have continued for some time. Yet, even if the campaign had been spread over two or three campaigning seasons and the Emperor's defeat deferred for two or three years, it is doubtful if the bloodletting would have been less than it was. The creation of the new Empire cost Italy just over 2,000 Italian and 1,600 Eritrean lives, and according to the Ethiopian Government 275,000 Ethiopians were killed in action.*

During the early months, De Bono's advance was little more than a glorified route march into unoccupied territory. Badoglio's brief to get the war over and done with meant bringing the Emperor's forces to battle, and if Haile Selassie had allowed the

---

* Italian casualties January 1, 1935–May 31, 1936: Regular Army and Blackshirts: 1,148 killed; 125 died of wounds, 31 missing. Workmen 453; Colonial troops 1,593.

The Ethiopian figures are taken from a memorandum presented to the Paris Conference in 1946. In it the following losses were recorded:

Killed in action	275,000
Patriots killed in battle (i.e., men killed during the occupation 1936–1941)	78,500
Women, children and others killed by bombing	17,800
Massacre of February 1937	30,000
Persons who died in concentration camps	35,000
Patriots executed by sentence of Summary Courts	24,000
Persons who died from privations due to the destruction of their villages	300,000
	760,300

The loss of 2,000 churches, 525,000 houses, and the slaughter or confiscation of 5,000,000 beef cattle, 7,000,000 sheep and goats, 1,000,000 horses and mules, and 700,000 camels was also claimed in this memorandum and a bill for reparations totaling £184,746,023 was presented to the Economic Commission for Italy.

Italians to be drawn into the heart of his country and then preyed on their long lines of communications, his downfall might have been postponed. But guerrilla warfare is effective only when the local population shields and supports its freedom fighters. As the population of the Ogaden resented the Emperor's role he would have had to sacrifice this part of his empire to the Italians, and without a change of heart at Geneva his total defeat would have come ultimately. By delaying the issue it is just possible that uneasy consciences might have turned support to his cause, but this is conjecture and as it was, by advancing to meet the invaders, the Ethiopian commanders played straight into Badoglio's hands. Consequently when the Rases and the Emperor committed their men to battle they did so in circumstances unfavorable to the Ethiopians. Ras Mulugeta's rout presaged the Emperor's own defeat, since the rapid series of blows which the Italians delivered after the success at Amba Aradam never gave the Ethiopians time to recover. How they might have put off the evil day was shown by Ras Imru's performance in the Tembien. The guerrilla fighting there was a constant source of ·discomfiture to Badoglio, and it was a long time before the Tembien area was finally cleared. This was the best form of defense the Ethiopians could have adopted, but events showed it could not be sustained and as his authority rested on the feudal power of the chiefs, Haile Selassie was not in a position to exercise any real control over the tactics they employed. Independent in peace, they were even more independent in war; jealous of their rights and of each other, reluctant to take orders, the chiefs fought for their own feudal domains, and the peoples' first loyalty was to their local chief—as illustrated by Gojjam's reluctance to take up arms on behalf of the man who had deposed Ras Hailu. The Emperor's cause was important only in so far as their territories were part of Ethiopia. How and where they fought they regarded as entirely their own affair, and the lack of mutual cooperation was illustrated by what happened in the Tigre battles. Internal troubles—not necessarily provoked by, ·but certainly fostered by, the Italians—made centralized control more difficult; Haile Selassie Gugsa's defection and the behavior of the people of Gojjam exemplify the seething turmoil of an unstable regime. In choosing his commanders the Emperor had to weigh up the loyalties of his subordinates, and setting Amhara nobles in authority over non-Amharic peoples was not conducive to patriotism.

In discipline, organization, equipment, and training, the Italians were vastly superior, and the supply problem—difficult for both sides—was such as to render prolonged operations by the Ethiopians well nigh impossible. For a few days the levies could live on the meager rations which they or their camp followers carried on their backs. But when these supplies were exhausted, they were compelled to live off the country, and this tended to restrict their movements. Individually the Ethiopians were courageous enough, and in the first flush of their attacks they fought with fanatical courage. But their tactics played straight into the Italians' hands, and mowed down by machine guns, bombed and shelled to pieces, it was inevitable that their morale would break. Only two of the senior Ethiopian commanders—Ras Imru in the north, and Dejiak Nasibu on the southern front—showed any skill; as generals the rest of the chiefs were incompetent.

With the quality and quantity of arms in their possession, superior organization, better generals, and the advantage of strategical initiative, the Italians ought to have been able to cut through Ethiopia like a knife through butter. Yet it took seven months from the outbreak of hostilities before Badoglio and Graziani reached their objectives. The greater part of this time can be accounted for by the "phony" war period covering the ponderous operations which gave the Italians Adowa and Makale, and it was January 1936 before the campaign really started to move. Once Badoglio's and Graziani's offensives started to roll forward in earnest, the duration of the war was calculable and it was nature which proved to be a more potent enemy than the Emperor's forces. Despite the extensive use of colonial units, large numbers of white troops were involved, and the Italians' ultimate success depended on moving them with their supplies and heavy equipment. To do this meant building roads and developing tracks to take vehicles; for this reason the campaign was as much a battle of roads as a trial of strength—presenting more challenges to the engineers than infantry objectives or targets for the guns.

Graziani's operations on the southern front, where the Ethiopians appear to have been better equipped, were virtually independent of the main conflict in the north. His main purpose was to engage Ethiopian forces which could otherwise have been deployed on the northern front, but his secondary objective was to cut the Djibuti–Addis Ababa railway. Although Graziani forestalled the Ethiopians on the two occasions they attempted an offensive against Italian Somaliland, in this section they undoubtedly showed considerably more initiative than their colleagues in the north. Nevertheless the first Italian offensive led to the rout of Ras Desta's army, and the second resulted in the break of Dejiak Nasibu's defensive positions, and the virtual destruction of his army.

In the heyday of the scramble for Africa the major powers had tacitly recognized that Ethiopia was Italy's prize—if she could get it. And, by implication, the treaty which brought Italy into the First World War had preserved her claim. Having got neither Ethiopia nor any worthwhile substitute from the postwar distribution of spoils, Italy felt that she had reason to feel aggrieved, and but for Ethiopia being a member of the League it is possible that she might have attacked Ethiopia without either Britain or France saying a word. Reflecting on their own colonial history and the political climate of the early thirties, it is logical to suppose that both would have found it expedient to hold their tongues and let Italy quietly settle her growing pains on the Ethiopian plateau. Thus it is particularly ironic that it was Italy who sponsored Haile Selassie's application to join the League, for undoubtedly it was Ethiopia's membership of the League and the "friendship" pact signed in 1928 that established a cast-iron case against the policy of aggression which Mussolini decided to adopt. As an invasion of Ethiopia meant abrogating the principles of the Covenant as well as tearing up the Friendship Pact, it would have been more logical—and certainly more honest—if Italy had left the League, denounced her agreements, and then prepared for war.

The crisis which arose out of the Walwal incident was ex-

tremely embarrassing for those of the British and French statesmen whose eyes were fixed apprehensively on Germany. From
their point of view Mussolini may be judged to have been saved
by German rearmament, which was rapidly reducing the margin
of safety in Europe—a margin already narrowed beyond danger
point by that Utopian belief in disarmament which reaches its
peak shortly before any great war breaks out. Fresh from his
negotiations in Rome, Pierre Laval was probably the most embarrassed of all, but to him a Franco-Italian entente was far more
important than Ethiopia's independence. Outside France, this
man has been universally condemned for the bargain he struck
with Mussolini in January 1935. Yet, in retrospect, he appears to
have displayed a patriotism truly French, and to have been animated by a love of country and of peace no less deep than that
motivating the statesmen of other nations. To suggest that he
was an austere and incorruptible patriot like Poincaré, or an international idealist like Briand, would be unjust—and it is equally
absurd to suggest that he was looking forward hopefully to a
German conquest of France in order to play the ignominious
and distressing role of Vichy jackal to the Nazi lions. Laval in
the thirties was striving to do the best for France, and if Mussolini wanted Ethiopia, so far as he was concerned this was a small
price to pay for Franco-Italian cooperation. Japan had already
violated the Covenant, so had Germany, and both had got away
with it, so there seemed little reason why Italy should not do the
same. It was unfortunate, but as Laval saw it the purpose of the
League was to preserve peace *in Europe;* to initiate measures
which would alienate and perhaps bring war with Italy over
Ethiopia would be to sacrifice the end for the sake of the means.
Furthermore, if France and Britain got involved in a war with
Italy, it was highly unlikely that Germany would be content to
look on.

Britain had no direct quarrel with Italy, whose projected
conquest of Ethiopia menaced no vital *material* British interest,
and it was the attitude of the British public which proved to be
the unexpected factor that Whitehall had to reckon with. The
collective security idea had had a stupifying effect on political

thought throughout Europe, more especially in Britain. It was assumed that mere condemnation by the League would frighten any European country out of any warlike designs; sanctions were a way of fighting without actually going to war, and although they had never been imposed on Japan, presumably this was because she was so far away. What people failed to appreciate was that the League was simply an agglomeration of member States, and that if those States were inadequately armed and, in the final analysis, not prepared to go to war, the League's condemnation would count for nothing with the totalitarian states. The responsibility for translating the League's decisions into positive action rested on the two leaders, Britain and France; the rest took their cue from them. The French Government was reluctant to do anything to antagonize its new-found friend and potential ally, and the British Government concluded that any League war would turn out primarily to be a war of Britain against Italy. Closing the sluice gate of Suez would precipitate Anglo-Italian hostilities, and Baldwin's ministers reckoned that for all its protestations the British public did not want a shooting war. There was also the practical consideration that even if a League war was short and victorious, it would probably cost a heavy price in destroyed or damaged ships of the Royal Navy, at a time when the German danger made that price too heavy to pay. Furthermore Hitler might also use a diversion in the Mediterranean to spread himself in central Europe.

Thus it could be argued that Baldwin's Government acted prudently, and faithfully interpreted the will of the British people; if it did it got small thanks for its pains. Where some criticism seems justifiable is in regard to both the Government and Opposition failing to make clear that Haile Selassie's Ethiopia was either a lost cause or that defending it would mean war. But in October 1935 there was no clear realization that Italy would attain a quick victory and subsequently that the sanctions imposed would fail to deter her. Baldwin justified his actions as the means to an end. When accused of dangerously delaying rearmament until 1936, his reply was that public opinion would not have accepted it sooner; in this he was right. The notorious resolution passed by the Oxford Union (subsequently adopted by a number of other university debating societies) "That this House will not fight for King or Country" reflected more than the whims of a generation of undergraduates, and many people in Britain in 1935 were opposed to rearmament on a large scale. Their opposition to such a program was based on a belief that if collective security were mobilized, Britain's arms contribution need not be excessive; concurrently it was also believed that the collective security which the League offered would also supply the means of introducing collateral disarmament. Certainly no intelligent person can fail to appreciate that the ultimate survival of humanity depends on the ability of the nations of the world to erect a law and enforce it; unfortunately more than blind faith in the ideals of a world organization is necessary. In December 1935, the Archbishop of York spoke prophetically when he said that he considered "it may be necessary to have another great and horrible war to establish the efficacy of the League of Nations." Whether the dictators would have been checked and tethered at that time if the members of the League had been prepared and willing to go to war for the principles of the Covenant can only be surmised. The fact is that Mussolini was saved by German rearmament and Hitler reaped the harvest of uncertainty which grew from the confusion over Ethiopia. Attempts to coerce Italy drove her into coalition with Germany, and whether it was ever possible to avoid the fatal denouement which emerged from the crisis is doubtful.

Because the will to enforce them was absent, the halfhearted sanctions invoked against Italy proved wholly ineffective. They could never have been anything else. Unless Haile Selassie could have been persuaded to make extravagant concessions, the real choice lay between war in the Mediterranean and the abandonment of all attempts to coerce Italy; no compromise solution was possible. In this case, effective coercion meant cutting off Italy's oil supply and bottling up the Suez Canal. By letting it be known that he would regard either of these measures as an act of war—and one which would provoke a kind of Italian Thermopylae—the Duce produced a powerful counterdeterrent. Theoretically, economic sanctions are a potent weapon; in practice, they are unlikely to prove to be so unless they are ruthlessly applied. If antisanctionist countries or self-seeking entrepreneurs are allowed to trade with the sanctioned victim, loopholes are bound to be punched in the sanctions' wall.

While the sanctions fiasco of 1935–36 did not bring the end of peace in Europe, it did—for all practical purposes—mark the end of the League of Nations. After May 1936 the League's influence steadily declined; in the later crises—that of Munich, for example—the League neither helped nor hindered. The imposing Palais des Nations, planned in brighter times, stood desolate, with its assembly halls empty, its well-stocked library provided by the Rockefeller Foundation rarely used. The flags of all nations still flew over it in 1939. But the League was doomed, and with the coming of the Second World War only the Secretariat—under orders to move at short notice to Vichy—remained.* Between 1936 and 1939 occasional attempts were made to rally its members, but disillusionment, defeatism, and demoralization had set in; international relations had reverted to the technique of the years preceding 1914.

The Italian occupation of Ethiopia lasted just over five years, and during their stay the colonizers conferred many obvious and acknowledged benefits on the country they had assaulted. A network of new roads, bridges, modern buildings, more and better hospitals were constructed, and schools were set up—although little was accomplished on the educational side, largely because there was not enough time. Under Italian rule Ethiopia was being unified, and development proceeded at a pace which it seems an independent Ethiopia cannot maintain. Whatever their motives and notwithstanding the impress of Fascism, the point must be made that it was the Italians who laid the foundations for Haile Selassie's modern state. Despite the many injustices committed against them, the Ethiopians were to reap considerable benefit from the Colonial Government of their country, for during the Italian occupation they developed a greater respect for

---

* Its last agenda was confined to "items relating to nutrition and the unification of level crossings."

law and order and a more modern attitude towards centralized government. Fortunately Mussolini's apartheid policy had little effect, and today Ethiopians show little of the color neurosis that poisons the rest of Africa; indeed greater problems than the color bar continue to be the ignorance, poverty, and tribal rivalries which existed long before the Italians invaded Ethiopia.

Five years of heavy expenditure and hard work brought Italy little benefit in return, and despite her efforts to subjugate the population, a revolt simmered in Ethiopia throughout the life of the Italian East Africa Empire. Except in Gojjam, the patriot activities were never much of a menace to the regime—indeed, by June 1940 the tide of rebellion was ebbing. (Not only were the patriot leaders disappointed that Italy had kept out of the European war, they were also horrified at the collapse of France. Educated in Djibuti schools, many of them had believed that France was the first military power in Europe.) Nevertheless they were a running sore, and the fact that a potential rebellion existed proved an important factor when Mussolini finally decided that the fortunes of Fascist Italy were irrevocably linked with those of Nazi Germany.

On July 2, 1940, Haile Selassie arrived in Khartoum, anxious to effect his restoration. As his arrival coincided with an Italian offensive, anything beyond the defense of the Anglo-Egyptian Sudan was little more than a rosy dream at that particular time. But plans were formulated, rifles and ammunition supplied to the rebellious elements in Gojjam, and Ethiopians who had sought refuge in the Sudan were trained and equipped for the war of liberation that was to come. Within six months, with the arrival in the Sudan of an infantry division from India and a startling victory in the Western Desert which had swept the Italian threat back along the North African coast, the military situation had improved, and straight from the battlefield of Sidi Barrâni the Fourth Indian Division was moved quickly to the Sudan. Thus in January 1941, British troops set out to recover the Emperor's lost territories. In the north, the Italians offered stubborn resistance at the Eritrean mountain fortress of Keren. But when this was overcome, five columns converged on Addis Ababa with astonishing speed; on April 6, 1941, General Cunningham's troops occupied Addis Ababa—and Haile Selassie's red war tent was pitched outside Debra Markos on the same day. (In 1936 it had taken the Italians six months to overcome the Ethiopians, while from the start of the British offensive in December 1940 less than four months elapsed.) Finally on May 5—after exactly five years of exile—Haile Selassie entered his capital in triumph.

The war was not over, for a large number of Italian troops had still to be rounded up. But the Emperor's return to Addis Ababa marked the birth of a new era for Ethiopia, and that night, wearing the uniform of a field marshal, he delivered from the balcony of the Imperial Palace an address which has come to be known as the "Great Mercy Proclamation."

People of my country . . . this day is a day on which a fresh chapter of this history of New Ethiopia begins. If we desire to be reminiscent of the affliction which befell Ethiopia during the past years we shall speak only of her recent history. When Ethiopia . . . was attacked in 1888 [1896 by the Gregorian Calendar] by Italy, who had harboured aggressive designs against her for many years before, with the intention of destroying her freedom, her brave sons fought at Adowa and she saved her independence. The Treaty of Uccialli in 1889 was not the only cause of the battle fought at Adowa. It was only a pretext for the constant desire that Italy had had of ruling Ethiopia. . . . When Italy began a war of aggression on Ethiopia . . . we went against her. . . . But as it was apparent she was bent on exterminating our people . . . we went to appeal to the League of Nations to claim justice. . . . How many are the young men, and women, the priests and the monks whom the Italians pitilessly massacred [during the years of occupation]. . . . The blood and bones of those who were killed with spades and pickaxes, of those . . . hammered to death . . . clubbed . . . stoned . . . burned alive . . . perished of hunger . . . have been crying for justice. But . . . people of my country, Ethiopia! . . . Today is a day on which Ethiopia is stretching her hands to God in joy and thankfulness . . . a day of rejoicing for us all. Therefore let us rejoice with our hearts . . . in the spirit of Christ. Do not return evil for evil. Do not indulge in atrocities. . . . Take care not to spoil the good name of Ethiopia by acts which are worthy of the enemy. . . .

The wheel had come full circle; the Duce's civilizing mission was over and many of the generation reaching maturity in the 1960s have never even heard of it. Yet this period of history has a moral particularly befitting a world that has changed so much since the thirties. The dangers of apathy and of desperate enthusiasms for simple solutions to complex problems, coupled with the need for considered concern, not only with the present but with the past that has molded us, and the future for which we are responsible: these surely are the lessons.

Appendixes

Agreement Between the United Kingdom, France, and Italy Respecting Ethiopia

SIGNED AT LONDON, DECEMBER 13, 1906

It being the common interest of France, Great Britain and Italy to maintain intact the integrity of Ethiopia, to provide for every kind of disturbance in the political conditions of the Ethiopian Empire, to come to a mutual understanding in regard to their attitude in the event of any change in the situation arising in Ethiopia, and to prevent the action of the three States in protecting their respective interests, both in the British, French and Italian possessions bordering on Ethiopia and in Ethiopia itself, resulting in injury to the interests of any of them, the Government of the French Republic, the Government of His Britannic Majesty, and the Government of Italy have assented to the following Agreement:

ARTICLE 1. France, Great Britain and Italy shall co-operate in maintaining the political and territorial *status quo* in Ethiopia as determined by the state of affairs at present existing, and by the following Agreements:

(*a*) The Anglo-Italian Protocols of the 24th March and 15th April, 1891, and of 5th May, 1894, and the subsequent Agreements modifying them, including the reserves formulated by the French Government in 1894 and 1895;

(*b*) The Anglo-Ethiopian Convention of 14th May, 1897, and its annexes;

(*c*) The Italo-Ethiopian Treaty of 10th July, 1900;

(*d*) The Anglo-Ethiopian Treaty of 15th May, 1902;

(*e*) The note annexed to the above-mentioned Treaty of 15th May, 1902;

(*f*) The Convention of 11th March, 1862, between France and the Dannakils;

(*g*) The Anglo-French Agreement of 2nd–9th February, 1888;

(*h*) The Franco-Italian Protocols of 24th January, 1900, and 10th July, 1901, for the delimitation of the French and Italian possessions on the littoral of the Red Sea and the Gulf of Aden;

(*i*) The Franco-Ethiopian Frontier Convention of 20th March, 1897.

It is understood that the various Conventions mentioned in this Article do not in any way infringe the sovereign rights of the Emperior of Abyssinia, and in no respect modify the relations between the three Powers and the Ethiopian Empire as stipulated in the present Agreement.

ARTICLE 2.   As regards demands for agricultural, commercial and industrial concessions in Ethiopia, the three Powers undertake to instruct their Representatives to act in such a way that concessions which may be accorded in the interest of one of the three States may not be injurious to the interests of the two others.

ARTICLE 3.   In the event of rivalries or internal changes in Ethiopia, the Representatives of France, Great Britain and Italy shall observe a neutral attitude, abstaining from all intervention in the internal affairs of the country, and confining themselves to such action as may be, by common consent, considered necessary for the protection of the Legations, of the lives and property of foreigners and of the common interests of the three Powers. In no case shall one of the three Governments interfere in any manner whatsoever, except in agreement with the other two.

ARTICLE 4.   In the event of the *status quo* laid down in Article 1 being disturbed, France, Great Britain and Italy shall make every effort to preserve the integrity of Ethiopia. In any case, they shall concert together, on the basis of the Agreements ennumerated in the above-mentioned Article, in order to safeguard:

(*a*)   The interests of Great Britain and Egypt in the Nile Basin, more especially as regards the regulation of the waters of that river and its tributaries (due consideration being paid to local interests), without prejudice to Italian interests mentioned in paragraph (*b*);

(*b*)   The interests of Italy in Ethiopia as regards Eritrea and Somaliland (including the Benadir), more especially with reference to the hinterland of her possessions and the territorial connection between them to the west of Addis Ababa;

(*c*)   The interests of France in Ethiopia as regards the French Protectorate on the Somali Coast, the hinterland of the Protectorate and the zone necessary for the construction and working of the railway from Djibouti to Addis Ababa.

ARTICLE 5.   The French Government communicates to the British and Italian Governments:

(*1*)   The Concession of the Franco-Ethiopian Railway of 9th March, 1894;

(*2*)   A communication from the Emperor Menelek dated 8th August, 1904, the translation of which is annexed to the present Agreement, inviting the Company to whom the above Concession was granted to construct the second section of the line from Dire Dawa to Addis Ababa.

ARTICLE 6.   The three Governments agree that the Djibouti Railway shall be prolonged from Dire Dawa to Addis Ababa, with a branch line to Harrar eventually, either by the Ethiopian Railway Company in virtue of the deeds enumerated in the preceding Article, or by any other private French Company which may be substituted therefor, with the consent of the French Government, on condition that the nationals of the three countries shall enjoy in all matters of trade and transit absolute equality of treatment on the railway and in the port of Djibouti. Goods shall not be subject to any fiscal transit duty levied for the benefit of the French Colony or Treasury.

ARTICLE 7.   The French Government will endeavour to arrange that an English, an Italian and an Abyssinian Representative shall be appointed to the Board of the French Company or Companies which may be intrusted with the construction and working of the railway from Djibouti to Addis Ababa. The British and Italian Governments will reciprocally endeavour to arrange that a French Director shall in like manner and on the same conditions be appointed to the Board of any English or Italian Company which has been or may be formed for the construction or working of railways running from any point in Abyssinia to any point in the adjoining English or Italian territory. It is likewise agreed that the nationals of the three countries shall enjoy in all matters of trade and transit absolute equality of treatment, both on the railways which may be constructed by English or Italian Companies, and in the English or Italian ports from which these railways may start. Goods shall not be subject to any fiscal transit duty levied for the benefit of the British or Italian Colonies or Treasuries.

The three Signatory Powers agree to extend to the nationals of all other countries the benefit of the provisions of Articles 6 and 7 relating to equality of treatment as regards trade and transit.

ARTICLE 8. The French Government will abstain from all interference as regards the Concession previously granted beyond Addis Ababa.

ARTICLE 9. The three Governments are agreed that all railway construction in Abyssinia west of Addis Ababa shall, in so far as foreign assistance is required, be carried out under the auspices of Great Britain. The three Governments are also agreed that all construction of railways in Ethiopia, joining the Benadir to Eritrea to the west of Addis Ababa, shall, in so far as foreign assistance is required, be carried out under the auspices of Italy.

The Government of His Britannic Majesty reserve to themselves the right, in case of need, to make use of the authorisation, granted by the Emperor Menelek on the 28th August, 1904, to construct a railway from British Somaliland through Ethiopia to the Sudanese frontier, on condition, however, that they previously come to an agreement with the French and Italian Governments, the three Governments undertaking not to construct without previous agreement any line entering Abyssinian territory or intended to join the Abyssinian lines, which would compete directly with those established under the auspices of any one of them.

ARTICLE 10. The Representatives of the three Powers will keep each other fully informed, and will co-operate for the protection of their respective interests. In the event of the British, French and

Italian Representatives being unable to agree, they will refer to their respective Governments, suspending all action meanwhile.

ARTICLE 11. Beyond the Agreements enumerated in Articles 1 and 5 of the present Convention, no Agreement concluded by any one of the Contracting Powers concerning Ethiopia shall affect the other Signatory Powers of the present Agreement.

Done at London, 13 December 1906

(*Signed*) E. GREY.
(*Signed*) PAUL CAMBON
(*Signed*) A. DI SAN GIULIANO.

ANNEX

[Translation of the Imperial Letter of August 8, 1904, authorising the Railway Company to undertake the Construction of the Line from Dire Dawa to Addis Ababa.]

The Lion, conqueror of the tribe of Judah, Menelek II, elect of Lord, King of Kings of Ethiopia to the French Minister Plenipotentiary at Addis Ababa,

Greeting!

In order that the Railway Company may lose no time unnecessarily, I inform you that it is my will that it forthwith commence work on the line from Dire Dawa to Addis Ababa.

As regards the terms of the contract, however, we shall come to an arrangement later with the Railway Company.

Written the 2nd Naasse, in the year of grace 1896 (*Abyssinian style*), in the city of Addis Ababa (*the 8th August, 1904*).

DECLARATION signed at London,

December 13, 1906.

The Italian Minister for Foreign Affairs states that Italy has Treaties with the Sultan of Lugh, the Sultan of Raheita, and the Dannakils respecting frontier questions. Inasmuch as these treaties must form the subject of negotiations with the Abyssinian Government, it is not possible to include them in the list contained in Article 1, but the Italian Government reserves to itself the right to communicate them to Great Britain and France after the termination of the negotiations.

His Majesty's Secretary of State for Foreign Affairs and the

French Ambassador take note of the declaration made by the Italian Minister for Foreign Affairs.

London, 13 December 1906

(*Signed*) E. GREY.

(*Signed*) PAUL CAMBON

(*Signed*) A. DI SAN GIULIANO.

Some Notes on the Constitution of the League of Nations and Extracts from the League Covenant

1. Membership

The founding members of the League of Nations—which ceased to exist when the United Nations Organization was founded after the Second World War—were the thirty-two signatories of the Treaty of Versailles: the United States of America, Belgium, Bolivia, Brazil, Britain, Canada, Australia, South Africa, New Zealand, India, China, Cuba, Ecuador,* France, Greece, Guatemala, Haiti, Hedjaz, Honduras, Italy, Japan, Liberia, Nicaragua, Panama, Peru, Poland, Portugal, Rumania, Yugoslavia, Siam, Czechoslovakia, and Uruguay. Thirteen other States—Argentina, Chile, Colombia, Denmark, Netherlands, Norway, Paraguay, Persia, Salvador, Spain, Sweden, Switzerland, and Venezuela—accepted an invitation to join. The original active membership of the League was forty-four (the United States not having ratified the peace treaty). However the Covenant of the League provided that any other "fully self-governing State, Dominion or Colony" might become a member of the League if its admission was agreed to by two-thirds of the Assembly, "provided that it shall give effective guarantees of its sincere intention to observe its

---

* Ecuador, which had signed but not ratified the peace treaties containing the Covenant, did not take up active membership until 1934.

international obligations and shall accept such regulations as may be prescribed by the League in regard to its military, naval and air forces and armaments."

Consequently Austria, Bulgaria, Costa Rica, Finland, Luxemburg, and Albania were elected members of the League by the First Assembly in 1920. Subsequently Esthonia, Latvia, Lithuania (1921); Hungary (1922); Ireland, Abyssinia (1923); Dominican Republic (1924); Germany (1926); Mexico (1931); Turkey, Iraq (1932); Union of Soviet Socialist Republics, Afganistan (1934), and Egypt (1937) were all admitted into the League.

On the other hand several countries withdrew from the League. The first, Costa Rica, ceased to be a member on January 1, 1927; Brazil ceased to be a member on June 13, 1928; Japan and Germany ceased to be members on March 26 and October 21, 1935, respectively. After that Guatemala, Honduras, Nicaragua, and Paraguay left the League. Then Austria, Ethiopia, Albania, and Czechoslovakia ceased to exist as independent States, and Italy, Chile, Salvador, Hungary, Peru, and Venezuela gave notice of withdrawal. The membership of Italy came to an end on December 11, 1939. Russia was expelled from the League three days later. The effective membership when the League disbanded was thus only forty-five.

2. Constitution of the League

The organs of the League were the Assembly, the Council, and the Permanent Secretariat. The Assembly consisted of delegations each comprising not more than three representatives of all the members of the League; each delegation had only one vote.

The Council comprised two kinds of members: the Great Powers belonging to the League, and nonpermanent members elected by the Assembly for a limited period. Originally it consisted of four permanent members—Britain, France, Italy, and Japan—and the first four nonpermanent members were Belgium, Brazil, Spain, and Greece. The original intention was that there should be five permanent members of the Council to provide a majority over the four nonpermanent members but the failure of the United States to ratify the peace treaties and its subsequent withdrawal from the League made the numbers of permanent and nonpermanent members equal. New permanent seats were created on the Council for Germany and the U.S.S.R. when they became members of the League and the number of nonpermanent members were increased to six in 1922, to nine in 1926, to ten in 1933, and to eleven in October 1936. (The last two seats were only provisional but in December 1939 the Council decided to continue them until 1942.)

The system under which selected nations had permanent seats on the Council—and yielded more power in consequence—is analogous to that of the members of the Security Council of the United Nations Organization. No doubt both are inconsistent with the theoretical equality of all States who are members of an organization for international understanding. In essence, of course, all States are *not* equal in importance, and the permanent seats of the Council of the League was an attempt to recognize the realities of the political strength, influence, and responsibilities of the countries which occupied them.

The Covenant provided that "the Assembly shall meet at stated intervals and from time to time as the occasion may require . . ." and the Assembly had an ordinary session once a year. Nearly all of its work was in fact done by Committees. On the other hand the Council met four times in a year—once in January, again in May (three days before the ordinary session of the Assembly), and twice in September. However the Council could decide, of its own volition, to meet at any time in extraordinary session and *had* to do so if any member of the League requested a meeting under the terms of Articles 11, 15, or 16 of the Covenant.

3. *The League Secretariat*

Articles 2 and 6 of the Covenant provided that the League shall have a permanent Secretariat, "which shall comprise a Secretary-General and such secretaries and staff as may be required." In its brief life the League had only two Secretaries-General. The first, Sir Eric Drummond (later the Earl of Perth), resigned in June 1933 when he was appointed British Ambassador in Rome—an appointment he held until 1939. He was succeeded by M. Joseph Avenol, the Frenchman who had been Deputy Secretary-General since 1923.

Unfortunately neither man was a particularly fortunate choice for an international organization. Lord Perth, who could not forget that he was a British official during his service at Geneva, considered that the League's job was to confine itself to routine and keep clear of matters which might upset established *principles*. No doubt Britain, who had as little faith in the League as Drummond, nominated him for the appointment because he was steeped in Palmerstonian tradition and could be relied on to restrain the League and counteract French influence among its members. Avenol, a reactionary with sympathies toward Italy's brand of fascism, was no improvement. Drummond had little faith in principles but Avenol had less.

4. *Revenue*

The income of the League was derived from the contributions of its members, who paid according to a scale fixed by the Assembly. A member State's contribution depended on its economic and financial resources and was fixed in "units." The highest contribution was that of the United Kingdom—108 units in 1938 (amounting to about two and a half million gold francs). The U.S.S.R. paid 94 units, France 80, Italy 56, India 49, China 42, Spain 40, and so on; at the other end of the scale eight small States paid only 1 unit each while Salvador's contribution was only 0.6 of a unit.

5. *The Covenant**

The Covenant of the League of Nations contained twenty-six Articles, which were also the first twenty-six Articles of the Treaty of Versailles. Because it was badly drafted, inconsistencies and ambiguities in the Articles gave rise to great difficulties and when it came to the test the Articles concerning dispute between members of the League, acts of aggression, war or threat of war, proved to be thoroughly unsatisfactory.

Article 15, which enabled any party to a dispute to submit the matter to the Council, was the best of them. Sensibly, it included the necessary provision that parties representing the dispute under consideration be excluded from voting in the Council or Assembly. On the other hand Article 11, which dealt with war or the threat of war, contained no such provision, so that no decision of the Council or the Assembly under this Article was valid unless the parties to the dispute agreed to it.†

Article 10 of the Covenant provided that in any case of aggression against the territorial integrity and existing political independence of any member of the League, or any threat of such aggression,

---

*Extracts of the relevant Articles of importance are given at the end of this appendix.

† This is the way the Council acted, although some eminent lawyers have held that as it cannot have been the intention of the authors of the Covenant to make a nonsense of the Article the Council took the wrong attitude.

"The Council shall advise upon the means by which the obligation of the members of the League to defend the victim of such aggression shall be fulfilled." Under this Article, therefore, it was the Council's duty to take the initiative whether or not the aggression was brought before it. (In fact the Council took no action except in cases where the victim of an aggression appealed to it.) One peculiarity about Article 10 was that no mention of the Assembly was made in it and so, unlike cases brought under Articles 11 or 15, which provide for the Assembly as well as the Council dealing with them, the Assembly had no means of bringing pressure to bear on the Council if it failed in its duty.

Articles 12 and 13, which dealt with disputes between members of the League, were contradictory. Under Article 12, the members of the League agreed "that if there should arise between them any dispute likely to lead to a rupture they will submit the matter either to arbitration or judicial settlement or to inquiry by the Council." Under Article 13, however, it was agreed that "whenever any dispute shall arise between them which they recognise to be suitable for submission to arbitration or judicial settlement, and which cannot be satisfactorily settled by diplomacy, they will submit the whole subject matter to arbitration or judicial settlement." (The phrase "or judicial settlement" was not part of the original text of the Covenant, but was added to these Articles and to the first paragraph of Article 15 in September 1924.) No doubt Article 12 was intended to deal with disputes of a political character and Article 13 with disputes of a judicial nature, but in practice it proved difficult to understand the difference between the two. Apart from there being no time limit for "the award of the arbitrary or the judicial decision" (which, vaguely, "shall be made in a *reasonable time*") the real flaw in Article 12 was that it did not bind members of the League to accept the decision of the arbitrators, the Court or Council, and allowed them to resort to war three months after the arbitrators' award, or the judicial decision, or the report by the Council.

Article 16 was the all-important Article dealing with sanctions. ". . . Should any Member of the League resort to war, in disregard of its covenants under Articles 12, 13 or 15, it shall *ipso facto* be deemed to have committed an act of war against all other Members of the League," which undertook immediately to apply economic and financial sanctions against the treaty-breaking member. Article 16 did not designate any authority to decide whether or not a break of the

Covenant had taken place. This was left to the decision of individual member States, and the disadvantages attached to such a principle are obvious. In October 1921 an amendment adding a new paragraph ("It is for the Council to give an opinion whether or not a break of the Covenant has taken place. In deliberations on this question, in the Council, the votes of Members of the League alleged to have resorted to war and of Members against whom such action was directed shall not be counted.") to Article 16 was adopted by the League, but as it was never ratified, the minor improvement it initiated did not come into force. This was an improvement on the original text of the Article but as the Council was empowered only to give an opinion whether a breach of the Covenant had occurred, it still left the way clear for a member to disregard the Council's opinion and to refuse to take action under Article 16. But, while members were mutually bound to support each other in any economic measures imposed under this Article, even as amended it remained ambiguous. On the question of Italy's aggression against Ethiopia the difficulties arising from the fact that paragraph 1 of Article 16 left the application of financial and economic sanctions to the individual members was overcome by setting up a Coordination Committee composed of all members of the League—the Assembly, in fact, under another name. Article 16 did *not* make it obligatory for members to impose military sanctions. The Council was empowered only "to recommend to the several Governments concerned what effective military, naval or air force the members of the League shall severally contribute to the armed forces to be used to protect the Covenants of the League" and there was no obligation to follow such a recommendation.

Needless to say, Article 18, which provided that every treaty or international arrangement entered into by a member of the League shall be registered by the League Secretaries, who would publish it, was never enforced. Subsequent to the drafting of the Covenant, it was maintained that the Article could not be enforced because it might not always be desirable to reveal certain international arrangements such as those providing financial assistance by one country to another. This is a cogent argument, but one which could have been overcome by specifying the categories of arrangement to be excluded from the Article. If the terms of the arrangements entered into in January 1935 by Laval for France and Mussolini for Italy had been made public early enough, the Ethiopian war might have been avoided.

Article 19 of the Covenant, providing that "the Assembly may from time to time advise the reconsideration by Members of the League of treaties which have become inapplicable and the consideration of international conditions whose continuance might endanger the world," remained a dead letter throughout the life of the League of Nations. Basically this was because the Article did not go far enough. Clearly it is as essential now as it was in the thirties that no nation, however justified in its grievances, should be allowed to take the law into its own hands and attempt to gain redress by force of arms. But this makes it necessary to have machinery for the redress of grievances. "Reconsideration" of treaties falls short of redress and where the Geneva Protocol of 1924 erred was in not providing machinery for effecting change by peaceful methods.

EXTRACTS FROM THE COVENANT OF THE LEAGUE OF NATIONS

"Article 5
1. Except where otherwise expressly provided in this Covenant or by the terms of the present Treaty, decisions at any meeting of the Assembly or of the Council shall require the agreement of all the Members of the League represented at the meeting."

"Article 10
The Members of the League undertake to respect and preserve as against external aggression the territorial integrity and existing political independence of all Members of the League. In case of any such aggression or in case of any threat or danger of such aggression the Council shall advise upon the means by which this obligation shall be fulfilled."

"Article 11
1. Any war or threat of war, whether immediately affecting any of the Members of the League or not, is hereby declared a matter of concern to the whole League, and the League shall take any action that may be deemed wise and effectual to safeguard the peace of nations. . . ."

"Article 12
1. The Members of the League agree that if there should arise between them any dispute likely to lead to a rupture, they will submit the matter either to arbitration *or judicial settlement* or to inquiry by the Council, and they agree in no case to resort to war until three months after the award of the arbitrators *or the judicial decision* or the report by the Council."

"Article 15

1. If there should arise between Members of the League any dispute likely to lead to a rupture, which is not submitted to arbitration *or judicial settlement* in accordance with Article 13, the Members of the League agree that they will submit the matter to the Council. Any party to the dispute may effect such submission by giving notice of the existence of the dispute to the Secretary General, who will make all necessary arrangements for a full investigation and consideration thereof.

2. For this purpose the parties to the dispute will communicate to the Secretary General, as promptly as possible, statements of their case with all the relevant facts and papers, and the Council may forthwith direct the publication thereof.

3. The Council shall endeavour to effect a settlement of the dispute, and if such efforts are successful, a statement shall be made public giving such facts and explanations regarding the dispute and the terms of settlement thereof as the Council may deem appropriate.

6. If a report by the Council is unanimously agreed to by the members thereof other than the Representatives of one or more of the parties to the dispute, the Members of the League agree that they will not go to war with any party to the dispute which complies with the recommendations of the report.

9. The Council may in any case under this Article refer the dispute to the Assembly."

"Article 16

1. Should any Member of the League resort to war in disregard to its covenants under Articles 12, 13 or 15, it shall *ipso facto* be deemed to have committed an act of war against all other Members of the League, which hereby undertake immediately to subject it to the severance of all trade or financial relations, the prohibition of all intercourse between their nationals and the nationals of the covenant-breaking State, and the prevention of all financial, commercial or personal intercourse between the nations of the covenant-breaking State and the nations of any other State, whether a Member of the League or not.

2. It shall be the duty of the Council in such case to recommend to the several Governments concerned what effective military, naval or air force the Members of the League shall severally contribute to the armed forces to be used to protect the covenants of the League.

3. The Members of the League agree, further, that they will mutually support one another in the financial and economic measures

which are taken until this Article, in order to minimise the loss and inconvenience resulting from the above measures, and that they will mutually support one another in resisting any special measures aimed at one of their number by the covenant-breaking State, and that they will take the necessary steps to afford passage through their territory to the forces of any of the Members of the League which are co-operating to protect the covenants of the League.

4. Any Member of the League which has violated any covenant of the League may be declared to be no longer a Member of the League by a vote of the Council concurred in by the Representatives of all the other Members of the League represented theron."

"Article 19
The Assembly may from time to time advise the reconsideration by Members of the League of treaties which have become inapplicable and the consideration of international conditions whose continuance might endanger the peace of the world."

"Article 20
1. The Members of the League severally agree that this Covenant is accepted as abrogating all obligations or undertakings *inter se* which are inconsistent with the terms thereof, and solemnly undertake that they will not hereafter enter into any engagements inconsistent with the terms thereof."

Notes on the Suez Canal Convention

The essence of the Suez Canal Convention of 1888 was contained in the first article:

> The Suez Maritime Canal shall always be free and open, in time of war as in time of peace, to all merchant or war vessels, without flag discrimination.
>
> Consequently, the high contracting parties agree in no way to prevent the free use of the Canal in time of war as in time of peace.
>
> The Canal shall never be used for the exercise of the right of blockade.

Signatories included Britain, France, Germany, Italy, and Turkey, and the argument about closing the Canal in 1935 centered on the undertaking quoted above. In actual fact Britain and France had closed the Canal to shipping of the Central Powers during the First World War—and in the Second World War Britain closed it to Germany and Italy again.

The Convention should have been revised because of Article 19 of the League Covenant, but in any case Article 20 should have provided legal justification for its closure had it been invoked.

Notes on the Italian Contingents in East Africa

1. *The Italian Army: General Categories*

   a) Regular army formations sent out from Italy, with all the usual ancillary and supporting units.
   b) Blackshirt Fascist Militia formations.
   c) Regular colonial units—mostly infantry but some cavalry and batteries of artillery—of local troops commanded by Italian officers. Troops from Eritrea were known as Askaris; those from Somaliland as Dubats.
   d) Libyan "volunteers," most of whom served in their own division under Graziani on the Italian Southern Front.

2. *The Advance on Adowa and Makale: Order of Battle*
   For this operation, General de Bono's force on the northern front was organized into three columns, each constituting one army corps. On the left (i.e., east) was the First Corps; in the center the Eritrean Corps; and on the right the Second Corps. The Order of Battle was as follows:

First East African Army Corps (General Somma)
    Sabauda Infantry Division (General Somma)
    Second (Twenty-eighth October) Blackshirt Division
    (114th, 116th, and 180th Legions)
        Sixth Group of Blackshirt battalions
        Tenth and Twenty-fifth Colonial battalions
        Scimenzana Band
        One 'group' (three squadrons) of light tanks*
        One 'group' of engineers
        Two 'groups' of lorries.
The Libyan Squadron of the Italian Air Force was put in
direct support of this corps for the operation.

Second East African Army Corps (General Maravigna)
    Gavinana Infantry Division (General Villa Santa)
    One battalion each of Savoia Grenadiers, Alpini, and Fron-
    tier Guard
    Third Askari Brigade (of four battalions) †
        Eighteenth and Twenty-third Colonial battalions
        Serae Band
        One 'group' of light tanks
        One 'group' of engineers
        Two 'groups' of lorries.

Eritrean Army Corps (General Pirzio-Biroli)
    First Askari Division (less the Third Askari Brigade)
    Second Askari Division
    First (Twenty-third March) Blackshirt Division
        First Eritrean 'group' of Blackshirt battalions
        Harrarno Band
        One 'group' of light tanks
        Four squadrons of Eritrean cavalry
        One 'group' of lorries.

---

*Each squadron had fifteen Fiat light tanks, which offered 13 mm. of armor
protection to its crew of two. Each tank carried two Fiat machine guns.
  † The Third Askari Brigade from the Eritrean Army Corps replaced the
Third (Twenty-first April) Blackshirt Division for this operation. The latter
had not all arrived from Italy by September 1935 and De Bono withdrew it into
reserve.

The three corps constituted de Bono's striking force. On the flanks of the front, troops were also deployed in the Eastern and Western lowlands.

Eastern Lowlands
Thirteenth and Twenty-sixth Colonial battalions
Libyan Battalion
Three irregular Bands (Massawa, Northern Danakil, and Southern Danakil)

Western Lowlands
Twenty-seventh and Twenty-eighth Colonial battalions
A mixed group of irregulars and Libyan volunteers backed by the Seventeenth Colonial Battalion. This force had horse and camel cavalry, armored cars and infantry.

3. *The Regia Aeronautica*

The Italian Air Force used the following types of aircraft in East Africa:

For bombing missions the principal machine was the Caproni Ca 101 three-engine monoplane of 700–900 h.p. With a range of 600 miles, and a cruising speed of 125 m.p.h., it could carry a payload of one ton.

Also used in a bombing role, but designated as strategical reconnaissance aircraft, were the Ca 111 and Ro 37 machines. The Ca 111 was a single-engined monoplane with a cruising speed of 140 m.p.h., capable of carrying a payload of about two tons, while the Ro 37 was a two-seater single-engined biplane with a one-ton payload. Both had an effective range of about 600 miles.

For tactical reconnaissance Ro 1, two- or three-seater single-engined biplanes, were used initially. As this machine could only carry just over a quarter of a ton at a speed of 120 m.p.h., and its range was limited to 350 miles, Fiat Cr 20 Scouts—fighter aircraft which were sent out to deal with the Ethiopian Air Force—were also used in this role.

In January 1935, S 81 three-engined monoplanes which could carry two tons of bombs at 186 m.p.h. to a range of 900 miles and Caproni Ca 133 machines with a similar performance were shipped out to the theater. (The intention had been to fly these more modern machines to Eritrea but this meant overflying the Sudan, and Mussolini deemed it wiser to send them by sea.)

4. *Transport Organization*

The number of men, animals, and motor vehicles transported to East Africa each month went on steadily increasing from February 1935 (5,890 men, 400 animals, and 82 motor vehicles) to September 1935 (51,743 men, 2,166 animals, and 660 motor vehicles), with a slight reduction during the month of July owing to the rainy season. This represented a monthly average from February 1935 to February 1936 of 24,902 men, 1,603 animals, and 417 motor vehicles. These figures refer to chartered steamers only and do not include the transport of men, animals, motor vehicles, and other material by ships of the regular services.

Up to the end of April 1936, 298,821 men, 19,233 animals, 5,000 motor vehicles, and 207,219 tons of material had been transported to East Africa by chartered steamers, in the proportion of five-sixths to Eritrea and one-sixth to Somalia.

In addition, 26,000 workmen were transported to East Africa and those who had completed their contract were repatriated.

Taking into account further movements of troops by sea in order to relieve garrisons, etc., the total for the year amounted to 360,000 men, 30,000 animals, 6,500 motor vehicles, and 3,000,000 tons of stores.

A naval officer was sent on board each of the chartered ships (a Captain or Commander for the larger transports, and a Lieutenant-Commander or Lieutenant for the smaller ones) together with some naval ratings.

In Naples, the home base of the expedition, a Naval Transport Office was set up under the command of a naval captain, with a staff of naval and military officers, to deal with the embarkation of troops, the loading and refuelling, etc., of the transports. Similar offices were created in Messina, Genoa, Leghorn, and Cagliari, while at the Ministry of Marine in Rome a special office was created to deal with the administrative work connected with the expedition.

5. *Medical Arrangements*

With the arrival of the first white troops in East Africa the Italians were faced with the problem of providing suitable hospital accommodation for cases of sickness caused by the climate—particularly at Massawa. The first measure taken was that of transforming a passenger ship into a floating hospital. Saloons were converted into operating rooms, dentists' offices, a bacteriological laboratory, etc., and equipped with modern medical fittings, and the holds were transformed into wards. It was also necessary to rig up special means of hoisting the sick on board from the boats taking them alongside so as to avoid the risk of jarring them in rough weather. Additional water tanks were fitted to bring the supply up to 2,000 tons, refrigerating machinery was installed, while the supply of medicines, bandages, linen, etc., enabled the hospital ship to remain at sea for six months with a full complement of patients.

The first hospital ship, the *Urania*, reached Massawa at the end of April 1935, where it was found that the alterations and medical organization were satisfactory. The following month it was decided to equip a second hospital ship and for this purpose the steamer *Tevere* was chosen. As a result of the experience already gained during the brief period of service of the *Urania*, the alterations in the *Tevere* were carried out quickly and easily and the final result was more satisfactory. In June the *Tevere* left Trieste for Massawa with accommodation for 600 patients, slightly more than the *Urania*, which had 550 beds.

The service of the *Tevere* at Massawa during the hottest months of 1935 proved that in spite of the precautions taken, the temperature in the wards remained much too high, and the patients suffered considerable discomfort. For these reasons the preparation of a third hospital ship, the *California*, was undertaken, and in this vessel a special plant was installed to keep the wards, operating rooms, laboratories, etc., at a maximum temperature of 60 to 70 degrees, according to requirements.

The *California* served at Massawa uninterruptedly for two months from August 15th to October 15th and the work of the medical staff during this period can be gathered from the following figures: patients treated, 1,863; days of treatment 14,868; discharged as cured 1,048; repatriated 666; general operations 200. (Among the patients treated were an officer and two men of the British merchant service who had been sent ashore sick when their ships called at Massawa.)

To prepare for future eventualities two other liners, the *Helouan* and the *Vienna*, were fitted out as hospital ships. These comprised all the improvements dictated by the experience gained during the previous six months' service in East Africa. Before the end of the campaign there were eight hospital ships in East African waters, *Urania, Tevere, California, Helouan, Vienna, Cesarea, Aquilea,* and

Gradisca, with a total accommodation of 5,000–6,000 beds. All the medical staff belonged to the Navy, with the exception of the V.A.D.s (Voluntary Aid Detachment), of whom there were eight to ten in each ship. In Naples, a special depot was set up to deal with all supplies for these ships.

NOTES

Chapter 1

1. League of Nations Official Journal, June 1935, pp. 736–37.
2. Reported in the *Times* (London), August 1, 1935.

Chapter 2

1. Treaty of London, April 26, 1915.
2. Article 119.

Chapter 4

1. Arnold J. Toynbee, *Survey of International Affairs 1935* (New York: Oxford University Press), ii, 17.
2. Quoted in the *Times* (London), August 1, 1935.

Chapter 5

1. *Manchester Guardian*, November 15, 1935.
2. League of Nations Official Journal, 1935, p. 1601.
3. Emilio de Bono, *Anno XIIII– The Conquest of an Empire* (London: Cresset Press, 1937), p. 13.
4. *Ibid.*, p. 57.
5. *The Unpublished Diary of Pierre Laval* (London: Falcon Press, 1948), p. 33.

6. The Earl of Avon, *The Eden Memoirs: Facing the Dictators* (London: Cassell & Co., 1962), p. 193.
7. The Earl of Avon, *op. cit.*, p. 192.
8. *Facing the Dictators*, pp. 241–42.
9. *The Mist Procession: The Autobiography of Lord Vansittart* (London: Hutchinson, 1958), p. 522.
10. *Morning Post* (London), September 17, 1935.
11. Hansard, *Parliamentary Debates:* 5th series, 1935.
12. Ian Colvin, *Vansittart in Office* (London: Gollancz, 1965), p. 60.
13. Vansittart, *op. cit.*, p. 520.
14. *Survey of International Affairs 1935* (New York: Oxford University Press).

Chapter 6

1. *The Ribbentrop Memoirs* (London: Weidenfeld & Nicolson, 1954), p. 65 f.
2. Viscount Templewood (Samuel Hoare), *Nine Troubled Years* (London: Collins, 1954).
3. Ian Colvin, *Vansittart in Office* (London: Gallancz, 1965), p. 66.
4. The Earl of Avon, *The Eden Memoirs: Facing the Dictators* (London: Cassell & Co., 1962), p. 223.
5. *Ibid.*, pp. 228–29.
6. Arthur W. Baldwin, *My Father: The True Story* (London: Allen & Unwin, 1955), pp. 207, 219; Keith Feiling, *The Life of Neville Chamberlain* (London: Macmillan, 1946), p. 262; Lord Robert Vansittart, *The Mist Procession: The Autobiography of Lord Vansittart* (London: Hutchinson, 1958), p. 503.
7. *Times* (London), July 27, 1934.

Chapter 7

1. Letter by Sir Hesketh Bell, *Times* (London), July 29, 1935.
2. Article in the *Times* (London), July 31, 1935.
3. *Times* (London), July 31, 1935; Special Correspondent at Addis Ababa, paraphrasing the Emperor's speech of July 18.
4. *Tribuna* (Rome), July 30, 1935, as quoted in the *Times* (London).
5. Emilio de Bono, *Anno XIIII: The Conquest of an Empire* (London: Cresset Press, 1937), p. 160.
6. *Times* (London), August 2, 1935.
7. Trans. by Janet Flanner, *New Yorker*.
8. *International Conciliation*, December 1934.

Chapter 8

1. David A. Talbot, ed., *Ethiopia Liberation Silver Jubilee* (Addis Ababa: Ministry of Information, 1966), p. 11.
2. George L. Steer, *Caesar in Abyssinia* (London: Hodder & Stoughton, 1936), p. 121.
3. *Ibid.*, p. 130.

Chapter 9

1. Webb Miller, *I Found No Peace* (London: Gollancz, 1937).
2. *Anno XIIII: The Conquest of an Empire* (London: Cresset Press, 1937), p. 243.
3. *Ibid.*, p. 249.
4. George L. Steer, *Caesar in Abyssinia* (London: Hodder & Stoughton, 1936), pp. 159, 164.
5. *Ibid.*, p. 164.
6. *Ibid.*, p. 165.
7. *Anno XIIII.*

Chapter 10

1. Robert Dell, *The Geneva Racket 1920–1939* (London: Hale, 1941), p. 126. `

Chapter 11

1. *The Mist Procession: The Autobiography of Lord Vansittart* (London: Hutchinson, 1958), p. 538.
2. *Ibid.*, p. 539.
3. *Ibid.*, p. 540.
4. *The Unpublished Diary of Pierre Laval* (New York: Scribners, 1948; London: Falcon Press, 1948), p. 31.
5. *Both Sides of the Curtain* (London: Constable, 1950).
6. Vansittart, *op. cit.*, p. 540.
7. Arthur W. Baldwin, *My Father: The True Story* (London: Allen & Unwin, 1955), p. 291.
8. Hansard, *The House of Commons Official Report*, Parliamentary Debates (December 10, 1935).
9. *Correspondence relating to the dispute between Ethiopia and Italy:* Cmd 5044 (1935) (London: Her Majesty's Stationery Office, 1935).
10. *Giornale d'Italia*, December 19, 1935.

Chapter 12

1. *The War in Abyssinia* (London: Mathuen, 1937), p. 38.
2. *Ibid.*
3. *Italy Against the World* (London: Chatto & Windus, 1937), p. 256.
4. *Waugh in Abyssinia* (London: Longmans, 1936), p. 127.

Chapter 13

1. Pietro Badoglio, *The War in Abyssinia* (London: Methuen, 1937), p. 66.
2. *Ibid.*
3. *Ibid.*, p. 65.
4. *Ibid.*, p. 67.
5. *Ibid.*
6. George L. Steer, *Caesar in Abyssinia* (London: Hodder & Stoughton, 1936), p. 260.

7. *Ibid.*, p. 262.
8. *Ibid.*, p. 264.
9. *Ibid.*, p. 266.
10. Badoglio, *op. cit.*, p. 85.
11. Leonard Mosley, *Haile Selassie: The Conquering Lion* (London: Weidenfeld & Nicolson, 1964), p. 213.
12. *Ibid.*, p. 214.
13. Steer, *op. cit.*, p. 275.
14. Kathleen Nelson & Alan Sullivan, eds., *John Melly of Ethiopia* (London: Faber & Faber, 1937), p. 240.

Chapter 14

1. Leonard Mosley, *Haile Selassie: The Conquering Lion* (London: Weidenfeld & Nicolson, 1964), p. 219.
2. George L. Steer, *Caesar in Abyssinia* (London: Hodder & Stoughton, 1936), p. 216.
3. *Ibid.*
4. Mosley, *op. cit.*, p. 220.
5. Pietro Badoglio, *The War in Abyssinia* (London: Methuen, 1937), p. 145.
6. *Ibid.*
7. *Ibid.*, p. 146.
8. Mosley, *op. cit.*, p. 225.
9. *Ibid.*
10. *The War in Abyssinia*, p. 146.
11. Mosley, *op. cit.*, p. 216.
12. *Ibid.*, p. 229.
13. Steer, *op. cit.*, p. 369.
14. *Ibid.*, p. 371.
15. *Giornale d'Italia*, May 6, 1936.

Chapter 15

1. Address at exhibition of the Catholic Press, Rome, May 12; reported in *Giornale d'Italia*.
2. *The Pope in Politics* (London: Lovat Dickson, 1937), pp. 128–29.
3. Letter to the author February 1968, from Commander P. A. R. Withers, D.S.O., D.S.C.
4. Mosley, *op. cit.*, p. 239.
5. Speech at 1900 Club dinner, June 10, 1936.
6. Ethiopia: *Liberation Silver Jubilee*, pp. 27–29.

Chapter 16

1. The Earl of Avon, *The Eden Memoirs: Facing the Dictators* (London: Cassell & Co., 1962), pp. 425–26.
2. G. Ward Price, *I Know These Dictators* (London: Harrap, 1937), p. 245.

BIBLIOGRAPHY

AFRICANUS. *Etiopia 1935; Panorama geo-politico.* Rome: Ardita, 1935.

AGOSTINO ORSINI DI CAMEROTA, PAOLA D'. *L'Italia nella politica africana.* Bologna: Cappelli, 1928.

ALBRECHT-CARRIE, RENÉ. *The Unity of Europe.* London: Secker & Warburg, Ltd., 1965.

ALFIERI, DINO. *Dictators Face to Face.* D. MOORE, trans. London: Elek Books Ltd., 1954.

ALOISI, POMPEO. *Journal 35 juillet 1932–14 juin 1936.* M. VAUSSARD, trans. Paris: Librairie Plon, 1957.

AMERY, LEOPOLD S. *My Political Life.* 3 vols. London: Hutchinson & Co., Ltd., 1953–55.

ARALDI, V. *Il Patto d'Acciaio.* Rome: Bianco, 1961.

ATTLEE, CLEMENT R. *As It Happened.* London: Wm. Heinemann, Limited, 1954.

AVON, THE EARL OF. *The Eden Memoirs: Facing the Dictators.* London: Cassell & Co., Ltd., 1962.

BADOGLIO, PIETRO. *The War in Abyssinia.* (First published in Italy under the title *La Guerra D'Etiopia* in 1936.) London: Methuen & Co., Ltd., 1937.

BAER, GEORGE W. *The Coming of the Italian-Ethiopian War.* Cambridge: Harvard University Press, 1967.

BALDWIN, ARTHUR, W. *My Father: The True Story.* London: George Allen & Unwin, Ltd., 1955. New York: Oxford University Press, 1955.

BALDWIN, STANLEY. *This Torch of Freedom.* London: Hodder & Stoughton, Ltd., 1935.

BASKERVILLE, BEATRICE. *What Next, O Duce?* London: Longmans Green & Company, 1937.

BASTIANINI, GIUSEPPE. *Uomini, case, fatti.* Milan: Vitagliano, 1959.

BASTIN, JEAN. *L'Affaire d'Ethiopie et les diplomates, 1934–1937.* Brussels: Universelle, 1937.

BECHTEL, GUY. *Laval vingt ans après.* Paris: Laffont, 1963.

BELOFF, MAX. *The Foreign Policy of Soviet Russia, 1929–1951.* 3 vols. London: Oxford University Press, 1947–1953.

——— *The Great Powers: Essays in Twentieth Century Politics.* New York: The Macmillan Company, 1959.

BENTWICH, NORMAN. *Ethiopia, Eritrea, and Somaliland.* London: Victor Gollancz, Ltd., 1945.

BERKELEY, GEORGE F. *The Campaign of Adowa and the Rise of Menelik.* London: Constable & Company, Ltd., 1902.

BERTONELLI, FRANCESCO. *Il Nostro mare* (2nd ed.). Florence: Bemporad, 1931.

BINCHY, DANIEL. *Church and State in Fascist Italy.* London: Oxford University Press, 1941.

BIRKENHEAD, THE EARL OF. *The Life of Lord Halifax.* London: Hamish Hamilton, Ltd., 1965.

BITETTO, PRINCE CARLO CITO DE. *Méditerranée–Mer Rouge: Routes impériales.* Paris: Grasset, 1937.

BLUM, JOHN M. *From the Morgenthau Diaries: Years of Crisis, 1928–1938.* Boston: Houghton Mifflin Company, 1959.

BONNET, GEORGES. *Le Quai d'Orsay sous trois républiques.* Paris: Fayard, 1961.

BOTTAI, GIUSEPPE. *Vent'anni e un giorna* (2nd ed.). Rome: Garzanti, 1949.

BOVA, PASQUALE. *Il Criterio "razziale" nella politica imperiale d'Italia.* Naples: Capocci, 1937.

BRIGGS, ASA. *They saw It Happen.* Oxford: Blackwell & Mott, Ltd., 1960.

BROAD, LEWIS. *Sir Anthony Eden.* London: Hutchinson & Co., Ltd., 1955.

BROGAN, D. W. *The Development of Modern France, 1870–1939.* London: Hamish Hamilton, Ltd., 1940.

BROOK-SHEPHERD, GORDON. *Dollfuss.* London: The Macmillan Company, 1961.

BUDGE, E. W. WALLIS. *A History of Ethiopia.* 2 vols. London: Methuen & Co., Ltd., 1928.

BULLOCH, ALLAN. *A Study in Tyranny.* New York: Harper and Brothers, 1952. London: Odhams Press Ltd., 1952.

BUXTON, DAVID. *Travels in Ethiopia.* London: The Drummond Press, 1949.

CAIOLI, ALDO. *L'Italia di fronte a Ginevra.* Rome: Volpe, 1965.

CASTELLI, GIULIO. *La Chiesa e il Fascismo.* Rome: Arnia, 1951.

CAVIGLIA, ENRICO. *Diario, aprile 1925–marzo 1945.* Rome: Casini, 1952.

CECIL, LORD ROBERT. *A Great Experiment.* London: Jonathan Cape, Ltd., 1941.

CHABOD, FEDERICO. *A History of Italian Fascism.* M. GRINDROD, trans. London: George Weidenfeld & Nicolson Ltd., 1963.

CHAMBRUN, CHARLES DE. *Traditions et souvenirs.* Paris: Flammarion, 1952.

CHAPLIN, W. W. *Blood and Ink (An Italo-Ethiopian War Diary).* New York: The Telegraph Press, 1936.

CHARLES–ROUX, FRANÇOIS. *Huit ans au Vatican, 1932–1940.* Paris: Flammarion, 1947.

CHATFIELD, LORD ERNLE. *The Navy and Defence, II: It Might Happen Again.* London: Wm. Heinemann, Limited, 1947.

CHEESMAN, R. E. *Lake Tana and the Blue Nile.* London: The Macmillan Company, 1936.

CHRISTOPOLOUS, G. *La Politique extérieure de l'Italie fasciste.* Paris: Rodstein, 1936.

CHURCHILL, RANDOLPH. *The Rise and Fall of Sir Anthony Eden.* London: MacGibbon & Kee Ltd.. 1959.

CHURCHILL, WINSTON. *The Gathering Storm.* London: Cassell, 1948.

CIANO, GALEAZZO. *Ciano's Diary, 1937–1938.* ANDREAS MAYOR, trans. London: Methuen & Co., Ltd., 1952.

—— *Diario, 1937–1938.* Bologna: Cappelli, 1948.

—— *L'Europa verso la catastrofe.* Milan: Mondadori, 1948.

CIMMARUTA, ROBERTO. *Ual Ual.* Milan: Mondadori, 1936.

CLONMORE, LORD. *Pope Pius XI and World Peace.* New York: E. P. Dutton & Co., Inc., 1938.

COLE, HUBERT. *Laval.* New York: G. P. Putnam's Sons, 1963. London: Wm. Heinemann, Limited, 1963.

COLVIN, IAN. *Vansittart in Office.* London: Victor Gollancz, Ltd., 1965.

COMRYN-PLATT, SIR T. *The Abyssinian Storm.* London: Jarrolds, Publishers, Ltd., 1935.

COOPER, ALFRED DUFF. *Old Men Forget.* London: Hart-Davis Ltd., 1953.

CORA, CIULIANO. *Attualitá del trattato italo-etiopico del 1928.* Florence: Stet, 1948.

———— "Un Diplomatico durante l'era fascista," *Storia e politica*, 5:88–93 (January–March 1966).

———— "Il Trattato italo-etiopico del 1928," *Rivista di studi politici internazionali*, 15:205–26 (April–June 1948).

CRISCUOLO, LUIGI. *After Mussolini . . . What?* New York: Wisdom, 1936.

CROCE, BENEDETTO. *A History of Italy, 1871–1915.* C. M. ADY, trans. Oxford: Oxford University Press, 1929.

CROSSMAN, RICHARD H. S. *Government and the Governed.* New York: G. P. Putnam's Sons, 1939. London: Christophers, Ltd., 1939.

CUNNINGHAM OF HYNDHOPE, LORD. *A Sailor's Odyssey.* New York: E. P. Dutton & Co., Inc., 1951.

CURREY, MURIEL. *A Woman at the Abyssinian War.* London: Hutchinson & Co., Ltd., 1936.

DALTON, HUGH. *The Fateful Years: Memoirs, 1931–1945.* London: Frederick Muller, Ltd., 1957.

D'AROMA, NINO. *Vent'anni insieme: Vittorio Emanuele e Mussolini.* Rome: Cappelli, 1957.

DEAKIN, F. W. *The Brutal Friendship: Mussolini, Hitler and the Fall of Italian Fascism.* London: George Weidenfeld & Nicolson, Ltd., 1962.

DE BEGNAC, YVON. *Palazzo Venezia: Storia de un regime.* Rome: La Rocca, 1950.

DE BONO, EMILIO. *Anno XIIII: The Conquest of an Empire.* London: The Cresset Press, Ltd., 1937.

———— *La Preparazione e le prime operazioni* (3rd ed.). Rome: Istituto Nazionale Fascista di Cultura, 1937.

DEGRAS, JANE. *Soviet Documents on Foreign Policy, 1917–1941.* 3 vols. London: Oxford University Press, 1951–1953.

DELL, ROBERT. *The Geneva Racket 1920–1939.* London: Robert Hale, Ltd., 1941.

DE TARR, FRANCIS. *The French Radical Party: From Herriot to Mendes-France.* London: Oxford University Press, 1961.

DI NOLFO, ENNIO. *Mussolini e la politica estera italiana, 1919–1933.* Padua: Cedam, 1960.

DORIGO, P. P. *Ginevra o Roma?* Pisa: Nistri-Lischi, 1934.

EDEN, ANTHONY. *See* AVON, The Earl of.

FAVAGROSSA, CARLO F. *Perche perdemmo la guerra.* Milan: Rizzoli, 1946.

FEILING, KEITH. *The Life of Neville Chamberlain.* London: The Macmillan Company, 1946.

FARAGO, LADISLAS. *Abyssinia on the Eve.* New York: G. P. Putnam's Sons, 1935.

FERMI, LAURA. *Mussolini.* Chicago: University of Chicago Press, 1961.

FLANDIN, PIERRE-ETIENNE. *Politique française, 1919–1940.* Paris: Nouvelles, 1947.

FOOT, MICHAEL R. *Armistice, 1918–1939.* London: George G. Harrap & Co., Ltd., 1940.

FULLER, MAJOR-GENERAL J. F. C. *The First of the League Wars.* London: Eyre & Spottiswoode, Ltd., 1936.

GARRATT, G. T. *Mussolini's Roman Empire.* London: Penguin Books Limited, 1938.

GIGLI, GUIDO. "Sguardo ai rapporti fra Badoglio e Mussolini fino alla crisi etiopici del 1935–36," Appendix 1, pp. 255–60 in V. VAILATI, *Badoglio risponde.* Miland: Rizzoli, 1958.

GILBERT, MARTIN, and GOTT, RICHARD. *The Appeasers.* London: George Weidenfeld & Nicolson Ltd., 1963.

GIRAUD, EMILE. *La Nullité de la politique internationale des grandes démocraties, 1919–1939.* Paris: Sirey, 1948.

GOIFFON, PAUL. *Les Clauses coloniales dans les accords franco-italiens de 7 janvier 1935.* Lyon: Rion, 1936.

GRAZIANI, RODOLFO. *Il Fronte sud.* Milan: Mondadori, 1938.

GREENFIELD, RICHARD. *Ethiopia: A New Political History.* London: Pall Mall Press Ltd., 1965.

GUNTHER, JOHN. *Inside Europe.* New York: Harper and Brothers, 1936. London: Hamish Hamilton, Ltd., 1936.

HAMILTON, EDWARD. *The War in Abyssinia.* London: The Unicorn Press, 1936.

HARRIS, JR., BRICE. *The United States and the Italo-Ethiopian Crisis.* Stanford: Stanford University Press, 1964.

HERRIOT, ÉDOUARD. *Jadis, II: D'une guerre a l'autre, 1914–1936.* Paris: Flammarion, 1952.

HIBBERT, CHRISTOPHER. *Benito Mussolini: The Rise and Fall of Il Duce.* London: Longmans, Green & Company, 1962.

HILLSON, NORMAN. *Geneva Scene.* London: Routledge & Kegan Paul, Ltd., 1936.

The History of The Times, IV, part 2: *The 150th Anniversary and Beyond, 1912–1948.* New York: The Macmillan Company, 1952.

HOARE, SAMUEL. *See* TEMPLEWOOD, Viscount.

HOLLIS, M. CHRISTOPHER. *Italy in Africa.* London: Hamish Hamilton, Ltd., 1941.

JARDINE, DOUGLAS. *The Mad Mullah of Somaliland.* London: Herbert Jenkins, Ltd., 1923.

JEMOLO, A. C. *Chiesa e stato in Italia dal risorgimento ad oggi.* Turin: Einaudi, 1955.

JESMAN, CZESLAW. *The Ethiopian Paradox.* London: Oxford University Press, 1963.

Jones, a. h. m., and Monroe, e. *A History of Ethiopia.* London: Oxford University Press, 1935.

Junod, marcel, dr. *Warrior without Weapons.* London: Jonathan Cape, Ltd., 1957.

King-Hall, stephen. *Our Times, 1900–1960.* London: Faber & Faber, Ltd., 1961.

Kirkpatrick, ivone. *Memoirs: The Inner Circle.* London: The Macmillan Company, 1959.

——— *Mussolini: A Study in Power.* New York: Hawthorn Books, Inc., 1964.

Lagardelle, hubert de. *Mission à Rome: Mussolini.* Paris: Plon, 1955.

La Pradelle, albert de. *Le Conflit italo-éthiopien.* Paris: Editions Internationales, 1936.

Laval, pierre. *The Unpublished Diary of Pierre Laval.* New York: Charles Scribner's Sons, 1948. London: Falcon Press, 1948.

Lawford, valentine. *Bound for Diplomacy.* London: John Murray, Ltd., 1963.

Legionarius (pseud.) *Las Razones por las cuales Italia levanta graves quejas contra Abisinia.* Rome: Ardita (no date).

Lewis, ioan m. *The Modern History of Somaliland.* London: George Weidenfeld & Nicolson, Ltd., 1965.

Livingstone, dame adelaide. *The Peace Ballot: The Official History.* London: Victor Gollancz, Ltd., 1935.

Ludwig, emil. *Gespräche mit Mussolini* (Trans. by eden and cedar Paul as *Talks with Mussolini.* London: George Allen & Unwin, Ltd., 1933.)

Lussu, emilio. *Marcia su Roma e Dintorni.* (Trans. by marion Rawson as *Enter Mussolini.* London: Methuen & Co., Ltd., 1936.)

Luther, ernest w. *Ethiopia Today.* California: Stanford University Press, 1958. London: Oxford University Press, 1958.

League of Nations Official Journal. Switzerland: June 1935.

Lytton, the earl of. *The Stolen Desert.* London: Macdonald & Co., Ltd., 1966.

McElwee, william. *Britain's Locust Years 1918–1940.* London: Faber & Faber, Ltd., 1962.

MacGregor, r. m. *Order or Disorder? Studies in the Decline of International Order, 1918–1936.* London: Gerald Duckworth & Co., Ltd., 1939.

MacGregor-Hastie, roy. *The Day of the Lion.* London: Macdonald & Co., Ltd., 1963.

Macleod, iain. *Neville Chamberlain.* London: Frederick Muller, Ltd., 1961.

Mallet, alfred. *Pierre Laval.* 2 vols. Paris: Dumont, 1955.

MANTOUX, PAUL, *et al.* *The World Crisis.* London: Longmans, Green & Company, 1938.

MARTELLI, GEORGE. *Italy Against the World.* London: Chatto & Windus, 1937.

MATHEW, DAVID. *Ethiopia: The Study of a Polity, 1540–1935.* London: Eyre & Spottiswoode, Ltd., 1947.

MATTHEWS, H. *Eyewitness in Abyssinia.* London: Martin Secker & Warburg, Ltd., 1937.

────── *Two Wars and More to Come.* New York: Carrich & Evans, 1937.

MEGARO, GAUDENS. *Mussolini in the Making.* London: George Allen & Unwin, Ltd., 1938.

MILLER, WEBB. *I Found No Peace.* London: Victor Gallancz, Ltd., 1937.

MONTI, A. *Gli Italiani e il canale di Suez.* Rome: Vittoriano, 1937.

MORGAN, THOMAS B. *Spurs on the Boot.* London: George G. Harrap & Co., Ltd., 1942.

MOSLEY, LEONARD. *Haile Selassie: The Conquering Lion.* London: George Weidenfeld & Nicolson Ltd., 1964.

MOWAT, CHARLES L. *Britain Between the Wars, 1918–1940.* London: Methuen & Co., Ltd., 1956.

MUGGERIDGE, MALCOLM. *The Sun Never Sets: The Story of England in the Nineteen Thirties.* New York: Random House, Inc., 1940. London: Hamish Hamilton, Ltd., 1940.

MUSSOLINI, BENITO. *Storia di un anno (Il tempo del bastone e della carota).* Verona: Mondadori, 1944.

MUSSOLINI, RACHELE. *Benito il mio uomo.* Milan: Rizzoli, 1958.

MUSSOLINI, VITTORIO. *Vita con mio padre.* Rome: Mondadori, 1957.

NELSON, KATHLEEN, and SULLIVAN, ALAN (eds.). *John Melly of Ethiopia.* London: Faber & Faber, Ltd., 1937.

NEUMANN, SIGMUND. *The Future in Perspective.* New York: G. P. Putnam's Sons, 1946.

NEWMAN, E. W. POLSON. *Ethiopian Realities.* London: George Allen & Unwin, Ltd., 1936.

────── *Italy's Conquest of Abyssinia.* London: Thornton Butterworth, Ltd., 1937.

NICHOLSON, NIGEL (ed.). *Harold Nicholson: Diaries and Letters 1930–1939.* London: William Collins Sons & Co., 1966.

PANKHURST, SYLVIA. *Ethiopia: A Cultural History.* Woodford Green: Essex, 1955.

PAUL-BONCOUR, JOSEPH. *Entre deux guerres.* 3 vols. Paris: Plon, 1945.

PEGOLOTTI, B. *Corsica, Tunisia, Gibuti.* Florence: Vallecchi, 1939.

PELLIZZI, CAMILLO. *Italy.* London: Longmans, Green & Company, 1939.

PERCY, LORD EUSTACE. *Some Memories.* London: Eyre & Spottiswoode, Ltd., 1958.

PERHAM, MARGERY. *The Government of Ethiopia.* London: Faber & Faber, Ltd., 1948.

PETERSON, SIR MAURICE. *Both Sides of the Curtain.* London: Constable & Company, Ltd., 1950.

PETRIE, SIR CHARLES, BT. *Lords of the Inland Sea.* London: Lovat Dickson, 1937.

—— *The Life and Letters of the Rt. Hon. Sir Austen Chamberlain.* 2 vols. London: Cassell & Co., Ltd., 1939, 1940.

PIGLI, MARIO. *Etiopia, l'incognita africana.* Padua: Cedam, 1935.

PIGNATELLI, LUIGI. *La Guerra dei sette mesi.* Naples: Mezzogiorno, 1961.

PRICE, G. WARD. *I Know These Dictators.* London: George C. Harrap & Co., Ltd., 1937.

QUARONI, PIETRO. *Diplomatic Bags.* ANTHONY RHODES, *trans. and ed.* London: George Weidenfeld & Nicolson Ltd., 1966.

REY, CHARLES F. *Unconquered Abyssinia as It Is Today.* London: Seeley, Service & Co., Ltd., 1923.

RIBBENTROP, VON, JOACHIM. *The Ribbentrop Memoirs.* London: George Weidenfeld & Nicolson Ltd., 1954.

RIDLEY, FRANCIS A. *Mussolini over Africa.* London: Wishart, 1935.

ROBERTSON, JOHN H. (John Connell, pseud.) *The "Office": A Study of British Foreign Policy and Its Makers, 1919–1951.* London: Wingate, 1958.

ROSSI, CESARE. *Trentatre vicende mussoliniane.* Milan: Ceschina, 1958.

ROTHERMERE, VISCOUNT. *Warnings and Predictions:* London: Eyre & Spottiswoode, Ltd., 1939.

ROWAN-ROBINSON, MAJOR-GENERAL H. *England, Italy, Abyssinia.* London: William Clowes & Sons Ltd., 1935.

ROWSE, A. L. *All Souls and Appeasement.* London: The Macmillan Company, 1961.

—— *The End of an Epoch: Reflections on Contemporary History.* London: The Macmillan Company, 1948.

SALTER, LORD ARTHUR. *Memoirs of a Public Servant.* London: Faber & Faber, Ltd., 1961.

SALVATORELLI, LUIGI. *Vent'anni fra due guerra.* Rome: Italiane, 1941.

—— and GIOVANNI, MIRA. *Storia d'Italia nel periodo fascista.* Rome: Einaudi, 1959.

SALVEMINI, GAETANO. *The Fascist Dictatorship in Italy.* London: Jonathan Cape, Ltd., 1928.

—— *Under the Axe of Fascism.* London: Victor Gollancz, Ltd., 1936.

—— *Prelude to World War II.* London: Victor Gollancz, Ltd., 1953.

SANDFORD, CHRISTINE. *Ethiopia Under Haile Selassie.* London: J. M. Dent & Sons, Ltd., 1946.

SARFATTI, MARGHERITA. *Dux.* (Trans. by FREDERIC WHYTE as *The Life of Benito Mussolini.* London: Thorton Butterworth, Ltd., 1935.)

SAVA, GEORGE. *A Tale of Ten Cities.* London: Faber & Faber, Ltd., 1942.

SEVERINO, BARONE BERNARDO QUARANTA DI SAN (ed. and trans.). *Mussolini as Revealed in His Political Speeches.* London: J. M. Dent & Sons, Ltd., 1923.

SIMON, VISCOUNT. *Retrospect.* London: Hutchinson & Co., Ltd., 1952.

SFORZA, COUNT CARLO. *Contemporary Italy.* London: Frederick Muller, Ltd., 1946.

SIMON, KATHLEEN. *Slavery.* London: Hodder & Stoughton, Ltd., 1929.

STEER, GEORGE L. *Caesar in Abyssinia.* Boston: Little, Brown & Company, 1937. London: Hodder & Stoughton, Ltd., 1936.

TAYLOR, A. J. P. *The Origins of the Second World War.* New York: Atheneum Publishers, 1962. London: Hamish Hamilton, Ltd., 1961.

TEELING, SIR LUKE WILLIAM. *The Pope in Politics.* London: Lovat Dickson, Ltd., 1937.

TEMPERLEY, ARTHUR C. *The Whispering Gallery of Europe.* London: William Collins Sons & Co., 1946.

TEMPLEWOOD, VISCOUNT. (SAMUEL HOARE.) *Ambassador on Special Mission.* London: William Collins Sons & Co., 1946.

―――― *Nine Troubled Years.* London: William Collins Sons & Co., 1954.

THOMAS, IVOR. *Who Mussolini Is.* London: Oxford University Press, 1942.

THOMPSON, GEOFFREY. *Front-Line Diplomat.* London: Hutchinson & Co., Ltd., 1959.

THOMSON, DAVID. *Two Frenchmen: Pierre Laval and Charles de Gaulle.* London: The Cresset Press, Ltd., 1951.

ULLENDORFF, EDWARD. *The Ethiopians.* London: Oxford University Press, 1960.

VALLE, P. A. DEL. *Roman Eagles Over Ethiopia.* Harrisburg, Pa.: Military Service Publishing Co., 1940.

VANSITTART, LORD ROBERT. *Lessons of My Life.* London: Hutchinson & Co., Ltd., 1943.

―――― *The Mist Procession: The Autobiography of Lord Vansittart.* London: Hutchinson & Co., Ltd., 1958.

VARE, DANIELE. *Twilight of the Kings.* London: John Murray, Ltd., 1948.

―――― *The Two Impostors.* London: John Murray, Ltd., 1949.

VILLARI, LUIGI. *Italian Foreign Policy under Mussolini.* New York: Devin-Adair, 1956.

VIRGIN, GENERAL ERIC. *The Abyssinia I Knew.* N. WALFORD, trans. London: The Macmillan Company, 1936.

WAUGH, EVELYN. *Waugh in Abyssinia.* London: Longmans, Green & Company, 1936.

WEINHOLT, CAPT. ARNOLD, D.S.O., M.C. *The Africans' Last Stronghold.* London: John Long, Ltd., 1938.

WISKEMAN, ELIZABETH. *The Rome-Berlin Axis.* London: Oxford University Press, 1949.

WOLFERS, ARNOLD. *Britain and France between Two World Wars.* New York: Harcourt, Brace & Company, Inc., 1940.

WOOLF, LEONARD. *The League and Abyssinia.* London: The Hogarth Press, Ltd., 1936.

WRENCH, JOHN EVELYN. *Geoffrey Dawson and Our Times.* London: Hutchinson & Co., Ltd., 1955.

YOUNG, G. M. *Stanley Baldwin.* London: Rupert Hart-Davis, Ltd., 1952.

YOUNG, WAYLAND H. *The Italian Left: A Short History of Political Socialism in Italy.* London: Longmans, Green & Company, 1949.

OFFICIAL RECORDS AND DOCUMENTS

1. *Published in Britain*
   House of Commons Official Report, Parliamentary Debates (Hansard). London: Her Majesty's Stationery Office.

League of Nations:
   Dispute between Abyssinia and Italy.
   Abyssinia Memo, January 1935;   Abyssinia Memo, May 1935; Italian Memo, September 1935.
   Request of the Abyssinian Government under Article II, paragraph 2, of the Covenant, 1935.

Foreign Office:
   Documents relating to the Dispute between Ethiopia and Italy. London: Her Majesty's Stationery Office, 1935.
   Correspondence respecting Abyssinian Raids and Incursions into British Territory. Cmd. 2553 (1925), Abyssinia No. 1. London: Her Majesty's Stationery Office, 1925.
   Correspondence respecting the Agreement between the United Kingdom and Italy of December 14-20, 1925, in regard to Lake Tsana. Cmd. 2792 (1927), Abyssinia No. 1. London: Her Majesty's Stationery Office, 1927.
   Documents on British Foreign Policy, 1919-1939, 3rd series, III-VI; 2nd series, VI, E. L. Woodward, R. Butler *et al.* (eds.). London: Her Majesty's Stationery Office, 1950-1953, 1957.

COLLIER, BASIL. *The Defence of the United Kingdom.* London: Her Majesty's Stationery Office, 1957.

HERTSLET, EDWARD. *The Map of Africa by Treaty.* 3 vols. London: His Majesty's Stationery Office, 1909.

2. *Published in Ethiopia*
   Documents on Italian War Crimes. 2 vols. Addis Ababa: Ministry of Justice, 1949–1950.

   TALBOT, DAVID A. (ed.). Ethiopia Liberation Silver Jubilee, 1966; Agriculture in Ethiopia, 1964; Public Health in Ethiopia, 1965; La Civilisation de l'Italie Fasciste en Ethiopie (2 vols., 1946). Addis Ababa: Ministry of Information.

3. *Published in Italy*
   La Campagne 1935–1936 in Africa Orientale, vol. 1.

   La Preparazione Militaire. Stato Ufficio Stories, 1939.

   Comando delle Forze Armate della Somalia. *La Guerre italo-etiopico: Fronte sud.* 4 vols. Rome.

   I Documenti diplomatici italiani. 6th series (1918–1922), vol. I, R. MOSCATI (ed.). Rome, 1955. 7th series (1922–1935), vols. I–IV, R. MOSCATI (ed.). Rome, 1953–1962. Ministero degli Affari Esteri.

   Italy and Abyssinia. Rome: Societa Editrice di Novissima, 1936.

   Italy and the Treaties. Rome: Pallotta, 1936.

   ANCHIERI, ETTORE. *Antologia storico-diplomatica.* Milan: Instituto per gli Studi di Politica Internazionale, 1941.

   CURATO, FEDERICO. *La Conferenza della pace.* 2 vols. Milan: Instituto per gli Studi di Politica Internazionale, 1942.

4. *Published in Switzerland*
   BUELL, RAYMOND L. "American Neutrality and Collective Security," *Geneva Special Studies,* VI, 6. Geneva: Geneva Research Council, 1935.

   ——— "The Suez Canal and League Sanctions," *Geneva Special Studies,* VI, 3. Geneva: Geneva Research Council, 1935.

   DEAN, VERA M. "The League and the Italian-Ethiopian Dispute," *Geneva Special Studies,* VI, 8. Geneva: Geneva Research Council, 1935.

   DE WILDE, J. "The International Distribution of Raw Materials," *Geneva Special Studies,* VIII, 5. Geneva: Geneva Research Council, 1936.

   HIETT, HELEN. "Public Opinion and the Italo-Ethiopian Dispute: The Activity of Private Organizations in the Crisis," *Geneva Special Studies,* VII, 1. Geneva: Geneva Research Council, 1936.

KOREN, WILLIAM. "The Italian-Ethiopian Dispute," *Geneva Special Studies,* VI, 4. Geneva: Geneva Research Council, 1935.

MISCELLANEOUS PUBLICATIONS

Survey of International Affairs 1935, vol. 2. Published for the Royal Institute of International Affairs by Oxford University Press.

AUER, PAUL DE. "The Lesson of the Italo-Abyssinian Conflict," *New Commonwealth Quarterly,* 1:1–19 (March 1936).

AVENOL, JOSEPH. "The Future of the League of Nations," *Royal Institute of International Affairs,* 13:143–58 (March–April 1934).

BARZINI, LUIGI. "Benito Mussolini," *Encounter,* 23:16–27 (July 1964).

BRADDICK, H. "A New Look at American Policy During the Italo-Ethiopian Crisis, 1935–36" *Journal of Modern History,* 34:64–73 (March 1962).

CHAMBERLAIN, AUSTEN. "The Permanent Bases of British Foreign Policy," *Foreign Affairs,* 9:533–46 (July 1931).

CLIFFORD, E. H. M. "The British Somaliland-Ethiopia Boundary," *Geographical Journal,* 87:289–302 (April 1936).

DUPUIS, C. "Lake Tana and the Nile," *Journal of the [Royal] African Society,* 35:18–25 (January 1936).

GARRATT, G. "Abyssinia," *Journal of the [Royal] African Society,* 36:36–50 (January 1937).

GATHORNE-HARDY, G. M. "The League at the Cross-Roads," *Royal Institute of International Affairs,* 15:485–505 (July–August 1936).

——— *A Short History of International Affairs 1920–1939.* Published for the Royal Institute of International Affairs by Oxford University Press, 1950.

——— and MITRAYNY, D. "Territorial Revision and Article 19 of the League Covenant," *Royal Institute of International Affairs,* 14:818–36 (November–December 1935).

GERAUD, ANDRÉ. "British Vacillations," *Foreign Affairs,* 14:584–97 (July 1936).

——— "France and the Anglo-German Naval Treaty," *Foreign Affairs,* 14:51–61 (October 1935).

——— "Gamelin," *Foreign Affairs,* 19:310–31 (January 1941).

LECHENBERG, H. P. "With the Italians in Eritrea," *National Geographic Magazine,* 68:265–96 (September 1935).

MAGISTRATI, MASSIMO. "La Germania e l'impresa italiana di Etiopia (Ricordi di Berlino)," *Rivista di studi politici internazionali,* 17:562–606 (October–December 1950).

MORI, RENATO. "L'Impresa etiopica e le sue ripercussioni internazionali," in AUGUSTO TORRE *et al.*, *La Politica estera italiana dal 1914 al 1943.* Rome, 1963.

New Statesman and Nation. "The Abyssinian Dispute: The Background of the Conflict," X:321–26 (September 7, 1935).

SCHAEFER, LUDWIG, F. (ed.). *The Ethiopian Crisis, Touchstone of Appeasement?* Published for the Carnegie Institute of Technology by D. C. Heath & Co., Boston, 1961. (This booklet comprises articles extracted from previously published documents whose authors are experts in the particular aspects for which they have been chosen.)

TOYNBEE, ARNOLD J. *Survey of International Affairs, 1935* (2 vols.), vol. II *Abyssinia and Italy.* Published for the Royal Institute of International Affairs by Oxford University Press, 1936.

VARE, DANIELE. "British Foreign Policy through Italian Eyes," *Royal Institute of International Affairs*, 15:80–102 (January–February 1936).

WALTERS, F. P. *A History of the League of Nations.* 2 vols. Published for the Royal Institute of International Affairs by Oxford University Press, 1952.

WHITE, F. *The Abyssinian Dispute.* League of Nations Union publication, London, 1935.

NEWSPAPERS AND MAGAZINES

Il Giornale d'Italia.
Il Popolo d'Italia.
Life, "Dino Grandi Explains," February 26, 1945.
Look, articles by Milton Bracker.
The *Times* (London).
The New York Times.

Index

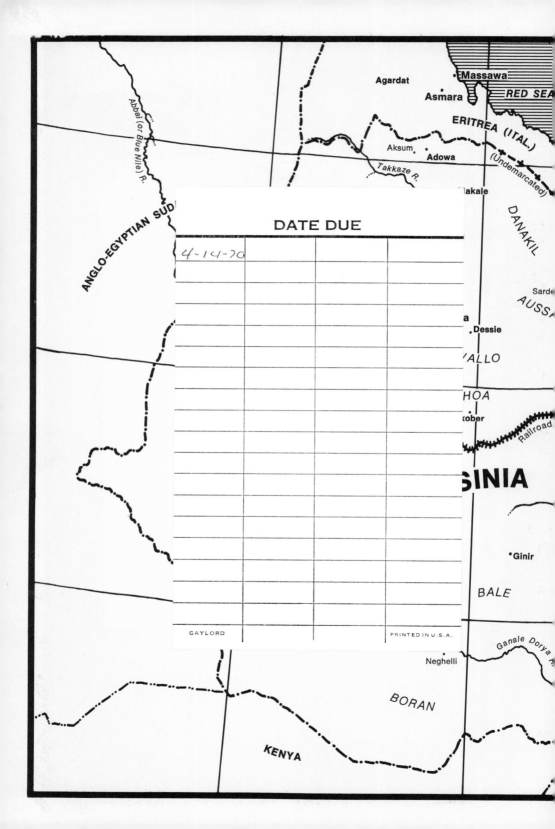